AUTISTIC SPECTRUM DISORDERS: EDUCATIONAL AND CLINICAL INTERVENTIONS

ADVANCES IN SPECIAL EDUCATION

Series Editor: Anthony F. Rotatori

Recently Published Volumes:

Volume 11: Issues, Practices, and Concerns in Special Education – Edited by Anthony F. Rotatori, John O. Schwenn, Sandra Burkhardt

Volume 12: Multicultural Education for Learners with Exceptionalities – Edited by Festus E. Obiakor, John O. Schwenn, Anthony F. Rotatori

Volume 13: Intervention Techniques for Individuals with Exceptionalities in Inclusive Settings – Edited by Festus Obiakor, Sandra Burkhardt, Anthony F. Rotatori, Tim Wahlberg

ADVANCES IN SPECIAL EDUCATION VOLUME 14

AUTISTIC SPECTRUM DISORDERS: EDUCATIONAL AND CLINICAL INTERVENTIONS

EDITED BY

TIM WAHLBERG

Psychology Department, Northern Illinois University, USA

FESTUS OBIAKOR

Department of Exceptional Children

University of Wisconsin-Milwaukee, USA

SANDRA BURKHARDT

Psychology Department, Saint Xavier University, USA

ANTHONY F. ROTATORI

Psychology Department, Saint Xavier University, USA

2001

JAI

An Imprint of Elsevier Science

Amsterdam – London – New York – Oxford – Paris – Shannon – Tokyo

ELSEVIER SCIENCE Ltd
The Boulevard, Langford Lane
Kidlington, Oxford OX5 1GB, UK

First edition 2001

Library of Congress Cataloging in Publication Data
A catalog record from the Library of Congress has been applied for.

British Library Cataloguing in Publication Data
A catalogue record from the British Library has been applied for.

ISBN: 0-7623-0818-4
ISSN: 0270-4013 (Series)

∞The paper used in this publication meets the requirements of ANSI/NISO Z39.48-1992 (Permanence of Paper).
Printed in The Netherlands.

CONTENTS

LIST OF CONTRIBUTORS

Michele A. Arthur	Department of Psychology Saint Xavier University, USA
Jeffrey P. Bakken	Department of Special Education Illinios State University, USA
Stacey J. Bock,	Department of Special Education Illinios State University, USA
Mary Ellen Bucci	Department of Psychology Saint Xavier University, USA
Sandra Burkhardt	Department of Psychology Saint Xavier University, USA
Julia A. Deisinger	Department of Psychology Saint Xavier University, USA
Mirah J. Dow	Library and Information Management Emporia State University, USA
Tina Taylor Dyches	Department of Counseling and Special Education, Brigham Young University, USA
Marlin Hoover	Clinical Psychologist, Hoover and Associates, Orland Park, Illinois, USA
Scott Jordan	Department of Psychology Illinios State University, USA
Teresa A. Mehring	The Teachers College Emporia State University, USA

Festus Obiakor — Department of Exceptional Children
University of Wisconsin-Milwaukee, USA

Anthony F. Rotatori — Department of Psychology
Saint Xavier University, USA

Tim Wahlberg — Psychology Department, Northern Illinois
University, USA

Lynn K. Wilder — Department of Counseling and Special
Education, Brigham Young University,
USA

PREFACE

This book is concerned with the study of children and adults with Autistic Spectrum Disorders (ASD). The book provides theoretical, educational and clinical perspectives to the study of individuals with ASD. The perspectives are based upon past and present theories of autism, educational practices over the past thirty years, and recent clinical innovations. The authors believe that this feature sets the book apart from other books in the field. Additionally, the term ASD recognizes that this is a very heterogeneous disorder that encompasses the classic autistic disorder and mild variants such as Asperger Syndrome and pervasive developmental disorder not otherwise specified. Presently, there exists a growing need for information to understand the complex educational and mental health needs of individuals with ASD. The content of this book is directed at meeting this need. For example, Section One of the book provides the reader with information concerned with theoretical aspects of the disorder including chapters on cognitive symptomology of autism, neurological implications and the aging process. Section Two of the book provides the reader with educational best practices including chapters on preservice and inservice training considerations, curriculum innovations, language development and text comprehension and multicultural concerns. Section Three of the book provides the reader with current clinical practices including chapters on assessment, counseling parents of children with ASD, recent innovations in counseling individuals with ASD, psychotropic management considerations, and a clinical synopsis of a comprehensive interview of a high functioning adult with autism. Unique to the book is a new theoretical model to ASD called The Control Theory of Autism and a discussion related to multicultural issues for students with autism.

PART 1: THEORETICAL ASPECTS

COGNITIVE THEORIES AND SYMPTOMOLOGY OF AUTISM

Tim Wahlberg

DEFICITS ASSOCIATED WITH AUTISM

Autism is a very perplexing psychological disorder that effects an estimated four in 10,000 children born in the United States (Happe & Frith, 1996; Wahlberg & Rotatori, 1996; Wing, 1993). It is a biological/neurological condition that is usually diagnosed before three years of age via the Diagnostic and Statistical Manual of Mental Disorders 4th Edition (DSM-IV, 1994). Three distinct criteria are outlined and used in the diagnosis of autism that are found within the diagnostic categories of the DSM-IV. These criteria are: (1) qualitative impairment in social interaction, (2) qualitative impairments in communication, and (3) restricted, repetitive, and stereotyped patterns of behavior, interests, and activities.

Qualitative impairment in social interactions consists of individuals with autism lacking the ability to engage in appropriate social interactions (see Hewitt, 1998; Mundy, 1995; Smith & Bryson, 1994; Wahlberg & Rotatori, 1996). This social inadequacy is witnessed early on in individuals with autism. For example, infants with autism show an impaired capacity to engage in social exchanges, such as mutual imitation (Smith & Bryson, 1994). This social inadequacy extends into childhood in the form of the inability to have friends and engage in appropriate social play with others (DSM-IV, 1994; Fotheringham, 1991; Happe & Frith, 1996; Wahlberg & Rotatori, 1996), and into adulthood in the form of a lack of strong social relationships (DSM-IV, 1994; Fotheringham, 1991; Happe & Frith, 1996; Wahlberg & Rotatori, 1996).

Autistic Spectrum Disorders: Educational and Clinical Interventions, pages 3–17.

ISBN: 0-7623-0818-4

Impairment in communication includes the lack of language and communication, and the inappropriate use of language (Happe, 1995; Happe & Frith, 1996; Mundy, 1995; Tager-Flusberg, 1991; Wahlberg & Rotatori, 1996) and the delayed onset of language (DSM-IV, 1994; Frith & Snowling, 1983; Happe & Frith, 1996; Minshew, Goldstein & Seigel, 1995; Prior & Hall, 1979; Tager-Flusberg, 1981a; Wahlberg & Rotatori, 1996). When language does develop it often takes the form of echolalia (repeating phrases) or parroting (repeating word for word what was said to them) (Happe & Frith, 1996; Minshew et al., 1995). Some high functioning individuals with autism are able to read text. However, research has shown that these individuals often exhibit distinct comprehension deficits when interpreting written text (Frith & Snowling, 1983; Goldberg, 1987; Happe, 1997; Minshew et al., 1995; O'Connor & Hermelin, 1994; Prior & Hall, 1979; Tager-Flusberg, 1981b; Yuill, Oakhill & Parkin, 1989).

Restrictive and repetitive forms of behavior can be best described as an inherent insistence on sameness (Happe, 1995; Happe & Frith, 1996; Wahlberg & Rotatori, 1996). Individuals with autism engage in activities, such as spinning the wheel of a toy car, for an extended period of time. The activity involves inappropriate play as well as a repetitive pattern of activity.

THEORETICAL ACCOUNTS FOR DEFICITS IN AUTISM

Cognitive oriented theories exist today that attempt to shed some light on this unique psychological disorder (see Wahlberg & Rotatori, 1996). Many of these theories postulate that various cognitive mechanisms appear to be malfunctioning, giving rise to the symptomology of autism (Happe & Frith, 1996; Mundy, 1995; Smith & Bryson, 1994). Four of these theoretical positions, namely: (1) theory of mind (Happe, 1993, 1994, 1995; Happe & Frith, 1996; Hughes & Russell, 1993; Karmiloff-Smith, Klima, Bellugi, Grant & Baron-Cohen, 1995; Phillips, Baron-Cohen & Rutter, 1998), (2) weak central coherence (Frith, 1989; Frith & Happe, 1994; Happe, 1997; Happe & Frith, 1996; Jarrold & Russell, 1997; Shah & Frith, 1993), (3) impaired executive function (Happe & Frith, 1996; Ozonoff, Pennington & Rogers, 1994; Pennington & Ozonoff, 1996), and (4) social impairment (Happe & Frith 1996; Hobson, 1993; Mundy, 1995) are discussed below.

Theory of Mind

One potential explanation of many of the symptoms of autism is that these individuals suffer from a weak theory of mind. Theory of mind can be best described as a person's ability to attribute mental states such as knowing and believing to other people, and within this, understand that other people have their own thoughts and beliefs about the world around them (Flavell & Miller, 1998; Happe, 1995; Happe & Frith, 1996; Smith & Bryson, 1994). It also involves ones understanding that individuals other than themselves are able to appreciate and evaluate the actions taken by other people and use this understanding to form mental concepts or ideas based on these actions (Happe, 1993; Hobson, 1994; Hughes & Russell, 1993; Phillips et al., 1998). Normal individuals (with a sound theory of mind) are able to understand that others may form different perspectives than theirs about other people or objects that exist within the environment. Individuals with autism have been hypothesized to suffer from a specific impairment in the ability to represent the mental states of themselves and others and to understand and predict behavior in terms of these states (Happe, 1993). They are unable to attribute mental states, such as knowing and believing, to other people. The mental states individuals with autism have are constrained by what is observable within the concrete, physical, environment.

One of the primary ways in which a child can demonstrate a theory of mind is through the administration of a false belief task (Flavell & Miller, 1998; Hughes & Russell, 1993; Phillips et al., 1998). The following is an example of a highly used false belief task:

> If three people are sitting in a room and a pen is placed into a box with a cover, all involved realize that a pen is in the box. One of the person's in the room is asked to leave and while out of the room, the pen is replaced with a pencil. Upon the persons return to the room, the question is posed, "What does the person who exited the room think is in the box?"

The correct answer is the pen. In order to pass a false belief task, such as the one above, one has to understand that the individual that left the room has no idea about the switch. In order to pass this task, individuals have to understand a belief that is different from their own. Normal children are typically able to pass first order false belief tasks consistently by 4 to 5 years of age (e.g. see Flavell & Miller, 1998; Phillips et al., 1998).

In order to assess the extent to which autistic individuals possess a theory of mind, Happe (1994) presented 18 high functioning individuals with autism, who ranged in age between nine and 45 years old, a false belief task. Happe found that six of the participants were unable to pass first order false belief tasks. These subjects averaged 17.6 years of age with a lower than average verbal IQ score ranging between 52 and 76.

Baron-Cohen, Leslie, and Frith (1985) conducted a study and found that children with autism were unable to predict where a protagonist would look for an object moved in his absence. In contrast, normal four year olds and children with Down's syndrome who were matched with the autistic participants were able to make the distinction. These results provided evidence of deficits in theory of mind for autistic children because the children with Down's syndrome passed the first order false belief tasks, while children with autism failed.

A weak theory of mind can be used to explain various symptomologies associated with autism, namely, the inability to share joint attention and perspectives (see Happe & Frith, 1996; Mundy, 1995), weak interpersonal relatedness (see Hobson, 1993), a dysfunction in the appreciation of the significance of incoming stimuli and attaching motivational value to stimuli (see Fotheringham, 1991), and imagination, communication, and socialization deficiencies (see Happe & Frith, 1996). For example, individuals with autism have a hard time coordinating objects and perspectives with others in the environment. Additionally, individuals with autism seem to lack the ability to share joint attention and perspectives (Happe & Frith, 1996; Mundy, 1995) and suffer from the ability to initiate joint shared attention relative to an object or event (see Mundy, 1995). Presumably, one needs an intact theory of mind in order to share the perspectives of others (i.e. joint attention). Theory of mind accounts for joint attention because individuals need to understand that others have perspectives in order to share that perspective.

A weak theory of mind deficit in individuals with autism may be due to joint attention problems as infants. They lack social reciprocity as infants, which can lead to a lack of understanding of the mental state of another individual which eventually leads to a theory of mind deficit later on in development. Another example which is closely related to joint attention, is that individuals with autism suffer from weak interpersonal relatedness (Hobson, 1993). Weak interpersonal relatedness is the inability to effectively coordinate perspectives of others to a shared object. Individuals need an intact theory of mind in order to be able to coordinate another person's perspective onto an object of interest. Furthermore, they would need to understand that others have perspectives different from their own in order to coordinate and share a perspective with another individual.

It has also been hypothesized that individuals with autism suffer from a dysfunction in the appreciation of the significance of incoming stimuli and attaching motivational value to the stimuli (Fotheringham, 1991). Within this hypothesis, Fotheringham believes that individuals with autism can not understand the significance of incoming stimuli and suffer difficulties in making meta-representations. Making meta-representations involves the process of forming beliefs about another person's mental state. Fotheringham believes this is accomplished by being able to put oneself in another's shoes and take his/her point of view. Again, it becomes apparent that one would need a sound theory of mind to understand the significance of incoming stimuli so as to attach motivational value to take another's point of view.

Happe and Frith (1996) argue that the theory of mind deficit can explain various symptomologies associated with autism. The researchers state that a deficit in theory of mind would explain the impairment's which individuals with autism have with imagination, communication, and socialization. Happe and Frith state that the key element which individuals with autism seem to suffer from is "mentalizing". A deficit in mentalizing is supported by the inability of individuals with autism to correctly complete a false belief task. Happe and Frith described this deficit as the "failure to attribute mental states independent of reality and of the child's own belief" (p. 1386). These researchers stress that this mentalizing deficit accounts well for the above three impairments.

Within all the aforementioned symptomologies associated with autism, it becomes apparent that a causal relationship exists. It seems that individuals with autism suffer from a weak theory of mind as well as the deficits that were mentioned above. As was pointed out, theory of mind can account for all of the previously mentioned deficits associated with autism.

Executive Function Deficits

Autistic individuals exhibit rigid repetitive behaviors, deficits in pretend play, as well as socially inappropriate behaviors (see Wahlberg & Rotatori, 1996). In order to explain these symptoms, the executive function theory has been proposed that describes the behaviors individuals with autism exhibit in terms of an impairment in executive processing (see Normal & Shallice, 1986). Executive function is described as the control of continuous planful behavior while engaging in future goal directed activities (Normal & Shallice, 1986). This process allows one to retrieve and use knowledge and prior experience as part of the planning and inhibiting of responses, while at the same time monitoring progress. Individuals with autism seem to exhibit certain skill deficits related to impairments in executive functioning. For example, they are unable to inhibit inappropriate responses while interacting with other individuals or to monitor responses while providing feedback to others.

Ozonoff, Pennington, and Rogers (1994) proposed that a number of symptoms individuals with autism demonstrate are related to executive function deficits. These researchers emphasize that executive function is the cognitive construct used to describe activities that involve higher level cognitive processes. These higher level cognitive processes can occur in many forms. An example of a higher level process includes the ability to inhibit inappropriate responses. Another process involves monitoring performance and using feedback. These executive functions are needed to monitor progress toward an end goal and use feedback to modify and make changes while obtaining that end goal. The ability to disengage from context is another process that falls under the executive function domain. It involves one's ability to use previously learned knowledge to interpret and understand a certain context of events, without the knowledge necessarily appearing within the context under interpretation. This process can be described as learning from your mistakes or learning from past experience and changing your perceived notion of a certain context. Another key element of executive function processes that is involved in all of the previously mentioned elements is flexibility. Executive function theorists classify flexibility as a higher level cognitive construct that normal individuals typically possess. To succeed and function in life people need to be flexible, to a certain degree, due to the fact that nothing in life is ever a "sure thing".

Ozonoff et al. (1994) state that "all executive function behaviors share the need to disengage from the immediate environment or external context and guide action instead by mental models or internal representations" (p. 1016). The researchers report that an individual's actions are guided by mental representations of context, rather than actual concrete components existing within the context itself. Individuals with an intact executive function mechanism are able to use higher level cognitive constructs to guide their actions, rather than relying solely on the immediate environment. A good example of this is the ability to inhibit inappropriate responses. Individuals are capable of responding to questions such as, "Do you like my new dress?", by disengaging from the immediate environment and answering, "yes." They may answer yes, even though they may not feel that way, because they do not want to hurt the other person's feelings. Many individuals with autism fail at this task. They would say exactly what they feel because they are unable to disengage themselves from the immediate environment and guide their actions by internal representations.

Normal individuals are capable of developing internal plans and actions, and then calling upon them for use in future contexts. By acting upon mental plans and actions individuals are not reflexive, or acting via a stimulus response domain, rather they are very interactive and flexible. They are able to formulate plans and future actions based on these mental representations they have created and stored in memory. Individuals are not forced to only act upon the given context or environment that presents itself. They are always using the executive function construct to interact and function in their everyday lives.

A feature included within all diagnostic criteria of autism is restricted repetitive and stereotyped patterns of behavior, interests, and activities. If individuals with autism suffer from executive function deficits, their behaviors would fit this criterion and be very rigid and odd. They would not be capable of being flexible or capable of disengaging from the immediate environment. Individuals with autism are often rigid and inflexible and are narrowly focused on details (Wahlberg & Rotatori, 1996). They show deficits in their ability to inhibit familiar or overlearned responses and often times perseverate for hours on certain objects. All this symptomology can be attributed to executive function deficits as previously described.

Ozonoff et al. (1994) tested the hypothesis that individuals with autism do indeed suffer from executive function deficits. In their study, individuals with autism and matched control participants were given a number of tasks to perform. Two information processing paradigms were used to examine three cognitive operations required in many traditional executive function measures. The first was a Go-No-Go task consisting of three conditions with a hierarchy of processing demands. The first neutral inhibition condition required subjects to respond to a neutral stimulus, while simultaneously inhibiting responses to another neutral stimulus; this condition required no shifting of cognitive set. The second proponent inhibition (i.e dominant) condition required inhibition of a previously reinforced well-learned response. The final flexibility condition necessitated frequent shifting from one response pattern to another, which placed high demands on cognitive flexibility (Ozonoff et al.). The second task was the H&S task. This task examined local-global processing (which is described as detail orientation as opposed to seeing the big picture). Participants were presented with large letters on a computer screen. Each of the large letters was, in turn composed of small letters. The small letters were either the same letter as the large pattern or different than the larger pattern. The ability to process small letters (local processing) was compared to the ability to attend to large letters (global processing). Three groups participated in the study: the experimental group consisting of those diagnosed with autism and two control groups, one diagnosed with Tourette's syndrome and the other that was developmentally normal.

Ozonoff et al. (1994) found that the performance of the autistic and the Tourette's syndrome groups were similar on tasks requiring inhibition of neutral stimuli and global-local processing, but differed on a measure of cognitive flexibility and on a task that appeared to require inhibition of inappropriate responses. Overall, the autistic participants were less flexible than the Tourette's syndrome group on the tasks performed. The ability to shift attention from various informational sets was also found to be lacking in the autistic group in comparison with the Tourette's syndrome group. Individuals with autism struggled with tasks that required the planned control of action as compared with the normal and Tourette's syndrome groups.

The restricted, repetitive, and stereotyped patterns of behavior individuals with autism exhibit are part of the diagnostic criteria used in identifying autism. Executive function deficits seem to explain these behavioral oddities found in autism that exist outside of the social realm. Suffering from deficits in executive functioning help to explain repetitive behavior (Turner, 1997), as well as deficits in pretend play (Jarrold, 1997). Further, Happe and Frith (1996) pointed out that individuals with autism have problems in planning and organization (Hughes, Russell & Robbins, 1994; Ozonoff et al., 1994; Prior & Hoffman, 1990), and switching set and perseveration (Hughes et al., 1994; Rumsey & Hamburger, 1988) which are also related to executive function deficits.

Central Coherence

Central coherence is another theory that explains various symptomologies associated with autism (Happe, 1997). This theory purposes that individuals with autism have a weak drive for central coherence, which is needed for general information-processing. This perspective is based on a body of research that centers around the relative failure of individuals with autism to extract and use global meaning from a situation or written context (see Happe, 1997). Frith (1989) states that the underlying cognitive deficit associated with autism is displayed by a failure to process information for meaning in context. Frith argues that individuals with autism are processing the information in a very different way than normal individuals. Due to their weak drive for central coherence individuals with autism are unable to derive overall meaning from a situation or written text. This weakness results in individuals with autism making less use of content while paying more attention to parts rather than wholes. For example, research has shown that individuals with autism are just as good at recalling meaningless information as they are at recalling meaningful information (Happe & Frith, 1996). In comparison, normal and mentally handicapped individuals showed a superior ability in processing meaningful and patterned information over random and meaningless stimuli (Hermelin & O'Connor, 1967). Within the same context, normal subjects typically extract the gist of a passage or story while forgetting the surface form (Bartlett, 1932), while children and adults with autism may retain the actual words used but fail to extract the meaning (Happe & Frith, 1996).

Frith and Happe (1994) proposed that the weak drive for central coherence theory can account for symptomology that does not quite fit under the theory of mind account for autism. Specifically, these researchers argue that high functioning adults with autism who can pass theory of mind tasks, continue to show patterns of performance characteristic of weak central coherence. An example of this would be their above average block design performance (Happe, 1994) and poor sentence-specified pronunciations of homographs (Happe, 1997). Other examples which support a weak drive for central coherence are their: savant skills (Grandin, 1995; Wahlberg & Rotatori, 1996), inherent insistence on sameness (DSM-IV, 1994; Happe & Frith, 1996; Wahlberg & Rotatori, 1996), specific odd interests (DSM-IV, 1994; Grandin, 1995; Powers, 1989), as well as poor comprehension of text (Frith & Snowling, 1983; O'Connor & Hermelin, 1994; Prior & Hall, 1979; Snowling & Frith, 1986; Tager-Flusberg, 1981b; Yuill et al., 1989).

Theorists have hypothesized that individuals with autism process information differently than normal individuals. Jarrold and Russell (1997) describe individuals with autism as processing information at an analytic rather than a global level. They assessed whether individuals with autism would rapidly and automatically enumerate a number of dots presented in a canonical form, or count each dot individually to obtain the total. Jarrold and Russell found that individuals with autism counted each dot individually, which suggests that they counted the dots at an analytic level rather than a global level. The researchers stated that this analytic performance by children with autism supports a weak drive for central coherence theory.

Processing information in such a manner causes impairments in making sense of stimuli and deriving meaning, consistency, and structure when processing information (Frith, 1989). Frith and Happe (1994) explain that individuals with autism may not show the normal bias towards processing certain types of information at a global level. The tendency to draw together diverse information and use this information to construct higher-level meaning in context is not present. Frith and Happe argue that instead of integrating low-level features into a coherent whole, individuals with autism may process information in a more piecemeal and bottom-up fashion. In other words, individuals with autism struggle to incorporate learned information when formulating higher level meaning.

There has been some speculation as to the mechanisms that support the weak drive for central coherence perspective. Experimental subjects' performance on the block design test has been used frequently to demonstrate a weak drive for central coherence. For example, researchers (Bolles & Goldstein, 1938; Nadel, 1938; Reissenweber, 1953; Shapiro, 1952) have reported that psychiatric patients and patients suffering from certain cerebral lesions perform poorly on the block design test (cited in Shah & Frith, 1993). Also, children with Williams syndrome are substantially impaired on this task (Bihrle, Bellugi, Delis & Marks, 1989). Kaplan (1983) found that different types of errors on the block design test can be distinguished in adult patients with left-hemisphere and right-hemisphere lesions (cited in Shah & Frith, 1993). In contrast, individuals with autism excel on the block design test (Shah & Frith, 1993).

Happe and Frith (1996) assessed evidence for the weak drive for central coherence theory in a recent study. The researchers presented individuals with autism and normal individuals various forms of text. The participants read sentences as well as paragraphs that were either meaningful or not meaningful. The researchers assessed comprehension by requiring participants to recall information the participants had previously read in various forms of text. Participants were asked to recall either the text itself or the underlying meaning of what they had read. Happe and Frith found that individuals with autism were able to recall the written text verbatim, but were unable to recall meaning of text they had read. Recall for both forms of sentences were equal (those that had underlying meaning and those that did not) for individuals with autism. Normal participants were found to recall sentences with underlying meaning better than meaningless sentences. This was also found to hold true for reading paragraphs. Individuals with autism were able to recall the text they read, but struggled to describe any underlying meaning or connotations made within the paragraph. Happe and Frith hypothesized that individuals with autism perform well on the recall of written text and block design tests because they are able to resist the overall pattern (the global picture) and perceive it instead in terms of individual cubes (the analytic level).

A weak drive for central coherence may lead to the development of certain brain anomalies in individuals with autism such as making interpretations at an analytic rather than global level. This way of processing information may lead to the various symptoms associated with autism such as: savant skills (Grandin, 1995; Wahlberg & Rotatori, 1996), inherent insistence on sameness (DSV-IV, 1994; Happe & Frith, 1996; Wahlberg & Rotatori, 1996), and specific odd interests (DSM-IV, 1994; Grandin, 1995; Powers, 1989). Processing information at an analytic rather than a global level could also have an impact on the poor text comprehension of individuals with autism (see Frith & Snowling, 1983; O'Connor & Hermelin, 1994; Prior & Hall, 1979; Snowling & Frith, 1986; Tager-Flusberg, 1981b; Yuill et al., 1989).

Social Impairment

Social impairment is a very highly researched and theoretically supported cognitive theory associated with the development of autism (see Happe & Frith, 1996; Hobson, 1993; Mundy, 1995). Theorists purposing a social impairment position hypothesize that autism is a direct manifestation of a problem with social insight. For example, Happe and Frith (1996) postulate that the root of autism may be a disorder of social insight. These researchers contend that this is the most successful cognitive account of autism to date. Similarly, Mundy (1995) debates the idea that the developmental anomalies in the neurological systems associated with autism may result in social disturbances known to be associated with individuals with autism. The researcher states that these anomalies may be directly associated with cognitive or affective processes related to social development.

Social impairment can be broken down to various subcomponents. The first subcomponent involves a lack of interpersonal relatedness (Hobson, 1993). This can be best described as an individual's failure to effectively coordinate perspective of others to a shared object. This hypothesis is based on the abilities of normally developing children in understanding that others like themselves are able to share perspectives on objects in a similar way. Normal children are able to mirror others and learn to interact with them, which in turn plays a very important role in their social development. If individuals with autism are unable to perform such tasks, their social development will suffer significantly. The interpersonal relatedness hypothesis suggests that this process takes place in the earliest months of life, and that children with autism are unable to perform these tasks at that time.

Researchers have explored interpersonal relatedness in older children with autism and found that they show an inability (relative to matched controls) at identifying emotions (see Hobson, 1994). It is hypothesized that individuals with autism are unable to recognize the emotional states of others because of their inability as children to understand that other individuals share thoughts and feelings relative to external stimuli.

Another subcomponent of social impairment, which normal children acquire and children with autism do not, is joint attention. This involves sharing the focus of attention, through eye contact or pointing, between an object and another person. Joint attention failure is considered a significant early indicator of autism and Mundy (1995) suggests that joint attention disturbances in children with autism "reflects a failure of the adequate development, or operation of social-emotional executive function" (p. 65). Mundy states that this failure results in an inadequate allocation of resource to social problem solving procedures, which in turn yields the developmental anomalies that exist within the social-cognitive systems of individuals with autism.

Fotheringham (1991) contends that the basic underlying deficit associated with autism is a dysfunction of the appreciation of the emotional significance of incoming stimuli and attaching motivational value to the stimuli. This researcher proposed that the basic deficit associated with individuals who have autism is found within their capacity to perceive and interpret social-emotional type stimuli, and it is this deficit that causes them difficulties in making meta-representations. Fotheringham describes Meta-representation as the process of forming beliefs about another person's mental state, by making representations or being able to put oneself in another's shoes and take on his or her point of view.

The final subcomponent of social impairments which is deficit in children with autism is imitation. This involves the ability of infants to imitate facial expressions of care givers. This early form of imitation (it is hypothesized) leads to later social understanding. Happe and Frith (1996) suggest that imitation may underlie social communication. These researchers stress that infants learn to share the emotional state felt by the other person by imitating various facial expressions. An early imitation problem may result in significant problems or delays in later social development. Smith and Bryson (1994) contend that the social deficit(s) of children with autism are associated with an imitative deficit. The researchers propose that this imitative deficit is diagnostic of a basic information processing problem rather than a social function deficiency. Smith and Bryson hypothesize that "the problem of imitation in autism may be due in part to impairment in the perceptual organization of movements, manifested in abnormal representations of actions" (p. 260).

All these theories of social impairment hypothesize that the underlying neurological anomalies associated with individuals having autism, in one way or another, deal with the acquisition of social insight. Due to these neurological anomalies, children with autism are unable to form a strong social understanding of others. While this process may occur within any of the above subcomponents of social impairment, the end result is autism. It is hypothesized that this lack of social understanding creates a barrier that forces these individuals to withdrawal from society and in turn to develop very odd stereotypical behaviors and very poor communication skills. This social impairment leads to problems in communicating and adapting in our society.

CONCLUSION

Many cognitive theories exist that attempt to explain why certain individuals develop autism. This chapter has attempted to give the reader a brief overview of some of the most prominent theoretical positions. Because individuals with autism differ considerably across the spectrum of the disorder, finding a theoretical position that fits all individuals with autism is very difficult. The fact that about 75% of individuals with autism are mentally retarded (Wahlberg & Rotatori, 1996) makes it more difficult to test these various theoretical positions.

Autism is described as a brain disorder causing certain neurological anomalies to develop. As researchers get more sophisticated in their scientific understanding of the human brain, society may learn more about why these individuals suffer from autism. For the time being, researchers are forced to theorize as to the "goings on" in the brains of individuals with autism. In general researchers have hypothesized about certain cognitive limitations individuals with autism suffer from and then try to find ways to assess these limitations through experimental research. The reader can see from the current discussion, that many different theoretical positions exist today that attempt to explain why individuals with autism develop abnormal behaviors. As researchers continue to work with individuals who are autistic, test them, and develop better means to assess their brain processing capabilities, the key to unlocking this very perplexing psychological disorder will become known. Until then, the world can only continue to speculate and wonder about autism and its development within the human species.

REFERENCES

American Psychiatric Association (1994). *Diagnostic and statistical manual of mental disorders (DSM-IV)* (4th ed). Washington, D.C.: Author.

Baron-Cohen, S., Leslie, A. M., & Frith, U. (1985). Does the autistic child have a 'theory of mind'? *Cognition, 21*, 37–46.

Bartlett, F. C. (1932). *Remembering: A study in experimental and social psychology*. Cambridge: Cambridge University Press.

Bihrle, A. M., Bellugi, U., Delis, D., & Marks, S. (1989). Seeing either the forest or the trees: Dissociation in visuospatial processing. *Brain and Cognition, 11*, 37–49.

Bolles, M., & Goldstein, K. (1938). A study of impairment of abstract behaviour in schizophrenic patients. *Psychiatric Quarterly, 12*, 42–65.

Flavell, J. H., & Miller, P. H. (1998). Social cognition. In: W. Damon, D. Kuhn, & R. S. Siegler (Eds), *Handbook of Child Psychology: Cognition, Perception, and Language* (Vol. 2, pp. 851–898). New York: John Wiley & Sons, Inc.

Fotheringham, J. B. (1991). Autism: Its primary psychological and neurological deficit. *Canadian Journal of Psychiatry, 36*, 686–692.

Frith, U. (1989). *Autism: Explaining the enigma*. Oxford: Basil Blackwell.

Frith, U., & Happe, F. (1994). Autism: Beyond "theory of mind." *Cognition, 50*, 115–132.

Frith, U., & Snowling, M. (1983). Reading for meaning and reading for sound in autistic and dyslexic children. *Journal of Developmental Psychology, 1*, 329–342.

Goldberg, T. E. (1987). On hermetic reading abilities. *Journal of Autism and Developmental Disabilities, 17*(1), 29 44.

Grandin, T. (1995). *Thinking in pictures and other reports from my life with autism*. New York: Doubleday.

Happe, F. G. (1993). Communicative competence and theory of mind in autism: A test of relevance theory. *Cognition, 48*, 101–119.

Happe, F. G. (1994). An advanced test of theory of mind: Understanding of story characters' thoughts and feelings by able autistic, mentally handicapped, and normal children and adults. *Journal of Autism and Developmental Disorders, 24*, 129–154.

Happe, F. G. (1995). The role of age and verbal ability in the theory of mind tasks performance of subjects with autism. *Childhood Development, 66*, 843–855.

Happe, F. G. (1997). Central coherence and theory of mind in autism: Reading homographs in context. *British Journal of Developmental Psychology, 15*, 1–12.

Happe, F. G., & Frith, U. (1996). The neuropsychology of autism. *Brain, 119*, 1377–1400.

Hermelin, B., & O'Connor, N. (1967). Remembering of words by psychotic and subnormal children. *British Journal of Psychology, 58*, 213–218.

Hewitt, L. E. (1998). Influence of question type on response adequacy in young adults with autism. *Journal of Communication Disorders, 31*, 135–152.

Hobson, R. P. (1993). Understanding persons: The role of affect. In: S. Baron-Cohen, H. Tager-Flusberg & D. Cohen (Eds), *Understanding Other Minds: Perspectives from Autism*. New York: Oxford University Press.

Hobson, R. P. (1994). On developing mind. *British Journal of Psychiatry, 165*, 577–581.

Hughes, C., & Russell, J. (1993). Autistic children's difficulty with mental disengagement from an object: Its implications for theories of autism. *Developmental Psychology, 29*(4), 498–510.

Hughes, C., Russell, J., & Robbins, T. W. (1994). Evidence for executive dysfunction in autism. *Neuropsychologia, 32*, 477–492.

Jarrold, C. (1997). Pretend play in autism. In: J. Russell (Ed.), *Autism as an Executive Disorder* (pp. 101–142). New York: Oxford University Press.

Jarrold, C., & Russell, J. (1997). Counting abilities in autism: Possible implications for central coherence theory. *Journal of Autism and Developmental Disorders, 27*(1), 25–37.

Kaplan, E. (1983). A process approach to neuropsychological assessment. In: T. K. Boll & B. K. Bryant (Eds), *Clinical Neuropsychological Brain Function: Research Measurement and Practice* (pp. 129–167). Washington, D.C.: APA.

Karmiloff-Smith, A., Klima, E., Bellugi, U., Grant, J., & Baron-Cohen, S. (1995). Is there a social module? Language, face processing, and theory of mind in individuals with Williams syndrome. *Journal of Cognitive Neuroscience, 7*(2), 196–208.

Minshew, N. J., Goldstein, G., & Siegel, D. J. (1995). Speech and language in high-functioning autistic individuals. *Neuropathology, 9*(2), 255–261.

Mundy, P. (1995). Joint attention and social-emotional approach behavior in children with autism. *Developmental Psychopathology, 7*, 63–82.

Nadel, A. B. (1938). A qualitative analysis of behaviour following cerebral lesions diagnosed as primarily affecting the frontal lobes. *Archives of Psychology*, Whole No. 224.

Norman, D. A., & Shallice, T. (1986). Attention to action: Willed and automatic control of behavior. In: R. J. Davidson, G. E. Schwartz & D. Shapiro (Eds), *Consciousness and Self-Regulation* (Vol. 4, pp. 1–18). New York: Plenum.

O'Connor, N., & Hermelin, B. (1994). Two autistic savant readers. *Journal of Autism and Developmental Disorders, 24*(4), 501–515.

Ozonoff, S., Pennington, B. F., & Rogers, S. J. (1994). Executive function deficits in high functioning autistic children: Relationship to theory of mind. *Journal of Child Psychiatry, 32*, 1081–1105.

Pennington, B. F., & Ozonoff, S. (1996). Executive functions and developmental psychology. *Journal of Child Psychology and Psychiatry, 37*(1), 51–87.

Phillips, W., Baron-Cohen, S., & Rutter, M. (1998). Understanding intention in normal development and autism. *British Journal of Developmental Psychology, 16*, 337–348.

Powers, M. D. (1989). *Children with autism*. Rockville, MD: Woodbine House Inc.

Prior, M. R., & Hall, L. C. (1979). Comprehension of transitive and intransitive phrases by autistic, retarded and normal children. *Journal of Communication Disorders, 12*, 103–111.

Prior, M. R., & Hoffman, W. (1990). Brief report: Neuropsychological testing of autistic children through an exploration with frontal lobe tests. *Journal of Autism and Developmental Disorders, 20*, 581–590.

Reissenweber, M. (1953). The use of modified block designs in the evaluation and training of the brain injured. *Psychological Monographs: General and Applied*, *67*, Whole No. 371, 1–28.

Rumsey, J. M., & Hamburger, S. D. (1988). Neurological findings in high-functioning autistic men with infantile autism, residual state. *Journal of Clinical and Experimental Neuropsychology*, *10*, 201–221.

Shah, A., & Frith, U. (1993). Why do individuals show superior performance on the block design task? *Journal of Child Psychiatry*, *34*(8), 1352–1364.

Shapiro, M. B. (1952). Experimental studies of perceptual anomaly: Two confirmatory and explanatory experiments. *Journal of Mental Science*, *98*, 605–617.

Smith, I. M., & Bryson, S. E. (1994). Imitation and action in autism: a critical review. *Psychological Bulletin*, *116*, 259–273.

Snowling, M., & Frith, U. (1986). Comprehension in 'hyperlexic' readers. *Journal of Experimental Psychology*, *42*, 392–415.

Tager-Flusberg, H. (1981a). On the nature of linguistic functioning in early infantile autism. *Journal of Autism and Developmental Disorders*, *11*, 45–56.

Tager-Flusberg, H. (1981b). Sentence comprehension in autistic children. *Applied Psycholinguistics*, *2*, 5–24.

Tager-Flusberg, H. (1991). Semantic processing in the free recall of autistic children: Further evidence for a cognitive deficit. *British Journal of Developmental Psychology*, *9*, 417–430.

Turner, M. (1997). Towards an executive dysfunction account of repetitive behaviour in autism. In: J. Russell (Ed.), *Autism as an Executive Disorder* (pp. 57–100). New York: Oxford University Press.

Wahlberg, T. J., & Rotatori, A. (1996). Various treatment modalities for autistic individuals. In: A. F. Rotatori, J. O. Schwenn & S. Burkhardt (Eds), *Advances in Special Education* (pp. 109–131). Greenwich, CT: JAI Press.

Wing, L. (1993). The definition and prevalence of autism: A review. *European Child and Adolescent Psychiatry*, *2*, 61–74.

Yuill, N., Oakhill, J., & Parkin, A. (1989). Working memory, comprehension ability and the resolution of text anomaly. *British Journal of Psychology*, *80*, 351–361.

THE CONTROL THEORY OF AUTISM

Tim Wahlberg

INTRODUCTION

The following chapter explores a theoretical hypothesis looking at the development of autism through a neurological perspective. This is accomplished by presenting the control theory of autism from a developmental neurological perspective, dealing with how an individual with autism neurologically develops the disorder. Many theoretical perspectives exist today that attempt to explain the difficulties associated with autism based on the behavioral manifestations of the disorder with the underlying notion that they are caused by a neurological deficit (Happe & Frith, 1996). While other researchers blame the disorder on a breakdown of an underlying neural mechanism. The control theory of autism will explain the syndrome as the developmental emergence of a functionally distinct neurobehavioral architecture. Specifically, "normal" neurobehavioral architectures develop in a manner geared toward incorporating more and more complex forms of unpredictability, while autistic architectures develop toward reducing the very thing the other is attempting to incorporate; namely, unpredictability. This chapter attempts to explain the development of this autistic architecture at a neurological level and tie this into the behavioral manifestations as well as the cognitive problems resulting from the irregular neurological development.

Autistic Spectrum Disorders: Educational and Clinical Interventions, pages 19–35.

ISBN: 0-7623-0818-4

INTRODUCTION TO THE NEUROBIOLOGY OF AUTISM

One of the primary criticisms of research into the neurobiological underpinnings of autism involves the fact that much of the research involves single primary deficit models (Minshew & Goldstein, 1998). Therefore, such research proposes, "a clinically apparent deficit in a single cognitive domain or modality as underlying the social, communication, and odd nonsocial behavior in autism" (p. 131). New neurobiological research is proposing that the deficits can be found in several higher order cognitive abilities (Minshew & Goldstein, 1998; Minshew, Johnson & Luna, 2001). Current research (see Minshew et al., 2001) is finding that individuals with autism seem to do well or even excel at tasks that are simple and do not involve a great deal of complex information processing such as intact functioning in attention, sensory perception, simple memory, simple language, rule governing, and visuospatial areas. Deficits seem to stem from tasks that require concept formation, complex memory, complex language, and skilled motor abilities (Minshew & Goldstein, 1998).

The neurological development of autism, as proposed by this chapter, provides a clear understanding of the deficits associated with autism, including these higher order deficits. It is accomplished by explaining and comparing the difference in normal versus autistic brain development. This comparison provides the reader with a clearer understanding of why individuals with autism develop the disorder and insight into their thinking and thought processing based on neurological manifestations.

Normal Neurological Development: The Adaptive Incorporation of Unpredictability

Figure 1 is a schematic regarding the neurological development of the human brain. The large arrow in the middle represents the process of brain development. The arrow signifies the fact that brain development at a neurological level can not be stopped, only hindered (e.g. brain damage of some sort) or sidetracked as it reaches the full normal neurological stage represented by the outer most portion of the diagram labeled "full neurological development". The brain early on learns to take in information and make sense of it. Matus (2000) describes brain development via neuronal circuits as being established in three distinct stages. The first stage involves the initial "wiring up" of the nervous system which takes place during embryogenesis. The second phase takes place after birth during a short critical period when synaptic connections are refined by sensory and motor experience. The third and final stage of development

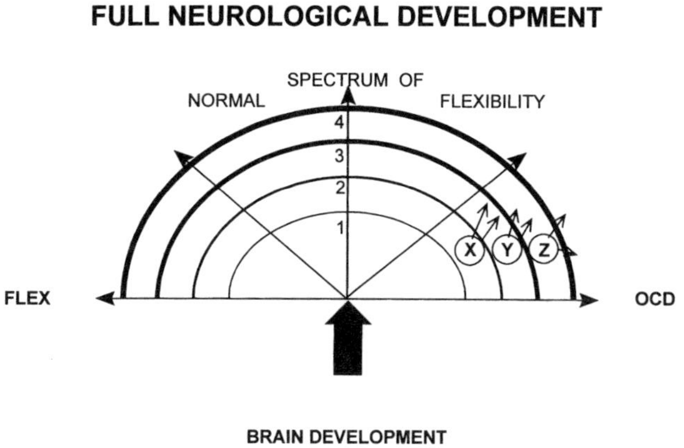

Fig. 1.

occurs in adulthood where brain plasticity is not as pronounced although changes in synaptic connectivity can occur.

The process of neurological interconnectivity of synaptic connections increases in complexity as an infant develops into adulthood. The point being made here, is that development at a neurological level is going to happen from conception to birth, and into adulthood. During this process, the brain learns to adapt and function within the surrounding environment.

The rings in Fig. 1 represent the stages of normal neurological development. Once the human brain is fully developed it has reached the external ring labeled Full Neurological Development. During this developmental process, neurons form connections and these connections are strengthened through a complex array of interactions.

The definition of Full Neuronal Development, within this theoretical position, involves the notion of ones ability to incorporate unpredictability as a means of functioning throughout life. It is the author's contention that in order to function at a relatively normal level in society one needs to be able to accommodate a certain level of unpredictability in everyday functioning. Adapting to unpredictability allows one to except change as well as to learn from experiences. A normal human brain allots for this function at a neurological level. In order to be considered able to handle unpredictability, one needs to be able to adapt to change and accept it. This acceptance of change does not necessarily mean one needs to like it, they just need to have the ability to adapt to it.

The Ability to Accommodate Unpredictability Requires Flexibility at a Neurological Level.

The two horizontal arrows in Fig. 1 represent brain development as well. The right horizontal arrow labeled OCD represents full brain development after the fourth ring, but with limited capacity to handle unpredictability. The label OCD represents the clinical diagnosis of obsessive compulsive disorder. Obsessive compulsive disorder is described as people whose brains are fully developed, but lack the ability to accommodate unpredictability in certain areas of functioning. These individuals often exhibit high levels of anxiety and rigidity. It is hypothesized that in order to calm themselves, these individuals may engage in ritualistic types of behavior. These behaviors involve routines that are never changing and consistent across time for each individual. Routines may be obsessions (e.g. reciting a long list created by the individual) or compulsions (e.g. excessively cleaning the house or washing ones hands because of a fear of germs). Individuals in the OCD section of Fig. 1 may be classified as extremely rigid persons who struggle with unpredictability, but are able to function in society (except of course in extreme cases).

The left horizontal arrow in Fig. 1 labeled **FLEX** represents full brain development after the fourth ring. The label **FLEX** represents individuals who are extremely flexible, able to handle large amounts of unpredictability in their daily lives, and have a sort of go-with-the-flow mentality. These are individuals who are unscathed by feelings of anxiety related to following a certain routine, ritual, or even rules that govern society. Such individuals are not necessarily pathological in nature, but they represent individuals in society who may not be considered highly functional. The author has often referred to individuals representative of this portion of the graph as being similar in functionality to the "Dead Heads" (individuals who used to follow the band the "Grateful Dead" around from concert to concert). These individuals for the most part had no jobs, no careers, and followed no strict routine and were only interested in attending the next "Grateful Dead" concert.

Normal functioning persons are represented in Fig. 1 between the two diagonal lines. Individuals represented in this section are described as having reached full neurological development and able to function within society by being flexible and adapting to various life changes (i.e. unpredictability) they encounter. This is where the majority of the population would fall. This is labeled the **Normal Spectrum of Flexibility**.

To reiterate, from conception individuals will develop at a neurological level and eventually reach full neurological development represented in Fig. 1 by the outer portion past the fourth ring. The important aspect represented in Fig. 1 involves the concept of flexibility. The human brain learns to neurologically adapt to change by forming a complex array of interconnections. It has the ability to do so and move on as well as learn from the experience. The unexpected does not force a complete shut down or overload of the system. In some cases individuals with fully neurologically developed brains struggle with flexibility (OCD) and in other cases seem to be overly flexible (**FLEX**).

It should be pointed out that the human brain *could* change and reorganize itself neurologically after it is fully developed. However, the farther along the brain is in its development (e.g. ring 1 vs. ring 4), the harder the changes may be. In fact, research (see Willott, 1999) is finding that neurological brain interconnectivity is not necessarily a Darwinian concept of the strongest surviving and the weakest dying, but rather the strongest connections flourishing and the weakest connections are present but not used.

AUTISTIC NEUROLOGICAL DEVELOPMENT

It is postulated that the development of the autistic brain follows the same simple rule put forward with normal brain development, namely, *that neurological brain development will happen and continue to happen until it is fully developed.* In the case of individuals with autism, the brain develops even though there may be certain neurological abnormalities encountered along the way. Unfortunately, as the autistic brain develops, adaptations to the neurological abnormalities occur. For example, individuals with autism have been found to have certain hyper/hypo sensitivities to various external/internal stimulation early on in neurological development (O'Neill & Jones, 1997). It is the very nature of these variable sensitivities that may actually constitute the problem lying at the root of autistic neurophysiology. Research suggests that about 25% of individuals afflicted with autism show distinct stimulation problems immediately after birth, whereas the other 75% show these problems around 18 to 24 months, but before the age of three years (Van Hasselt & Hersen, 1994). This problem may occur into adulthood as many high functioning individuals with autism describe feeling over-stimulation in some fashion (Grandin, 1995).

This sensitivity to stimuli involves the perception of information entering the brain. The perception involves nerve cells, nuclei, nerve endings, efferent and afferent nerves, and brain tissue. Therefore, perception is a neurological function (Cruickshank, 1981). The brain is able to integrate information from separate sensory systems into a comprehensive awareness of the external environment. The nervous system deals with a multitude of sensory information at any given moment (Stein & Meredith, 1990). The sensory problems of individuals with autism are not found within the neurons receptor cites but in the parts of the brain that are responsible for reading the messages sent by the nerves to the brain. In other words, when an individual with autism is tactually over-stimulated, the nerve endings in the skin are not hypersensitive to touch, the problem lies in the brains reading of the information sent to it by the nerve ending at the skin. The brain interprets this information in the above example at a very amplified level. This leads to perceiving the information sent as over-stimulating and possibly in other cases as under-stimulating. What autism researchers are finding is that the brain tissue, or the processing of the information is the problem for persons with autism as opposed to problems with their nerve endings (Minshew & Goldetein, 1998; Minshew, Goldstein & Siegel, 1997). The problem does not seem to be in information acquisition but rather information analysis, understanding, and evaluation (Minshew & Goldstein 1998). This is supported by researchers who postulate that deficits in sensory modulation are manifested behaviorally by overactivity and underactivity to stimuli (Dunn, 1997; Ornitz, 1992) and that the problems lie in the modulation of sensory input (Rapin, 1991).

This difficulty during the sensory-motor stage of development may indeed lead to the "construct" known as autism spectrum types of disorders. Neurologically, the sensory stage of development is the first stage of brain development and begins after conception in utero. The variability in the autistic disorder may be a direct reflection of the amount of sensory-motor difficulty each individual is experiencing and being forced to deal with at a neurological/brain level in early development. The more problems the system has at this level, the more "energy" (see Vandervert, 1995 for a detailed description of energy and the human brain) the brain is forced to use to handle the problems that under normal conditions wouldn't require extra energy or effort to process. This energy will undoubtedly have to be absorbed from another system or function that the brain would normally have the energy to carry out. This difficulty may lead to the higher level conceptualization problems that individuals with autism have (Minshew & Goldstein, 1998; Minshew, Johnson & Luna, 2001). The hypothesis being that higher level processing requires more energy while at the same time, lower level processes need to be functional. If problems exist in lower level processes, the brain will use the given amount of energy it has to compensate and deal with the lower level problems. Unfortunately, this results in the brain taking potential energy away from higher level functionality.

As one might imagine, brain development at a neurological level would involve massive neurological transformations in order to accomplish "learning" in a productive normal fashion. The problem comes in when the brain, for whatever reason, is not utilizing its given "energy" efficiently. Vandervert

(1995) discusses what he refers to as the maximum-power principle. In this principle, he states that the "systems that survive in the competition among alternative choices are those that develop [retool algorithms for] more power inflow and use it to meet the need of survival" (p. 83). If something is not working or processing information correctly in the brain, the brain is forced to utilize the energy it has to adjust to the problem and attempt to function, regardless. While we describe children and adults as being extremely resilient to difficulties they encounter developmentally, their biological system (the human brain) has a breaking point and it is unable to handle any more perturbations or overload. Once this point is reached, the brain must react and take action to protect and adapt to the problem. In the case of individuals with autism, the brain does react to the problems it is faced with. It does so whether the problem is in the actual "hard wiring" of the brain (i.e. a genetic component), the chemical make-up of the brain, or brain damage that may have occurred in utero or early in life. What ever the cause of the damage or problem in the brain, the brain will learn to cope and survive utilizing the energy and capacity it has to function to its fullest potential.

The development of the autistic brain can be demonstrated by the circles labeled X, Y, and Z in Fig. 1. As the autistic brain develops, the sensory information is being interpreted differently than in normal brain development. In many cases, this interpretation of stimuli can result in painful experiences or hypersensitivity. This can be seen in children with autism's unpleasant reactions to noise, touch, food, etc. What the brain is forced to do is *adapt* to these perceptual processing problems and do so while continuing to develop neurologically. This adaptation is represented in Fig. 1 by the three circles labeled X, Y, Z. These circles represent the autistic brain adapting to the perceived over or under-stimulating environment. In doing so, their brains learn effective ways to keep out or screen sensory stimulation they deem as incomprehensible or even painful. In the processing or handling this information, they are not taking in or processing external information as normal children do. They seem to spend the same amount of time and energy working at keeping the external stimulation out, as normal individuals spend absorbing and learning the information.

During development, the rings will get neurologically stronger and more developed (as seen in Fig. 1 by the changing thickness of rings 1 through 4). Another way to think about this is that the neurological interconnectivity within the brain strengthens over time. This makes early intervention critical for individuals with autism or related disorders. It is at the earliest stages of the neurological development of autism that the most significant changes are seen to occur from various types of interventions (e.g. Lovaas, 1987). With early intervention, the impact on the neurological connectivity of the brain seems to happen faster as the brain is in a very "plastic" malleable stage. Brain plasticity is described as a time during which neurological interconnections are made and enhanced with relative ease in comparison to a more developed brain where established connections are harder to change. The short arrows coming from the circles labeled X, Y, and Z in the Fig. 1 represent neurological changes in the brain leading to more normal neurological development following an intervention of some sort.

It is hypothesized that as an individual with autism ages, the compensatory neurological interconnections for their processing problems become stronger. Changes can and are made with older individuals with autism, but it is more difficult in comparison to young children with autism. It is hypothesized that some forms of treatment are beneficial to individuals with autism because they are forced, at a neurological level, to take in and process information that they would not likely do on their own. This results in new neurological connections that allow individuals with autism to learn different ways of handling and processing information as opposed to totally becoming withdrawn from the external environment which may be what their brains want to do. In effect their brains are forced toward the external ring in Fig. 1.

The amount of over or under-stimulation may be directly related to the severity of ones autism and may account for the large variability found within individuals diagnosed with the autism spectrum disorder. As individuals with autism age, they must adapt to their sensory processing problems. Individuals with autism who are unable to adapt because of the magnitude of their problems may represent persons diagnosed with mental retardation or those that deteriorate with time and end up institutionalized. In essence their brains can't learn to adapt or handle the processing problems to function in society. Possible adaptations are represented in Fig. 1 by the three circles. The circles represent neurological development and degree of autism. A mildly autistic individual would be represented with the third circle labeled Z (i.e. a lesser degree of processing difficulty at the sensory-motor stage of development). Individuals with high functioning autism, Asperger's Disorder, or Pervasive Developmental Disorder (PDD) may fall into this section of the graph. In many cases these individuals have a large amount of anxiety and are extremely rigid (as with OCD individuals). Individuals with autism in this section of the Figure, however, are still distinguishable diagnostically from OCD individuals. As the circles representing neurological development move inward (Z to Y to X) the degree of autism increases (mild, moderate, severe). In other words, severely autistic individuals would be represented by circle X. Another way to interpret this is that the innermost circle in Fig. 1 represents the farthest point from normal neurological development and cases with the greatest amount of sensory processing problems.

HOW DO THESE PROBLEMS IN BRAIN DEVELOPMENT LEAD TO AUTISM?

As individuals with autism learn to process and screen stimulation from conception on, they do so at a huge neurological expense. The brain is provided with a certain amount of energy to perform tasks needed to prosper, survive, and develop. Higher functioning human brains learn to utilize the energy and perform certain functions without expending large amounts of energy in the process (i.e. human brains become "efficient"). Think about the process the human brain goes through as it learns and becomes familiar with mathematical operations. We first learn what a number is and what it represents (one apple). We then learn that numbers can be manipulated. For example, physically taking one apple and placing it next to another apple gives you two apples. Therefore, $1 + 1 = 2$. As these concepts begin to make sense, less energy/effort is required to perform them. So, rather than holding up two fingers and counting them (i.e. one plus one equals two) children are able to calculate the problem "in their heads" so to speak. As a young child learns his/her "times tables" they do so in a very structured rigid manner, usually through rote memorization. When first tested on their times tables they may need to use a paper and pencil to perform the task of $8 \times 8 =$___. They may have to draw out the numbers and attempt to add them together.

As individuals with autism adapt, they block out stimuli that is incomprehensible to them and learn stimuli at a very concrete, simplistic level in order to function and understand the world around them. Information that is never changing and concrete is what individuals with autism crave to function. In order to make sense of the information presented, the brain of an individual with autism learns to break down stimuli into simple concrete never changing information (i.e. removing unpredictability) which in turn creates comprehensibility and simplicity for him/her in a complex world. Individuals with autism want to be able to process information in a very black and white concrete way. This provides stability for individuals with autism. Due to their processing pattern, the brain of individuals with autism is forced to use much more energy in processing information than normal individuals. In doing so, energy needed to understand higher level conceptualization can be compromised.

As an individual with autism develops, he/she appears to acquire skills that serve to block out sensory stimulation. This blocking of input could be described as the active reduction of abstractions into simpler structures (i.e. actively reducing the unpredictability or flexibility). To facilitate the readers understanding, flexibility/unpredictability could be considered "abstract" and non-flexibility/predictability could be considered "concrete". These acquired skills may take the form of self-stimulation behaviors that are commonly observed in individuals with autism. It is believed that individuals with autism may engage in these behaviors to remove stimuli that are unpleasant to process while at the same time having the effect of calming them. When individuals with autism stimulate themselves, they appear to be in their "own world". A world that they create for themselves as a way to cope with what they are unable to understand.

Individuals with autism create ways to understand environments that lack consistency and concreteness. They do this in a way which simplifies inconsistencies and transforms complex environment information into black and white terms. Their goal is to create an environment that is uniform and consistent, in order to have predictability in their lives. When individuals with autism become confused, disoriented, or anxious, they often resort to something that is consistent and concrete. In doing so they remove unpredictability, and this is calming. Information is better understood for individuals with autism when presented and interpreted in such a manner. Because large amounts of energy are used to "control" for external stimulation, little energy is left for functional learning and normal developmental progression. Individuals with autism therefore, learn simple concrete ways of maneuvering through life. Individuals with severe autism often resort to rather violent means of "control". This can often time take the form of self-injurious behaviors. In contrast higher functioning individuals with autism find other control behaviors to remove themselves from an over-stimulating environment such as hand flapping, rocking, staring at something for hours or even the development of savant skills. Engaging in these control behaviors remove the individuals with autism from any external problematic or confusing stimulation.

SIMPLE RATHER THAN COMPLEX INFORMATION PROCESSING

As a child with autism develops neurologically, his/her brain learns to handle incoming information in a simplistic manner. This may involve actively preventing the development of abstractions (i.e. breaking down information into black and white characteristics) while providing a means of comprehensibility to individuals with autism, which is calming to them. During this process, neurological advanced interconnections/interconnectivity may be lacking. For example, Bauman and Kemper (1997) have found that individuals with autism are lacking in the branching of nerve endings (dendrites) in comparison with controls (as can be seen in Fig. 2). This lack of dendritic complexity may lead to decreased flexibility that in turn may lead to a preference for concrete stimuli. This makes sense if individuals with autism process information, in a very

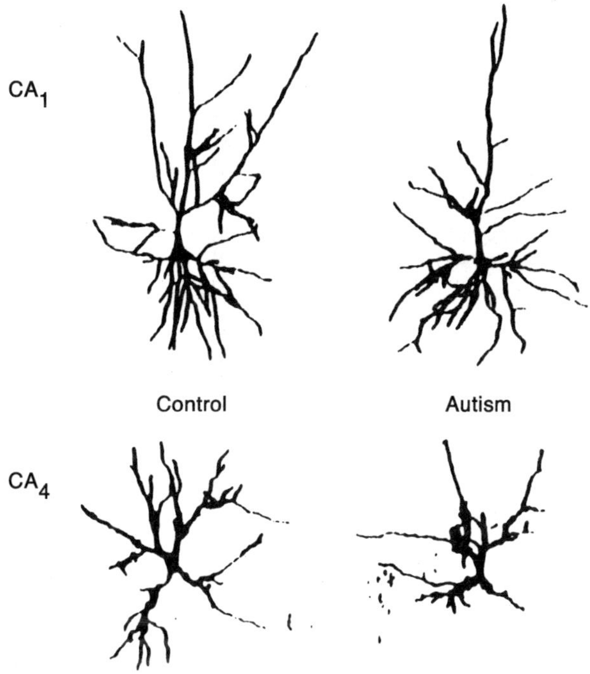

Fig. 2. Camera lucida drawings of glogi-Stained neurons from CA4 and CA1 subfields of the hippocampus. Note the stunting of some of the dendritic arbors in the cells from the autistic brain and the limited amount of secondary and tertiar branching in these neurons.

Reprinted from *Neurobiology of infantile Autism* H. Naruse & E. M Ornitz (Eds.), Kemper, T. L., & Bauman, M. L. Neuropatholgy of infantile autism. (pp 43–57) 1992, with permission from Elsevier Science.

concrete, black and white manner. Interestingly Temple Grandin (1995), who is autistic, stated that individuals with autism process information in either picture or number form. This makes sense as they are two highly concrete ways of seeing and processing information in the world. Grandin described how she would process hearing the word "dog" as seeing physically a picture of her first dog in her head, not as thinking about a four legged, domesticated furry animal. Other individuals with autism think in numbers and use numbers to solve environmental problems in order to get through life. Numerical thinking is a very factual concrete way of processing information. A way of processing

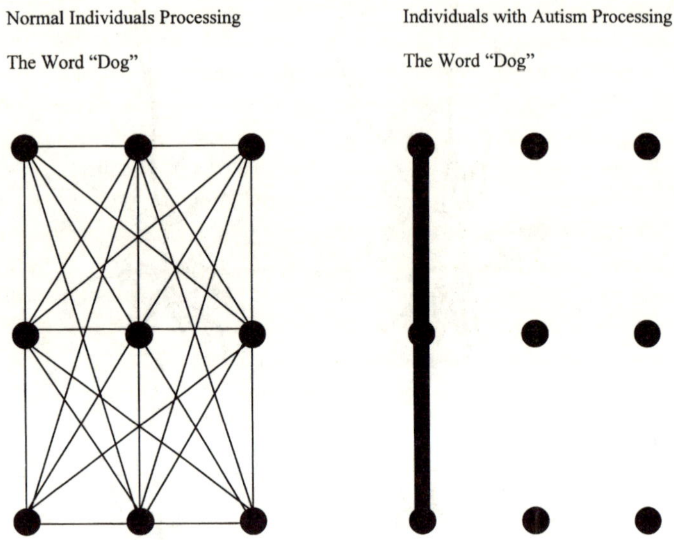

Fig. 3.

information is represented in Fig. 3. As can be seen in Fig. 3, one way of interpreting neurological functioning is to show the firing of neurons when the word dog is heard by normal individuals and individuals with autism. As hypothesized, individuals with autism make fewer neurological connections than normal individuals when thinking of the word "dog".

This simplistic way of processing information becomes problematic for individuals with autism when the information is complex. The definition of complex information in cognitive theory as described by Minshew and Goldstein (1998) is: "the number of elements contained in the stimulus material as well as the multiplicity of cognitive processes involved in task performance" (p. 134). Due to the manner in which the autistic brain develops and the resulting information comprehension problem, higher level cognitive tasks become very difficult to process and understand for individuals with autism. For example, individuals with autism struggle with social situations and communication, because both are very complex tasks. Even if one tries to create concrete rules to follow in social situations and communications, a social interaction is never the same. This can be illustrated with an example of social boundaries. Social proximity is not always consistent and varies from culture to culture. There is no universal rule that governs proximity. So in order for an individual to use appropriate social proximity when interacting with another individual, one needs to pay attention to the social interaction as it unfolds. If an individual gets a "sense" that he/she is to close to another individual while engaging in conversation, one will probably move back during the interaction. A similar illustration would involve a person following distinct facial cues to gain social information. As individuals speak and interact their faces are full of nonverbal expression. For individuals with autism, processing nonverbal facial expressions can be uncomfortable and problematic because they are trying to transform these expressions into concrete consistent cues during an interaction. It may be that these minor changes in facial expression during a social interaction lead individuals with autism to struggle with eye contact. This struggle may lead an individual with autism to look at something other than the person's face or eyes while interacting and carrying on a conversation in order to avoid becoming ever whelmed by the interaction. Language is another extremely difficult form of social interaction to follow. Individuals with autism seem to interpret language in a very literal sense (as seen in Fig. 3). Therefore "slang" expressions are very difficult for them to understand because often times it does not have a literal interpretation.

Complex sensory information may overload individuals with autism. The over-stimulation caused by the environment can cause individuals with autism to shutdown and remove themselves from the problematic stimulation. In some case this may be as easy as walking away, but in other cases it may not be an option. When leaving is not an option, individuals with autism may resort to self-stimulation behaviors which help them cope with over-stimulation. The behaviors exhibited may range from hand flapping to reciting or memorizing facts in their heads. In such situations an individual with autism copes with the stress to his/her system by removing the stimulation that stresses the system. This process allows their brains to become "efficient" and "effective" at reducing informational complexity (abstraction). As their brains learn to do this, individuals with autism compromise other important life functioning aspects they could be attending to. In effect individuals with autism increase their neurological interconnections to carry out this stimulus removal function but sacrifice their enabling skills to interact socially.

NEUROLOGICAL IMPLICATIONS OF TREATMENT

Behavioral therapy has been shown to be an effective treatment for children with autism (Lovaas, 1987). It may be effective due to the simplicity of the therapy. For example, tasks are broken down onto the simplest form of understandability and are presented a number of times in a very concrete, black and white fashion. This may be very appealing to individuals with autism because of the way they process information. The end goal of treatment is to get individuals with autism to become less rigid and more spontaneous when processing information and interacting with others.

The drug Secretin has been found to offer some relief (Horvath, Stefanatos, Sokoloski, Wachtel, Nabors & Tildon, 1998) to certain individuals with autism (although with very limited research). Secretin is a drug used primarily to conduct tests of the digestive and/or gastrointestinal system. Would this drug help certain individuals with autism? The gastro-intestinal track is directly tied into the brain via neurological connections that tell the brain what is happening when digesting food and sends a signal when a problem occurs. Even though this process takes place at an unconscious level the brain is involved. If individuals with autism are suffering gastro-intestinal "overload", the brain would have to utilize its given energy to "deal with" the problems it is experiencing internally in the intestines and stomach. When the drug is administered it seems to help children with autism function better. It is hypothesized that Secretin is freeing up energy in the brain or "space" to be used in another fashion, such as for speech. Research with Secretin is currently underway and the results discussed here are used solely in a theoretical manner based on rather limited findings to date.

Anytime energy is freed up in the brain of an individual with autism, the potential for progress in increased. This may be done with medication (Wahlberg & Rotatori, 1996), vitamins or supplements (Menage, Thinbault, Barthelemy, Lelord & Bardos, 1992), or through some intervention or treatment as previously described (Grandin, 1995; Lovaas, 1987; Wahlberg & Rotatori, 1996). Many effective types of interventions exist for the treatment of individuals with autism (see Wahlberg & Rotatori, 1996).

EXPERTS AT SAMENESS

Individuals with autism seem to become experts at "sameness" and concrete, black and white informational processing. They develop skills in areas that follow rules or that are never changing. Savants are said to make up a small proportion of the autistic population, but most savants are classified as having a spectrum disorder. When we think of a savant skill, we usually see skills in the area of calendars (see Spitz, 1995), music, math, memorizing long lists of names, reading (in some cases being hyperlexic) or train schedules, just to name a few. What do all of these areas have in common? They are concrete in nature. Calendars of the past will never change, basic mathematical or reading rules never change, the number of notes the human ear can hear or the number of keys on the piano keyboard will never change.

Savants are motivated to spend time learning these tasks. Hard concentrated effort is put into learning to perform these tasks with relative ease. If one thinks of doing mathematical times tables as discussed earlier, one can become good and efficient at performing these tasks. Similarly, individuals with autism become good and efficient at concrete tasks and in some cases savants become exceptionally good at one task. The human brain is capable of becoming extremely efficient at performing tasks. The difference with savants, might be due to the amount of "motivated" effort they put into learning these tasks. Research on "experts" indicates that motivated effort of 10 years and/or 10,000 hours of practice in a specific skill is needed (Ericsson, Krampe & Tesch-Romer, 1993). Once this time period is reached, one is said to be an expert in that area or field (Ericsson & Charness, 1994). If an individual with autism finds an area of interest, it is easy to see how a skill in that area can become highly developed. For example, an individual with autism may be motivated to keep out environmental stimuli that are incomprehensible or painful and if memorizing calendars allows him/her to do this, it makes sense that he/she would.

If early neurological development were effected in individuals with autism as previously described, then it would make sense that they would have problems with social interactions, communication, and display odd behaviors and interests (as per the diagnostic criteria in the DSM-IV, 1994). Due to their unique neurological development individuals with autism are not as interested in the outside world as normal children. If this is indeed the case, they would not be interested in learning to communicate or interact with others. Also, they would withdraw into their own worlds which they are able to control. We can control ourselves and our actions for the most part, but we can not control the actions and thoughts of others around us. Since humans in general are considered social creatures, anything that appears asocial in development would be considered odd or different (i.e. the behavioral oddities associated with autism). Most children as they develop, do so within a social context, responding to caregivers and in doing so learn from others within their immediate environment. Humans are motivated neurologically to do so, unfortunately this is not the neurological course of development for individuals with autism.

CONCLUSION

Because of the problems with the neurological processing of incoming information in individuals with autism, problems develop in their first/earliest stages of brain development. Individuals with autism are forced to learn to function in some manner despite the problems they have at understanding and/or processing the incoming sensory information and stimulation. We are starting to see much clearer that there are various parts of the brain of individuals with autism that are seemingly effected such as the frontal lobes, the cerebellum, and the cerebral cortex (see Autism: Neurological Implications and the Aging Process, this volume, for a detailed description). Early brain development involves the Purkinje cell dendrites within the cerebellum and the cerebellum develops very rapidly during the early postnatal period. Therefore, sensory-motor developmental problems may have an impact on these areas of brain development. Research is showing that individuals with autism are having trouble making higher level inferences and performing higher level tasks because of the neurological problems previously described (Minshew & Goldstein, 1998). The aforementioned sensory-motor processing problems may lead to a direct decrease in neurological interconnectedness, which in turn infringes on higher level neurological development and processing and leads us to the construct known as autism.

REFERENCES

American Psychiatric Association (1994). *Diagnostic and statistical manual of mental disorders (DSM-IV)* (4th ed). Washington, D.C.: Author.

Bauman, M., & Kemper, L. (1997). Neuroanatomic observations of the brain in autism. In: M. L. Bauman & T. L. Kemper (Eds), *The Neurology of Autism* (pp. 45–65). Baltimore, MD: John Hopkins University Press.

Cruickshank, W. M. (1981). A new perspective in teacher education: The neuroeducator. *Journal of Learning Disabilities*, *14*(6), 337–367.

Dunn, M. (1997). Neurophysiological observations in autism and implication for neurological dysfunction. In: M. L. Bauman & T. L. Kemper (Eds), *The Neurology of Autism* (pp. 45–65). Baltimore, MD: John Hopkins University Press.

Ericsson, K. A., & Charness, N. (1994). Expert performance. *American Psychologist*, *49*(9), 725–747.

Ericsson, K. A., Krampe, R. T., & Tesch-Romer, C. (1993). The role of deliberate practice in the acquisition of expert performance. *Psychological Review*, *100*(3), 363–406.

Grandin, T. (1995). *Thinking in pictures and other reports from my life with autism*. New York: Doubleday.

Happe, F. G., & Frith, U. (1996). The neuropsychology of autism. *Brain*, *119*, 1377–1400.

Horvath, K., Stefanatos, G., Sokoloski, K. N., Wachtel, R., Nabors, L., & Tildon, J. T. (1998). Improved social and language skills after secretin administered in patients with autistic spectrum disorders. *Journal of the Association for Academic Minority Physicians*, *9*, 9–15.

Kemper, T. L., & Bauman, M. L. (1992). Neuropathology of infantile autism. In: H. Naruse & E. M. Ornitz (Eds), *Neurobiology of Infantile Autism*. (pp. 43–57). Amstredam: Elsevier Science Publishers.

Lovaas, O. I. (1987). Behavioral treatment and normal educational and intellectual functioning in young autistic children. *Journal of Consulting and Clinical Psychology*, *55*, 3–9.

Matus, A. (2000). Actin-based plasticity in dendritic spines. *Science*, *290*(5492), 754–758.

Menage, P., Thinbault, G., Barthelemy, C., Lelord, G., & Bardos, P. (1992). CD4 + CD45RA + T lymphocyte deficiency in autistic children: Effect of a pridoxine-magnesium treatment. *Brain Dysfunct*, *5*, 326–333.

Minshew, N. J., & Goldstein, G. (1998). Autism as a disorder of complex information processing. *Mental Retardation and Developmental Disabilities*, *4*, 129–136.

Minshew, N. J., Goldstein, G., & Siegel, D. J. (1997). Neuropsychological functioning in autism: Profile of a complex information processing disorder. *Journal of the International Neuropsychological Society*, *3*, 303–316.

Minshew, N. J., Johnson, C., & Luna, B. (2001). The cognitive and neural basis of autism: A disorder of complex information processing and dysfunction of neocortical systems. *Mental Retardation and Developmental Disabilities*, *23*, 111–138.

O'Neill, M., & Jones, R. S. P. (1997). Sensory-perceptual abnormalities in autism: A case for more research? *Journal of Autism and Developmental Disorders*, *27*(3), 283–292.

Ornitz, E. M. (1992). A behaviorally-based neurophysiological model for dysfunction of directed attention in infantile autism. In: H. Naruse & E. M. Ornitz (Eds), *Neurobiology of Infantile Autism* (pp. 89–110). Amstredam: Excerpta Medica.

Rapin, I. (1991). Autistic children: Diagnostic and clinical features. *Pediatrics*, (Suppl.), 87, 751–760.

Spitz, H. H. (1995). Calendar calculating idiot savants and the smart unconscious. *New Ideas In Psychology*, *13*, 167–182.

Stein, B. E., & Meredith, M. E. (1990). Multisensory integration: Neural and behavioral solution for dealing with stimuli from different sensory modalities. In A. Diamond (Ed.), *The Development and Neural Bases of Higher Cognitive Functions* (pp. 51–70). New York: Annals of the New York Academy of Sciences.

Van Hasselt, V. B., & Hersen, M. (1994). *Advanced abnormal psychology*. New York: Plenum Press.

Vandervert, L. R. (1995). From idiots savants to Albert Einstein: A brain-algorithmic explanation of savant and everyday performance. *New Ideas in Psychology*, *14*, 81–92.

Wahlberg, T. J., & Rotatori, A. (1996). Various treatment modalities for autistic individuals. In: A. F. Rotatori, J. O. Schwenn & S. Burkhardt (Eds), *Advances in Special Education* (pp. 109-131). Greenwich, CT JAI Press.

Willott, J. F. (1999). *Neurogerontology: Aging and the nervous system*. DeKalb, IL: Northern Illinois University: VCB Custome Packets.

AUTISM: NEUROLOGICAL IMPLICATIONS AND THE AGING PROCESS

Tim Wahlberg

INTRODUCTION

Autism is a very perplexing psychological disorder that effects an estimated four in 10,000 children born in the United States (Wahlberg & Rotatori, 1996). Autism can be defined as "a developmental disorder which usually becomes evident before the age of three years. It is a neurological or brain disorder in which the behavior, communication, and social interactions are the primary disabilities" (National Information Center for Children and Youth with Disabilities, 1993, p. 1). Three distinct criteria are outlined and used in the diagnosis of autism within the diagnostic categories of the Diagnostic and Statistical Manual of Mental Disorders, Fourth Edition (DSM-IV, 1994). These three criteria are as follows; (1) qualitative impairment in social interaction, (2) qualitative impairments in communication, and (3) restricted repetitive and stereotyped patterns of behavior, interests, and activities. Qualitative impairment in social interactions takes the form of individuals with autism lacking the ability to engage in appropriate social interactions (Hewitt, 1998; Mundy, 1995; Smith & Bryson, 1994; Wahlberg & Rotatori, 1996). This social inadequacy is witnessed early on in individuals with autism. For example, infants with autism show an impaired capacity to engage in social exchanges, such as mutual imitation (Smith & Bryson, 1994). This social inadequacy extends into

Autistic Spectrum Disorders: Educational and Clinical Interventions, pages 37–51.

ISBN: 0-7623-0818-4

childhood in the form of the inability to have friends and engage in appropriate social play with others (DSM-IV, 1994; Fotheringham, 1990; Happe & Frith, 1996; Wahlberg & Rotatori, 1996), and into adulthood in the form of a lack of strong social relationships (DSM-IV, 1994; Fotheringham, 1990; Happe & Frith, 1996; Wahlberg & Rotatori, 1996). Impairment in communication includes not only the lack of language and communication, but the inappropriate use of language (Bartak, Rutter & Cox, 1975; Bartak, Rutter & Cox, 1977; Cantwell, Baker & Rutter, 1978; Happe, 1995; Happe & Frith, 1996; Lord, 1985, 1996; Mundy, 1995; Ramberg, Ehlers, Nyden, Johansson & Gillberg, 1996; Simmons & Baltaxe, 1975; Tager-Flusberg, 1981a; Wahlberg & Rotatori, 1996). Individuals with autism often exhibit a delayed onset of language (Carpuralo & Cohen, 1977; DSM-IV, 1994; Frith & Snowling, 1983; Happe & Frith, 1996; Prior & Hall, 1979; Tager-Flusberg, 1981b; Tager-Flusberg et al., 1990; Wahlberg & Rotatori, 1996). When language does develop it often takes the form of echolalia (repeating phrases) or parroting (repeating word for word what was said to them) (Happe & Frith, 1996). Some high functioning individuals with autism are able to read text. Research has shown that these individuals often show distinct comprehension deficits when interpreting written text (Frith & Snowling, 1983; Happe, 1997; O'Connor & Hermelin, 1994; Prior & Hall, 1979; Snowling & Frith, 1986; Tager-Flusberg, 1981b; Yuill, Oakhill & Parkin, 1989). Also, restrictive and repetitive forms of behavior can be best described as an inherent insistence on sameness (Happe, 1995; Happe & Frith, 1996; Wahlberg & Rotatori, 1996). When individuals with autism engage in activities, such as spinning the wheel of a toy car for an extended period of time, the activity involves inappropriate play as well as a repetitive pattern of activity.

A number of theories exist to date that attempt to explain how individuals with autism come to acquire the disorder (see Happe & Frith, 1996). Since autism is classified as a neurological disorder, many researchers are attempting to shed some light on what portions of their brains are functioning incorrectly, causing autism to develop (see Bauman & Kemper, 1985; 1994a, b; Minshew & Goldstein 1998). Other theories do not attempt to explain the neurological anomalies, but rather explain how individuals with autism function as a result of such disturbances in the brain (see Happe & Frith, 1996). These theories are labeled "cognitive theories of autism".

The cognitive oriented theories that exist today attempt to shed some light on this unique psychological disorder. Many of these theories postulate that various cognitive mechanisms appear to be malfunctioning, giving rise to the symptomology of autism (Baron-Cohen, Leslie & Frith, 1985; Frith, 1989; Frith & Happe, 1994; Happe, 1994; Happe & Frith, 1996; Jarrold & Russell, 1997;

Mundy, 1995; Mundy, Sigman & Kasari, 1990; Ozonoff, Pennington & Rogers, 1991; Smith & Bryson, 1994). Other theories postulate that the symptoms associated with autism occur because of various strategies individuals with autism employ in order to better understand sensory information they acquire from the environment (see Wahlberg, 2000).

This chapter begins by explaining how autism develops in children at the neurological level. Then various neurological findings associated with individuals with autism are explored. The final emphasis of the chapter is devoted to the neurological development of autism, and on how an individual with autism's brain changes neurologically as they age.

CONTROL THEORY

As mentioned previously, very few theories exist that attempt to describe the neurological development of autism. Neurological deficits in individuals with autism are generally taken as a given, and research and theories tend to focus on the behavioral manifestations of the neurological anomalies inherent in individuals with autism. Wahlberg (2000) has used clinical findings, previous knowledge, and current research to develop a theory that attempts to explain the development of autism at the neuronal level starting at birth. This researcher has postulated a theory that attempts to explain how autism manifests itself in certain individuals (see also The Control Theory of Autism, this volume). His theory is an attempt to "bridge the gap" between theories that exist to date.

Wahlberg (2000) postulates that individuals with autism suffer from environmental over-stimulation (O'Neill & Jones, 1997) which leads to many, if not all, of the symptoms associated with autism. Wahlberg indicates that this over-stimulation forces individuals with autism to process incoming stimuli in a very different manner, than normal individuals. This researcher argues that the brain of an individual with autism learns to think and handle information in a very different manner due to environmental over-stimulation. His theory is referred to as the Control Theory of autism.

O'Neill and Jones (1997) state that abnormalities in sensory or perceptual experiences can occur in the following areas, perception of sound, vision, touch, taste, smell, as well as kinesthetic and proprioceptive sensation. This stimulation may include hyper- and/or hyposensitivity to stimulation. According to O'Neill and Jones these stimulation distortions may lead individuals with autism to have problems in the processing of incoming sensory information.

Wahlberg (The Control Theory of Autism, this volume) describes over-stimulation as the effect environmental stimuli has on the neuronal activity within the human body. An example of over-stimulation would be wearing a wooly sweater without a tee shirt underneath. To most individuals this would be very over-stimulating to the tactile senses in the human body. This feeling is produced by the activation of neurons in the body that describe the "feel" of the sweater to the brain. The brain then suppresses this activation of the senses through chemical exchanges. This suppression is what allows us to wear clothing and not feel it unless we consciously think about it. This term is referred to as habituation (Willott, 1999). In the above example, the body may not be able to suppress the high level of over-stimulation produced by the sweater (i.e. it is to stimulating for suppression to take hold). Wahlberg hypothesizes that this over-stimulation of the senses is what causes individuals to develop autism and the various symptoms associated with it. In essence individuals with autism are unable to suppress the incoming stimuli and as information enters their respective "field", it does so much in the same way the sweater does for normal individuals, as over-stimulating, but to a much greater effect. Normal individuals have control over the sweater example as they can take it off or put on a tee shirt. In contrast individuals with autism can not take off clothing that is over-stimulating to them as many may be walking around with no clothes on. This example can be applied to all forms of incoming stimuli entering the bodies sensation field such as sight, sound, touch, and smell.

Wahlberg (2000) hypothesizes that individuals with autism learn to take in information in such a way as to screen out anything in the environment that is over stimulating. Within this information processing paradigm, individuals with autism learn to perceive information in a manner that is recognizable and understandable to them without the information over-stimulating them. Individuals with autism learn to control their surrounding environment in such a way as to make it understandable and less painful. They in turn learn very effective strategies that suppress over-stimulating events that surround them. These strategies, it is argued, are manifested in many of the odd behaviors classic to individuals with autism, such as stereotypic behaviors. For example, individuals with autism often will begin to stimulate themselves, when over-stimulated, by flapping their hands in front of their faces. In essence, they are removing themselves from whatever is over-stimulating them in the environment.

Individuals with autism learn to control over-stimulating environmental stimuli very early on in life. For example, infants with autism avoid eye contact and tense up when held (Van Hasselt & Hersen, 1994; Wahlberg & Rotatori, 1996). This is evident in almost 25% of cases of autism. Additionally, children with autism are often found sitting in a corner by themselves, almost as if they are attempting to tune out the external environment that they deem to be over-stimulating. Similarly, the way children with autism play with toys is suggestive of a form of control over the environment as they will take a toy car, turn it over, and spin the tires for extended periods of time. In doing so they are controlling the action of the toy, as well as tuning out external stimuli that they perceive as over-stimulating. All these interactions effect the way children with autism interact and draw information from their environment.

Wahlberg (2000) argues that individuals with autism can be over-stimulated by the external environment in a number of ways via tactile, auditory, or visual stimuli. Their reaction to controlling this over stimulation leads to brain development that is different than typical normal brain development. During normal brain development in childhood, individuals are attempting to acquire information dealing with every aspect of the world around them. In contrast individuals with autism expend the same amount of energy learning to remove the over-stimulating environment around them. They attempt to find ways to "tune out" the external, at times painful, environmental stimulation. Whereas in normal brain development, children take in information, the brains of individuals with autism tune out over stimulating external stimulus. The brain of an individual with autism continues to develop and learn to harness the energy it's provided, but it learns to screen out information deemed over-stimulating or painful by developing very concrete ways of processing information to make it meaningful without being painful or over-stimulating. This process results in the individual with autism appearing rigid and inflexible, socially inept, and lacking proper communication skills. The focus for individuals with autism becomes "sameness". They crave information that is consistent and concrete. Individuals with autism focus on environmental stimuli that are concrete, such as numbers, or calendars because they never change.

Recently, Wahlberg (1996) tested a child with autism's ability to control a short-term memory task (see A Case Study in the Dynamics of Autism, this volume). The researcher used the Sternberg short-term memory task to assess both normal children and a child with autism's reaction times and delay times in completing the task. All subjects were asked to complete a task that required them to respond to a probe that either appeared in a previously presented word or did not. This response was referred to as a reaction time response. Subjects in the study had to press a button to initiate the next trial. This was referred to as the delay time. Upon analysis of the subjects reaction and delay times, Wahlberg and Jordan found that the child with autism had a longer overall delay time, while at the same time having a very structured set of data. In other words, the child with autism was controlling the task. The researcher reported that the length of the delay time represents the child's apprehension in initiating the next trial as it represented an unknown set of new variables. Wahlberg concluded that the subject's control of the unknown next trial placed him in an awkward and uncomfortable position due to his craving for sameness.

Wahlberg (2000) hypothesizes that the over stimulation felt by individuals with autism causes them to attempt to create order within the chaos of the world. They do this by filtering the information they take in. In essence individuals with autism take "flexible" information that is and filter it to make it more "concrete". The over-stimulation they experience forces them to control the influx of information, while at the same time feeding their desire for "sameness". This insistence on sameness is paramount in the diagnosis of autism and it is referred to as rigid stereotypic behavior. This is what Wahlberg found in his study where the child with autism controlled the task and at the same time controlled how he was processing information.

NEUROLOGICAL RESEARCH

Happe and Frith (1996) carried out an extensive literature review dealing with neurological findings related to individuals with autism. The authors found that research conducted with autistic individuals used in vivo imaging and/or post-mortem autopsies at both the macro and microscopic levels of exploration. Happe and Frith pointed out that some of the research reviewed did not have adequate comparison groups and that in some cases the documentation of the subjects was not always complete.

Happe and Frith (1996) reported the most solid finding to date is the presences of cytoarchitectonic peculiarities in the limbic system and cerebellum. Bauman and Kemper (1985, 1994a; as cited in Happe & Frith, 1996) found increased cell packing, reduced cell size and reduced connections in many parts of the limbic system when viewing whole brain serial sections of individuals with autism. The researchers reported additional abnormalities in the cerebellum and inferior olive of the brainstem in the form of lower Purkinje cell counts. Similarly, Bauman (1991) found Purkinje cell loss in the preserved olivary neurons, multiple areas of the brain showing increased cell-packing density with reduced neuronal cell size and an absence of obvious gliosis. Bauman stated that all the aforementioned abnormalities were, "consistent with a curtailment of the normal development of portions of the limbic system and cerebellar circuits" (p. 794). This researhcer stressed that the preserved olivary neurons suggested the process which caused these abnormalities began or occurred before birth. Also, Kemper and Bauman (1993) reported evidence that abnormalities in the brains of individuals with autism were found to exist primarily in two areas, namely the limbic system in the forebrain and the cerebellum and related inferior olive in the hindbrain.

Happe and Frith (1996) reported that structural MRI studies have reported mixed results. For example, some research showed that not all subjects with autism have abnormalities and no single abnormality characterizes all subjects with autism (Happe & Frith, 1996). Hashimoto et al. (1995) (as cited in Happe & Frith, 1996) found morphological abnormalities of the cerebellum and brainstem. These researchers used extremely young children with autism which was important to rule out the possibility that similar abnormalities in adults are late appearing or secondary to consequences of autism.

Happe and Frith (1996) also reviewed literature focused on structural PET scans and EEGs. The researchers found that these areas of investigation were inconclusive in regards to individuals with autism. For instance, one of the cited PET scan studies reported that elevated glucose utilization in widespread brain regions showed considerable overlap between individuals with autism and the matched controls (Rumsey, Rapoport & Sceery, 1985), whereas Herold, Frackowiak, Le Couteur, Rutter & Howlin (1988) found no differences in resting blood flow and oxygen consumption between individuals with autism and matched controls. Happe and Frith concluded that the EEG studies do not provide any independent evidence concerning the biological nature of autism but they may be important to assess seizure activity in individuals with autism.

Seigel, Nuechterlein, Abel, Wu, and Buchsbaum (1995) found that individuals with autism showed negative correlations of medial frontal cortical glucose metabolic rate (GMR) with attentional performance. In this study subjects performed a test of sustained attention, the degraded stimulus continuous performance test (CPT), during a 35 minute 18-flouro-2-deoxyglucose uptake period preceding positron emission tomographic (PET) scan acquisition. PET with 18-fluoro-2-deoxyglucose (FDG) is a brain imaging technique which measures regional brain glucose metabolic rate summed over a 35 minute FDG tracer uptake period. Seigel et al. concluded that neuronal inefficiency in that region may contribute to poor performance and subcortical damage may be an important factor in attentional dysfunction in individuals with autism.

Bailey's (1993) literature review concerning the neurology of autism indicated that post mortem studies did not find any gross pathology. There were findings of alterations in cell packing (Bauman, 1991), as well as reported morphology in the hippocampus and related limbic structures (Raymond, Bauman & Kemper, 1989). Also, Bailey reported cerebellum abnormalities in studies with mentally retarded individuals with autism (see Bauman, 1991; Ritvo et al., 1986; Williams, Hauser, Purpura, Delong & Swisher, 1980).

Bailey also reviewed neuroimaging studies that found a wide variety of macroscopic abnormalities. These abnormalities were found in the dilation of the various ventricles (Bauman & Kemper, 1985; Campbell et al., 1982; Hauser, Delong & Rosman, 1975; Jacobson, Le Couteur, Howlin & Rutter, 1988), basal ganglia abnormalities (Gaffney, Kuperman, Tsai & Minichin, 1989; Jacobson et al., 1988) as well as diverse cortical malformations (Piven et al., 1990). Similar findings were reported in a review by Ciaranello and Ciaranello (1995).

FUTURE NEUROLOGICAL RESEARCH

The fact that autism is characterized as a neurological disorder creates a very difficult paradigm for researchers. Technology limits our understanding of the human brain and its development. Further complicating the issue is the fact that individuals with autism are very different with respect to their abilities and prognosis. The aforementioned research does not provide a very clear, pronounced understanding of the neurological implications of autism. Research is currently underway that is attempting to provide new information in regards to the neurology of autism.

For example, Carlucci (1999) reports that Minshew and her colleagues have recently received a grant from the National Institutes of Health (NIH) to conduct research in the area of autism. There are a number of researchers working with Minshew on neurology and autism. Minshew (as cited in Carlucci, 1999) states that, "contemporary theories hypothesize deficits in complex or higher order cognitive abilities and disturbances in the development of neural networks that link brain regions to subserve complex cognitive functions" (p. 8). Minshew feels that the deficits seen in individuals with autism are due to the 'wiring' or connections between brain regions, as opposed to the deficits being caused by one region alone (which is in agreement with the control theory of autism previously mentioned).

Minshew (as cited in Carlucci, 1999) has used functional magnetic resonance imaging (fMRI) to study the amygdala, which is involved in emotion, and the hippocampus, which is involved in memory. This researcher has found that these two brain regions are smaller in individuals with autism. Minshew hypothesized that this finding may explain why individuals with autism have problems experiencing and/or understanding subtle emotions and remembering complex information.

Researchers (see Carlucci, 1999) at the University of Pittsburgh (also part of the research team) approach autism, "as a disorder of complex information processing resulting from the abnormal development and dysfunction of neocortical systems" (p. 8). Their research has suggested that abnormalities do exist in the circuitry of the neocortical systems, but not in the brainstem or cerebellum. These findings have led them to the hypothesis that abnormalities associated with autism involve the neocortical systems.

Carpenter and Just (as cited in Carlucci, 1999) are using fMRI to focus on language comprehension, visuospatial processing and executive processing in individuals with autism. These researchers are interested in studying the prefrontal cortex. Preliminary research findings suggests that when high functioning individuals with autism are given complex sentences to comprehend, their left prefrontal cortex, which provides executive support, is activated. Such activation did not occur with matched control subjects. The researchers concluded that a complex sentence is much harder for individuals with autism to solve in comparison to control subjects who perform the task more automatically.

Sweeney (as cited in Carlucci, 1999) is looking at the reflexive and voluntary eye movements in people with high functioning autism. This researcher is investigating the basic motor control of eye movements in terms of velocity and latency and the executive and attentional factors regulating these movements. Sweeney's preliminary results suggest that individuals with autism do not have difficulties with eye movements controlled by the cerebellar vermis as previous research has suggested. In contrast Sweeney found that individuals with autism experience problems on the eye movement tasks due to aspects of the prefrontal cortex. In fact, Sweeney found that individuals with autism had great difficulty if they were told to look toward a remembered location or if they were asked to stop themselves from looking at suddenly appearing lights.

AUTISM AND THE AGING PROCESS

No research has addressed the issue of the effects of aging on individuals with autism. This is due to a number of reasons. First, autism was discovered to exist as its own entity in 1943 when Kanner labeled a group of children as having this condition. Even if these children identified by Kanner were followed throughout their lives, they would only be in their late '50s or early '60s. Thus, the construct known as autism has not really been around long enough to address the effects aging have on these individuals. Second, researchers have struggled to pinpoint what portions of the brain are malfunctioning. Without being able to figure out where the problems lie, it is hard to study the effects of the aging process on individuals with autism. Finally, it is hard to find concrete results on the effects of aging on normal individuals to compare them with individuals with autism (Willott, 1999).

Knowing the above, the only alternative is to speculate on the effects aging may have on individuals with autism by examining brain findings that have been found to show certain anomalies. These findings of anomalies will be compared to findings found with normal individuals in regards to the aging process. In order to take on such a task, an attempt will be made to incorporate information that exists to date on this question in normal individuals. This information has been reported in a newly published book entitled: *Neurogerontology: Aging and The Nervous System* by Willott (1999).

The first area of focus is the relationship between sensory abilities and aging. As proposed in the Control Theory, individuals with autism are hypothesized to experience sensory overload due to environmental stimulation. For individuals with autism, how would this sensory overload be dealt with as they aged? Willott (1999) stated that hearing as a sensory experience declines in normal people with age. The researcher reported that nearly 25–50% of normal aged individuals have a clinically significant hearing loss that can be detected in routine hearing tests. Such a hearing loss may help individuals with autism to better deal with over stimulating auditory sounds as it would reduce painful environmental stimuli.

Another sensory area addressed by Willott (1999) involves the somato-sensation system which is concerned with touch, pressure, vibration, heat, cold, pain, joint position, and musculoskeletal movement. This researchers reported that aging is usually accompanied by some losses in these areas (citing Corso, 1981; Kenshalo, 1979; McBride, 1988; Stevens & Cruz, 1996; Verrillo & Verrillo, 1985; Weisenberger, 1996). If this is indeed the case, then aging individuals with autism who suffer from tactile sensory overload would seem to benefit from the decreased sensitivity. If individuals with autism are hyperactive in somatosensory systems, then it may be safe to speculate that these sensations would decrease with age in regards to the magnitude of the effect it has on their bodies. This effect would also carry over into individuals with autism who are hypersensitive to olfactory and gustation senses. These may be especially important for individuals with autism who have been reported to have odor fetishes as well as those with digestive problems and picky diets (Wahlberg & Rotatori, 1996).

Willott (1999) addressed the effects aging has on learning and memory. One area of the brain that he reported to have an effect on learning is the hippocampus. Willott reported that some studies have shown that as normal individuals age, the number of neurons in the hippocampus may actually decrease. More importantly this research pointed out that this neuronal loss may lead to physiological alterations that occur in the hippocampus which can effect learning and memory. As reported earlier, research (Bailey, 1993; Carlucci, 1999) had found that individuals with autism have a smaller than normal hippocampus which may lead to their lack of emotionality or understanding of complex information. Thus, one might hypothesize that individuals with autism would show an increased deficiency in emotionality and understanding complex information with age.

Another area addressed by Willott (1999) involves the decline of emotionality with age. One portion of the brain that is a key limbic structure for behaviors and experiences that involve emotionality is the amygdala. This portion of the brain has been linked to learning and memory that may have emotional significance. As stated earlier, research (Carlucci, 1999) with individuals with autism has reported that their amygdala is smaller than normal individuals. Therefore, it may be safe to postulate that individuals with autism become more unemotional with age due to their amygdala being smaller to begin with.

The prefrontal regions of the cerebral cortex have also been attributed to learning and memory functioning (Willott, 1999). As stated earlier individuals with autism have problems with executive functions that involve complex tasks which are attributed to prefrontal cortex malfunctioning. Willott (1999) addressed this deficiency as it pertains to the aging process in a model developed by Moscovitch and Winocur (1992) in which they reported that the frontal lobes in conjunction with the hippocampus appear to be involved in the "application of remembered events to the organization of behaviors in a current context" (p. 359). Willott pointed out that the ability of the cerebral cortex to function normally often diminishes with age leading to problems with memory in aged individuals.

This memory deficit is present in individuals with autism and creates a problem in their handling of past information and using the information in a present context. Since this brain region diminishes with age, it is likely that it will lead to further problems experienced by individuals with autism. In essence individuals with autism would get progressively worse at handling this type of information or in solving complex tasks.

Another interesting finding explored by Willott (1999) was related to aging and the plasticity of synapses and dendrites in the aging nervous system. Willott stated that much of the capacity for synaptic plasticity is retained in older brains. If we revert back to the "Control Theory" of autism, one has to ask the question of whether or not this applies to individuals with autism? Control Theory makes the argument that the brains of individuals with autism suffer from being inflexible in its interpretation of incoming information. A person with autism develops into an individual that is not open to change or diversion from information they experience. In fact, they are very rigid when it comes to any changes or to acquiring new information. Wahlberg (2000) argues that this rigidity gets accentuated with age. Thus individuals with autism do not seem to develop this ability to be flexible which is needed to lead a productive life. In contrast, normal individuals have this synaptic plasticity seemingly all their lives.

CONCLUSION

After theorizing about the aging process in individuals with autism it is apparent to the reader that many questions are left unresolved. At this stage researchers can postulate their "best guesses" as to the development of the brain's of individuals with autism, and further speculate about the changes that individuals with autism experience as they age. Many of the theoretical hypothesizes formulated in this chapter are based on scientific research and clinical experience working with individuals with autism. Since no research exists to date that sheds any light on aging and autism, researchers and clinicians are left with behavioral observations of aging individuals with autism.

Autism has been described in this chapter as a brain disorder causing certain neurological anomalies to develop. As researchers get more sophisticated in their scientific understanding of the human brain, they will be able to apply their understanding to learn more about why these individuals suffer from autism. For the time being, researchers are forced to theorize as to the "goings on" in the brains of individuals with autism. The author hypothesized about certain cognitive limitations individuals with autism seem to suffer from. Future researcher needs to find ways to assess these limitations through experimental research. Such information will assist researchers and clinicians in assessing changes in the brains of individuals with autism as they age. Until then, researchers and clinicians can only speculate and wonder about autism and its development within the human species.

REFERENCES

American Psychiatric Association (1994). Diagnostic and statistical manual of mental disorders. *American Psychiatric Association.*

Bailey, A. J. (1993). The biology of autism. *Psychological Medicine*, *23*, 7–11.

Baron-Cohen, S., Leslie, A. M., & Frith, U. (1985). Does the autistic child have a 'theory of mind'? *Cognition*, *21*, 37–46.

Bartak, L., Rutter, M., & Cox, A. (1975). A comparative study of infantile autism and specific developmental receptive language disorder: I. The children. *British Journal of Psychiatry*, *126*, 127–145.

Bartak, L., Rutter, M., & Cox, A. (1977). A comparative study of infantile autism and specific developmental receptive language disorder: III. Discriminant functional analysis. J*ournal of Autism and Childhood Schizophrenia*, *7*, 383–396.

Bauman, M. L. (1991). Microscopoc neuroanatomic abnormalities in autism. *Pediatrics*, *87*, 791–796.

Bauman, M., & Kemper, T. L. (1985). Histoanatomic observations of the brain in early infantile autism. *Neurology*, *35*, 866–874.

Bauman, M., & Kemper, T. L. (1994a). Neuroanatomic observations of the brain in autism. In: M. L. Bauman & T. L. Kemper (Eds), *The Neurobiology of Autism*. Baltimore: Johns Hopkins University Press.

Bauman, M., & Kemper, T. L. (1994b). *The Neurobiology of Autism*. Baltimore: Johns Hopkins University Press.

Campbell, M., Rosenbloom, S., Perry, R., George, A., Kricheff, I., Anderson, L., Small, A., & Jennings, S. (1982). Computerized axial tomography in young autistic children. *American Journal of Psychiatry*, *139*, 510–512.

Cantwell, D. P., Baker, L., & Rutter, M. (1978). A comparative study of infantile autism and specific developmental receptive language disorder. IV. Analysis of syntax and language function. *Journal of Child Psychology and Psychiatry, 19,* 351–363.

Carlucci, D. (1999). Brain wiring in autism. Research probes cognitive processing in people with high-functioning autism and Asperger's syndrome. *Advance for Speech-Language Pathologists and Audiologists, 9*(1), 6–9.

Carparulo, B. K., & Cohen, D. J. (1977). Cognitive structures, language, and emerging social competence in autistic and aphasic children. *Journal of the American Academy of Child Psychiatry, 16,* 620–645.

Ciaranello, A. L., & Ciaranello, R. D. (1995). The neurobiology of infantile autism. *Annual Review of Neuroscience, 18,* 101–128.

Corso, J. F. (1981). *Aging sensory systems and perception.* New York: Praeger.

Fotheringham, J. B. (1990). Autism: Its primary psychological and neurological deficit. *Canadian Journal Of Psychiatry, 36,* 686–692.

Frith, U. (1989). *Autism: Explaining the enigma.* Oxford: Basil Blackwell.

Frith, U., & Happe, F. (1994). Autism: Beyond "theory of mind." *Cognition, 50,* 115–132.

Frith, U., & Snowling, M. (1983). Reading for meaning and reading for sound in autistic and dyslexic children. *Journal of Developmental Psychology, 1,* 329–342.

Gaffney, G., Kuperman, S., Tsai, L., & Minchin, S. (1989). Forebrain structure in infantile autism. *Journal of the American Academy of Child and Adolescent Psychiatry, 28,* 534–537.

Happe, F. G. (1994). An advanced test of theory of mind: Understanding of story characters' thoughts and feelings by able autistic, mentally handicapped, and normal children and adults. *Journal of Autism and Developmental Disorders, 24,* 129–154.

Happe, F. G. (1995). The role of age and verbal ability in the theory of mind tasks performance of subjects with autism. *Childhood Development, 66,* 843–855.

Happe, F. G. (1997). Central coherence and theory of mind in autism: Reading homographs in context. *British Journal of Developmental Psychology, 15,* 1–12.

Happe, F. G., & Frith, U. (1996). The neuropsychology of autism. *Brain, 119,* 1377–1400.

Hashimoto, T., Tayama, M., Murakawa, K., Yoshimoto, T., Miyazaki, M., & Harada, M. (1995). Development of the brainstem and cerebellum in autistic patients. *Journal of Autism and Developmental Disorders, 25,* 1–18.

Hauser, S., Delong, G., & Rosman, N. (1975). Pneumographic findings in the infantile autism syndrome: A correlation with temporal lobe disease. *Brain, 98,* 667–688.

Herold, S., Frackowiak, R. S., Le Couteur, A., Rutter, M., & Howlin, P. (1988). Cerebral blood flow and metabolism of oxygen and glucose in young autistic adults. *Psychological Medicine, 11,* 317–330.

Hewitt, L. E. (1998). Influence of question type on response adequacy in young adults with autism. *Journal of Communication Disorders, 31,* 135–152.

Jacobson, R., Le Couteur, A., Howlin, P., & Rutter, M. (1988). Selective subcortical abnormalities in autism. *Psychological Medicine, 18,* 39–48.

Jarrold, C., & Russell, J. (1997). Counting abilities in autism: Possible implications for central coherence theory. *Journal of Autism and Developmental Disorders, 27*(1), 1997.

Kanner, L. (1943). Autistic disturbances of affective contact. *Nervous Child, 2,* 217–250.

Kemper, T. L., & Bauman, M. L. (1993). The contribution of neuropathologic studies to the understanding of autism. *Behavioral Neurology, 11*(1), 175–187.

Kenshalo, D. R. (1979). Changes in the vestibular and somesthetic systems as a function of age. In: J. M. Ordy & K. Brizzee (Eds), *Sensory Systems and Communication in the Elderly* (pp. 269–282). New York: Raven.

Lord, C. (1985). Autism and the comprehension of language. In: E. Schopler & G. Mesibov (Eds), *Communication Problems in Autism* (pp. 257–281). New York: Plenum Press.

Lord, C. (1996). Language in high-functioning adolescents with autism: Questions about deviance and delay. In: D. Cicchetti & S. L. Toth (Eds), *Adolescence: Opportunities and Challenges* (pp. 149–165). Rochester, New York: University of Rochester Press.

McBride, M. (1988). The somatosensory system. In: M. Abramson & P. M. Lovas (Eds), *Aging and Sensory Change. An Annotated Bibliography* (pp. 30–36). Washington, D.C.: Gerontological Society of America.

Minshew, N. J., & Goldstein, G. (1998). Autism as a disorder of complex information processing. *Mental Retardation and Developmental Disabilities Research Reviews*, *4*, 129–136.

Moscovitch, M., & Winocur, G. (1992). The neuropsychology of memory and aging. In: F. I. M. Craik & T. A. Salthouse (Eds), *The Handbook of Aging and Cognition* (pp. 315–372). Hillsdale, NJ: Erlbaum.

Mundy, P. (1995). Joint attention and social-emotional approach behavior in children with autism. *Developmental Psychopathology*, *7*, 63–82.

Mundy, P., Sigman, M., & Kasari, C. (1990). A longitudinal study of joint attention and language development in autistic children. *Journal of Autism and Developmental Disorders*, *20*, 115–128.

O'Connor, N., & Hermelin, B. (1994). Two autistic savant readers. *Journal of Autism and Developmental Disorders*, *24*(4), 501–515.

O'Neill, M., & Jones, R. S. P. (1997). Sensory-perceptual abnormalities in autism: A case for more research? *Journal of Autism and Developmental Disorders*, *27*(3), 283–292.

Ozonoff, S., Pennington, B. F., & Rogers, S. J. (1991). Executive function deficits in high functioning autistic children: Relationship to theory of mind. *Journal of Child Psychiatry*, *32*, 1081–1105.

Piven, J., Berthier, M., Startstein, S., Nehme, E., Pearlson, G., & Folstein, S. (1990). Magnetic resonance imaging evidence for a defect of cerebral cortical development in autism. *American Journal of Psychiatry*, *147*, 734–739.

Prior, M. R., & Hall, L. C. (1979). Comprehension of transitive and intransitive phrases by autistic, retarded and normal children. *Journal of Communication Disorders*, *12*, 103–111.

Ramberg, C., Ehlers, S., Nyden, A., Johansson, M., & Gillberg, C. (1996). Language and pragmatic functions in school-age children on the autism spectrum. *European Journal of Disorders of Communication*, *31*, 387–414.

Raymond, G., Bauman, M., & Kemper, T. (1989). The hippocampus in autism: Golgi analysis. *Annals of Neurology*, *26*, 483–484.

Ritvo, E., Freeman, B., Scheibel, A., Duong, T., Robinson, H., Guthrie, D., & Ritvo, A. (1986). Lower Purkinje cell counts in the cerebella of four autistic subjects: Initial findings of the UCLA-NSAC autopsy research report. *American Journal of Psychiatry*, *143*, 862–866.

Rumsey, J. M., Rapoport, J. L., & Sceery, W. R. (1985). Autistic children as adults: Psychiatric, social, and behaviral outcomes. *Journal of the Amercian Academy of Childhood Psychiatry*, *24*, 465–473.

Siegel, B. V., Nuechterlein, K. H., Abel, J., Wu, J. C., & Buchsbaum, M. S. (1995). Glucose metabolic correlates of continuous test performance in adults with a history of infantile autism, schizophrenics, and controls. *Schizophrenia Research*, *17*, 85–94.

Simmons, J. Q., & Baltaxe, C. A. (1975). Language patterns of adolescent autistics. *Journal of Autism and Childhood Schizophrenia*, *5*, 333–351.

Smith, I. M., & Bryson, S. E. (1994). Imitation and action in autism: A critical review. *Psychological Bulletin*, *116*, 259–273.

Snowling, M., & Frith, U. (1986). Comprehension in 'hyperlexic' readers. *Journal of Experimental Psychology*, *42*, 392–415.

Stevens, J. C., & Cruz, L. A. (1996). Spatial acuity of touch: Ubiquitous decline with aging revealed by repeated threshold testing. *Somatosensory and Motor Research*, *13*, 1–10.

Tager-Flusberg, H. (1981a). On the nature of linguistic functioning in early infantile autism. *Journal of Autism and Developmental Disorders*, *11*, 45–56.

Tager-Flusberg, H. (1981b). Sentence comprehension in autistic children. *Applied Psycholinguistics*, *2*, 5–24.

Tager-Flusberg, H., Calkins, S., Nolin, I., Baumberger, T., Anderson, M., & Chadwick-Denis, A. (1990). A longitudinal study of language acquisition in autistic and Down syndrome children. *Journal of Autism and Developmental Disorders*, *20*, 1–22.

Van Hassalt, V. B., & Hersen, M. (1994). *Advanced abnormal psychology*. New York: Plenum Press.

Verrillo, R. T., & Verrillo, V. (1985). Sensory and perceptual performance. In: N. Charness (Ed.), *Aging and Human Performance* (pp. 1–46). Chichester: Wiley.

Wahlberg, T. J. (1996). A child with autism's reaction time in a short term memory visual test as compared to a normal population of children. Masters Thesis. Saint Xavier University, Chicago, IL.

Wahlberg, T. J. (2000). How individuals with autism think and process information: A theoretical perspective. Paper read at the Arkansas State School Psychology Conference, Little Rock, Arkansas.

Wahlberg, T. J., & Rotatori, A. (1996). Various treatment modalities for autistic individuals. In: A. F. Rotatori, J. O. Schwenn & S. Burkhardt (Eds), *Advances in Special Education* (pp. 109–131). Greenwich, CT JAI Press.

Weisenberger, J. M. (1996). Touch and proprioception. In: J. E. Birren (Ed.), *Encyclopedia of Gerontology* (Vol. 2, pp. 591–603). San Diego: Academic Press.

Williams, R., Hauser, S., Purpura, D., Delong, G., & Swisher, C. (1980). Autism and mental retardation. *Archives of Neurology*, *37*, 749–753.

Willott, J. F. (1999). *Neurogerontology: Aging and the nervous system*. DeKalb, IL: Northen Illinois University: VCB Custome Packets.

Yuill, N., Oakhill, J., & Parkin, A. (1989). Working memory, comprehension ability and the resolution of text anomaly. *British Journal of Psychology*, *80*, 351–361.

A CASE STUDY IN THE DYNAMICS OF AUTISM

Tim Wahlberg and Scott Jordan

INTRODUCTION

Throughout the course of any given day, people find themselves engaged in a complex array of unpredictable environmental events – a toothbrush isn't where it is supposed to be, a strong wind pushes a hiker in the wrong direction, or a stranger interrupts a conversation, just to name a few. When faced with such disturbances, most people deal with them. They search for the toothbrush, walk against the wind, or ask the stranger to wait his turn. As a matter of fact, most people integrate such unpredictability into their actions so naturally, it appears as though their actions anticipate the unexpected. In short, they demonstrate behavioral flexibility – the ability to express fluid action patterns that take into account and reflect the inherent unpredictability of moment-to-moment living.

Given the key role behavioral flexibility plays in normal functioning, the present chapter presents a unique theoretical approach to describing why autistic persons' actions seem to lack it. The approach is unique because it avoids the tendency to model autism as a mental disorder that gives rise to bizarre behaviors. Instead, we adopt a systems perspective and model autism as a dynamic coordination of environmental-neurological-cognitive-behavioral systems that function synergistically at multiple nested time scales. To be sure, we model "normals" in the same way. The uniqueness of autistic systems derives from the types of coordinations they tend to maintain. Whereas "normal" systems tend to maintain coordinations that necessitate engagement of the

Autistic Spectrum Disorders: Educational and Clinical Interventions, pages 53–65.

ISBN: 0-7623-0818-4

unpredictable, autistic systems maintain coordinations that avoid it. In short, autistic systems actively work toward sameness.

To present this systems approach to autistic inflexibility, we begin with a description of the types of coordinations autistic persons often express. We then interpret these coordinations within a systems approach to emerging mind developed by Vandervert (1996). We do because Vandervert's approach is grounded in the conceptual framework of Dynamical Systems Theory (DST), which is a method of analysis that focuses on describing the types of patterns a system produces over time, both qualitatively and quantitatively. In light of such a description, one can say something about a system's relative level of flexibility. Given this method of analysis, we then use it to test the behavioral flexibility of a person with autism. In conclusion, we examine the implications of the DST-based approach for future research on autism.

Inflexibility in Autism

Behavioral inflexibility is included in almost all descriptions of autism. Kanner (1943), for example, described youngsters with autism as, "children who exhibit: (a) serious failure to develop relationships with other people before 30 months of age, (b) problems in development of normal language, (c) ritualistic and obsessive behaviors ("insistence in sameness"), and (d) potential for normal intelligence" (p. 3).

The Individuals with Disabilities Education Act (IDEA) (1990) describes autism as:

> A developmental disability significantly affecting verbal and nonverbal communication and social interaction, generally evident before age 3, that adversely affects a child's performance. Other characteristics often associated with autism are engagement in repetitive activities and stereotyped movements, resistance to environmental change or change in daily routines, and unusual responses to sensory experiences (34 C.F.R. section 300.7 [b] [1] [1992]).

DSM-IV characterizes children with autism by severe deficits in a number of areas: language development, attachment to their parents, self care skills, toy play, interactions with peers, and attentiveness to their surroundings. They may express high rates of aggression directed against themselves or others, and self-stimulatory behaviors such as repeatedly rocking their bodies and flapping their hands.

Although behavioral inflexibility figures prominently in all of the above-mentioned descriptions, its treatment as a sub-component makes the inflexibility appear symptomatic of some "real" underlying disorder. In our systems-based approach, we treat inflexibility in terms of the types of relationships (i.e. coordinations) persons with autism tend to maintain.

Inflexibility, therefore, refers not only to specific coordinations maintained at the behavioral scale, such as self-abuse and hand-flapping, it also refers to more general ways of engaging the environment such as maintaining constant room arrangements (i.e. the individual scale) or avoiding other people (i.e. the social scale). The disorder, therefore, is not seen as residing at only one level of the autistic coordination. Rather, the disorder is seen as an actively maintained means of existing as a system that avoids the unpredictability of daily life. Inflexibility, therefore, emerges naturally at many levels of scale (e.g. the behavioral, the individual, and the social) as the autistic system works toward maintaining sameness in a world that constantly denies it.

Although we adopt a systems approach to autism and focus on inflexibility, we do not intend to avoid or minimize the pain and suffering that accompany it. Rather, our intent is to broaden the perspective utilized in its description. By modeling autism as an actively maintained coordination of environmental-neurological-cognitive-behavioral systems, we explicitly acknowledge the active participation of all these different levels in the maintenance of the disorder. Thus, within our systems approach, autism is described as a qualitatively distinct way of being, and the emotional distress is regarded as what it "feels" like to be a human being whose struggle to produce sameness is constantly thwarted.

Ciaranello and Ciaranello (1995) and Mundy (1995) describe autistic behaviors in a manner that is consistent with our approach. That is, they describe autistic behaviors in terms of their social-emotional content. Behavioral excesses include the following: (a) self-stimulatory behavior, which consists of repetitive ritualistic behavior that gives the child internal pleasure (e.g. rocking, stacking, balancing, lining up objects, or spinning); (b) negativistic behavior, which consists of noncompliance and tantrums; (c) aggression, including aggression towards self, others, and property; (d) rigidity/insistence on sameness, in which the child does not like anything to change; and (e) sensitivity to external stimuli. Behavioral deficits include the following: (a) receptive language – the child does not understand instruction (e.g. come here, sit down, or get your shoes); (b) expressive language – the child does not understand how to give verbal gestures (e.g. what is your name); (c) social/emotional attachment – the child has neither fear of strangers nor separation anxiety; (d) play behavior – the child does not play like normal children and does not have any friends, he/she sits passively and does not want to share; (e) attention – eye contact is almost nonexistent; (f) failure to develop proper self help skills – the child can not drink from a cup or use the bathroom; and (g) apparent sensory deficit– the child is thought to be deaf at first, and does not react to pain.

Collectively, these descriptions of autistic behavior are consistent with our systems-based approach because they do not treat the social-emotion-behavioral aspects of autism as separate symptoms of an underlying disorder. Rather, they focus on the social-emotional consequences of the behaviors the autistic must produce in order to sustain sameness.

Autism as the Dynamic Struggle for Sameness

Given that most persons maintain coordinations with the world that necessitate engagement of the unpredictable, the question arises as to how a system that struggles for sameness could ever emerge. Vandervert (1996) argues that the ontogenic (i.e. developmental) processes underlying the emergence of autism are one and the same as those underlying the emergence of "normal" individuals, as well as genius individuals such as Albert Einstein. Specifically, Vandervert argues that during early development, brain processes, what he refers to as "neuroalgorithms", are "driven" to abstract patterns from the evolutionarily older brain processes involved in perception. By "mining" repetitive perceptual neuropatterns, these newly developing neuroalgorithms come to be "about" world patterns the developing person continuously encounters in daily life. It is Vandervert's contention that these abstracted world patterns eventually form the bedrock of ones concepts, what he refers to as "conceptual primitives" (also see Mandler, 1988, 1992). Examples of such primitive concepts include prepositions such as "in", "on", "over", and "under".

Once these abstract neuroalgorithms have developed, the driving process of neuro-development mines them as well, resulting in the development of neuroalgorithms that are about states even more abstract than the neuro-algorithms from which they were initially mined. This recursive process (i.e. mining the results of mining) continues to be driven and, over time, gives rise to the highly complex neuro-cognitive architecture we commonly refer to as a mind. In short, mental development is a bootstrapping process in which the developing brain continuously feeds upon the products of its own work.

As Vandervert (1996) applies these ideas to the development of an autistic mind, he begins with Spitz's (1995) assertion that the savant powers of certain autistics are the result of hard, concentrated effort and the eventual mapping of such effort onto the neural processes of the unconscious. In Vandervert's framework, the "unconscious" refers to the conceptual-level neuroalgorithms that autocatalytically emerge during neural development. Thus, for example, as a calendar savant repeatedly exposes him/herself to the extremely predictable regularity of calendar systems, developing conceptual-level neuroalgorithms abstract the perceptual patterns available, and, as a result, come to reflect the predictable regularity of calendar systems. In short, a neuroarchitecture (i.e. a "mind") emerges that is "about" regularity and predictability.

To be sure, no one knows why a developing human would repeatedly expose him/herself to regularity. If the autocatalytic thesis is correct, however, such a tendency would be maintained because it somehow "pays for" itself. It may be the case, for example, that during development, an individual struggles to maintain a regular, predictable stream of input because at some level in the system, there is something noxious about unpredictability (Wahlberg & Rotatori, 1996). The actual level would be unimportant, for since the entire system is recursively autocatalytic, the dynamics of later-developing levels could only be "about" (i.e. emerge from) pre-existing levels. Thus, as a result of unpredictability being noxious at some level in the architecture, later-emerging levels would pay for themselves by reducing the impact of noxious unpredictability. As a result, autistic cognitive dynamics and autistic behavioral dynamics would be autocatalytically selected and sustained. In short, an environmental-neural-behavioral-cognitive coordination would emerge that was "about" producing and maintaining sameness.

Measuring the Autistic Struggle for Sameness

A major difference between the present approach to emerging mind and more traditional approaches, is the type of interactions that are assumed to take place between perceptual, cognitive, and behavioral systems. In traditional approaches, what one might refer to as computational approaches (Clark, 2000), perception, cognition and behavior tend to be modeled as input, computation and output, respectively (Jordan, 1999). Such modeling derives from information-processing theory (IPT), and leads one to treat interactions between system levels in terms of informational exchange. As a result, research based on IPT tends to utilize reaction time (RT) paradigms in order to measure the temporal dynamics of information exchange. From the resultant RT data, one makes inferences about the functional structure of the information-processing architecture that produced the RTs.

In the present approach, perception, cognition and behavior are modeled as energy-transformation systems that function at different levels of scale and afford an individual a means of maintaining increasingly complex coordinations with the environment (Järvilehto, 1998; Jordan, 1998, 1999, 2000; Vandervert, 1999). Behavioral systems, therefore, allow an individual to control relationships among body parts (e.g. walking, running, jumping). Perceptual systems allow one to embed behavioral systems in larger scale coordinations that include the immediate environment (e.g. walking toward a table), and cognitive systems allow one to embed behavioral/perceptual systems in coordinations whose scale is virtual (e.g. walking toward a table in order to wait on a friend).

By focusing on energy transformation, as opposed to information exchange, the present approach explicitly acknowledges the fact that biological systems live in a thermodynamically open world whose moment-to-moment states are highly unpredictable, at all levels of scale. The complexity of the coordinations one can maintain with the environment, therefore, will be dictated by the degree to which the inherent unpredictability of the natural world can be reflected in the ones functioning. This emphasis on hierarchical system dynamics leads to different research strategies than IPT, for what is most important in the present approach is the complexity of the coordinations one maintains with the environment. Thus, instead of measuring the temporal dynamics of information exchange, the present approach focuses on measuring functional complexity.

Given our assertion that the hallmark of autistic functioning is the active maintenance of sameness, an autistic confronted with an unpredictable situation should express a lower level of functional complexity than a 'normal' person. For by working to avoid versus engage unpredictability, the autistic prevents the complexities of the avoided event from manifesting themselves in his/her functionality. In short, by acting to avoid complexity, the autistic renders him/herself functionally simple.

To measure functional complexity, we utilized a technique recently reported by Cooney and Troyer (1994). Specifically, these researchers asked young children and adults to participate in a Sternberg (1966, 1970) reaction-time task. During every trial of the task, a set of letters appeared on a computer monitor for 2 seconds. Two seconds later, another letter appeared (what is referred to as the "probe") and the participant's task was to indicate, as quickly and accurately as possible, whether or not the probe matched any of the letters in the previously-presented set. Participants did so by pressing buttons. The time passing between the onset of the probe and the moment of the participant's button press was measured in milliseconds, and was referred to as the reaction time (RT). Participants completed 240 correct trials.

In addition to determining the central tendency and variability of the RTs, Cooney and Troyer (1994) examined the complexity of the trial-to-trial changes in the value of the RTs. This technique for measuring a system's complexity was initially reported by Packard, Crutchfield, Farmer and Shaw (1980), "The basic idea is that the evolution of any single component of a system is determined by the other components with which it interacts. Information about the relevant components is thus implicitly contained in the history of any single component" (p. 54).

The implications for measuring the complexity of autistic functioning are straightforward. If one is to produce a series of correct responses, one must continuously engage a multi-scale constellation of unpredictable disturbances. Thus, we assumed that if an autistic person were to actually complete the task, their resulting data streams would be dominated by their struggle against unpredictability and, as a result, be less-complex than those produced by 'normal' persons. In other words, their struggle for sameness would motivate them to avoid engaging the total constellation of multi-scale disturbance that had to be dealt with in order to produce a correct response on every trial. Thus, on some trials, they might simply guess, in order to avoid disturbances to the transformations involved in actually determining whether or not the probe matched any of the letters in the set.

To test this idea, we asked a four-year, eleven-month old boy, who had been diagnosed with autism at the age of two years, to participate in an RT task that was based on the paradigm used by Cooney and Troyer (1994). Specifically, a set of letters appeared on a computer monitor for two seconds, and was followed, two seconds later, by a probe letter. The participant's task was to indicate via button presses whether or not the probe matched any of the letters in the set. The letter set was the same on every trial, and one experimental session entailed 240 correct responses. After the session, we determined the complexity estimates for the RT streams.

We manipulated the difficulty of the task by using different letter sets. Thus, in one session the letter set was the consonant string LGB, while in another it was the word CAR. Due to the well-known Word-Superiority effect (McClelland & Rumelhart, 1981; Prinzmetal, 1992) we assumed the session involving the consonant string would be the more difficult of the two. In energy-transformation terms, this means that determining whether or not a probe letter matches any of the letters in LGB is more difficult than making such a determination for CAR because the latter is already a part of the developed neurocognitive architecture. Working successfully with LGB, therefore, requires the utilization of neurocognitive structures that are not needed when working with CAR. This increase in necessary systems naturally increases the potential for disturbance. Thus, a person with autism should react to this increase in unpredictability by becoming less functionally complex. RT streams garnered from the more difficult session, therefore, should be less complex than those garnered from the easier session.

As an additional index of the autistic struggle for sameness, we asked the participant to control the trial-to-trial progression of the experiment. Specifically, after pressing a button to indicate whether or not there had been a set-probe match, the participant was to press another button in order to begin the next trial. We referred to the time passing between these two button presses as the delay-time (DT). Upon the completion of a session, we determined the complexity of the trial-to-trial changes in the DT. Since producing this second button press actually served to initiate another trial and the need to once again engage the constellation of unpredictable disturbances associated with successfully completing a trial, we assumed a person with autism would find this interval quite challenging. Thus, we assumed the autistic struggle for sameness would fully express itself in the dynamics of this interval and, as a consequence, result in DT strings that were functionally rather simple. Finally, as a basis of comparison, we compared the data from our participant with autism to data obtained from two individuals who had completed the same task as part of a different experiment (Jordan, 1997). One was a 1st grade girl, and the other, a 5th grade boy.

The first result to note is that our participant with autism did not complete the session involving the consonant string LGB. Given that he was able to complete the session involving CAR, we assume the LGB set was too difficult. Thus, our analysis focuses on the CAR session. Table 1 lists descriptive performance measures for each of the three participants. While the 1st and 5th grader both had extremely low error rates (i.e. 2 and 1 errors, respectively), the participant with autism produced 18 errors and had a larger RT average than those of the other two participants. Also, his average DT was dramatically larger. Collectively, these data indicate that the task was more challenging for the participant with autism.

Figure 1 depicts the complexity estimates for the RTs (top) and the DTs (bottom). The autistic participant's complexity estimates are lower than those of the other participants, especially in the DTs. This is consistent with out assertion that the autistic struggle for sameness would manifest itself most robustly in the DT dynamics, for it was during the DTs that the participant had the greatest opportunity to avoid unpredictability. During RTs, the transformations involved in determining the set-probe match were, for the most part, unconscious. Thus, the only conscious control the participant had during RTs was determining whether or not to allow the unconscious transformations to continue. According to our systems approach, saying that unconscious processes were able to determine the probe-set match, is roughly the same as saying that the unconscious transformations dealt with all the disturbances encountered while determining the probe-set match. In systems terms therefore, these disturbances, which played

Table 1. Descripitve Data.

Participant	Errors		Reaction Time (RT)	Delay Time (DT)
Autistic	18	*M*	863.18	4401.55
		SD	243.72	5731.18
1st grader	2	*M*	781.76	291.60
		SD	258.25	128.35
5th grader	1	*M*	605.07	648.48
		SD	113.01	207.90

themselves out at unconscious time scales, were reflected in the length of the RT and, as a result, made the RT stream rather complex. The fact that the participant with autism made 18 errors, however, indicates that on roughly seven percent of the trials he did not allow the unconscious processes to complete their work. That is, he guessed. By guessing, he avoided certain unpredictable events at the unconscious level and, as a result, reduced the complexity of his RT stream.

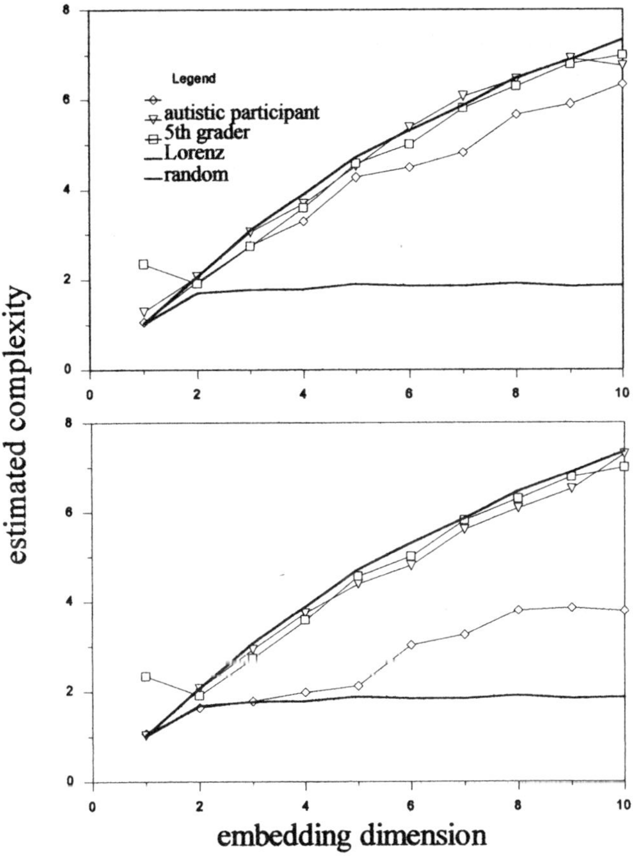

Fig. 1. Estimated complexity as a function of embedding dimension for the RT data (top) and the DT data (bottom) of all three participants. The 5th grader's data are represented by triangles, the 1st grader's by squares, and the autistic participant's by diamonds. The upper and lower lines without any symbols represent complexity estimates for the random number stream and the Lorenz data, respectively. These two lines are provided as a frame of reference.

During DTs, the participant had a greater degree of conscious control over the engagement of unpredictability because he could inhibit the second, trial initiating button-press as long as he wanted. If what he had really wanted to do was avoid the unpredictability of impending trials; the decision regarding whether or not to start one would have been both taxing and difficult. As a result, the act of making such a decision, time and time again, would have come to dominate the length and the complexity of his DTs. In systems terms, the increased influence of one level of the autistic system (i.e. the decision making level) over all others during the DT, would have reduced the magnitude of impact the other levels could have on the DT. As a result, the trial-to-trial pattern in DTs would have been dictated by trial-to-trial changes in the autistic participant's ability to decide whether or not to initiate another trial. Due to the extreme influence of this one level of the system, the resulting DT pattern would be much less complex than those produced by participants who had no problem dealing with unpredictability embodied in trials.

Figure 2 illustrates the extreme pattern of behavior the autistic participant had to produce in order to control his engagement of unpredictable, RT-related disturbance. Specifically, Fig. 2 depicts two 1st return maps. In the top return map, the coordinates of the graph space are large enough to hold all of the autistic participant's DTs. The scale is in milliseconds and ranges from 0 to 35 seconds. The DTs of the other two participants are present, but are very difficult to see (i.e. the squares and triangles in the lower-left corner of the space). In the bottom return map, the coordinates of the graph space range from 0–1000 milliseconds. We used this magnified scale to reveal the different temporal scales at which the different participants were behaving.

In the bottom return map, one can see that the 1st and 5th grader produced DTs falling mainly within a range of 300 to 600 milliseconds. One can see in the top graph, however, that the autistic participant produced DTs that transcended time scales ranging from tenths-of-seconds to tens-of-seconds. In terms of the actual experimental situation, this means that on some trials, the autistic participant waited only a few tenths of a second to initiate a subsequent next trial, while on others, he waited as long as thirty seconds. The other two participants, on the other hand, kept their DTs under one second.

When one combines Figs 1 and 2 it becomes clear that the autistic participant's DT data are not extremely variable because they are *more* complex. On the contrary, they are extremely variable because they are *less* complex. By struggling to maintain a coordination with the environment that was explicitly devoted to avoiding unpredictability, the autistic participant's DT behavior became slave to the dynamics of choosing when and whether when to start

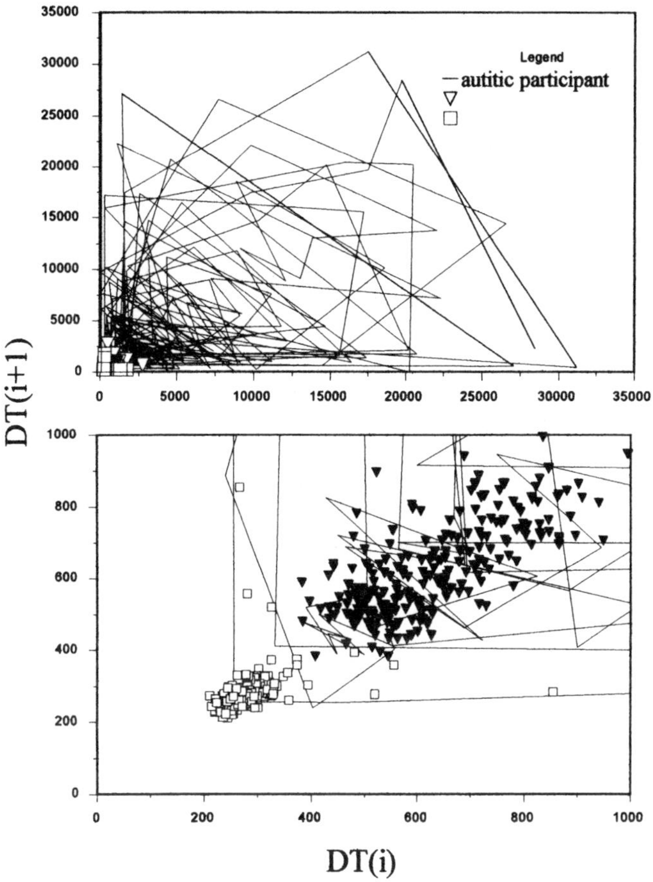

Fig. 2. 1st return maps for all three participants at a larger (top) and smaller (bottom) time scale. The 5th grader's data are represented by triangles, the 1st grader's by squares, and the autistic participant's by lines.

Printed with permission from New Ideas In Psychology.

another trial. Needing to have so much conscious control over every single action, he, in short, rendered himself functionally simple.

CONCLUSIONS

The present paper proposed a systems-theoretical approach to the emergence and maintenance of autism. In addition, we tested the utility of this approach via the utilization of systems-theoretical techniques for data analysis. Complexity estimates garnered from a participant with autism were much lower than those garnered from two 'normal' participants. In addition, the return maps of the participant with autism were more variable, yet less complex, than those of the other two participants. In summary, we interpreted these data to indicate that while struggling for sameness, the participant with autism exercised an extreme degree of conscious control over the decision whether or not to start another trial. As a consequence, his behavior was dominated by the dynamics of this decision making process, thus rendering him functionally simple.

To be sure, the data we have presented only represent the performance of one individual with autism. Thus, we are well aware of the need for further research utilizing larger sample sizes. Regardless of our small n however, the correlation integrals and the return maps did capture and reveal robust individual differences that would have been missed had we relied solely on traditional statistical methods. Given the potential promise of this systems-theoretic approach, perhaps it is time to give the dynamic approach a try.

REFERENCES

American Psychological Association (1993): *Diagnostic and statistical manual of mental disorders*, (5th ed., revised). Washington, D.C.: Author.

Ciaranello, A. L., & Ciaranello, R. D. (1995). The neurobiology of infantile autism. *Annual Review of Neuroscience*, *18*, 101–128.

Clark, A. (2000). *Mindware*. Oxford: Oxford University Press.

Cooney, J. B., & Troyer, R. (1994). A dynamic model of reaction time in a short-term memory task. *Journal of Experimental Child Psychology*, *58*, 200–226.

Education for All Handicapped Children Act of 1975, P.L. 94–142, United States Code, 20, sections 1401 et seq.

Järvilehto, T. (1998). Efferent influences on receptors in knowledge formation. *Psycoloquy*, *9*(41), *Efference Knowledge*, (1).

Jordan, J. S. (1997). Variations in the complexity of reaction-time and delay-time attractors as a function of set-size and set-type. Paper presented at the Seventh annual meeting of the Society for Chaos Theory in Psychology and the Life Sciences, Milwaukee, Wisconsin.

Jordan, J. S. (1998). Intentionality, perception, and autocatalytic closure: A potential means of repaying psychology's conceptual debt. In: J. S. Jordan (Ed.), *Systems Theories and a priori Aspects of Perception* (pp. 181–208). North-Holland: Elsevier.

Jordan, J. S. (1999). Cognition and spatial perception: Production of output or control of input? In: G. Aschersleben, J. Muesseler, & T. Bachmann (Eds), *Cognitive Contributions to the Perception of Spatial and Temporal Events* (pp. 69–90). North Holland: Elsevier.

Jordan, J. S. (2000). The role of "control" in an embodied cognition. *Philosophical Psychology*, *13*, 233–237.

Kanner, L. (1943). Autistic disturbances of affective contact. *Nervous Child*, *2*, 217–250.

Mandler, J. (1988). How to build a baby: On the development of an accessible representational system. *Cognitive Development*, *3*, 111–136.

Mandler, J. (1992). How to build a baby: II. Conceptual primitives. *Psychological Review, 99*, 587–604.

McClelland, J. L., & Rumelhart, D. E. (1981). An interactive activation model of context effects in letter perception: Part 1. An account of basic findings. *Psychological Review, 88*(5), 375–407.

Mundy, P. (1995). Joint attention and social-emotional approach behavior in children with autism. *Developmental and Psychopathology, 7*, 63–82.

Packard, N. H., Crutchfield, J. P., Farmer, J. D., & Shaw, R. S. (1980). Geometry from a time series. *Physical Review Letters, 45*(9), 712–716.

Prinzmetal, W. (1992). The word-superiority effect does not require a T-scope. *Perception & Psychophysics, 51*(5), 473–484.

Spitz, H. (1995). Calendar calculating idiots savants and the smart unconscious. *New Ideas in Psychology, 13*, 167–182.

Sternberg, S. (1966). High-speed scanning in human memory. *Science, 153*, 652–654.

Sternberg, S. (1970). Memory scanning: Mental processes revealed by reaction-time experiments. In: J. S. Antrobus (Ed.), *Cognition and Affect* (pp. 13–58). Boston, MA: Little, Brown.

Vandervert, L. R. (1996). From idiots savants to Albert Einstein: A brain-algorithmic explanation of savant and everyday performance. *New Ideas in Psychology, 14*, 81–92.

Vandervert, L. R. (1999). Maximizing consciousness across the disciplines: Mechanisms of information growth in general education. In: J. S. Jordan (Ed.), *Modeling Consciousness the Disciplines* (pp. 3–25). Lanham, MD: University Press of America.

Wahlberg, T. J., & Rotatori, A. (1996). *Advances in special education: Assessment and Psychopathology issues in special education*. Greenwich, CT: JAI Press Inc.

PART 2: EDUCATIONAL CONSIDERATIONS

PREPARING FUTURE TEACHERS FOR STUDENTS WITH AUTISTIC SPECTRUM DISORDERS

Teresa A. Mehring and Mirah J. Dow

INTRODUCTION

> Good teachers are to education what education is to all other professions – the indispensable element, the sunlight and oxygen, the foundation on which everything else is built. They are central to assuring excellence and rigor in the educational experience of every young person in America (Milken, 1999, p. 3).

The past decade has witnessed an incredibly intense national quest to improve education for students. Never before in the history of our country has the education of teachers been such a key focus of public interest (e.g. the 2000 presidential contest between Governor George W. Bush and Vice President Albert Gore). Americans view improving the quality of education as the most pressing issue confronting the nation, and the public considers improving the quality of teaching as the most important way to improve public education (Haselkorn & Harris, 1998).

A quality teacher preparation program for those who instruct students with autism must consider several factors: the demands of twenty-first century classrooms; elements of effective teacher preparation; special education legislation related to teacher preparation; the influence the Council for Exceptional Children (CEC) standards have on the preparation of special education teachers; and the special knowledge and skills teachers of students

Autistic Spectrum Disorders: Educational and Clinical Interventions, pages 69–88.

ISBN: 0-7623-0818-4

with autism must possess. Individuals interested in teacher preparation must also realize that the molding of a teacher does not begin and end with the four or five years the prospective teacher spends on the university campus. Effective teaching requires support and mentoring, particularly during the first one to three years of teaching. Although university teacher preparation has been the accepted means through which individuals gain the requisite knowledge and skills leading to a license to teach, growing supply and demand concerns as well as a growing dissatisfaction with the monopoly colleges of education have had on the preparation of teachers has led to alternative licensure programs. This chapter provides a concise review of each of these elements as related to teacher preparation for students with autism.

DEMANDS OF TWENTY-FIRST CENTURY CLASSROOMS

Schools are now expected to ensure that all students learn and perform at high levels. Rather than merely "cover the curriculum," teachers are expected to find ways to support and connect with the needs of all learners. This new mission for education requires substantially more knowledge and radically different skills for teachers. The kind of teaching required to meet these demands for more thoughtful learning cannot be produced through teacher-proof materials or regulated curricula. In order to create bridges between common, challenging curriculum goals and individual learners' experiences and needs, teachers must understand cognition and the many different pathways to learning. They must understand child development and pedagogy as well as the structures of subject areas and a variety of alternatives for assessing learning (Darling-Hammond, 1990). This is especially true for teachers who provide instruction for students with autism. Children and adolescents with autism experience major challenges in communicative and social interaction. Their unique cognitive, learning, sensory processing, movement, rhythm, communication, and social/emotional characteristics require special understanding and individual assessment before education and training can be effectively designed and implemented (Graczyk et al., 1996).

If all children are to be effectively taught, teachers must be prepared to address the substantial diversity in experiences children bring with them to school – the wide range of languages, cultures, exceptionalities, and learning repertoire of teaching strategies. In addition, teaching for universal learning demands a highly developed ability to discover what children know and can do, as well as how they think and how they learn, and to match learning and performance opportunities to the needs of individual children.

"Effective" teaching behaviors vary for different subject areas and grade levels, for students at different developmental stages and with different cognitive and psychological characteristics, and for different learning outcomes. Teaching is an intense activity and teachers must simultaneously juggle subject matter; the lesson's underlying cognitive, social, and affective goals; the management of time, materials, and equipment; and the needs and responses of individual students. They must be aware of how students are working and be alert to signs of misunderstanding or confusion while seizing the "teachable moment" for pursuing a key point when students are ready to grasp it. They must skillfully manage transitions among activities so as not to lose students' attention and momentum. Teachers of students with autism must be particularly knowledgeable about effective instruction strategies. It is not uncommon for their students to experience difficulty in attending to and/or focusing on the task at hand. Teachers of students with autism must plan specific programs and strategies for enabling students to attend to tasks and to identify and focus on salient stimuli and cues (Simpson & Myles, 1998). According to Olley (1992), "One of the most commonly heard comments about students with autism is that they are not motivated to engage in education or treatment programs" (p. 11). Students with autism can be withdrawn, preoccupied, unmotivated to explore new situations or environments, and may appear to be uninterested in learning activities (Hardman et al., 2000; Koegel & Koegel, 1996; Simpson & Myles, 1998). Such lack of motivation creates problems for educators because motivation is key to learning. Considerable time must be spent teaching generalization and transfer of information to novel settings, individuals and other conditions. Providing opportunities for students with autism to practice skills in novel ways, including community and classroom settings, is a necessary component of effective instruction for students with autism (Simpson & Myles, 1998).

The setting in which instruction is provided also influences the content and teaching strategies employed. The U.S. Office of Education (1997) estimated that one out of every four students with autism are served in resource room programs while an estimated 58% are educated in full-time special education classrooms. Special educators who serve students in these settings must demonstrate collaboration between regular classroom teachers and other professionals. According to Drew and Hardman (2000), resource room teachers must be capable of providing services which "may range from assisting a teacher in the use of tests or modification of curriculum to direct instruction with students in the regular classroom" (p. 242).

In addition to structuring encounters with important ideas and useful tasks, good teachers must cheer up children who are discouraged, rechannel the energies of those who are aimless or nonproductive, and challenge those who are bored. They must listen to students to understand what the students know and think, evaluate papers and performances, give assignments that move students forward, and provide feedback that offers constructive information and direction. In addition, they must be well organized and able to concentrate to keep all of these balls in the air at once, yet their structures must be permeable, allowing them to maintain an openness to unexpected events, problems, and opportunities. Teachers of students with autism must be particularly resourceful. Children and youth with autism are frequently described as exhibiting social impairments, being socially unresponsive, and having difficulty relating to other people. They may display self stimulatory behaviors, resist change, demonstrate obsessive and ritualistic behaviors, or respond unusually to the environment (Ricks, 1989; Schreibman, 1988; Szatmari et al., 1990).

What teachers know and do is the most important influence on what students learn (National Commission on Teaching and America's Future, 1996). Research has discovered a great deal about effective teaching and learning. "We know that students learn best when new ideas are connected to what they already know and have experienced; when they are actively engaged in applying and testing their knowledge using real-world problems; when their learning is organized around clear, high goals with lots of practice in reaching them; and when they can use their own interests and strengths as springboards for learning" (Woolfolk, 1998, p. 72). We also know that expert teachers use knowledge about children and their learning to fashion lessons that connect ideas to students' experiences. They create a wide variety of learning opportunities that make subject matter come alive for young people who learn in very different ways. They know how to support students' continuing development and motivation to achieve while creating incremental steps that help students progress toward more complicated ideas and performances. They know how to diagnose the source of problems in students' learning and how to identify strengths on which to build. These skills make the difference between teaching that creates learning and teaching that just marks time (Darling-Hammond, 1995). This kind of teaching requires high levels of knowledge and skill. To be effective, teachers must know their subject matter so thoroughly that they can present it in a challenging, clear, and compelling way. They must also know how their students learn and how to make ideas accessible so that they can construct successful "teachable moments". According to Darling-Hammond (1996), "teacher knowledge of subject matter, student learning, and teaching methods are all important elements of teacher effectiveness" (p. 96). At a time when all students must meet higher standards for learning, access to good teaching is a necessity, not a privilege to be left to chance (National Commission on Teaching and America's Future, 1996).

Simpson and Myles (1998) stated, "The skill depth and breadth of education personnel are the most significant variable accounting for gains made by persons with autism" (p. 18). Instruction and management strategies must be explicitly taught to enable educators to be effective with students with autism, followed by modeling and practice in field placement with students with autism (Smith et al., 1998). Teachers who work with children and youth with autism should be well trained special educators who have acquired the requisite knowledge, skills, and experiences (Siegel, 1996). Although not all students with autism will be included within general education classrooms, Simpson and Myles advocate that teachers of students with autism should possess skills and experiences needed to effectively collaborate with general educators and other school and non-school professionals. Successful education of children and youth with autism and pervasive developmental disorders can be challenging for even the most skilled and dedicated professional. "Significant gains can and do occur when teachers of students with autism possess the necessary depth and breadth in the knowledge and skills needed to provide appropriate instruction" (Simpson & Myles, 1998, p. 18).

The traditional system of certification based upon completion of specified courses in state-approved programs of study has left most practitioners, members of the public, and policymakers unconvinced that licensing standards separate out those who can teach responsibly from those who cannot (Darling-Hammond, Wise & Klein, 1995). Despite the many examples to the contrary, the conventional wisdom among many veteran practitioners is that the teacher education courses they experienced too rarely helped them in their practice. Most members of the public continue to think professional training requirements for teachers are weaker than those of other professions such as medicine. Many policymakers' suspicions lead them to create special routes into teaching that avoid teacher education and standard licensing because they believe these are unnecessary (Darling-Hammond, Wise & Klein, 1995). Special route preparation programs for teachers of students with autism are particularly problematic. Many current programs leading to certification in autism have been criticized because of the lack of in-depth study in specialized autism-related instruction and management programs. According to Simpson and Myles (1998), future teachers of students with autism who complete these programs are not adequately prepared for the many challenges that will occur on a daily basis. Alternative routes to teacher certification will be discussed later in this chapter.

ELEMENTS OF EFFECTIVE TEACHER PREPARATION

A large number of studies have found positive relationships between education coursework and teacher performance in the classroom. Three specific types of study appear to be important: subject matter, teaching pedagogy, and clinical experiences. These three elements of study are particularly important for teachers preparing to teach students with autism. Schulman (1987) classified the elements of teaching knowledge as:

(1) Content knowledge.
(2) General pedagogical knowledge including principles and strategies for classroom organization and management.
(3) Curriculum knowledge, including materials and programs.
(4) Pedagogical content knowledge, an amalgam of content and pedagogy that is a teachers' special form of professional understanding.
(5) Knowledge of learners and their characteristics.
(6) Knowledge of educational contexts, including the characteristics of classrooms, school, communities, and cultures.
(7) Knowledge of educational ends, purposes, and values, and their philosophical and historical grounds.

The American Association for Colleges of Teacher Education (AACTE) also articulated a knowledge base for all beginning teachers. According to the AACTE, beginning teachers should possess knowledge about learners and learning (includes knowledge about developmental needs of students and students with special needs); knowledge about curriculum and teaching (includes knowledge about classroom organization and management); knowledge about social foundations of education (includes knowledge about collaboration, ethics, and legal rights and responsibilities); knowledge about subject matter; and knowledge about the liberal arts and sciences (Reynolds, 1989).

The model standards which are having the most pronounced impact on teacher preparation are those developed by the Interstate New Teacher Assessment and Support Consortium (INTASC) (1999). INTASC was founded in 1987 by Connecticut and California to create performance based initial licensure standards. The INTASC standards have now been adopted by virtually every state in the country and provide a common set of standards upon which teacher licensure and assessments governing entry to the profession can be based upon (Darling-Hammond, 1995).

A number of capabilities and dispositions that are related to educator preparation are also important to teacher performance. Research on teachers' attitudes and dispositions has found that flexibility increases teacher effectiveness

(Darling-Hammond, 1995; Darling-Hammond, Wise & Pease, 1993; Schalock, 1979; Walberg & Waxman, 1983). This finding is consistent with other research on effective teaching which suggests that an effective teacher is one who molds and adjusts his or her teaching to fit the demands of each student, topic, instructional method, and teaching goal. Given the multidimensionality, simultaneity, and immediacy of classroom events, it is not surprising that teachers who are flexible, adaptable, and creative are more effective in producing positive student learning outcomes (Bents & Bents, 1990; Berliner, 1987, 1992; Rottenberg & Berliner, 1990). Teachers' attitudes – specifically their feeling of efficacy or beliefs in their ability to help students learn – have also been found to be strongly and consistently related to teacher performance and student outcomes (Darling-Hammond, 1995). Teachers who believe they can help their students achieve are more effective than teachers who are less certain of their influence.

The psychological atmosphere of the classroom for students with autism in great part is influenced by specific teacher characteristics including dispositions, competencies, skills, and actions. (Smith et al., 1998). The teacher's personal philosophy about education, discipline, and curriculum weigh heavily as factors which contribute to the learning of students with autism (Simpson & Myles, 1998). The types of expectations a teacher holds for students can significantly influence learner outcomes. According to Smith et al. (1998), "An understanding teacher more effectively meets students instructional and curriculum needs. Teachers play a very critical role in creating a positive classroom environment" (p. 36). Smith et al. (1998) stressed three critical elements which influence the classroom learning of students with autism: teacher attitude (the way the teacher views the student), teacher expectations (teachers who have high expectations are more likely to inspire better performance), and teacher competence (the teacher's knowledge and skill in teaching students with autism).

The opportunity to apply knowledge about teaching in the complex, real world of classrooms under supervised guidance has been found to be a critical key in the effective preparation of teachers (Darling-Hammond, 1995). Although many applied skills must ultimately be learned in practice, it is clear that unsupervised on-the-job experience is, in and of itself, insufficient to support teacher learning and teacher effectiveness, as it can lead as frequently to the adoption of regressive and ineffective methods as to the acquisition of appropriate strategies.

Sewell (1999) summarized expectations for competent teachers included within 1999 IDEA Regulations (20 U.S.C 1400): "Competent teachers are expected to have excellent instructional skills and the ability to plan and design curriculum. They are expected to have knowledge in their fields to teach the full range of students from the most gifted to those most in need of individualized instruction. They must expect all students to reach their full potential" (p. 3).

SPECIAL EDUCATION LITIGATION AND LEGISLATION

Another major variable which has influenced the preparation of special education teachers is federal legislation. The history of special education, especially with regard to the right to a free appropriate public education, is related to the civil rights movement. *Brown v. Board of Education of Topeka*, 347 U.S. 483 (1954) is the landmark case which challenged the segregation of students according to race. The Supreme Court, in its ruling in the Brown Case, declared that education must be made available to all children on equal terms (Heward, 2000). One of the most historically significant cases which examined segregated education based upon disability was the 1972 class action suit *Pennsylvania Association for Retarded Children (PARC) v.* the *Commonwealth of Pennsylvania*. Heward summarized key arguments and findings in the PARC case: "The lawyers and parents supporting PARC argued that even though the children had intellectual disabilities, it was neither rational nor necessary to assume they were ineducable and untrainable" (p. 16). Because the state was unable to prove that the children were, in fact, ineducable or to demonstrate a rational need for excluding them from public school programs, the court decided that the children were entitled to receive a free appropriate public education.

Public Law 85-926, enacted in 1958, provided training fellowships for individuals willing to teach students with mental retardation. Public Law 87-276 (1961) supported the preparation of teachers of students who were deaf, speech pathologists, and audiologists. Public Law 88-164 (1963) expanded federal preparation programs for special education professionals in all areas of disabilities. The Vocational Rehabilitation Act of 1973 (P.L. 93-112) established a precedent that individuals with disabilities cannot be excluded from participation in, denied benefits of, or be subjected to discrimination under any program or activity receiving federal financial assistance. The legislation which has had the most profound impact on the preparation of special education teachers is Public Law 94-142 passed in 1975. The mandate for free appropriate education (including related services) for all students with disabilities created a demand for special educators. This piece of legislation also laid the groundwork for standards based teacher preparation for special education teachers (Hallahan & Kauffman, 2000). In 1986, Congress amended P.L. 94-142 to include provisions for preschool age students with disabilities. Public Law 99-457 mandated the provision of a free appropriate public education and all other provisions guaranteed under P. L. 94-142 to children with disabilities ages 3 to 5. This legislation also mandated an Individual Family Service Plan (IFSP) for infants and toddlers with disabilities. An IFSP is similar to an

Individual Education Program (IEP) in that it requires assessment and statements of goals, needed services, and plans for implementation. The IFSP also requires more involvement of the family, coordination of services, and plans for making the transition into preschool.

In 1990, P.L. 94-142 was reauthorized again and given a new name – the Individuals with Disabilities Education Act (IDEA). IDEA mandated the inclusion of plans for transition from school to work for older students with disabilities as part of the IEP. IDEA also stressed nondiscriminatory and multidisciplinary assessment of educational needs, parent involvement in developing each child's educational program, education in the least restrictive environment, and IEP (Hallahan & Kauffman, 2000). IDEA also added autism as a category of disability to the existing law. Hardman et al. (2000) summarize the definition for autism included within IDEA: "Autism is a developmental disability that primarily results in significant deficits in verbal and nonverbal communication and social interactions" (p. 397). The most recent reauthorization of this legislation took place in 1997, when Congress passed P.L. 105-17, calling it IDEA 97. This legislation represented a sustained commitment to require schools, employees, and government agencies to recognize the abilities of individuals with disabilities (Hallahan & Kauffman, 2000). One of the major provisions of IDEA 97 is that students with disabilities are entitled to appropriate education services in settings that best meet their individual needs and which offer the greatest opportunity for contact with students without disabilities. Simpson and Myles (1998) reported that in 1998, 4.7% of students with autism were being served in general education classrooms while 6.9% were being served in resource rooms. The current trend in educational placement for students with autism is toward greater inclusion in the general education setting (Simpson & Myles, 1998).

Special educators are likely to be more involved in working in inclusive settings in the future. The 1997 IDEA reauthorization requires that special educators be more knowledgeable about the general education curriculum. Specifically, special education teachers are expected to know about legal matters, behavior management, and how to make accommodations to meet student's needs.

PROFESSIONAL STANDARDS IN SPECIAL EDUCATION

The work of Schulman, AACTE and INTASC applies to the preparation of all teachers. What special knowledge and skills are required of those who choose to teach children and youth with exceptional needs? The founders of the Council for Exceptional Children (CEC) declared in 1922 that one of its primary purposes was to "establish professional standards in the field of special education" (CEC, 1998, p. 1). In the 1700s and 1800s, new teachers learned their skills directly from their 'masters' – de L'Epee, Braille, Itard, Pereire, Seguin, Montessori, Bell, Gallaudet and Howe. As special schools and classes expanded around the turn of the century, the need for teachers with specialized preparation grew. School based training programs such as the summer session offerings at New Jersey's Vineland Training School, were created to equip preservice and inservice teachers with skills to 'teach' children with mental retardation. "Penn State provided a summer session (1897) for teachers of "backward" children; the University of California (1918) initiated a program for the teachers of children who were blind and a Department of Special Education was established at Miami University in Ohio (1919). Teachers College at Columbia University (1920) developed a program to prepare teachers of gifted children. By 1929, the United States Office of Education (U.S.OE) reported 43 training institutions offering special education courses" (CEC, 1998, p. 32). Continued growth in the number of special education teacher training programs has continued to increase steadily over the past sixty years. Today, there are over 900 colleges and universities which offer degrees in special education (CEC, 1998). Simpson and Myles (1998) reported that "There are only a handful of legitimate autism preservice personnel preparation programs in the country" (p. 18). Siegel (1996) stated that "Students with autism should have a teacher who has specialized training or previous experience working with children with autism. Most states have no specific statewide teaching credential for autism" (p. 213).

As the number of training programs for special education teachers grew, the need for consistency across programs also grew. "In 1965, CEC held a conference on professional standards at which participants drafted statements of standards. These early professional standards included directives to ensure a basic level of standards (mandates from the field) related to teachers' educational programs, certification and accreditation, continuing education special education doctoral programs, and ethics of behavior" (CEC, 1998, p. 103). Several revisions in the CEC standards followed in 1973 resulting in increased emphasis on preparing teachers to meet the needs of students with exceptionalities in less restrictive educational settings and on performance criteria. In 1976, CEC became a member of the National Council for the Accreditation of Teacher Education (NCATE). This affiliation resulted in CEC establishing a process in 1986 to conduct standards based folio reviews which are used in many states as a part of the NCATE accreditation review. From 1986 to 1996, the CEC standards have undergone considerable review and revision. While CEC has specified standards for 'special educators', there are no standards specifically developed for teachers of students with autism.

In 1998, The Council for Exceptional Children (CEC) articulated specific competencies for special educators in its book, *What Every Special Educator Must Know: The International Standards for the Preparation and Licensure of Special Educators*. The 1998 CEC standards delineate the code of ethics expected of those in the profession, standards for professional practice, recommendations for what states should require for initial teacher licensure, standards for special education teacher preparation programs, and a summary of the knowledge and skills that beginning special educators should possess. The knowledge and skill standards have the most significant influence on what university based teacher preparation programs need to include within the curriculum for special education teachers. Core knowledge and skills essential for all beginning special education teachers include the following:

- Philosophical, historical, and legal foundations of special education
- Characteristics of learners
- Assessment, diagnosis and evaluation
- Instructional content and practice
- Planning and managing the teaching and learning environment
- Managing student behavior and social interaction skills
- Communication and collaborative partnerships
- Professionalism and ethical practices

Because almost all special educators will have students who will receive their instruction in special education as well as general education classroom settings, prospective special educators need to be able to apply the specific knowledge and skill competencies delineated in the eight categories listed above to students who are served in both general and special education settings.

Several authors have identified general topics which should be included within a training program for teachers of students with autism: receptive and expressive communication skills; social interaction strategies for varied settings; basic problem solving strategies for improving quality of life at home, school, and in the community; and information regarding positive behavioral supports (Carr et al., 1999; Cohen & Volkmar, 1997; Dunlap et al., 1994; Siegel, 1996). Designing an educational program for students with autism can present unique challenges for administrators and teachers. An effective classroom must include a physical structure that enhances learning opportunities. According to Simpson and Myles (1998), "Candidates pursuing teacher certification to teach students with autism should, at the very least, learn about instructional approaches that facilitate language acquisition, behavior management, social skills, and targeted academic goals" (p. 55). The specific topics they suggest should be incorporated within the teacher preparation program include: behavioral strategies, functional communicative abilities, social skills training strategies, and sensory integration techniques. Smith et al. (1998) suggested that designing education programs for students with autism requires use of many different strategies and techniques. They stated "Effective teachers must keep in mind that no single approach is right for every student. The curriculum must be individualized and customized for each student" (p. 91). Knowing how to individualize the curriculum and instructional procedures should be a key component of all preparation programs for teachers of students with autism.

The recently adopted NCATE 2000 standards place a much greater emphasis on what teacher candidates and graduates of teacher preparation programs know and can do relative to producing learning in Preschool through grade 12 learners rather than the course of study an individual progresses through as they complete a teacher preparation program. This transition will undoubtedly have a significant impact not only on the CEC standards, but also on the types of evidence which will be required in folio reviews to document student learning.

PREPARING TEACHERS OF STUDENTS WITH AUTISM

Children and youth with autism are classified using different terms, including *pervasive developmental disorder, autistic-like, higher functioning autism disorder, Asperger syndrome, Rett's disorder, and childhood disintegrative disorder* (Simpson & Zionts, 2000). General characteristics which apply to children and youth with the label of autism include social interaction impairments, qualitative communication impairments, and repetitive, restricted, ans stereotyped interests, activities, and patterns of behavior (Simpson & Zionts, 2000). In addition, individuals with autism may also have cognitive delays (including intellectual and learning problems), social adaptation difficulties (withdrawal, social deficits, and social ineptness), and motor delays (walking, crawling, and writing) (Trevarthen et al., 1998).

Until 1990, autism was generally viewed as either a form of severe emotional disturbance or mental retardation. With the passage of the Individuals with Disabilities Education Act in 1990, autism became a specific category of exceptionality. Currently as many as 67 per 1,000 individuals are being identified with autism-related disorders (Simpson & Zionts, 2000). It is a lifetime disorder that begins in childhood. "Most children with autism show signs of the disorder by 2 to 3 years of age. Many children with autism are described by their parents as different' from other children from the time they are born. On the other hand, some children with autism appear to develop normally for several years, except perhaps for relatively minor problems such as language delays, before showing significant signs of autism. Some children with higher functioning autism may not be diagnosed until they begin school" (Simpson & Zionts, 2000, p. 42).

Although curriculum and procedures will vary with individual needs, all children and youth diagnosed as having autism will require and benefit from education and training. Some children with autism are educated in regular classrooms. Others may require special education services designed for students with mild learning disabilities and social difficulties. Still other children and youth diagnosed as having autism may require a special education program designed for students with autism or moderate to severe disabilities (Hallahan & Kauffman, 2000; Heward, 2000). In light of the wide variability of characteristics and functioning levels of children and youth who have autism, teacher preparation programs must require prospective teachers to possess a broad knowledge base and demonstration of widely varied skills. Simpson and Zionts (2000) stated that regardless of whether the teacher of a child with autism is a general or special educator, special training is needed. They explained that "The educator needs to learn how to be a careful observer and recorder of the children's social and academic behaviors. This individual must be able to communicate to the parent and other team members regarding each student's progress in very specific terms" (p. 79). According to Simpson and Zionts, teachers should possess competence in twelve specific areas:

(1) Behavior management and social interaction enhancement techniques for students with autism.
(2) Speech and language development techniques for students with autism.
(3) Nonverbal communication techniques for students with autism.
(4) Ability to develop curricula for students with autism.
(5) Evaluation and assessment techniques for students with autism.
(6) Expressive therapy (e.g. art and music) programming for students with autism.
(7) Daily living skill programming for students with autism.
(8) Self-care skill programming for students with autism.
(9) Working with parents and families of students with autism.
(10) Directing and supervising classroom paraprofessionals.
(11) Vocational programing for students with autism.
(12) Community and independent living programming for students with autism.

While acknowledging parental views regarding the knowledge and skills needed by teachers of students with autism, Quill (1995) argued that:

> The teachers responsibility begins with the first day of school. The teachers goals should be to recognize how the child responds to different sensory stimuli, identify the child's learning, identify activities and interests that motivate the child, develop a reward system based on the child's interests, evaluate the child's current skills, set educational objectives

> for the year, and design a home-school communication system. Give the child the same things that every child needs from an education: opportunities to grow and to become as capable, as independent, and as happy as it is within his nature to become! (pp. 68–69).

Educational programs for children and youth with autism are usually very structured to enable more productive and adaptive functioning for the individual (Smith et al., 1998; Simpson & Myles, 1998). Structure often involves using task analysis and shaping, use of routines, and specific arrangement of the classroom's physical environment (Siegel, 1996; Simpson & Myles, 1998; Smith et al., 1998). Although instruction should be tailored to the unique needs of each student, six basic skill areas are usually emphasized: behavior and social skills, communication and language skills, self-help and independent living skills, prevocational and vocational skills, academic skills, and motor skills. Functionality (toilet training, eating, grooming, social interaction, language, and community living) is the primary skill emphasized in programs for children and youth who have severe autism (Koegel & Koegel, 1996). Basic attending and learning skills frequently are integrated into the student's curriculum.

Donnelly and Levy (1995) and Pratt (1996) believe that high-functioning students with autism and/or Asperger syndrome should be included in the general education classroom with age level peers. Being included and surrounded by typical behavior models is essential for social growth, educational challenge, and motivation. According to Donnelly and Levy, "There must be an awareness of the needs of these high-functioning students. Frequently collaborative services between the regular teacher, learning specialist, language therapist, motor specialist, gifted education teacher and/or counselor are required in the areas of language and communication, sensory development, social skills, behavior, academics, motor, and functional skills" (p. 87). Pratt (1996) recommended that high functioning students with autism should have access to all curricular and extracurricular options within the general education setting. She stresses selecting courses and instruction which will promote individual success. Simpson and Myles (1998) summarized specific skills which should be stressed in the instructional program for high functioning students with autism: "communication, including pragmatic use of language, literal interpretation, comprehension, and conversation; positive behavioral support techniques; and social skills training including how to make friends, rules of proximity, how to read social situations, and making accurate judgements about specific situations" (p. 167).

Teachers of students with autism must possess the knowledge, skills, and dispositions described in this section if they intend to provide effective instruction to the students entrusted to their care. Teacher preparation programs must be responsible for requiring each teacher candidate to demonstrate competence in each of these areas before recommending that the candidate be certified or licensed to teach students with autism.

INDUCTION AND SUPPORT PROGRAMS

Few experiences in life have such a tremendous effect on the personal and professional life of a teacher as that first year of teaching. The first year of teaching is both an exhilarating and physically and emotionally exhausting experience, complete with unexpected events that may never have been discussed in the teacher preparation program. These initial experiences are imprinted as beginning teachers gain new ideas about teaching, students, the school environment, and their role as teachers (Conderman & Stephens, 2000). First year induction and support programs, professional opportunities for reflection and dialogue, and other avenues for individualized or small-group support focusing on specific issues are just a few ways for beginning teachers to sustain their enthusiasm and love for teaching. Early career teachers need to learn about specific policies and issues affecting the district or school, and maintain a healthy emotional balance while making the transition to the level of professional educator. Successful mentoring programs encourage the development of a relationship between mentor and mentee that provides assistance tailored to the needs and challenges of the beginning teacher. Gold (1996) enumerated the goals that mentoring programs should offer: assistance for new teachers; expansion on what was learned in the preservice program; and help in reducing attrition by preventing the loss of talented and skilled teachers.

Special educators must assume many roles as they work with parents and other family members, community agencies, administrators, general educators, and other support personnel. Beginning teachers, however, may lack ability, confidence, or experience with specific communication, team building, and collaborative decision-making skills. To effectively establish partnerships, preservice teachers must master collaborative skills (Dow & Mehring, 2000). Preservice teacher education programs can develop this foundation by providing authentic collaborative experiences throughout coursework and field experiences. Mentoring programs can continue this support by including opportunities for the beginning special education teacher to observe and reflect on in preparation for developing successful collaborative partnerships.

ALTERNATIVE ROUTES TO TEACHER CERTIFICATION

Numerous sources have documented the growing gap between teacher supply and demand, especially in selected subject areas and in certain regions of the nation (Hirsch, Koppich & Knapp, 1999). It is estimated that in the next decade, American school districts will need to hire 2.2 million new teachers (220,000 a year) into a professional that now totals 2.7 million (Feistritzer, 1999). Kansas provides a good illustration of this concern. Fifty-nine percent of the teacher vacancies in Kansas between 2000 and 2006 will be special education positions (Pochowski, 2000). In the fall of 2000, there were over 250 special education classrooms in Kansas which in November still did not have a certified special education teacher. Similar conditions exist throughout the U.S. The specific supply and demand data related to the number of teachers of autism needed to fill classrooms during the next decade is unknown. Simpson and Myles (1998), however, through summarizing prevalence figures for autism over the past 40 years, provide an estimated trend regarding a growing need for teachers of students with autism. "In 1966, the estimated prevalence of autism was 4 to 5 per 10,000 births. In 1998, the prevalence of autism is estimated to be 15 to 20 out of every 10,000 births. As many as 67 per 1,000 individuals are identified annually as having autism or autism-related disorders" (p. 17). Bullock and Simpson (1990) reported that there is currently a shortage of teachers and other professionals trained to work with students with autism. It is anticipated that this shortage will increase over the next decade given the increasing trends identified above.

Supply and demand issues as well as a growing voice of concern related to the monopoly that university based teacher preparation programs have in regulating who is awarded a license to practice teaching have resulted in a growing number of alternative certification programs. At the writing of this chapter, 115 alternative programs exist in over 40 states (Feistritzer, 2000). Such programs generally 'prepare' teachers through a two or three week session of summer study followed by immersion into the classroom the following fall. While districts who hire individuals prepared by alternative routes to certification are supposed to provide a mentoring program, the depth and quality of such support has been questioned. For well over a decade, studies of teachers admitted through quick-entry alternate routes have frequently noted that the candidates have difficulty with curriculum development, pedagogical content knowledge, attending to students' differing learning styles and levels, classroom management, and student motivation (Adams, Hutchinson & Martray, 1980; Darling-Hammond, 1995; Glassberg, 1980; Taylor & Dale, 1971). Novice teachers without full training show more ignorance about student needs and differences and about the basics of teaching than do trained beginning teachers (Rottenberg & Berliner, 1990). Feistreitzer (2000) indicated that approximately 125,000 teachers have been certified through alternative routes, with 24,000 receiving certification in 1998–1999 alone. With increasing reliance on alternative teacher certification to rebuild the teaching workforce, it has become more critical than ever to examine how school districts and state policymakers can ensure that nontraditional programs produce quality teachers. The licensing of teachers through alternative routes should be a major concern when used as a means to provide special education teachers – especially those needing the specialized knowledge and skill required to effectively teach students with autism. Individuals licensed through alternative systems may lack the content, pedagogy, and clinical experiences needed to successfully 'teach' students with disabilities.

SUMMARY

A great deal has been learned about autism and childhood developmental disorders since the 1960s. No longer is the teaching of children with developmental disorders nebulous or a matter of guesswork,. The special education field has become better delineated, and its goals have been clarified. Teaching materials and techniques are constantly improving and expanding.

In the 1960s, teachers had to teach children with autism with intuition and often with handmade materials (Cohen & Volkmar, 1997). Teachers now have textbooks and workbooks especially geared for students with developmental disabilities and autism, as well as other teaching aids such as computers, cassettes, television, videocassette recorders, and copying machines. A generation of teachers has developed and refined teaching approaches such as behavior modification, signing, inclusion, prevocational and vocational training, special physical education and special techniques for music, art, and recreation. Special educators have been joined by occupational therapists, physical therapists, music and dance therapists, and specialists in other disciplines. They all work together in addressing the difficult task of communicating with, enhancing the general learning potential of, and otherwise solving or alleviating developmental problems of children and youth with autism.

The college student who today contemplates teaching children with autism has a good chance of making a realistic decision. A variety of classes and programs for individuals with developmental disabilities can be observed in private schools, public school general and special education programs, state sponsored service centers, and early intervention programs. From these observations, the aspiring future teacher can decide whether she or he has the capabilities and personality traits needed to be a successful teacher of individuals with autism.

All the progress made in the past 25 years has still not made teaching an easy job. Anyone starting off on a career of teaching individuals with autism or other disabilities often feels lost, not knowing which way to turn, where to go, or what to do. Physical endurance, emotional stability, flexibility, ability and willingness to improvise, and respect for the value of one's own intuition are all needed to work with children who have developmental disabilities. Various methods of research, new interventions and treatments are becoming available. These methods will ultimately have an impact on teachers and teaching methods. Even now, they are raising questions and beginning to bring about change. The basic necessary approach to teaching, however, has not changed: each child's strengths must be analyzed and used.

Children with autism present unique and challenging qualities for instruction. Hardman et al. (2000) summarized it well when they stated: "These students need creative and innovative teachers with positive attitudes" (p. 269). Preparing an increasing supply of well trained professionals to serve the needs of students with autism is, by any standard, a daunting challenge.

REFERENCES

Adams, R., Hutchinson, S., & Martray, C. (1980). A developmental study of teacher concerns across time. Paper presented at the annual meeting of the American Educational Research Association, Boston, MA.

Bents, M., & Bents, R. (1990). Perceptions of good teaching among novice, advanced beginner and expert teachers. Paper presented at the annual meeting of the American Educational Research Association, Boston, MA.

Berliner, D. (1987). In pursuit of the expert pedagogue. *Educational Researcher*, *15*, 5–13.

Berliner, D. (1992). Exemplary performances: Studies of expertise in teaching. Collected Speeches. Washington, D.C.: National Art Education Association.

Bullock, L., & Simpson, R. (1990). *Critical issues in special education: Implications for personnel preparation*. Denton, TX: University of North Texas Press.

Carr, E. G., Horner, R. H., Turnbull, A. P., Marquis, J. G., McLaughline, D. M., McAtee, M. L.,Smith, C. E., Ryan, K. A., Ruef, M. B., Doolabh, A., & Braddock, D. (1999). *Positive behavior support for people with developmental disabilities: A research synthesis*. Washington, D.C.: American Association on Mental Retardation.

Cohen, D., & Volkmar, F. (1997). *Handbook of autism and pervasive developmental disorders* (2nd ed.). New York: John Wiley & Sons.

Conderman, G., & Stephens, T. (2000). Voices from the field: Reflections from beginning special educators. *TEACHING Exceptional Children*, *33*(1), 16–21.

Council for Exceptional Children (1998). *What every special educator must know: The international standards for the preparation and licensure of special educators* (3rd ed.). Reston, VA: Author.

Darling-Hammond, L. (1990). Teacher supply, demand, and standards. *Educational policy*, *3*(1), 1–17.

Darling-Hammond, L. (Fall, 1995). Restructuring schools for student success, *Daedalus*, *1*(24), 53–162.

Darling-Hammond, L. (1996). Teaching and knowledge. In: John Sikula (Ed.), *Handbook of Research on Teacher Education* (2nd ed.). New York: Association of Teacher Educators.

Darling-Hammond, L., Wise, A., & Klein, S. (1995). *A license to teach: Building a professional for 21st century schools.* Boulder, CO: Westview Press.

Darling-Hammond, L., Wise, A., & Pease, R. (1993). Teacher evaluation in the organizational context: A review of the literature. *Review of Educational Research, 53*(3), 285–328.

Dow, M., & Mehring, T. (2000). Helping parents to maximize the potential of their child with exceptionalities. In: F. Obiakor, S. Burkhardt, A. Rotatori & T. Wahlberg (Eds), *Intervention Techniques for Individuals with Exceptionalities in Inclusive Settings.* Greenwich, CT: JAI Press.

Drew, C. J., & Hardman, M. L. (2000). *Mental retardation: A life cycle approach.* Columbus, OH: Merrill-Prentice Hall.

Donnelly, J. A., & Levy, S. M. (1995). Strategies for assisting individuals with high functioning autism and/or Asperger syndrome. 1995 National Conference on Autism Proceedings. Greensboro, NC: Future Education, Inc.

Dunlap, G., DePerczel, M., Clarke, S., Wilson, S., White, R., & Gomez, A. (1994). Choice making and proactive behavioral support for students with emotional and behavioral challenges. *Journal of Applied Behavioral Analysis, 27*, 505–518.

Graczyk, M., McGinnity, K., Negri., G., & Shoultz, M. (1996). *Strategies to support individuals with autism. 1996 Autism Society National Conference Proceedings.* Milwaukee, WI: Omni Press.

Feistritzer, C. E. (1999, May). Teacher quality and alternative certification programs. Paper presented to House Committee on Education and the Workforce Subcommittee on Post-secondary Education, Training and Life-long learning, Washington, D.C.

Feistritzer, C. E. (2000, February). *Alternative teacher certification: A state-by-state analysis.* Washington, D.C.: The National Center for Education Information.

Glassberg, S. (1980). A view of the beginning teacher from a developmental perspective. Paper presented at the annual meeting of the American Educational Research Association, Boston, MA.

Gold, Y. (1996) Beginning teacher support: Attrition, mentoring, and induction. In: J. Sikula (Ed.), *Handbook of Research on Teacher Education* (2nd ed., pp. 548–594). New York: Simon & Schuster.

Graczyk, M., McGinnity, M., Negri, N., & Shoultz, M. (1996). *Strategies to support individuals with autism. 1996 Autism Society Conference Proceedings.* Madison, WI: Omni Press.

Hallahan, D. P., & Kauffman, J. M. (2000). *Exceptional children* (6th ed.). Boston, MA: Allyn and Bacon.

Hardman, M. L., Drew, C. J., Egan, M. W., & Wolf, B. (2000). *Exceptional Children.* Boston, MA: Allyn and Bacon.

Haselkorn, D., & Harris, L. (1998). *The essential profession: A national survey of public attitudes toward teaching, educational opportunity, and school reform.* Belmont, MA: Recruiting New Teachers.

Heward, W. L. (2000). *Exceptional children: An introduction to special education* (6th ed.). Columbus, OH: Merrill-Prentice Hall.

Hirsch, E., Koppich, J., & Knapp, M. (1999, December). *State action to improve teaching. Teaching Quality Policy Briefs, 1.* Seattle, WA: Center for the Study of Teaching and Policy.

Interstate New Teacher Assessment and Support Consortium (1999). *Standards for beginning teacher licensing and development: A resource for state dialogue.* Washington, D.C.: Council of Chief State School Officers.

Koegel, R., & Koegel, L. (1996). *Teaching children with autism.* Baltimore, MD: Brookes Publishing Company.

Milken, L. (1999). A matter of quality: A strategy for assuring the high caliber of America's teachers. Santa Monica, CA: Milken Family Foundation.

National Commission on Teaching and America's Future. (1996). *What matters most: Teaching for America's future*. New York: Teachers College Press.

Olley, J. G. (1992). Autism: Historical overview, definitions, and characteristics. In: D. E. Berkell (Ed.), *Autism: Identification, Education and Treatment* (pp. 3–20). Hillsdale, NJ: Erlbaum.

Pochowski, A. (2000, November). Kansas special education supply and demand issues. Paper presented to the Kansas Educate America Act State Panel Meeting, Topeka, KS.

Quill, K. (1995). *Teaching children with autism: Strategies to enhance communication and socialization*. New York: Delmar Publishers.

Pratt, C. (1996). Practical instructional strategies for learners with autism. 1996 Autism Society Conference Proceedings. Madison, WI: Omni Press.

Reynolds, M. (1989). *Knowledge base for the beginning teacher*. New York: Permagon Press.

Ricks, D. M. (1989). Vocal communication in pre-verbal normal and autistic children. In: N. O'Connor (Ed.), *Language, Cognitive Deficits and Retardation*. London: Butterworth.

Rottenberg, C., & Berliner, D. (1990). Expert and novice teachers' conceptions of common classroom activities. Paper presented at the annual meeting of the American Educational Research Association, Boston, MA.

Schalock, D. (1979). Research on teacher selection. In: D. C. Berliner (Ed.), *Review of Research in Education*, Vol. 7. Washington, D.C.: American Educational Research Association.

Schriebman, L. (1988). *Autism, developmental clinical psychology and psychiatry*. Newbury Park, NJ: Sage Publications.

Schulman, L. (1987, January). Knowledge and teaching: Foundations of the new reform. *Harvard Educational Review*, *57*, 1–22.

Sewall, A. M. (1999). New frames for an undefined future. *Phi Kappa Phi Journal*, *79*(1), 3–4.

Siegel, B. (1996). *The world of the autistic child*. New York, NY: Oxford University Press.

Simpson, R., & Myles, B. (1998). *Education children and youth with autism*. Austin, TX: PRO-Ed.

Simpson, R., & Zionts, P. (2000). *Autism: Information and resources for professionals and parents* (2nd ed.). Austin, TX. PRO-Ed.

Smith, T. E., Polloway, E. A., Patton J. R., Dowdy, C. (1998). *Teaching students with special needs* (2nd ed.). Boston, MA: Allyn and Bacon.

Szatmari, P., Tuff, L., Finlayson, M. A., & Bartolucci, G. (1990). Asperger's syndrome and autism: Comparisons on early history and outcome. *Developmental Medicine and Child Neurology*, *31*, 130–136.

Taylor, J., & Dale, R. (1971). *A survey of teachers in the first year of service*. Bristol, England: University of Bristol, Institute of Education.

Trevarthen, C., Aitken, K., Papoudi, D., & Robarts, J. (1998). *Children with autism*. Philadelphia, PA: Jessica Kingsley Publishers.

U.S. Department of Education (1994). *Sixteenth annual report to Congress on the implementation of the Individuals with Disabilities Education Act*. Washington, D.C.: Author.

U.S. Department of Education (1997). *Preliminary results from the study of personnel needs in special education*. Washington, D.C. Author.

Walberg, H., & Waxman, H. (1983). Teaching, learning, and the management of instruction. In: D. C. Smith (Ed.), *Essential knowledge for beginning educators*. Washington, D.C.: American Association of Colleges for Teacher Education and ERIC Clearinghouse on Teacher Education.

Woolfolk, A. (1998). *Educational psychology*. Boston: Allyn and Bacon.

INSERVICE TRAINING FOR EDUCATORS OF INDIVIDUALS WITH AUTISM

Mirah J. Dow and Teresa A. Mehring

INTRODUCTION

Much about inservice education has been linked to discussions of school improvement and the raising of educational standards. It is not always clear from school improvement literature that teacher or student improvement efforts are intended to include the needs of individuals with autism. What is clear is that effective staff development utilizes a variety of staff development approaches to accomplish the goals of improving instruction and student success, provides follow-up necessary to ensure improvement, and requires knowledge and use of the stages of group development to build effective, productive, collegial teams. Research-based and experiential knowledge recognizes that students with autism and their teachers can "fit" into the nationwide movement to improve schools and educational outcomes for students. In this chapter, we discuss inservice training as a survival "tool" for educators who teach and support students with autism in today's schools and communities. First, we present "inservice" in the context of "inclusion". Following a brief review of autism and related disabilities, we identify on-the-job-learning models of inservice including the "information utility" model of inservice.

Autistic Spectrum Disorders: Educational and Clinical Interventions, pages 89–107.

ISBN: 0-7623-0818-4

AN ENRICHED IMAGE OF INSERVICE

Inservice training is typically offered to professional educators who already have significant knowledge and skills in a specific area and who need additional and/or specialized information on a given topic. "Inservice" is a term ascribed to education and training that is undertaken by professional educators who are involved in doing professional work. Inservice education, commonly called "inservice training," is typically offered during short sessions, several hours or days, while a "substitute" fills in for the professional or paraprofessional participating in the training. Inservice training has been used to improve the knowledge and skills educators need to effectively include children with disabilities in both regular and special education settings (Bennett, Rowe & DeLuca, 1996; Burke, 1996; Heimann, Nelson, Tjus & Gillberg, 1995; Herron, & Buss, 1991; Kamps, Walker, Maher & Rotholz, 1992; Madfes & Shulman, 2000; Munson, 2000; Sigafoos, Kerr, Roberts & Couzens, 1994; Stefanich, 1998; Swan & Brown, 1989; Williams, 1993). Inservice training is extremely helpful to teachers who discover for the first time that they must share responsibilities of educating students with autism and other severe disabilities.

Providing educators with additional information and instruction beyond certification requirements is essential in today's schools where teachers are expected to include all students. The movement for inclusion in the general classroom of children with identified disabilities has progressed from a theoretical argument to practical reality (Friend & Cook, 1993). Inclusion implies more than just change in teaching; it represents a paradigm shift in which all students learn in the same environment, and the focus is on effective instruction (Gartner & Lipsky, 1987; Lipsky & Gartner, 1996). For children with autism, experiencing effective instruction in public school, opposed to idle time spent at home or in state institutions, requires that educators and family members have access to specialized inservice training and information. Underlying the process of inclusion of all children is the assumption that general classroom teachers have a certain amount of knowledge about special education, students, teaching techniques, and curriculum strategies. Another assumption is that the classroom teacher is willing to change from the old to the new paradigm. According to Malarz (1996), as teachers use new models of classroom organization, assessment, and delivery of instruction, staff development and support for both general and special educators becomes critical.

Inclusion of children with autism may occur in various individualized placements such as regular classrooms, special education rooms, or some combination of regular and special education settings depending on the severity of the disability and the needs of the student. Preparing competent teachers to be accountable for their shared instructional responsibilities of children who begin life with what Wing (1988) called "autism spectrum disorder" is currently a challenge faced by many school systems and teacher training programs. Inservice training for educators of children with autism can provide time for learning about the nature of the disability, discovering the preferences, priorities and concerns of the individual with the disability, and time for adapting curriculum and instruction to match learning strengths, needs and interests of the student. Inservice training, which includes time for collaboration among professionals with a variety of disciplinary backgrounds, and information that can be quickly assimilated and later distributed, is needed to produce competent teachers of students with autism.

COMPETENT TEACHERS OF STUDENTS WITH AUTISM: A REQUIREMENT OF ALL SCHOOLS

Competent teachers are expected to have excellent instructional skills and the ability to plan and design curriculum. They are expected to have knowledge in their fields to teach the full range of students from the most gifted to those most in need of individualized instruction. They must expect all students to reach their full potential (Sewall, 1998). These expectations of teachers are reemphasized in the 1999 Individuals with Disabilities Education Act (IDEA) Regulations (20 U.S.C 1400), which calls teachers to even higher levels of competence in preparing students with disabilities for employment and independent living than was required in the 1990 IDEA. The competence that teachers are expected to bring about in students requires changes in the way educators access and use information.

It is no longer acceptable for districts to limit educational access simply by pointing to the limitations of existing staff (U.S. Reports, Vol. 526, Cedar Rapids Community School District v. Garret F., Docket 96-1793, March 3, 1999). Today, there are higher demands on professors of teacher education to cover content and recommended instructional practices. Teacher training programs have limited time to spend on all disability specific information. Faculty in public schools sometimes lack necessary skills to participate in adapting local, outcomes-based curriculum to match individual needs and abilities of students with the greatest needs. Employing competent educators, in this case, requires that school districts and teacher training institutions engage in new, cost-effective partnerships with each other and the public that produce accountable, competent teachers of students most severely effected by developmental disabilities.

In addition to ascertaining the core knowledge and skills identified by Mehring and Dow in this book, special educators must recognize and correctly describe children with autism spectrum disorders. Although teachers lack the medical credentials to diagnosis autism, inservice training should be designed to teach educators accurate and effective use of various diagnostic descriptors. Following is a brief overview of terms and characteristics that competent teachers and informed family members should know and use. We recommend general and special educators become familiar with current descriptive information related to autism spectrum disorders. We believe this descriptive information provides foundational knowledge for understanding the "information utility" model for on-the-job-learning described in this chapter.

AUTISM SPECTRUM DISORDERS

The term "spectrum of autism" was used by Lorna Wing (1988) to capture the idea of a range of manifestations of the same disability according to intellectual ability and age. Children with autism spectrum disorders include those sometimes diagnosed before 3 years of age with a regulatory disorder, or multisystems developmental disorder (Zero to Three, National Center for Infants, Toddlers, and Families), and who are later diagnosed with pervasive developmental disorder (American Psychiatric Association, 1994) including autism disorder, Rett's disorder, childhood disintegrative disorder, Asperger's disorder and pervasive developmental disorder not otherwise specified. According to the definition set forth in the Diagnostic and Statistical Manual-Fourth Edition, pervasive developmental disorders are characterized by severe and pervasive impairment in several areas of development including social interaction skills, communication skills, or the presence of stereotyped behaviors, interest, and activities (American Psychological Association, p. 6).

Autism and Asperger's Disorders

Both behaviorally defined syndromes, autism and Asperger's disorders are characterized by uneven developmental profiles created by disturbances in communication, social interaction, and perceptual organization. The primary distinction in the two disorders is that people with autism experience significant deficits in language development (some are non-verbal and experience mental retardation) while those with Asperger's disorder have only mild language impairments or peculiar ways of using language. These conditions are now considered to be the most serious, life-long developmental disabilities. However, the conditions can be alleviated somewhat by age and through the benefits of a range of educational and therapeutic interventions including various strategies for adapting to the social world (Baron-Cohn, 1996; Myles & Simpson, 1997; Simpson & Myles, 1998).

Rett's Disorder (RD)

Also called Rett's Syndrome, RD is diagnosed primarily in females. In children with Rett's disorder, development proceeds in an apparently normal fashion over the first six to 18 months at which point parents notice a change in their child's behavior and some regression or loss of abilities, especially in gross motor skills such as walking and moving. This is followed by an obvious loss in abilities such as speech, reasoning and hand use. The repetition of certain meaningless gestures or movements is an important clue to diagnosing Rett's disorder; these gestures typically consist of constant hand wringing or hand-washing (Moeschler, Gibbs & Graham, 1990).

Childhood Disintegrative Disorder (CDD)

An extremely rare disorder, CDD is a clearly apparent regression in multiple areas of functioning (such as the ability to move, bladder and bowel control, and social and language skills) following a period of at least 2 years of apparently normal development. By definition, CDD can only be diagnosed if the symptoms are preceded by at least 2 years of normal development and the onset of decline is prior to age 10 years (American Psychiatric Association, 1994).

Pervasive Developmental Disorder Not Otherwise Specified (PDDNOS)

Children with PDDNOS either: (a) do not fully meet the criteria of symptoms clinicians use to diagnose any of the four specific types of pervasive developmental disorder (PDD) specific types, or (b) do not have the degree of impairment described in any of the four PDD types. According to the DSM-IV, this category should be used "when there is a severe and pervasive impairment in the development of social interaction or verbal and nonverbal communication skills, or when stereotyped behavior, interest, and activities are present, but the criteria are not met for a specific PDD, Schizophrenia, Schizotypal Personality Disorder, or Avoidant Personality Disorder" (American Psychiatric Association, 1994, pp. 77–78).

These brief descriptions of autism spectrum disorders can be useful to educators in assessing student needs for referral to medical and mental health professionals (physicians, psychiatrists and clinic psychologists), and for diagnostic evaluations. They will also be helpful to educators, school counselors, and parents in selecting specialized inservice training and information. The good news is that the knowledge and skills needed to facilitate improvements in individuals with autism spectrum disorders is the same knowledge and skill needed to instruction and support many individuals with severe neurological disabilities. It is also important to emphasize that competent teachers of students with autism are likely to be competent teachers of many other students as well. Competent teachers of students with autism value individualized education that serves to adapt and modify content, instructional methodologies, assignments, and evaluation processes based on the student's intellect and cognitive style, culture, interests, and goals.

MODELS OF INSERVICE TRAINING

Inservice training as professional development has traditionally taken the form of workshops, study groups, conference sessions, and university courses taken for credit or non-credit. In addition to these traditional forms of inservice training, new approaches are also emerging as educators recognize their own needs for professional growth and change. One such approach is called "job-embedded" learning. According to Wood and McQuarrie (1999), "job-embedded learning is one of the most promising new approaches to professional growth. Job-embedded learning is the result of educators sharing what they have learned from their teaching experiences, reflecting on specific work experiences to uncover new understanding, and listening to colleagues share best practices they have discovered while trying out new programs or planning and implementing a project. Study groups, action research, and reflective logs are formal structures created to promote job-embedded learning" (p. 10).

Research indicates that simply holding inservice sessions with presentation of information alone is not enough to produce competent teachers (National Staff Development Council, 1995). Teaching behavior cannot be changed with "one shot" training on a "hot topic" (Mehring, 1997, p. 1). "When efforts cease following training workshops, 90% of the investment in the improvement of instruction is lost" (National Staff Development Council, 1995). Follow-up sessions and repeated use of the new skills soon after training are necessary if workshop participants are to retain the skills in their teaching repertoires (Joyce & Showers, 1988; Wells-Welsh, 1988). As shown in Table 1, presentation and demonstration of information through workshops, conferences, or even college course work result in increased knowledge but relatively little skill acquisition or classroom application. For staff development activities to make a significant difference in classroom applications by teachers, presentation must be accompanied by demonstration, practice, feedback and coaching (Mehring).

Research on staff development is one source of information about the nature of effective inservice training, and it is the source that we will draw on most heavily here. According to the National Staff Development Council (1995), the

Table 1. Training Effectiveness: Degree of Proficiency Attained in Knowledge, Skills, and Application from Staff Development Activities.

	Knowledge	Skills Acquisition	Classroom Applications
Presentation of Information	40–80%	10%	5%
Presentation + Demonstration	80–85%	10–40%	5–10%
Presentation + Demonstration + Practice and low-Risk Feedback	80–85%	80%	10–15%
Presentation + Demonstration + Practice/Feedback+Coaching	90%	90%	80-90%

Adapted from Fullan, 1991; National Staff Development Council, 1995; and Joyce and Showers, 1988.

characteristics of productive inservice programs include: (1) connectedness to school settings and to schoolwide efforts; (2) involvement of teachers as planners; (3) proving choice and differentiated learning opportunities; (4) use of demonstration, supervised practice, and feedback as a part of training; and (5) ongoing assistance and support.

Inservice training for teachers of students with autism must: (1) address specific aspects of the neurological disabilities in autism spectrum disorders; (2) connect classrooms and communities; and (3) offer teachers multiple and on-going opportunities for learning, feedback, networking, and rejuvenation. We feel that the concept of "job-embedded" learning suggests that almost any interaction between two or more educators can provide an opportunity for learning. We agree with Wood (1999) that both formal activities designed to promote learning and the formal and informal interacts within a school can be employed to promote valuable professional learning (p. 10). We are recommending an "information utility" model for in-service training and information services for teachers of students with autism spectrum disorders. Just as an electric company and Internet provider supplies unlimited opportunities for resources to power ones' computer (as long as the utility bill is paid), the "information utility" model offers unlimited opportunities for teachers and parents to have resources that will "power" their knowledge and skills with students with autism.

INFORMATION UTILITY MODEL FOR INSERVICE EDUCATION

The "information utility" model is a comprehensive in-service model which focuses on the needs of people most directly effected by the disability. The "information utility" model, when utilized, can provide "staying power" for teachers, parents and others who otherwise are at high risk of becoming overwhelmed by the high demands of teaching students with autism. We regard a specialized teacher as an "information professional" who provides access to disability specific information, and customizes responses to match users' learning styles and interests in specific disability issues. This model can be used by educators in special education cooperatives and university-based programs to improve teacher knowledge and instructional competence in teaching students with autism. Ideally, this model proactively eliminates the need for valuable resources to be exhausted in dispute resolution through remedies such as mediation, due process, or law suits. The "information utility" model is comprised of three essential components: information philosophy (a new foundation for special education), information services (access and dissemination of current and customized information) and inservice training (on-the-job-learning in recommended practices). Each component is contingent upon the other and emphasizes teacher and student learning.

Information Philosophy

Behind the practice of teaching is a philosophy, or set of beliefs, which influences the way teachers go about their work. Competent teachers take time to think about their own teaching and to articulate beliefs central to their practices with students. They know the structure of knowledge in their disciplines. This knowledge provides them with cognitive road maps to guide the assignments they give students, the assessments they use to gauge student progress, and the questions they ask in the give-and-take of classroom life. The following brief comparison of industrial era and information age philosophy, disciplinary knowledge and practice that will help the educator to assess her/his own information philosophy, and when necessary, provide the basis for moving forward into information age thinking and practices.

Industrial Era Philosophy

Until this decade, many teacher education programs, and recommended teacher practices with special education populations, have been premised on the foundational view of knowledge and science (Bledstein, 1976; Haskell, 1984). According to Bogdon and Knoll (1988), Bodgan and Kugelmass (1984), Mercer (1973), Skrtic (1986, 1988, 1991), and Thomlinson (1982) special educators utilized the biology and psychology disciplines related to human pathology. Assumptions of special educators include four key principles. First, disabilities are pathological conditions that students have. Second, differential diagnosis is objective and useful. Third, special education is a rationally conceived and coordinated system of services, which benefit diagnosed students. And forth, progress results from incremental technological improvements in diagnosis and instructional interventions. Educators relied primarily on theory derived from quantitative studies that sought empirical truth, and attempted to explain cause and effect relationships between specific interventions and student behaviors. Teachers were ultimately responsible for determining what and how to teach students. With these assumptions, teachers performed their duties in schools according to a "professional model" (Shein, 1972, pp. 8–9), which established a hierarchical order for having information and implied rules for using information. The industrial era professional model forced teachers to operate near the bottom of a pyramid-shaped configuration comprised of strict divisions between U.S. Department of Education, State Departments of Education, local administrators, teachers, school staff, and consumers of education including students and their family members. In contrast, information era philosophy rejects the industrial era tendency to locate teachers and their students with disabilities outside significant problem-solving/decision making and instead places value on information seekers (regardless of status or background) and locates seekers of information in the center of communities of learners.

Information Era Philosophy

A new philosophy of information has recently emerged that expands concepts of teaching and learning, changes assumptions behind professional work, practices of educators, and locates students, teachers and other key support persons on a more level playing field. Mason, Mason and Culnan (1995) pointed out five core beliefs of the information era philosophy, which provide the philosophical foundation for the "information utility" model we are suggesting for teachers of students with autism spectrum disorders.

1. Information must be Accessible

In the context of developmental disabilities, this belief asserts that all information about disability and intervention choices is available to the seeker regardless of the seeker's role with a person with a disability. There are no content secrets to be kept by educators and other professionals from others outside the education establishment. Access to information makes it possible for all stakeholders to participate in decision-making.

2. Information must be Repackaged to Match the User's Needs

Swift progress into the information era presents educators with the daunting task of selecting from abundance of print and on-line sources. Publications contain descriptions of neurological conditions and how to improve perceptions and behaviors of students who experiencecertain brain-based conditions. Some teachers and teacher educators have a wealth of background knowledge about such topics as diagnostic criteria, or biological treatments and educational therapies. These teachers simply need help to synthesize current research and to apply it to a specific situation. Other teachers and parents have had very little exposure to developmental disabilities and require significant guidance to gain a new focus. Understanding the background knowledge, experiences, abilities, and interest levels of a teacher is central to improving teachers' practices with students.

3. Information Resources must be User-Friendly

People who need to know about autism spectrum disorders are often facing persistent frustration. For resources to make a positive difference, the format must contain easy to use details that "speak" to the user and consequently make life easier, not more difficult. Print and on-line resources such as newsletters, brochures and directories are needed with visual appeal that "draws" the information seeker to an author's message. People who function as resources must indicate immediate understanding, genuine concern, communicate empathy, and be willing to treat every request as urgent. Convenient information services need to be available beyond typical work hours and during scheduled breaks from direct intervention and support of students.

4. The Role of the Information Professional is to Cost-effectively get the Right Information, at the Right Time, to the User

While consultants are often referred to as "experts" in one disability area or another, the label "expert" in the past has implied a narrow, expensive application of knowledge, skills and work. Applied to an "information utility" within a special education cooperative or university, the information "expert" must be prepared to communicate effectively within various academic disciplines and with decision-makers throughout the school environment. This "expert" teacher can facilitate on-the-job-learning and can cost-effectively become a member of a student's instructional team without building up an additional bureaucratic layer of expensive labor. This role moves beyond that of typical district consultant who attends Individualized Education Plan (IEP) meetings, makes recommendations, and interacts with specific teachers and/or students a few hours each week. Recognized as a local "information professional," this "expert" teacher makes significant contributions to on-the job-learning in district or university-based programs. The information professional is able to so because she/he: (a) possesses knowledge of typical development and various behaviorally diagnosed disorders, (b) understands the organization and management of classrooms, school systems, and social services, (c) uses technology to access, create, disseminate and store instructional materials, (d) is sensitive to various cultures, learning styles and lifestyles, and (e) has excellent interaction skills with students with challenging behaviors, their teachers and related service providers, parents or primarily caregivers. This person should be selected on the basis of her/his characteristics and because of her/his extraordinary ability to facilitate interactions that will serve to rejuvenate those most directly involved with students with autism.

5. Asking for Help is a Sign of Human Strength, not a Weakness

Competent educators and education institutions strive to stay on the "cutting edge" of technology, teacher skills, software, and facilities. Networking between people who share understanding of and commitment to people with autism spectrum disorders is essential to achieving best practices. Information seekers, regardless of their credentials or length of experience, are encouraged through the "information utility" to ask for help and to know that dialog among people with a common purpose is the way to maintain "staying power." Table 2 describes six major changes from industrial age philosophy and practice to information era philosophy and practices of educators.

Competent teachers are aware of industrial era and information age philosophies and practices of teachers, think about the beliefs behind their practices, and change their briefs and practices to achieve a match between practices and student needs. For teachers to prepare students with autism spectrum disorders for life beyond school, teachers must believe in the significance of their involvement and have access to specialized information services.

Information Services

Through the "information utility" model, on-the-job learning is facilitated by an information professional (specialized teaching) operating from a central location within the special education cooperative or university-based program. Primary service objectives of the "information utility" are consistent with the autism spectrum disorder policy of independence, productivity and inclusion. As a result, information professionals must:

1. listen to information seekers and answer questions;
2. increase public awareness of autism spectrum disorders;
3. provide informational and instructional materials in the format that best fits the information seeker's needs;
4. facilitate on-the-job learning opportunities; and
5. provide consultation and networking opportunities.

Users of a "information utility" created for the benefit of individuals with autism spectrum disorders are most often teachers and related service providers

Table 2. Comparison of Industrial Age and Information Era Philosophy and Practice of Educators.

Industrial Age Philosophy and Practice	Information Era Philosophy and Practice
Only professionals have and use information to inform others.	Information is accessible to everyone Information professionals facilitate access
Information available in one format (usually print).	Information packaged to match users' needs.
Publications about developmental disabilities available in professional terminology.	Resources are user-friendly.
Libraries with books and journals cataloged and arranged on shelves. Approved patrons come to the library to borrow items located in the library.	Technologically modern information centers with special collection communication software, database, search engines. The role of the information professional is to cost-effectively get the right information, at the right time, to the user.
Professionals, people with developmental disabilities, and their family members are separated from each other and from policy makers and program administrators by hierarchical organization structure.	Organization and management allows for interaction, adaptation and accommodation of environments.
Asking for help is an indication of human weakness	Asking for information is an indication of human strength.

(occupational and physical therapists; speech-language pathologists; adaptive physical education specialist; art and music therapists; and assistive technology and transition coordinators). However, individuals with disabilities and their family members, peers and neighbors, school counselors, school administrators, mental health and social service providers, and members of the medical community all utilize the center's services. Through "client-centered diagnosis" (Grover & Carabell, 1995, p. 4), the seeker's unique needs are established and responses are determined. This results in satisfied users who value such specialized attention and who return to the "utility" for assistance. Knowledge of seeker needs is used to improve the match between the clients and the information sources and inservice training.

Just as the electric utility company makes power available to consumers, the "information utility" makes available various information resources to teachers.

A special collection of books, journal, handbooks, and videos is loaned and used to increase knowledge about autism spectrum disorders and strategies for improving interactions with students. It is a great benefit to those who engage in on-the-job learning to discover others who are comfortable with people with autism spectrum disorders and develop networks of support providers who share similar preferences, priorities, and concerns. Through sharing common purposes, information seekers can be rejuvenated in what will otherwise become very intense and stressful work.

Inservice Training

For inservice training to make a significant difference in classroom applications, presentation must be accompanied by demonstration, practice, feedback, and coaching. In the "information utility" model, strategies are utilized in developing information philosophy and information services to increase access and dissemination of information. Research indicates that successful inservice training is most likely to result from training sessions that address the individual needs of participants (Berman & McLauglin, 1978; Lawrence, 1974). According to Siedow (1985), "the effects of inservice are likely to be more lasting when teachers are allowed to ask for the kinds of inservice they need and to participate actively throughout the inservice series" (p. 8). "Participants in inservice should initially voice their needs, participate in sessions, and engage in follow-up activities once the training is completed. Practical needs of teachers and their students are the basis for planning and conducting inservice sessions" (p. 4). The "information utility" model is based on Siedow's inservice principles as outlined below:

- Assessment of the needs of potential participants forms the basis of the inservice program. This process begins with the writing and administration of an information needs assessment that is used to identify the needs of potential participants, their students, supervisors, administrators, and family members who will benefit from inservice.
- Objectives for inservice training are developed on the basis of needs of participants and their students. They are formulated both in terms of the ultimate outcomes for students and the immediate outcomes related to teacher practices.
- Content of sessions is based on objectives established from the needs assessment. This content includes relevant and potentially effective instructional strategies which stand a reasonable chance of being successfully implemented in classrooms.

- Methods of presenting content and staffing for sessions involve teachers as adults responsible for their own learning. Modeling of strategies applied to specific content areas, opportunities for reflecting on ideas, and discussion of relative merits of strategies are all methods by which adults learn and become willing to try new ideas and strategies. Instructional methods are successfully presented by experienced teachers, university professors, or consultants selected for their specialization in aspects of teaching and support of individuals with autism spectrum disorders.
- Evaluation of individual sessions and of long-term programs is essential to measure accomplishment of objectives and also to assess further needs of participants.
- Follow-up activities are conducted to extend techniques learned and to modify them as needed in specific situations. Meetings between individual participants and presenters, small group discussions, and reunion sessions of participants are used to insure that inservice has lasting effects.

These principles form the logical basis for the "information utility" model of inservice, or on-the-job learning. They are in concert with Hudson's (1981) findings on effective inservice education.

Topics for Inservice Training

Information needs assessments (Dow, 1999) revealed several topics of interest to potential users of a "information utility" developed for teachers of students with autism. The topics that have been identified are consistent with the deficits that individuals with autism spectrum disorders experience: communication, self-care, social skills, and problem-solving skills. Participants frequently want to: (a) improve receptive and expressive communication skills; (b) improve the individual's participation and interaction in various natural environments; and (c) improve basic problem-solving skills necessary for quality of life at home, school and in the community. Not surprisingly, they want to have access to current information related to research investigating the cause(s) of autism spectrum disorders, demographic information, and "the-state-of-autism" information related to other similarly situated individuals. Also, they want to observe actual instruction in providing positive behavioral supports (Carr et al., 1999; Dunlap et al., 1994; Koegel, Koegel & Dunlap, 1996). In addition, they want to learn more about instruction in organizing and structuring environmental and tasks (Hodgdon, 1995; Schopler, Lansing & Waters, 1983; Sewell, 1998) that will make sense to the person with autism. Gray (1995) emphasized that teachers and parents want to learn to teach social skills and how to adapt general education curriculum for students with autism.

CONCLUSION

Children with autism spectrum disorders can benefit from a range of educational and therapeutic interventions (Baron-Cohn, 1996; Myles & Simpson, 1997; Simpson & Myles, 1998). Despite the challenges, general and special educators need to prepare student who are most in need of individualized instruction for life beyond the formal school years. As educators begin to recognize their own needs for professional growth and change in the ways they think and practice their skills with students with autism, on-the-job learning is an approach to inservice education wherein learning occurs as teachers and administrators engage in their daily work activities. In this chapter, we have extended the concept of "job-embedded" learning by presenting a model that can be used by local special education cooperatives and/or university programs to meet the continuous needs of teachers of students with autism spectrum disorders. This model, the "information utility" model, emphasizes the way teachers think about their work (information philosophy), access and share information (information services) and instructional practices of teachers (inservice training). An information professional, or specialized teacher, functions through a centralized location within a special education cooperative or university-based program to provide on-the-job learning in the form of study and problem-solving groups, and networking. The "information utility" learning is a new paradigm for staff development that will help shape professional learning in today's schools. It presents educators with an alterative to workshop-based professional development. It changes thinking about work as completing tasks to viewing daily experiences as opportunities to learn.

We have found through information needs assessments (Dow, 1999) that topics of interest to teachers and parents of students with autism spectrum disorders tend to mirror the deficits represented in the diagnostic criteria. In addition, educators and parents want to know more about what autism is, what is causing it, and how it directly and indirectly impacts lives. Teachers and parents also want to know more about how to provide positive behavioral supports that will improve opportunities for individuals with autism in their schools, homes, and communities. Additionally, they want to become effective in adapting and modifying general education curriculum so to make time spent in school more satisfying for students with autism and to enable these students to accomplish requirements for completion of high school programs.

More can be learned about the "information utility" model of inservice by investigating specialized information centers for autism. Examples of statewide inservice and information centers that operate like "information utilities" and provide on-the-job learning and disability specific information in the area autism spectrum disorder include: Autism and Asperger's Resource Center, University of Kansas; Division TEACCH, a Public Health Program at the University of North Carolina School of Medicine at Chapel Hill; Indiana Resource Center on Autism; Kansas Resource Center on Autism, Emporia State University; Project ACCESS at Southwest Missouri State University; Project CREST, Bowling Green State University in Ohio; The Center for Technology in Education (CTE), a partnership between Johns Hopkins University and the Maryland State Department of Education; The Curriculum Development in Teaching Science to Students with Disabilities project in Iowa; the Georgia Psychoeducational Network Program; and The Center for Collaborative Educational Leadership (LEAP) University of Colorado at Denver, Colorado.

REFERENCES

Alexander, D., Cowdry, R. W., Hall, Z. W., & Snow, J. R. (1996). The state of science in autism: A view from the National Institutes of Health. *Journal of Autism and Developmental Disorders*, *26*(2), 117–154.

American Psychiatric Association (1994). *Diagnostic and statistical manual of mental disorders* (4th ed.). Washington, D.C.: Author.

Baron-Cohn, S. (1996). *Mindblindness: An essay on autism and theory of mind*. Cambridge, MS: MIT Press.

Bennett, T., Rowe, V., & DeLuca, D. (1996). Getting to know Abby. *Focus on Autism and Other Developmental Disabilities*, *11*(3), 183–188.

Berman, P., & McLaughlin, M. W. (1978). *Implementing and sustaining innovations. Federal programs supporting educational change*, (7). Santa Monica, CA: Rand Corporation.

Bledstein, B. J. (1976). *The culture of professionalism: The middle class and the development of higher education in America*. New York: W. W. Norton.

Bogdon, R., & Knoll, J. (1988). The sociology of disability. In: E. L. Meyen & T. M. Skrtic (Eds), *Exceptional Children and Youth: An Introduction* (pp. 449–477). Denver, CO: Love.

Bogdon, R., & Kugelmass, J. (1984). Case studies in mainstreaming: A symbolic interactionist approach to special schooling. In: L. Barton & S. Tomlinson (Eds), *Special Education and Social Interests* (pp. 173–191). New York: NY: Nicholas.

Burke, J. C. (1996, March). Preparing school systems to deliver a hybrid education program for students with autism via distance learning classrooms, in-class teleconferencing, and listserv technology. Retrieved October 22, 2000, from Firstsearch database (ERIC, Accession ED394755) on the Internet: http://newfirstsearch.oclc.org

Carr, E. G., Horner, R. H., Turnbull, A. P., Marquis, J. G., McLaughline, D. M., McAtee, M. L., Smith, C. E., Ryan, K. A., Ruef, M. B., Doolabh, A., & Braddock, D. (1999). *Positive behavior support for people with developmental disabilities: A research synthesis*. Washington, D.C.: American Association on Mental Retardation.

Developmental Disabilities Reform Act, KSA 39-1801–39-1810.

Dow, M. J. I. (1991). Toward a technology of behavioral support for individuals with autism: An ideal information system. (Doctoral dissertation, Emporia State University, 1999).

Dunlap, G., DePerczel, M., Clarke, S., Wilson, D., Wright, S., White, R., & Gomez, A. (1994). Choice making and proactive behavioral support for students with emotional and behavioral challenges. *Journal of Applied Behavioral Analysis*, *27*, 505–518.

Friend, M., & Cook, L. (1993). Inclusion. *Instructor*, *103*, 52–56.

Fullan, M. (1991). *The new meaning of educational change*. New York, NY: The Teachers College Press.

Gartner, A., & Lipsky, D. K. (1987). Beyond special education: Toward a quality system for all students. *Harvard Educational Review*, *57*, 367–395.

Gray, C. (1995). Social stories and comic strip conversations: *Unique methods to improve social understanding*. Arlington, TX: Future Horizons.

Grover, R., & Carabell, J. (1995). Toward a better information service: Diagnosing information needs. *Special Libraries*, *86*, 1–4.

Haskell, T. L. (1984). *The authority of experts: Studies in history and theory*. Bloomington: Indiana University Press.

Heimann, M., Nelson, K. E., Tjus, T., & Gillberg, C. (1995). Increasing reading and communication skills in children with autism through an integrative multimedia computer program. *Journal of Autism and Other Developmental Disorders*, *5*, 459–480.

Herron, E., & Buss, J. R. (1991, March 17). Project ACCESS: Providing support and technical assistance to rural schools serving students with Autism. Missouri. Retrieved October 22, 2000, from Firstsearch database (ERIC Accession ED342578) on the Internet: http://newfirstsearch.oclc.org

Hodgdon, L. A. (1995). *Visual strategies for improving communication. Vol. 1: Practical supports for school and home*. Troy, MI: QuirkRoberts Publishing.

Hudson, J. M. (1981). Inservice best practices: The learnings of general education. *Journal of Research and Development in Education*, *14*, 1–10.

Individuals with Disabilities Education Act of 1990. *Federal Register*, *57*(189), September 29, 1992.

Individuals with Disabilities Education Act of 1999. Federal Register, (20 U.S.C 1400).

Joyce, B., & Showers, B. (1988). *Student achievement through staff development*. White Plains, NY: Longman Press.

Kamps, D., Walker, D., Maher, J., Rotholz, D. (1992). Academic and environmental effects of small group arrangements in classrooms for students with autism and other developmental disabilities. *Journal of Autism and Developmental Disabilities*, *2*, 277–293.

Koegel, L. K., Koegel, R. L., & Dunlap, G. (Eds) (1996). Positive behavioral support: *Including people with difficult behavior in the community*. Baltimore, MD: Paul H. Brookes.

Lawrence, G. (1974). Patterns of effective inservice education: A state of the art summary of research on materials and procedures for changing teacher behaviors in inservice education. Tallahassee, FL: Florida State Department of Education.

Lieberman, A. (1999). Networks. *Journal of Staff Development*, *20*(3), 43–44.

Lipsky, D. K., & Gartner, A. (1996). Inclusion, school restructuring, and the remaking of American society. *Harvard Education Review*, *66*, 762–796.

Madfes, T. J., & Shulman, J. (2000). Dilemmas in professional development: A case-based approach to improving practice. California. Retrieved November 3, 2000, from Firstsearch database (ERIC, Accession ED440099) on the Internet: http://newfirstsearch.oclc.org

Malarz, L. (1996). Using staff development to create inclusive schools. *Journal of Staff Development*, *17*, 8–11.

Mason, R. O., Mason, F. M., & Culnan, M. J. (1995). Ethics of information management. Thousand Oaks, CA: SAGE.

Mehring, T. (1997). Strengthening the application of SIM through peer coaching. *Stratenotes, 6*, 1–5.

Mercer, J. (1973). *Labeling the mentally retarded: Clinical and social system perspectives on mental retardation*. Berkeley: University of California Press.

Moeschler, J., Gibbs, E., & Graham, J. (1990). *A summary of medical and psychoeducation aspects of Rett Syndrome*. Lebonon, NH: Clinical Genetics and Child Development Center.

Munson, B. R. (2000, February). Character education: The missing ingredient of preservice teacher education programs. Oregon. Retrieved November 3, 2000, from Firstsearch database (ERIC, Accession ED440069) on the Internet: http://newfirstsearch.oclc.org

Myles, B. S., & Simpson, R. (1997). *Asperger syndrome: A guide for educators and parents*. Austin, TX: Pro-Ed.

National Center for Infants, Toddlers, and Families (1994). *Zero to three: Diagnostic classification of mental health and developmental disorders of infancy and early childhood*. Arlington, VA: Author.

National Staff Development Council (1995). *Standards for staff development*. Oxford, OH: National Staff Development Council.

Schopler, E., Lansing, M. & Waters, L. (1983). *Teaching activities for autistic children,* Vol. III. Austin, TX: Pro-Ed.

Sewall, A. M. (1999). New frames for an undefined future. *Phi Kappa Phi Journal*, *79*(1), 3–4.

Sewell, K. (1998). Breakthroughs: How to reach students with autism: A hands-on manual and video for teachers and parents. Vernon,WI: Attainment Co., Inc.

Shein, E. H. (1972). *Professional education: Some new directions*. New York: McGraw-Hill.

Siedow, M. D. (1985). Inservice education for content area teachers: Some basic principles. In: M. D. Siedow, D. M. Memory & P. S. Bristow (Eds), *Inservice Education for Content Area Teachers* (pp. 1–7). Newark, NJ: International Reading Association.

Sigafoos, J., Kerr, M., Roberts, D., & Couzens, D. (1994). Increasing opportunities for requesting in classrooms serving children with developmental disabilities. *Journal of Autism and Developmental Disabilities*, 631–645.

Simpson, R., & Myles, B. S. (Eds) (1998). *Educating children and youth with autism*. Austin, TX: Pro-Ed.

Skrtic, T. M. (1986). The crisis in special education knowledge: A perspective on perspective. *Focus on Exceptional Children*, *18*(7), 1–16.

Skrtic, T. M. (1991). *Behind special education: A critical analysis of professional culture and school organization*. Denver, CO: Love..

Skrtic, T. M. (1995). *Disability and democracy: Reconstructing (special) education for postmodernity*. New York: Teachers College Press.

Stefanich, G. P. (1998). Curriculum development in teaching science to students with disabilities. Iowa. Retrieved October 22, 2000, from Firstsearch database (ERIC, Accession ED420940) on the Internet: http://newfirstsearch.oclc.org

Swan, W. W., & Brown, C. L. (Eds) (1989). The Georgia Psychoeducational Network (GPN) Research Report, 1989. Georgia. Retrieved October 22, 2000, from Firstsearch database (ERIC, Accession ED398682) on the Internet: http://newfirstsearch.oclc.org

Tomlinson, S. (1982). *A sociology of special education.* Boston, MA: Routledge & Kegan Paul.

U.S. Reports, 527, 96-1793 (March 3, 1999). Cedar Rapids Community School District v. Garret, F.

Watson, L., Lord, C., Schaffer, B., & Schopler, E. (1989). Teaching spontaneous communication to autistic and developmentally handicapped children. Austin, TX: Pro-Ed.

Wells-Welsh, S. (1988). Improving instruction through peer coaching. Paper presented at the Fourth Learning Exchange Designing Excellence in Education National Conference, Kansas City, MO.

Williams, E. U. et al. (1993, March). Rural necessity as the mother of invention: Using collaboration to extend services to Autism and low-incidence handicaps. Ohio. Retrieved October 22, 2000, form Firstsearch database (ERIC, Accession ED358992) on the Internet: http://newfirstsearch.oclc.org

Wood, F. H., & McQuarrie, F. (1999). On-the-job-learning. *Journal of Staff Development, 20*(3), 10–13.

Wing, L. (1988). The continuum of autistic characteristics. In: E. Schopler & G. B. Mesibov (Eds), *Diagnosis and Assessment in Autism* (pp. 91–110). New York: Plenum Press.

DEVELOPING APPROPRIATE CURRICULUM FOR STUDENTS WITH AUTISM SPECTRUM DISORDERS

Jeffrey P. Bakken and Stacey J. Bock

INTRODUCTION

Leo Kanner (1943) first described the unique characteristics of a disability that caused children to be seemingly unattached, by choice, to the world around them. The characteristics that were first described included extreme autistic aloneness, lack of meaningful language, desire for the maintenance of sameness, strong relation to objects, and a general lack of relation to people. Within a year, Kanner published a short paper in which he named the new disorder "early infantile autism" (Rimland, 1964). Since this time, a half of a century of work has further contributed to the understanding of the disorder; however, Kanner's ability to accurately observe and record behavior allowed his original description to withstand the test of time (Donnellan, 1985).

Kanner's anecdotal characteristics were elaborated and developed into diagnostic criteria in the Diagnostic and Statistical Manual of Mental Disorders, third edition (DSM III) (American Psychiatric Association, 1980). With the revision of the DSM III-R, Autistic Disorder was placed under the umbrella term of Pervasive Developmental Disorders (PDD). Also found under the umbrella are the strikingly similar disorders, Asperger's Disorder and Pervasive Developmental Disorder – Not Otherwise Specified. Because these disorders present varying degrees of impairment in three distinct areas, behavior,

Autistic Spectrum Disorders: Educational and Clinical Interventions, pages 109–132.
2001 by Elsevier Science Ltd.
ISBN: 0-7623-0818-4

communication and socialization, there are calls for professionals to address the disorders as Autism Spectrum Disorders (ASD) (Wetherby & Prizant, 2000). The origination of the terminology can first be seen in a question that Kanner posed in his follow-up study of the eleven children who were seen in his clinic. Kanner stated, "It is well known in medicine that any illness may appear in different degrees of severity . . . Does this possibly apply to early infantile autism?" (Kanner, 1971, p. 145).

The research community generally agrees with Kanner's idea that ASD is a continuum-based disorder with some individuals falling on the severely affected end and some individuals falling on the mildly affected end. Which end the individual falls impacts the outcome or prognosis for that individual (Nordin & Gillberg, 1998). Individuals who display high-functioning or Asperger–type characteristics of autism are typically found on the mildly affected end of the continuum where a larger percentage of individuals lead good productive adult lives (Gillberg, 1992, 1996). In fact, the majority of this group holds down jobs, gets married, and has children (Larsen & Mouridsen, 1997). Individuals with more severe or Kanner-type autism are found on the severely affected end where only a small percentage go on as adults to live and work independently and only a few percent are married or carrying on serious relationships (American Psychiatric Association, 1994; Gillberg, 1992). These results are based upon the characteristics associated with autism and on the predictors of cognitive abilities and language acquisition (American Psychiatric Association, 1994; Gillberg, 1992; Larsen & Mouridsen, 1997; Venter, Lord & Schopler, 1992). For instance, children with an IQ above 70 who obtain speech by age six have a good prognosis and individuals with an IQ below 50 who fail to obtain speech by six have a relatively poor prognosis (Gillberg, 1993). In addition to the possibility of a relatively poor prognosis, other puzzling components of ASD are the behavior and learning issues that are somewhat unique to the disorder. The range of splinter skills that are often exhibited by children with ASD can give educators and parents a false estimation of overall ability. These issues have led parents, researchers and educators on an exhaustive search of systematic educational programming for children with ASD.

The search for sound educational programming for children with ASD has brought about impassioned debate from professionals since the 1970s. It has been a tendency of these professionals to ascribe to certain programs related to strict methodologies that have had an apparent positive influence on autistic behaviors. Many of these programs have placed an emphasis on curing or normalizing individuals with autism so they can lead productive lives in an inclusive community. These issues have fueled trials of interventions in the fields of education, psychology, and medicine. This climate has caused the field of autism spectrum disorders to become inundated with widespread use of invalidated or controversial practices (Simpson & Myles, 1998). The field is full of promising practices for educating children and youth with ASD and there is general agreement that it is too premature to say that one treatment is better than another (Greenspan & Wieder, 1999). With this in mind, the remainder of this chapter addresses promising practices that can be loosely categorized into the following areas: instruction to facilitate language growth or instruction, behavior management, social skills, and strategies for addressing targeted academic skills. It concludes with guidelines for selecting program elements.

STRATEGIES TO FACILITATE LANGUAGE ACQUISITION AND GROWTH

Children with ASD exhibit a variety of language disorders ranging from a total absence of verbal language to recitation of a monologue in an area of obsessional interest. Common communication concerns include lack of verbal communication, immediate and delayed echolalia, rote communication patterns, lack of conversation initiation or maintenance, immature rhythm, literalness, inability to recognize social cues and nuances, and topic perseveration. To address these communication concerns, the following promising practices are currently being researched in the field. These interventions can be categorized into two methodologies; language interventions in the natural context and language instruction in a structured trial format.

Language Intervention in Natural Context

Natural Language Teaching

Koegel, Koegel, and Surratt (1992) investigated whether or not the incorporation of parameters of natural language interactions and motivational techniques might reduce disruptive behavior during language teaching tasks. Three preschool children participated in this investigation which systematically examined to what effect a natural language teaching paradigm may have on disruptive behavior. The two different treatment conditions were analog and natural language teaching (NLT). Results indicated that during the NLT sessions all three children evidenced much less disruptive behavior than during the analog sessions. The results of this investigation are consistent with previous literature showing that teaching language to autistic children in a natural teaching context typically produces more correct target behavior than an analog approach.

Language Experience Approach

Shepherd and Arther (1986) described the use of a modification of the language experience approach (LEA) called "experience language (EL)" with an autistic-like person and provided some suggestions for how to use EL. The EL is for children who seem to have much potential but have problems communicating. Below are suggestions for teaching atypical children:

(1) One's concept of utilizing EL needs to be broader than teaching the child to read using already developed oral skills. Teachers should work on all language areas at all times, stimulate in all areas of communication, and model, demonstrate, and give examples.
(2) Teachers should begin with maximum assistance and work toward independence in stages.
(3) Teachers should start work with the non-communicating child as soon as possible.
(4) Care should be given from the beginning to establish a routine that will be standard enough to be helpful and yet flexible. Changes should be planned so that changes become vital part of routine. Teachers should systematically vary the procedures.
(5) Teachers should not make assumption about visual or auditory abilities (acuity or perception), and have eyes, ears, and vocal apparatus checked.
(6) Teachers should use instant (Polaroid) pictures that provide a concrete, immediate, stationary reference point when language is being evoked, concerning a particular experience.
(7) Color might be helpful in teaching students.
(8) Teachers should know what is going on in the child's life. For example, daily notes between teachers and parents might help.
(9) Teachers should clean up the handwriting.
(10) Teachers should allow children to trace with a felt tip marker the manuscript they have provided. They should provide a manuscript for coping that leaves space directly below the original. Later, entire paragraph may be copied from the top to the bottom of the sheet.
(11) Teachers should make cardboard strips for word banks only as long as needed for the word.

Milieu Teaching

Cavallaro (1983) discussed milieu teaching which incorporates naturally occurring opportunites throughout the school day to teach generalized language use. More specifically, it is referred to as incidental teaching. Goals of milieu teaching include teaching children that language can be used to obtain objects and attention, and what types of language is appropriate in different social contexts.

Choral Responding

Kamps, Dugan, Leonard and Daoust (1994) investigated the use of small group instructional strategies to increase student responding with 24 elementary students with autism and developmental disabilities. The strategies included choral responding, student-to-student responding, material rotation, and random unpredictable trials. The results of the study showed that there were increased opportunities to respond and increased levels of responding and academic engagement. In addition, students in the study made higher gains on tests and showed a decrease in passive and inappropriate behaviors.

Behavior Chain Interruption Strategy

Using an A-B design, Sigafoos and Littlewood (1999) investigated the effectiveness of the behavior chain interruption strategy (BCIS). A young child with autism was taught to ask for more playing time on playground equipment when he was interrupted. The BCIS is one strategy that can be implemented to instruct communication skills in the context of natural routines. As part of the program, children spend 30 minutes each day on the school playground. Play was interrupted from one to three times for each playground time. Initially, the teacher waited only five seconds for the student to make a correct response; saying, "play" when he was interrupted. After three days of using the five second delay procedure, the delay interval was increased to 10 seconds in an attempt to fade the imitative prompt and promote more spontaneous requesting. During baseline or during the five second delay procedure there were no correct responses. After the implementation of the 10 second delay, correct response increased to a high level after approximately 100 instructional trials. This high level of correct responses was maintained over the remaining sessions and in the final phase with the new teacher.

Language in a Structured Trial Format

Picture Exchange Communication System

Bondy and Frost (1994) described the Picture Exchange Communication System (PECS) and gave examples of long-term outcome measures for children who have been instructed with this system at the Delaware Autistic Program (DAP). The PECS is a communication training system geared for children under the age of five. Components of this program include backward chaining, repeated discrete trails, incidental training, shaping, and anticipatory or delayed prompting. Over the past five years at the DAP, 85 children classified as autistic were taught to communicate with PECS as their initial communicative modality. Steps of PECS include:

Phase 1:	*Teaching the Physically Assisted Exchange*. Requesting via picture exchange.
Phase 2:	*Expanding Spontaneity*. Trainers gradually move away from the child and move the communication board farther from the child.
Phase 3:	*Simultaneous Discrimination of pictures* from which requests are made.
Phase 4:	*Building Sentence Structure*. Requesting with a phase "I want ____." The picture exchange is maintained, teaching to place pictures on "sentence strip."
Phase 5:	Responding to"*What do you want?*" Providing opportunities for spontaneous direct requesting.
Phase 6:	*Commenting in Response to a Question*. Reinforcing requests and comments appropriately to teach a new communicative function.
Beyond Phase 6:	*Introducing Additional Language Concepts*. Teaching new vocabulary concepts, spontaneous comments, and "yes/no" question discrimination.

Schwartz, Garfinkle, and Bauer (1998) examined the PECS as a way of teaching functional communication skills to young children with severe communication delays. They also presented data of the overall efficacy of the PECS as a functional communication system. Initially, the data were divided into unsuccessful communication and successful communication. A constant comparative method (Glaser, 1978) was implemented to sort the data. Data were collected during free-choice activities and snack time in the same condition setting. Results indicated that PECS use generalizes to untrained settings and may have concomitant effects on the untrained language functions.

Sign Language

Bonvillian and Nelson (1976) studied the effects of a six-month instructional sign program on a nine-year-old, nonverbal child with autism. The instructional program consisted of daily half-hour sessions in which the therapist molded the correct signs with child's hands and the child independently imitating the therapist's signs. The desired behavior was reinforced with a token economy system. Through the program, based upon American Sign Language, the child learned to communicate extensively and produced many spontaneous signs and sign combinations. With the increase of communication, parents reported that the child had a decrease in toileting accidents and a lessening of tantrums in school as well as a lessening of stereotypic and bizarre movements and gestures.

In a summary of seven studies involving 52 nonverbal children with autism, Carr (1979) found that mute (nonverbal) and echolalic children may constitute distinct subgroups when evaluating language pre-training characteristics. He noted that mute children may benefit more from sign language training and echolalic children may benefit more from speech training. In addition, he found that after sign language training children with autism showed an increase in spontaneous communication, a decrease in self-stimulatory behavior, and an improvement in social skills.

Language Shaping Technique

Wolf-Schein (1995) described the SMILE method (structured methods in language education). SMILE develops a hierarchy of skills progressing from phonology to morphology to syntax. The approach incorporates the following: development of attention, specific and consistent teaching methodology, use of structure and routine, immediate reinforcement, successive approximations leading to exact repetition, pattern practice and substitution/transformation drills, and ongoing attention to generalization. SMILE is introduced in individual tutoring sessions or in small groups of not more than three pupils. During the beginning of the school day is when the major lesson takes place. Teaching begins with short lessons (five to 10 minutes) gradually increasing the lessons to a maximum of 30 minutes. When natural language or whole word approaches are not effective, SMILE may be beneficial.

Semantic/Pragmatic Language Instruction

Beisler and Tsai (1983) piloted a program to increase the communication skills of five children with autism, ranging in age from 36 to 68 months, by establishing reciprocal communicative exchanges. The children participated in the program for six weeks during an inpatient stay at the Iowa Autism Program, Child Psychiatry Service. The methods used in the study included intensive modeling of verbal responses with joint activity routines and a reinforcement system that provided fulfillment of the intent of the child's communication. Results of the study showed an overall increase in the mean length of response, in the mean receptive language level, and in the mean number of semantic-grammatical rules expressed.

Ogletree, Fischer, and Sprouse (1995) investigated a treatment program designed to facilitate semantic/pragmatic language development in a female with high-functioning autism. A single-subject, multiple-baseline across behaviors design was implemented. Each treatment session began with a two- to five-minute review of the treatment target. Sessions continued with the subject selecting and viewing two- to four-minute segments (i.e. vignettes) of Disney videotapes. These were incorporated into treatment due to subject's intense interest in Disney characters and the ease with which videos allowed for repeated viewings of treatment targets). Videotapes were cued to scenes depicting positive illustrations of treatment. After viewing and discussing a video, the subject and the clinician role-played the segment, allowing teaching and demonstration opportunities. Finally, the target was reviewed, followed by the re-initiation of the treatment sequence with other video segments. Results indicated that increases were seen in appropriate gazing behaviors, appropriate response time and appropriate topic maintenance.

APPROACHES FOR MANAGEMENT OF BEHAVIOR

Children with ASD often have a myriad of behavior concerns that include rigidness or an insistence on sameness, stereotyped or restricted play or interests, repetitive nonfunctional motor movements, aggression, and self-injurious behavior. Behavior management interventions to address these areas of concern can be categorized into environmental supports and self-management strategies.

Environmental Supports

Classroom Engineering

In an ABAB design, Duker and Rasing (1989) investigated the effects of redesigning the physical environment (i.e. the classroom arrangement) on the occurrence of self-stimulation, on-task behavior, inappropriate behavior, and inactivity. Three developmentally disabled males with autistic-type behaviors were included in the study. During baseline, the classroom space was left as it usually was while during treatment conditions all decorations and extraneous information on the walls and ceilings were removed and all colors were changed to a unicolor theme. In addition, some things were actually covered up (e.g. cupboard and sink). Results indicated a decrease of self-stimulation and inactivity and an increase of on-task behavior while inappropriate behavior remained unchanged across the experimental conditions.

Visual Strategies

Roberson, Gravel, Valcante, and Mauer (1992) explained in detail the use of pictures in task analysis to teach complex tasks to students with multiple disabilities. Any skill that can be analyzed into component steps can be taught through picture task analysis. Picture task analysis is cost and time efficient, serves as a memory aid, and enhances receptive communication. The steps for constructing picture task analysis only requires the following; (a) photographs, (b) manila folders, or another medium on which to mount the photo, (c) glue, and (d) clear contact paper or lamination to protect the photographs. These steps are as follows:

(1) An appropriate skill is selected from the student's IEP and broken down into component steps suitable for the student's abilities.
(2) A symbol system is selected.
(3) The necessary materials are gathered.
(4) A photograph is taken of each step in the task analysis.
(5) The photos are arranged and secured in sequential order on a manila folder.
(6) Numbers depicting the sequence of steps are written and arrows are drawn to direct the learner's attention.
(7) A description of the behavior in each photograph is written below the photo.
(8) The picture task analysis is laminated to preserve the photo.

The duration of each step depends on the abilities, disabilities, and learning patterns of the students. The teacher gradually fades his or her presence.

Pierce and Schreibman (1994) investigated the efficacy of pictorial self-management to teach daily living skills to three children with autism. A multiple baseline probe design across behaviors, systematically replicated across the three children was implemented. Picture stimuli were color six inch by four inch prints of selected steps from a task analysis of the target behaviors or of an object that would be used in the target behavior. Pictures were placed into a photo book. Each child had his own book. First, children were taught to discriminate pictures depicting steps in the target skills. Next, they were taught to pick their own reinforcer, independently turn pages in the picture book, perform motor actions and self-reinforce. Finally, the therapist's presence was faded. Results indicated that children with autism could successfully use pictures to manage their behavior in the absence of a treatment provider, generalize their behavior across tasks and settings, and maintain behaviors at a two-month follow-up.

Bryan and Gast (2000) investigated the effectiveness of a two-component teaching package (graduated guidance and visual activity schedules) in teaching young children with autism to increase on-task and on-schedule behavior. An ABAB withdrawal design was implemented with four children with autism. Each child had his/her own picture book. A graduated guidance procedure was implemented. This involved the teacher providing a controlling prompt, a moment-to-moment decision about what type of prompt was then provided and gradually prompts were faded in frequency and intensity until the student completed the sequence independently. Results indicated that student performance increased to criterion levels after the introduction of the graduated guidance procedure, student performance maintained when the picture book was available and dropped when it was not available and student performance generalized to novel activities.

Choice-making

Moes (1998) investigated the performance of children with autism during teacher-assigned academic tasks and whether choice making was an appropriate and effective antecedent intervention. Four children with autism placed in full-inclusion educational settings participated in this study. As part of the students' curriculum, they were given weekly homework assignments. All sessions consisted of academic tasks assigned by each student's teacher as homework expected to be completed outside of class. An A-B-A-B design was selected for two participants and a B-A-B-A design for the other two to investigate the effects of choice-making (student versus tutor). Each child was seen twice a week for a total of 20 homework sessions. Each phase consisted of five sessions. Demands to complete homework activities were given, characterized by the following types of prompting sequences: verbal prompt, verbal and gestural prompt, and verbal and physical prompt. All participant responses were reinforced with immediate social praise only if they were completed following a verbal or verbal and gestural prompt within five seconds of the prompt delivery. Results indicated that all four participants showed more favorable patterns of correct responding during choice conditions when compared to no-choice conditions. All four children engaged in less disruptive behavior in choice conditions when compared to no-choice conditions, however, the magnitude of differences varied somewhat across participants. Overall, the rates of homework completion appeared to be greater in choice conditions than in no-choice conditions. In addition, it was only under choice conditions that participants completed all assigned homework within the allotted time (20 minutes) for data recording.

Self-Management Strategies

Koegel and Koegel (1999) discussed research from the University of California, Santa Barbara, which focused on pivotal areas as the thrust of interventions. Pivotal areas are defined as those that, when changed, generally produce large collateral improvements in other areas such as multiple cues, motivation, self-management, and self-initiation. The goals of providing intervention in pivotal areas are to; (1) instruct the child how to be responsive to the many different learning opportunities and social interactions that occur in the natural environment every day, (2) decrease the need for constant attention by an intervention provider, and (3) decrease the number of services that remove the child from the natural environment. The emphasis of this program targets inclusive settings the child is involved with including the children's homes, community preschools, regular education school programs, and after school activities. The goal is to provide the most effective intervention possible within a relatively small number of hours of direct contact with a highly skilled specialist. Teaching individuals to discriminate and choose their own target behaviors, independently identify the occurrence or absence of that behavior (self-monitoring), and self-recruit reinforcement allows individuals with disabilities to become actively involved in the intervention process and more involved in their home, classroom, and community environments. Self-initiations can enable the child to be successful in a multitude of natural environments throughout their day, without the need for adult initiated interventions.

About a decade ago, Koegel and Koegel (1990) investigated whether students with severe autism could learn to use a self-management treatment package to reduce their stereotypical behaviors within a multiple baseline across subjects design with withdrawals. Four students with severe autism were included in this investigation. Students were taught to identify their stereotypic and appropriate behaviors through modeling of these behaviors by a treatment provider. The treatment provider then presented different behaviors, and students had to identify if they were stereotypical or appropriate. Students were then taught to self-monitor (place a mark in a box on a piece of paper) behaviors with the help of the treatment provider. When an alarm sounded (from a watch) students marked if any stereotypical behaviors had occurred since the last time the alarm sounded. The treatment provider initiated verbal prompts to students to self-monitor and gradually faded prompts so students were doing it independently. Results indicated that all students learned to use self-management procedures to greatly reduce stereotypical behaviors.

Koegel, Koegel, and Carter (1999) addressed effective teaching interactions with a focus on pivotal target behaviors in the treatment of individuals with autism. Repeatedly, it has been shown that choice can decrease disruptive behaviors and increase adaptive behaviors such as task engagement. Choice, to some degree, can be incorporated in almost all activities or academic topics. Effective interventions for multiple cue teaching can be divided into two general approaches. The *within-stimulus prompts* are exaggerations of relevant components of a stimulus, which are slowly faded throughout the learning exercise. Another approach, a *conditional discrimination* is one that requires responding on the basis of multiple cues. Research investigations have verified that if a child is repeatedly exposed to this type of instruction as opposed to a single-cue instruction, the child eventually learns to respond to an increased number of cues. A child's attention appears to become more normalized as they learn to respond on the basis of multiple cues in their environment, allowing more cues in their environment to become functional, thereby leading to enhanced learning and generalization. The general skill of self-initiated learning is classified as a pivotal response because widespread learning for typical development may require self-initiated interactions. The self-management generally refers to a procedure in which individuals are taught to discriminate their own target behaviors and to record the occurrence or absence of that target behavior (self-monitoring). Self-management has been shown to be effective for increasing on-task behavior, decreasing disruptive behavior, and eliminating time spent in time out for children with autism in full inclusion settings.

Stahmer and Schreibman (1992) implemented a self-management treatment package to three children with autism to play appropriately in the absence of a treatment provider. Four areas were investigated: self stimulation, approapriate play, inappropriate behavior, and other behavior. A single-subject multiple baseline design across subjects was implemented. Training was based on procedures outlined by Koegel and Koegel (1990). Results indicated that the children learned to exhibit appropriate play skills in unsupervised settings and these play skills were also generalized to new settings. In addition, two students maintained their gains at a one-month follow-up and self-stimulatory behaviors decreased as appropriate play increased. In a related study, Mancina, Tankersley, Kamps, Kravits and Parrett (2000) investigated the effects of a self-management program to reduce high rates of inappropriate vocalizations (e.g. tongue clucking, and humming) of a 12-year old girl with autism. A multiple baseline design across settings was implemented. Training was based on procedures outlined by Koegel and Koegel (1990). Results indicated that when self-management was applied to inappropriate vocalizations the occurrences of these vocalizations decreased.

Koegel, Koegel, Hurley and Frea (1992) investigated whether the self-management strategy could be implemented to produce extended improvements of responsiveness to verbal initiations from others (community, home, and school settings) without the presence of a treatment provider. Four students with autism participated in this investigation using a multiple baseline design across settings and subjects. Each child was taught to discriminate correct and incorrect responses. Each student had a wrist counter and each time they correctly responded they were taught to tally on the wrist counter. Reinforcers were given for each correct response. Gradually reinforcers were faded and students were taught to self-monitor independently and self-reinforce. Results indicated that children with autism that displayed severe social skill deficits could learn to implement the self-management strategy to improve responsivity to others in multiple settings and this was associated with a reduction in disruptive behavior.

Self-Regulation Strategies

Gerdtz (2000) investigated the behavioral treatment implemented to decrease the disruptive classroom behaviors of a 16-year-old male high school student with autism. A simple, progressive, muscle-relaxation technique based on deep breathing and systematic tensing and untensing of bodily extremities was taught to the student. Trends in the data from the daily data sheets were recorded as no problem days (less than five redirections from staff needed), mild-problem days (six to 10 redirections), moderate problem days (classroom activities disrupted in at least one class period, 11 to 15 redirections), and severe-problem days (all instances of physical aggression or attempted aggression, any referral to school office, or any behavior that would ordinarily result in suspension from school). Trends were reviewed monthly and compared from month to month. Results indicated that seriously disruptive behaviors were reduced to zero frequency, and the frequency of less severe disruptive behaviors was also reduced (No problem days: the first month was 20% and the last month was about 90%). A review of the school records indicated that no suspensions for problem behaviors occurred during the intervention period and he maintained good grades in both classes. The father of the student reported that severity and frequency of problem behaviors at home had also declined during the course of the intervention although behaviors at home were not specifically targeted.

SOCIAL INTERACTION STRATEGIES

Deficits in social interaction are likely the most debilitating for an individual with ASD. General social isolation is a result of lack of skills in the areas of reciprocal interactions, sharing enjoyment, interests or achievements, and impairment in the use and understanding of nonverbal gestures. Techniques to address social interactions include: peer mediated instruction, pivitol response training, play-based therapy, music therapy, and social stories.

Peer-Mediated Instruction

Odom and Watts (1991) found an increase in social interactions, in a study involving three children with autism and four nondisabled peers in an integrated preschool setting. The study consisted of four phases which involved training peers in social interaction strategies and providing verbal prompts when needed, a non verbal prompt setting, a corresponding training/visual feedback (CTVF) package, and the discontinuation of the peer-initiation strategy with continued CTVF support. In the setting where teachers provided verbal prompts, results indicated that students increased initiations but they did not increase initiations when verbal prompts were removed. Results also indicated that the implementation of the CTVF package was successful with considerable increases in peer initiations even when the peer-initiation intervention was removed.

Kamps, Leonard, Vernon, Dugan, Delquadri, Gershon, Wade and Folk (1992) examined the use of social skills groups to improve social interactions for first-grade students with autism and their nondisabled peers in an integrated classroom. Training of students and peers was undertaken addressing initiating, responding, and keeping interactions going; greeting others and talking about a variety of topics; giving and accepting compliments; sharing and taking turns; helping others and asking for help when needed; and including other students in activities. A multiple baseline across subjects design was implemented and results indicated that students' increased in frequency the duration and amount of time involved in social interactions as well as the interaction between peers. In addition, results were maintained in play groups and during follow-up when students were monitored and given feedback.

Pierce and Schreibman (1997) investigated peer-implemented pivotal response training (PRT) with eight typical peers and two children with autism to assess the effects of employing multiple peer trainers on the generalization of treatment effects. Peers were taught PRT strategies during training which consisted of didactic instruction, modeling, role playing, and corrective feedback. Results indicated that after treatment the two students with autism engaged in increased levels of social behavior. Later, Laushey and Heflin (2000) investigated whether a peer buddy approach would enhance non-adult-directed interactions. Students with and without autism were trained to interact in dyads through an ABAB design. Training involved all students being trained to stay with, play with and talk to a buddy (English, Goldstein, Kaczmarak & Shafer, 1996) in dyads that changed daily. Results indicated that training students with autism using this peer buddy approach significantly increased their appropriate social interactions; and follow-up data on one of the students indicated the generalization of appropriate social interactions to a new classroom environment.

Pivotal Response Training

Stahmer (1995) implemented pivotal response training (PRT) to teach seven children with autism to engage in symbolic play behaviors. A single subject multiple baseline design across subjects was implemented. Treatment sessions lasted one-hour, three times a week. Treatment was modified to use symbolic play as a target behavior instead of language. To gain access to toys, students were required to engage in symbolic play. Play and appropriate symbolic actions were modeled by the experimenter. This was repeated until children responded. Responses from the child were reinforced with opportunities to play and with praise. As children improved at symbolic play it was expected that they also engage in more complex play. Results indicated that before training or after a control condition, children rarely exhibited symbolic play. After training using PRT, all children learned to perform creative and complex symbolic play actions at similar levels to that of language-matched typical controls. In addition, after training, interaction skills improved.

Play-based Therapy

Baker, Koegel, and Koegel (1998) investigated whether an intervention based on incorporating an autistic child's obsessive behavior into an appropriate social game would increase the percent of time engaged in social interactive play. Three children who were diagnosed with autism participated in this study. Each obsession theme was incorporated into a common playground game in accordance with the rules of the playground, the age of the children, and without limitation to the number of children who could participate. The intervention consisted of an adult prompting, as well as any group of non-disabled peers who showed interest and approached the activity. Participation in the game was voluntary (participants varied from day to day) and no extrinsic reinforcers were provided. The types of prompting were performed one to two times during the initial days of intervention, fading during the remaining one to two days of the intervention phase. At that point, all of the children's selection of and participation in games and activities were entirely independent and voluntary, with no adult prompting. Data were collected on time engaged in social play interactions in obsession and nonobsession theme games and subjective ratings of child affect. Results indicated that all three children showed increases in their appropriate social behavior during the intervention, maintenance, and follow-up phases.

Jahr, Eldevik, and Eikeseth (2000) investigated procedures for acquisition, transfer and maintenance of cooperative play in children with autism. Behavior modeling was used as the basic component in this study. Five boys and one girl with autism participated in this study. Prior to the involvement in this study, all participants had received a minimum of six months of one-to-one behavioral treatment. When not receiving the one-to-one treatment, they were mainstreamed with their regular peers (except for two participants who took part in the residential program with their peers and staff). During probing and training, a minimum of 40 different toys were present. Prior to training, a list of scripted play episodes, which covered a range of topics was developed for each participant. All six participants received training with modeling, verbal description, and imitation. Training sessions lasted approximately 60 minutes and were conducted daily during weekdays. Seven days (range one to 18) was the average number of days in training across participants. Programmed consequences were verbal praise and access to favorite snacks every five minutes for compliance during training. Prior to training, none of the participants evidenced consistent cooperative play. Results indicated that all participants demonstrated cooperative play during probe sessions conducted in novel settings and with peers not associated with training. Further, they maintained cooperative play during follow-up at the average of 10 months (range 6–16 months) after training.

Music Therapy

Wimpory, Chadwick and Nash (1995) investigated the effect of Musical Interaction Therapy (MIT) on the social and symbolic development of a young female with autism who was described as "almost totally non-communicative" by her mother. A teaching film was used to introduce MIT. The musician and child's mother conducted 20-minute MIT sessions at home twice a month for seven months. Sessions involved repetitive yet varied runs of mother-child games of swinging, patting, tickling, blowing, stroking, vocalizing, action-rhymes, and singing. Spontaneously composed simple songs about her actions to give her joint attention and enable her participation were developed as were familiar lap games. The music reflected and highlighted the mood, timing, and meaning of the dyad's activities. For example, if the child happened to skip, the mother and the musician also skipped together and sang "skip, skip, skip away" with timing appropriate to the actions. As soon as the child stopped skipping, the music and singing paused in anticipation of her next move. The (harp) music became quieter if the child avoided her mother and more exciting if she approached her. An A-B-C design was implemented. Data were collected primarily from home visits. Results indicated that the student was more social as a result of MIT. A two-year follow-up confirmed that these positive changes were sustained as the child no longer showed frequent social withdrawal.

Kennedy and Shukla (1995) investigated autism and social interaction over the last 35 years. An important aspect of a person's environment is the consistency with which contingencies of reinforcement are delivered. If a person has difficulty learning, then the establishment of relevant behavior-environment relations is limited, and learning is slowed. One strategy that has been effective at overcoming possible learning difficulties is to arrange for very clear and unambiguous reinforcement contingencies for specific responses. It was also discovered that careful attention must be made in arranging a person's environment so that they could make contact with the relevant reinforcement contingencies, and hence, learn. One suggestion was that social interaction could be taught. The initial target responses selected for instruction were those that served as prerequisites for more complex social interaction. Complex imitative and interactive skills could be taught using systematic environmental manipulations similar to the initial studies of children with autism. If prerequisite social behaviors could be established without difficulty, then more complex analyses of social behavior appeared possible. Several developments have been attributed to the emergence of the proposition that peers could serve as effective models for social interaction for children with autism. Application of the peer-as-social-agent strategy also is evidenced in how teachers physically included students with and without disabilities in classrooms to reduce social deficits. The primary focus of each of these various intervention strategies is to present ample opportunities for children to engage in social communication making language learning situationally relevant and functional. The proposition that behavior may serve a communicative function is fairly recent. An important implication of this theory is that behavioral interventions need to focus on the social functions of behavior. By focusing on the social/communication basis of behavior not typically considered social, researchers have established a new set of techniques for dealing with problematic behavior. These emerging propositions are helping to extend the notion of social interaction into new areas that all have the common theme of improving socially valid outcomes for people with autism. The literature on how to obtain and continually receive the various benefits associated with social relationships is only beginning to emerge.

Social Stories

Swaggart, Gagnon, Bock, Earles, Quinn, Myles and Simpson (1995) explained the use of social-story intervention programs to teach appropriate social behavior to three children with autism. Each social story was written in a book format that consisted of a front cover and five story pages. Each page contained one or two sentences and a corresponding photo or icon. The program's classroom teacher and paraprofessional, along with four graduate students working in the classroom developed the stories. One student did not adapt well to changes in routine and had a history of physical aggression, another preferred solitary play and tended to ignore others around him, and the last student's social interactions consisted primarily of attempting to choke others or knock them down. Results indicated, after implementing social stories, that all three students improved desired behaviors.

Kuttler, Myles, and Carlson (1998) investigated the effects of social stories in reducing precursors to tantrum behavior for a 12-year old boy with autism in two social environments: morning work time and lunchtime. Social stories are written by professionals, parents, and caregivers to describe social situations, relevant cues, and desired responses to a given situation. Two different social stories were introduced for the two most difficult settings throughout the student's school day, morning work and lunchtime. He needed constant prompting to: (a) wait, (b) transition from one environment to the next, (c) know when he earned a sticker, and (d) remember. Each sentence, along with its corresponding icon, was placed on white tag-board. The tag-board strip was laminated and bound by two metal rings on the left-hand side in book form. An ABAB design was implemented. During baseline, the traditional classroom interventions were provided: the classroom picture schedule, the student's sticker/point chart, and verbal and physical prompting from the staff. During the intervention phases, the social stories were read to the student immediately prior to work time and lunchtime by classroom staff. Results indicated that the implementation of the social stories had significant effects on the reduction of tantrum behaviors during morning work time and during lunchtime.

Hagiwara and Myles (1999) investigated the implementation of multimedia social stories. The multimedia social story intervention was created by Hagiwara (1998) to allow students to learn new skills through social stories presented on a computer. Three elementary-age students with autism participated in this study. Materials included: (a) Macintosh™ computer systems for developing the multimedia social story program and executing the study in the students' classroom; (b) a video camcorder to capture students' actions on camera; (c) social stories created jointly by students' teachers, paraprofessionals, and the investigator to address students' needed skills, and (d) the multimedia social story programs developed for each participant. Teachers and paraprofessionals were taught how to interpret a functional analysis, clearly define targeted behaviors, and design a social story. The multimedia social story programs were developed by the investigator using the HyperCard™ (Apple Computer, 1994) software. The format of this program was book-like, which contained text of the social stories; movies of the participants' actions corresponding to social story sentences; audio capability that read aloud sentences using a synthesized computer voice; and a navigational button clickable by the participants. Each student operated the multimedia social story program once a day. Washing their hands and being on-task were the behaviors students tried to improve. Results indicated that the intervention using the multimedia social story program increased the skill levels of some of the participants in certain settings. Moreover, some students showed generalization of newly acquired information to other settings.

Sugai and Lewis (1996) discussed strategies and structures necessary for fostering social competence in all children, and in particular children who are at-risk of academic or social failure. Successful social skills instruction is directly related to the extent to which general and special educators can conduct accurate and functional assessments. In regards to social skills, there are many facets that include: (a) social skills assessments used to screen the general social competence of individual students or groups of students, (b) assessment strategies used to collect information about the nature of a student's social skill problem, (c) social skills assessments conducted to assist in selecting and modifying curriculum and design and delivery of instruction, and (d) assessment information used to monitor and evaluate the progress students make in their social skills instruction. Methods of social skills assessment, at a minimum, should focus on directly observing the student's behaviors and his or her interactions with others. To determine if the problem is a skill deficit or a performance problem, observations also should take place in settings where the student is not having social skills problems. Observations in multiple settings are always warranted. One of the most important and desirable outcomes of a social skills training program is generalized responding. Although the empirical identification of effective generalization strategies is relatively meager, some promising techniques can be employed to promote generalized responding throughout the social skills program. Since the research evidence about effective generalization strategies is limited, the development of specific interventions for direct implementation in the target generalization setting is needed.

GUIDELINES FOR SELECTING CURRICULUM

Deciding on specific programs, program elements, or instructional strategies to use with children with ASD causes distress for educators and parents because the field is full of promising practices as well as controversial therapies. Recently, professionals in the area of ASD addressed this issue by studying common elements of programming, providing guidelines for program selection, addressing questions for intervention discussion, and discussing the tenets of best practice that should be addressed when making program decisions (Dawson & Osterling, 1997; Freeman, 1997; Heflin & Simpson, 1998; Prizant & Rubin, 1999). For instance, Dawson and Osterling identified six common elements of programming. These common elements include curriculum that addresses attending, imitation, use and comprehension of language, play, and social interactions; structured teaching environments; classrooms with predictability and routine; functional approach to behavior; transition planning; and family involvement. It is felt that these common elements should be used as a starting point or a foundation for program development (Anderson & Romanczyk, 1999; Schwartz, Sandall, Garfinkle, & Bauer, 1998). In addition, it is highly likely that these common elements represent many effective approaches embedded in programs with strict methodological underpinnings.

Freeman (1997) noted that program evaluators should: (a) approach any new treatment with hopeful skepticism, (b) beware of any program or techniques that is said to be appropriate for every person with autism, (c) beware of any program that thwarts individualization and potentially results in a harmful program decision, (d) be aware that any treatment represents one of several options for a person with autism, (e) be aware that treatment should always depend on individual assessment information that points to it as an appropriate choice for a particular child, (f) be aware that no new treatment should be implemented until its proponents can specify assessment procedures necessary to determine whether it will be appropriate for an individual with autism, (g) be aware that debates over use of various techniques are often reduced to superficial arguments over who is right, moral, ethical, and who is a true advocate for the children, and (h) be aware that often new treatments have not been validated scientifically. Heflin and Simpson (1998) offered critical questions that could guide intervention discussions, namely: What are the anticipated outcomes of the programming? What are the potential risks? How will the option be evaluated? What proof is available that the option is effective? What other options would be excluded if this option were chosen? Additionally, Prizant and Rubin (1999) identified tenets of best practice and recommendations for selecting interventions and treatments. These tenets include: (a) matching intervention approaches to individualized learning traits and developmental level, (b) basing interventions upon current knowledge of child development, (c) including approaches that directly address the ASD characteristics displayed, and (d) creating approaches that use a variety of sources.

CONCLUSION

Autism Spectrum Disorders is considered one of the most complex groups of developmental disorders (Greenspan & Weider, 1999) for various reasons including the possibility of a relatively poor outcome, the unique learning and behavioral characteristics associated with the disorder, and the widespread use of invalidated or controversial practices. Promising practices are found in the field of ASD; however there is still great contention among professionals regarding appropriate educational programming. In this chapter, we have presented a brief overview of methods/strategies for teaching students with autism as well as various types of curricula that are currently available. The review of information provided is only the beginning step in deciding programmatic elements for students with autism and careful consideration should be given when selecting program elements that will specifically address students' individual learning and behavioral needs.

REFERENCES

American Psychiatric Association (1980). *Diagnostic and statistical manual of mental disorders* (3rd ed.). Washington, D.C.: Author.

American Psychiatric Association (1994). *Diagnostic and statistical manual of mental disorders* (4th ed.). Washington, D.C.: Author.

Anderson, S. R., & Romanczyk, R. G. (1999). Early intervention for young children with autism: Continuum-based behavioral models. *The Journal of the Association for Persons with Severe Handicaps*, *24*(3), 162–173.

Apple Computer (1994). *Hypercard* [Computer Software]. Cupertino, CA: Author.

Baker, M. J., Koegel, R. L., & Koegel, L. K. (1998). Increasing the social behavior of young children with autism using their obsessive behavior. *The Journal of the Association for Persons with Severe Handicaps*, *23*, 300–308.

Beisler, J. M., & Tsai, L. Y. (1983). A pragmatic approach to increase expressive language skills in young autistic children. *Journal of Autism and Developmental Disorders*, *13*, 287–303.

Bondy, A. S., & Frost, L. A. (1994). The picture exchange communication system. *Focus on Autistic Behavior*, *9*(3), 1–20.

Bonvillian, J. D., & Nelson, K. E. (1976). Sign language acquisition in a mute autistic boy. *Journal of Speech and Hearing Disorders*, *41*, 339–347.

Bryan, L. C., & Gast, D. L. (2000). Teaching on-task and on-schedule behaviors to high-functioning children with autism via picture activity schedules. *Journal of Autism and Developmental Disorders*, *30*, 553–567.

Carr, E. G. (1979). Teaching autistic children to use sign language: Some research issues. *Journal of Autism and Developmental Disorders*, *9*, 345–359.

Cavallaro, C. C. (1983). Language intervention in natural settings. *Teaching Exceptional Children*, *15*(3), 65–70.

Dawson G., & Osterling, J. (1997). Early intervention in autism. In: M. J. Guralnick (Ed.), *The effectiveness of early intervention* (pp. 307–326). Baltimore, MD: Paul H. Brookes.

Donnellan, A. M. (1985). *Classic readings in autism*. New York: Teacher's College Press.

Duker, P. C., & Rasing, E. (1989). Effects of redesigning the physical environment on self-stimulation and on-task behavior in three autistic-type developmentally disabled individuals. *Journal of Autism and Developmental Disorders*, *19*, 449–460.

English, K., Goldstein, H., Kaczmarak, L., & Shafer, K. (1996). "Buddy skills" for preschoolers. *Teaching Exceptional Children*, *28*(3), 62–66.

Freeman, B. J. (1997). Guidelines for evaluating intervention programs for children with autism. *Journal of Autism and Developmental Disorders, 27*, 641–651.

Gerdtz, J. (2000). Evaluating behavioral treatment of disruptive classroom behaviors of an adolescent with autism. *Research on Social Work, 10*(1), 98–110.

Gillberg, C. (1992). Autism and autistic-like conditions: Subclasses among disorders of empathy. *Journal of Child Psychology and Psychiatry, 33*, 813–842.

Gillberg, C. (1993). Autism and related behaviours. *Journal of Intellectual Disability Research*, 37, 343–372.

Gillberg, C. (1996). The long-term outcome of childhood empathy disorders. *European Child and Adolescent Psychiatry, 5*, 52–56.

Glaser, B. (1978). *Theoretical sensitivity: Advances in methodology of grounded theory*. Mills Valley, CA: Sociology Press.

Greenspan, S. I., & Wieder, S. (1999). A functional developmental approach to autism spectrum disorders. *The Journal of the Association for Persons with Severe Handicaps, 24*(3), 147–161.

Hagiwara, T. (1998). *Multimedia social story intervention for students with autism*. Unpublished doctoral dissertation, University of Kansas, Lawrence.

Hagiwara, T., & Myles, B. S. (1999). A multimedia social story intervention: Teaching skills to children with autism. *Focus on Autism and Other Developmental Disabilities, 14*, 82–95.

Heflin, L. J., & Simpson, R. L. (1998). Interventions for children and youth with autism: Prudent choices in a world of exaggerated claims and empty promises. Part II: Legal/policy analysis and recommendations for selecting interventions and treatments. *Focus on Autism and Other Developmental Disabilities, 13*, 212–220.

Jahr, E., Eldevik, S., & Eikeseth, S. (2000). Teaching children with autism to initiate and sustain cooperative play. *Research in Developmental Disabilities, 21*, 151–169.

Kamps, D. M., Dugan, E. P., Leonard, B. R., & Daoust, P. M. (1994). Enhanced small group instruction using choral responding and student interaction for children with autism and developmental disabilities. *American Journal on Mental Retardation, 99*(1), 60–73.

Kamps, D. M., Leonard, B. R., Vernon, S., Dugan, E. P., Delquadri, J. C., Gershon, B., Wade, L., & Folk, L. (1992). Teaching social skills to students with autism to increase peer interactions in an integrated first-grade classroom. *Journal of Applied Behavior Analysis, 25*, 281–288.

Kanner, L. (1943). Autistic disturbances of affective contact. *Nervous Child, 2*, 217–250.

Kanner, L. (1971). Follow-up study of eleven autistic children originally reported in 1943. *Journal of Autism and Childhood Schizophrenia, 1*(2), 119–145.

Kennedy, C. H., & Shukla, S. (1995). Social interaction research for people with autism as a set of past, current, and emerging propositions. *Behavior Disorders, 21*(1), 21–35.

Koegel, R. L., & Koegel, L. K. (1990). Extended reductions in stereotypic behavior of students with autism through a self-management treatment package. *Journal of Applied Behavior Analysis, 23*(1), 119–127.

Koegel, L. K., & Koegel, R. L. (1999). Pivotal response intervention I: Overview of approach. The *Journal of the Association for Persons with Severe Handicaps, 24*(3), 174-185.

Koegel, R. L., Koegel, L. K., & Carter, C. M. (1999). Pivotal teaching interactions for children with autism. *School Psychology Review, 28*, 576–594.

Koegel, L. K., Koegel, R. L., Hurley, C., & Frea, W. D. (1992). Improving social skills and disruptive behavior in children with autism through self-management. *Journal of Applied Behavior Analysis, 25*, 341–353.

Koegel, R. L., Koegel, L. K., & Surratt, A. (1992). Language intervention and disruptive behavior in preschool children with autism. *Journal of Autism and Developmental Disorders, 22*(2), 144–153.

Kuttler, S., Myles, B. S., & Carlson, J. K. (1998). The use of social stories to reduce precursors to tantrum behavior in a student with autism. *Focus on Autism and Other Developmental Disabilities*, *13*(3), 176–182.

Larsen, F., & Mouridsen, S. (1997). The outcome in children with childhood autism and asperger syndrome originally diagnosed as psychotic. A 30-year follow-up study of subjects hospitalized as children. *European Child and Adolescent Psychiatry*, *6*, 181–190.

Laushey, K. M., & Heflin, L. J. (2000). Enhancing social skills of kindergarten children with autism through the training of multiple peers as tutors. *Journal of Autism and Developmental Disorders*, *30*(3), 183–193.

Mancina, C., Tankersley, M., Kamps, D., Kravits, T., & Parrett, J. (2000). Brief report: Reduction of inappropriate vocalizations for a child with autism using a self-management treatment program. *Journal of Autism and Developmental Disorders*, *30*, 599–606.

Moes, D. R. (1998). Integrating choice-making opportunities within teacher-assigned academic tasks to facilitate the performance of children with autism. *The Journal of the Association for Persons with Severe Handicaps*, *23*, 319–328.

Nordin, V., & Gillberg, C. (1998). The Swedish version of the childhood autism rating scale in a clinical setting. *Journal of Autism and Developmental Disorders*, *28*(1), 69–75.

Odom, S. L., & Watts, E. (1991). Reducing teacher prompts in peer-mediated interventions for young children with autism. *The Journal of Special Education*, *25*(1), 26–43.

Ogletree, B. T., Fischer, M. A., & Sprouse, J. (1995). An innovative language treatment for a child with high-functioning autism. *Focus on Autistic Behavior*, *10*(3), 1–10.

Pierce, K. L., & Schreibman, L. (1994). Teaching daily living skills to children with autism in unsupervised settings through pictorial self-management. *Journal of Applied Behavior Analysis*, *27*(3), 471–481.

Pierce, K., & Schreibman, L. (1997). Multiple peer use of pivitol response training to increase social behaviors of classmates with autism: Results from trained and untrained peers. *Journal of Applied Behavior Analysis*, *30*(1), 157–160.

Prizant, B. M., & Rubin, E. (1999). Contemporary issues in interventions for autism spectrum disorders: A commentary. *The Journal of the Association for Persons with Severe Handicaps*, *24*(3), 199–208.

Rimland, B. (1964). *Infantile autism*. New York: Meredith.

Roberson, W. H., Gravel, J. S., Valcante, G. C., & Mauer, R. G. (1992). Using a picture task analysis to teach students with multiple disabilities. *Teaching Exceptional Children*, *24*(4), 12 15.

Schwartz, I. S., Garfinkle, A. N., & Bauer, J. (1998). The picture exchange communication system: Communicative outcomes for young children with disabilities. *Topics in Early Childhood Special Education*, *18*(3), 144–159.

Schwartz, I. S., Sandall, S. R., Garfinkle, A. N., & Bauer, J. (1998). Outcomes for children with autism. *Topics in Early Childhood Special Education*, *18*(3), 132–143.

Shepherd, T. R., & Arther, B. (1986). Experience language: An autistic case example. *Academic Therapy*, *21*, 605–613.

Sigafoos, J., & Littlewood, R. (1999). Communication intervention on the playground: A case study on teaching requesting to a young child with autism. *International Journal of Disability, Development, and Education*, *46*, 421–429.

Simpson, R. L., & Myles, B. S. (1998). Controversial therapies and interventions with children and youth with autism. In: R. L. Simpson & B. S. Myles (Eds), *Educating children and youth with autism: Strategies for effective practice* (pp. 315–331). Austin, TX: Pro-Ed.

Stahmer, A. C. (1995). Teaching symbolic play skills to children with autism using pivotal response training. *Journal of Autism and Developmental Disorders*, *25*(2), 123–141.

Stahmer, A. C., & Schreibman, L. (1992). Teaching children with autism appropriate play in unsupervised environments using a self-management treatment package. *Journal of Applied Behavior Analysis*, *25*, 447–459.

Sugai, G., & Lewis, T. J. (1996). Preferred and promising practices for social skills instruction. *Focus on Exceptional Children*, *29*(4), 1–16.

Swaggart, B. L., Gagnon, E., Bock, S. J., Earles, T. L., Quinn, C., Myles, B., & Simpson, R. L. (1995). Using social stories to teach social and behaviorial skills to children with autism. *Focus on Autistic Behavior*, *10*(1), 1–15.

Venter, A., Lord, C., & Schopler, E. (1992). A follow-up of high-functioning autistic children. *Journal of Child Psychology and Psychiatry*, *33*, 489–507.

Wetherby, A. M., & Prizant, B. M. (2000). Introduction to autism spectrum disorders. In: A. M. Wetherby & B. M. Prizant (Eds), *Autism spectrum disorders: A transactional developmental perspective* (Vol. 9, pp. 1–7). Baltimore, MD: Paul H. Brookes.

Wimpory, D., Chadwick, P., & Nash, S. (1995). Brief report: Musical interaction therapy for children with autism: An evaluative case study with two-year follow-up. *Journal of Autism and Developmental Disorders*, *25*, 541–552.

Wolf-Schein, E. G. (1995, July). *Structured methods in language education: SMILE.* Paper presented at the 18th International Congress on Education of the Deaf, Tel-Aviv, Israel. (ERIC Reproduction Service # ED 391 282).

LANGUAGE DEVELOPMENT AND TEXT COMPREHENSION IN INDIVIDUALS WITH AUTISM

Tim Wahlberg

INTRODUCTION

One of the primary characteristics of the Autism syndrome is impairment in language functioning (see Tager-Flusberg, et al., 1990; Vetter, 1995) which may take the form of a delay in, or total lack of, the development of spoken language (DSM-IV, 1994). Individuals with autism, who do acquire language (about 35–40%), display impairments in the ability to initiate or sustain a conversation with others (DSM-IV, 1994). The language acquired can also take the form of stereotyped and repetitive use of language (DSM-IV, 1994). This is often referred to as "parroting" (repeating what is being said to them) or "echolalia" which involves delayed repetition of whole phrases or even conversations (Caparulo & Cohen, 1977; Happe & Frith, 1996; Wahlberg & Rotatori, 1996).

Mesibov, Adams, and Klinger (1997) stated that, "one of the most consistent patterns among children with autism is significantly delayed language development" (p. 1). In fact research has shown that 35–40% of individuals with autism fail to develop functional and communicative language at all during their lifetimes (Mesibov et al., 1997; Rutter, 1978). Individuals with autism who do develop language often display patterns of strengths and weaknesses

Autistic Spectrum Disorders: Educational and Clinical Interventions, pages 133–150.

ISBN: 0-7623-0818-4

associated with language (Frith & Snowling, 1983; Goldberg, 1987; Mesibov et al., 1997; O'Connor & Hermelin, 1994; Tager-Flusberg, 1981a, b).

Individuals with autism seem very capable at operating in the visual-spatial aspects of the world, but show large deficits in social-communicative behaviors (Lord, 1996). While some individuals with autism develop language and learn to function in society, many are challenged by learning to read and understand text (see Happe, 1994; Prior & Hall, 1979; Snowling & Frith, 1986; Tager-Flusberg, 1981b). Normal individuals that come in contact with a high functioning individual with autism often assume that they are capable individuals that have no problems comprehending what is being said to them or what they read. This assumption occurs because individuals with autism can have normal or above normal IQ's, and superficially appear to understand and comprehend the world around them.

This chapter describes communication patterns that individuals with autism display as they develop language. The first part of the chapter examines three areas of language development, namely, semantic aspects, pragmatic aspects, and comprehension. The second part of the chapter discusses text comprehension in individuals with autism. This is followed by a brief description of the current ways in which text comprehension is assessed in normal individuals. Next, exploratory research related to the assessment of reading comprehension in individuals with autism is examined. This section includes the most promising methodological techniques. Also, the issue of the ability of individuals with autism to read written text and understand the message that is being portrayed will be addressed. Finally, the chapter concludes with future research possibilities.

COMMUNICATION PATTERNS

Semantic Aspects of Language

Children with autism often times use a limited range of words during conversations with parents or caregivers. Parents report that their autistic child does not use fully the vocabulary they have developed (Mesibov et al., 1997). This lack of vocabulary usage limits the ability of individuals with autism to communicate their wants and needs in everyday life. The language they use often displays two peculiar characteristics, namely, pronoun reversal and echolalia and/or parroting (Mesibov et al., 1997; Happe & Frith, 1996; Wahlberg & Rotatori, 1996). Pronoun reversal involves referring to others as "I" and referring to themselves as "you". Lee, Hobson, and Chiat (1994) conducted a study assessing the use of pronouns in individuals with autism. The participants were presented with different pictures and asked to respond appropriately to the pictures based on the prompt they were given by the experimenter. The researchers found that individuals with autism were significantly less likely to use the pronoun "me" in a visual perspective taking task. Also, lower ability autistic participants were more likely to use their own proper names rather than personal pronouns in certain photograph naming tasks. Lastly, the autistic participants were less likely than controls to employ the pronoun "you" to refer to the experimenter.

Another peculiarity seen in individuals with autism's language involves "parroting" or "echolalic" speech utterances (Carparulo & Cohen, 1977; Mesibov et al., 1997; Wahlberg & Rotatori, 1996). Parroting is best described as repeating, verbatim, what has been said. For example, individuals with autism might respond to the phrase, "It is a beautiful day, don't you think?" with "It is a beautiful day, don't you think?" Echolalia is the verbatim repetition of some previously heard words or phrases (Carparulo & Cohen, 1977; Happe & Frith, 1996; Mesibov et al., 1997; Wahlberg & Rotatori, 1996). Schuler and Prizant (1985) reported that approximately 85% of individuals with autism who develop speech are echolalic.

Carparulo and Cohen (1977) reported that echolalia plays a part in the language difficulty individuals with autism have with pronoun reversal. They described echolalia as an individual using "fixed verbal codes" (p. 627). Individuals with autism seem to echo what they have heard at other times. Carparulo and Cohen stated that pronoun reversal fits into this category of repeating what has been said previously. For example, if a parent says to their young child with autism, "Do you want a cookie?", the child with autism may respond with, "Do you want a cookie?" at a later date when he/she wants a cookie. This form of echolalia is different from parroting in that it has linguistic and/or communicative intentions.

Mesibov et al. (1997) also reported that echolalia is a way in which individuals with autism may communicate with others. The researchers stated that echolalia is an important precursor in the development of more advanced language. Mesibov et al. argued that echolalic individuals seem to use this form of language as a means to communicate basic wants and needs with others in the environment. The development of echolalia makes these individuals appear very odd and robotic, but it seems to be an attempt by individuals with autism to engage in communication. On the other hand, Carparulo and Cohen (1977) argued that echolalia plays a minimal role in linguistic progression.

Tager-Flusberg (1981a) reviewed a number of studies assessing the semantic abilities of individuals with autism. The researchers found that autistic children have deficits in certain aspects of semantic processing, which may be tied to impairments in higher level conceptualization. This supports a model proposed by Bartolucci and Albers (1974) which suggested that autistic children may be deficient in handling deitic categories of language. Deitic categories are terms that shift in meaning as a function of space, time, or person. An example of this would be using the terms "come here" or "over there" in a sentence. To understand what is meant by this term, one must understand the context and relationship one has with the speaker in regards to oneself as the listener. DeVilliers and DeVilliers (1974) pointed out that communication using deitic categories is complex because they have no fixed referents and are dependent on the relationship between the speaker and the listener.

Pragmatic Aspects of Language

Language impairments in individuals with autism are most pronounced in their social or pragmatic use of language (Tager-Flusberg, 1989). Many aspects of the conversational skills of verbal individuals with autism are noticeably problematic (see Cantwell, Baker & Rutter, 1978; Dobbinson, Perkins & Boucher, 1998; Hewitt, 1998; Mesibov et al., 1997; Schairer & Nelson, 1996). These problematic conversational skills include the use of irrelevant detail (Mesibov et al., 1997), perseveration on specific topics (Dobbinson et al., 1998; Mesibov et al., 1997), problems with longer utterances (Hewitt, 1998; Schairer & Nelson, 1996), queries requiring inference (Dobbinson et al., 1998; Hewitt, 1998), indirect requests for information (Hewitt, 1998), inappropriate shifting of topics (Dobbinson et al., 1998; Schairer & Nelson, 1996)), pausing (Dobbinson et al., 1998), turn taking (Schairer & Nelson, 1996), complex interpretive linguistic skills (Minshew, Goldstein & Siegel, 1995), ignoring the initiations introduced by others (Mesibov et al., 1997), and a lack of strategy for repair when there are problems in their conversations (Dobbinson et al., 1998).

Irrelevant Detail

The use of irrelevant details occurs when an individual with autism provides information in a conversation that offers no relevant detail to the topic at hand (Mesibov et al., 1997). For example, an individual with autism may provide the telephone number of a person he/she is speaking about in a conversation. This is very similar to inappropriately shifting of topics during a conversation (Dobbinson et al., 1998; Schairer & Nelson, 1996). For example, individuals with autism often add irrelevant information during a conversation and then continue to address this irrelevant information (such as talking about the specific numbers that make up the person's phone number, as previously mentioned above). They may perseverate on "their" chosen topic of choice whether or not it brings any bearing into the ongoing conversation (Dobbinson et al., 1998; Mesibov et al., 1997).

Complex Utterances

Individuals with autism typically have problems with following longer or complex utterances, made by other parties during a conversation (Hewitt, 1998; Minshew et al., 1995; Schairer & Nelson, 1996). For example, individuals with autism may appear as if they are not paying attention in a long or complex utterance because they got lost as the person spoke. At other times, individuals with autism will pause for extended periods of time during conversation making it awkward for the other individual carrying on the conversation (Dobbinson et al., 1998).

Social Rules

Individuals with autism may also have trouble taking turns during conversation (Schairer & Nelson, 1996). Tager-Flusberg (1993) hypothesized that people with autism are unaware of the social rules that govern social conversations (as cited in Mesibov et al., 1997). They may ignore intonation introduced by others during conversation (Mesibov et al., 1997). Also, individuals with autism seem unaware of the social delicacies associated with carrying on a reciprocal conversation with another individual. Additionally, these individuals stumble when things go awry during a conversation, because they are unable to repair the conversation (Dobbinson et al., 1998). Furthermore, social queries requiring inferences (Dobbinson et al., 1998; Hewitt, 1998) and indirect requests for information (Hewitt, 1998) may cause an individual with autism to struggle and appear lost during a conversation because the conversing requires information that is not concrete or literal.

Concrete and Literal Comprehension

Language comprehension in individuals with autism is often described as concrete and literal (Koegel, Camarata, Koegel, Ben-Tall & Smith, 1998; Mesibov et al., 1997). They do not use the semantic content of language (for meaning) any more effectively than when they produce language (Mesibov et al., 1997). Individuals with autism are unable to use underlying semantic knowledge to aid in the interpretation of language. This problem can be debilitating for individuals with autism because people often assume that they comprehend everything that is being said to them, when in reality they do not. Thus, people may perceive individuals with autism as being aloof, odd or stubborn (Mesibov et al., 1997). Furthermore, people often do not understand that individuals with autism have this inherent inability to understand certain aspects of conversations.

COMMUNICATIVE/COMPREHENSION ASPECTS OF LANGUAGE

Most studies that assess language in individuals with autism use an interview format to make inferences about their comprehension and language abilities (Cantwell, et al., 1978; Dobbinson et al., 1998; Hewitt, 1998; Minshew et al., 1995; Shairer & Nelson, 1996; Tager-Flusberg et al., 1990). Such a format allows researchers to assess an individual with autism's language capabilities in a seemingly "normal" arena. Most research to date assesses individuals with autism's conversations in this manner.

Hewitt (1998) assessed conversational speech in individuals with autism who were asked to engage in simple sentences about their lives. The researcher found four types of questions that showed a higher than normal failure-rate for individuals with autism in comparison with their overall rate for response to conversational questions. The four questions that Hewitt found to be problematic were: more than seven words in length, multiclausal, requiring inference, and indirect requests for information. Dobbinson et al. (1998) found similar results when they analyzed conversations between an experimenter and a woman with autism. The researcher reported that the autistic woman struggled with topic movement and inference production. She also displayed a tendency to repeat syntactic constructs and lexical items.

Schairer and Nelson (1996) assessed both written and oral conversations with individuals with autism and found that staying on topic was difficult in oral conversations. The researchers reported that it was easier for individuals with autism to stay on topic when writing out conversations. Schairer and Nelson reported that individuals with autism performed better in the written form of conversation, even though they provided more conversation in the oral form.

Minshew et al. (1995) assessed the oral receptive conversations of high functioning individuals with autism. The researchers found that these individuals showed evidence of normal lexicon, fund of semantic knowledge, and grasp of basic rules of grammar and phonetics. Speech was also found to be normally fluent. However, the researchers reported that more complex or interpretive language abilities were significantly impaired. All of the individuals that participated in the study had histories of early language deficits (per the diagnostic criteria). The study's findings suggested that early language deficits can evolve into less apparent deficits in older high functioning individuals with autism that acquire speech. However, these individuals still demonstrate some language-related problems in processing complex and interpretive language.

Tager-Flusberg et al. (1990) followed the language acquisition of six autistic and six Down syndrome children over the course of 12 to 26 months. The researchers collected language samples at home while the children interacted with their mothers. Tager-Flusberg et al. found that the majority of the children with autism followed the same general developmental path in the acquisition of grammatical and lexical aspects of language as the Down syndrome children and normal children reported in previous research (Bates, Bretherton, & Snyder, 1988; Brown, 1973; McCarthy, 1930; Paul, 1987; Peters, 1983). This finding suggests that children with autism are able to acquire certain developmental aspects of language. Tager-Flusberg et al. (1990) concluded that these children were able to follow some of the "rules" that govern our language, but the researchers did not address comprehension of the language that was used during conversation.

Cantwell et al. (1978) assessed the language abilities of 12 autistic and 12 dysphasic children by examining language samples taken between the child and their caregivers. Dysphasic children have normal non-verbal intelligence and a severe developmental impairment in language comprehension. The main difference found between the two groups of subjects was in the form of functional language usage. Over half of the autistic group showed an appreciable amount of delayed echolalia, thinking aloud/action accompaniments or metaphorical language, while none of the dysphasic group did so. The echoing was distinguished by two characteristics: (1) the inappropriateness of what was said, and (2) the echoing by the child of what he himself (rather than someone else) had just spoken. The researchers found that autistic children's language differs most markedly in having components that are both inappropriate and egocentric. In fact, the researchers stressed that it is the deviance of spoken language rather than the delay in its development that was the most characteristic of children with autism. Another interesting finding, which corresponds to the previously mentioned research, is that the two groups did not differ on syntactical usage as determined by morphological, transformational and phrase structure rules. However, children with autism were significantly less likely to make spontaneous remarks and significantly more likely to use delayed echoes, thinking aloud/action accompaniments, and inappropriate echoes.

TEXT COMPREHENSION WITH NORMAL INDIVIDUALS

Text comprehension in normal individuals is achieved by using two types of assessment methodologies: on-line processing and off-line processing (Balota,

Flores d'Arcais & Rayner, 1990; Keenan, Potts, Golding & Jennings, 1990; Magliano & Graesser, 1991). Over the past ten years researchers have examined text comprehension extensively using these two means of assessment (Balota et al., 1990). The following brief review will give the reader an idea of the components involved in both on-line and off-line means of assessing text comprehension.

On-Line Processing

The on-line process of collecting text comprehension information involves assessing what is happening while the individual is actually reading the text in order to tap the readers developing representation of the meaning of the text. It is done to see if the reader is using knowledge about unspecified information such as why events have happened in the text and what may happen next (see Graesser & Clark, 1985; Keenan et al., 1990; Olson, Duffy & Mack, 1984). This process of assessment can be done using many different techniques. One technique is reading time (Keenan et al., 1990; Magliano & Graesser, 1991). Reading times can be assessed as the subject reads the text. Text segments that can be used to collect reading times include: words, phrases, sentences, and passages. Times are taken once the subject has completed the segment of the text the researcher is interested in measuring (Keenan et al., 1990; Magliano & Graesser, 1991). The two most popular text segments used in assessing reading times are sentence reading and word reading (Magliano & Graesser, 1991).

Latency measures are another form of an on-line comprehension measure (Keenan et al., 1990; Magliano & Graesser, 1991). It involves the reader completing a sentence and then being presented with a target (e.g. letter string). The reader is required to make some response to the target (e.g. deciding if the target is a word or not). Targets are either related or not related to the text. Response latencies are recorded and compared for each target. It is hypothesized that words related to the text or sentence will result in a shorter response time for the reader. This process involves the "priming" of the target word. It is done via words or the sentence previously read creating a faster response time for related target words because of the similarities the target word may have with the text (Magliano & Graesser, 1991).

Assessing information while the subject reads the text is another form of on-line comprehension (Magliano & Greasser, 1991). Subjects can be asked specific questions regarding what they are thinking about or inferences they are making while they are reading the selected text (Keenan et al., 1990). Additionally, subjects are asked to provide information regarding their thought processes as they read and comprehend text.

Off-Line Processing

The off-line process of collecting text comprehension information involves the subject performing comprehensive tasks after he/she has finished reading (Magliano & Graesser, 1991). This time frame may be immediately after the individual has finished reading the text, or a few moments, days, or weeks afterwards. Subjects are asked questions pertaining to the text they have read. At times subjects are asked to recall what they have read via a summarization of the text or passage. This is known as "free recall". Subjects may also use other forms of off-line comprehension such as cued recall, recognition, speeded recognition, and word completion (see Magliano & Graesser, 1991 for a detailed description). An elaboration of these forms of recall is not warranted due to the fact that it does not appear in the comprehension research dealing with individuals with autism.

READING COMPREHENSION IN AUTISM

Off-Line Text Comprehension with Autistic Individuals

Tager-Flusberg (1981b) was interested in addressing whether or not children with autism use strategies while comprehending sentences. The researcher created a methodology that required the participants to "act out" sentences that were read to them. This allowed the researcher to assess the comprehension of the sentences immediately after they were read to the subjects. Two groups of subjects were used in the experiment, namely, autistic and normal children. The normal children ranged in age from three to four years and the autistic group ranged in age from eight to eleven years. Participants were matched based on tests of verbal and nonverbal ability.

The participants were instructed to "do as I say" and act out the sentences that were read to them by the experimenter. The children were given toys that corresponded with the nouns used in the sentences. Participants were instructed to use the toys to act out the sentences. Sentences were created and reversed with respect to subject and object, with an active and passive version of each, for a total of 24 sentences. The sentences were also rated on a probability level based on the action portrayed in the sentence making semantic sense. An example of a low rated probability level sentence would be, "The dog pats the mother." The children's responses were scored based on being correct, reversed, ambiguous, self (child acted out), other, and no response.

Tager-Flusberg (1981b) found that the autistic participants with higher mental age scores performed better on the sentence comprehension task than the autistic subjects with lower mental age scores. Nonverbal mental age did not predict comprehension. The overall findings suggested that the autistic group's overall sentence comprehension score was significantly lower than the matched normal three and four year olds. Tager-Flusberg reported that the autistic group used word-order strategies in sentence comprehension, however, the researcher was not convinced that the autistic subjects incorporated the probable-event strategy. The probable-event strategy required the individual to rely on information they already knew about the world form past experiences to interpret sentences describing semantically biased events (i.e. the dog pats the mother). Children two or three years of age can use this strategy (see Bever, 1970; Strohner & Nelson, 1974). The word-order strategy, which is used in slightly older children, is a comprehension strategy in which a noun-verb-noun sequence is interpreted as agent-action-object (Bever, 1970; Slobin, 1973).

Tager-Flusberg (1981b) ran a second experiment to further assess the finding that the autistic participants were not likely to use a probable-event strategy. The same subjects were used in the second experiment. Four different word series were constructed from two nouns and a transitive verb. Participants were presented each of six possible word orders, reversing the order of nouns, creating 24 items. The four series were derived from the sentences used in the first experiment. One series was unbiased and the other three series were semantically biased. Each participant was again asked to act out the sentence that was presented to him/her. All participants were told that this time the sentences might sound a bit funny. The participants were instructed to try and guess what was being said and act it out. The scoring was the same as in the first experiment.

The results from the second experiment confirmed the finding in experiment one. Children with autism were comparable to normal controls in their: (1) sensitivity to word order, (2) use of a word-order strategy, and (3) sensitivity to the semantic bias of the items. They were not, however, sensitive to the probability level, and were much less likely to use a probable-event strategy. The children with autism were unable to incorporate knowledge about the way objects or people relate to one another. For example, the autistic participants were unable to incorporate the idea that a girl can hold a baby but the converse is highly unlikely and implausible. In contrast the normal participants were able to make these distinctions.

Prior and Hall (1979) conducted a study using off-line procedures to assess the verbal comprehension of transitive and intransitive phrases by autistic, mentally retarded, and normal children. Participants were given transitive or intransitive phrases and then asked to identify the correct corresponding picture out of four presented. A transitive phrase is one that requires a direct object after subject and verb whereas an intransitive phrase is one that does not take a direct object. Prior and Hall found that normal children correctly identified 84.6% of the target phrases, children with retardation 80.4%, and children with autism 68.5%, respectively. The children with autism made more errors in identifying the target phrases of all types in all conditions. Prior and Hall stated that it is clear from the findings that children with autism have difficulty in identifying word combinations which lead to comprehending relationships between agents, actions, and objects. The researchers concluded that children with autism do not differ in their approach to language acquisition but they are grossly retarded in language comprehension even when their level of single word comprehension is similar to that of normal and retarded controls.

Individuals with autism are often times labeled as hyperlexic, meaning that they are able to read text but unable to comprehend what they have read. Snowling and Frith (1986) conducted a study assessing the comprehension abilities of autistic and hyperlexic individuals. The researchers compared and contrasted eight children with autism ranging in age from 11 to 19 years with eight children that were mildly educationally retarded. Participants were matched for chronological age, mental age, and reading age. The participants in the study were presented two parallel versions of the Bishop's Test for the Reception of Grammar (1982). Sentences were presented in order of increasing difficulty. Subjects were required to select one of four pictures that corresponded with the test sentence that was either presented in spoken or written form. The children with autism and matched controls were found to be equally competent in their ability to understand sentences of a wide range of grammatical contrasts. Their performance was not impaired based on whether the sentences were read or listened to by the participants. Snowling and Frith concluded that any comprehension impairments in reading found in the participants was due to language delay which raises the issue that comprehension may be only as good as verbal ability allows it to be.

Snowling and Frith (1986) conducted another experiment assessing story text comprehension in individuals with autism. The two stories used had approximately a six or seven year old reading ability. After the text was read, two different types of questions were asked of the subjects. The first type of question required the subject to remember factual detail provided by the specific sentences in the text. The second type of question invited general knowledge to be brought to bear in answering the question. Thirty-two comprehensive questions were devised, 16 concerned with the first text and 16 concerned with the second. Half of the sentences tested the children's memory for particular information in the story that they had read. The remaining questions were devised on an a priori basis to tap the children's ability to give reasoned answers on the basis of what they had read with the possibility of using general knowledge if they wished. All the answers were scored as correct or incorrect in terms of the stories by three raters. As in the previous experiment, the Snowling and Frith found that the autistic and nonautistic retarded participants of relatively high verbal ability performed identical to each other and as well as normal controls. For all these participants, the general questions were easier than factual questions. All the groups used general knowledge to supplement their memory for, or understanding of, a text. Snowling and Frith concluded that the findings suggested that verbal ability alone cannot fully account for text comprehension in individuals with autism.

Snowling and Frith (1986) did report that autistic and retarded children within the low verbal ability range did no better on the general knowledge than the factual questions. In fact, these participants answered both questions poorly. The researchers stressed that low ability autistic and retarded children are unable to integrate different sources of information simultaneously. Therefore, preexisting knowledge, if any, is not accessed during reading and new facts are not well represented which leads to the story not being understood.

Happe (1994) conducted a study assessing individuals with autism's ability to provide context-appropriate mental state representations for story character's non-literal utterances. Their performance was compared to normal and mentally handicapped controls. The stories consisted of 24 short vignettes that were accompanied by a picture and two test questions, a comprehensive question and a justification question. There were 12 types of stories: lie, white lie, joke, pretend, misunderstanding, persuade, appearance/reality, figure of speech, sarcasm, forget, double bluff, and contrary emotions. The participants were read the stories and then asked to answer the two questions at the end of each story dealing with the story character's non-literal utterances. The comprehensive question asked, "Is it true, what X said?" The justification question asked, "Why did X say that?" Subjects were also tested on theory of mind tasks.

Happe (1994) found that all participants with autism were impaired in providing context-appropriate mental state explanations for the story characters non-literal utterances when compared to the normal and mentally handicapped matched controls. Furthermore, the researcher found that even those autistic participants that passed all the theory of mind tasks showed impairments on the more naturalistic story materials relative to matched normal controls. Happe reported that the subjects with autism's performance on the stories was closely related to performance on standard theory of mind tasks and hypothesized from these results that individuals with autism have a specific impairment in extracting meaning in context, and a preference for processing local versus global information (see also Frith, 1989).

Minshew et al. (1995) compared interpretive linguistic skills of 62 high-functioning individuals with autism to 50 control participants matched for age, gender, IQ, race, education, and family socioeconomic distribution. The researchers studied both basic and complex interpretive linguistic skills. A number of tests were given to assess comprehension in the study, but the most significant tests required off-line comprehension strategies. These tests included the Woodcock Reading Mastery Test – Revised (Woodcock, 1987) and the Test of Language Competence (Wing & Secord, 1985). These tests were used because they involved the answering of questions in reference to passages or text that had to be read by the participants. Minshew et al. found that the autistic participants' complex or interpretive language abilities were significantly impaired in comparison to the matched controls. The autistic group struggled with comprehension that involved complex interpretive information which is required for conceptualization, reasoning, logical analysis, and inferencing. Minshew et al. reported that the autistic participants evidenced normal abilities in: lexicon, fund of semantic knowledge, and grasp of the basic rules of grammar and phonetics. This study supports earlier findings that individuals with autism seem to grasp the basic rules that govern reading and communication, but fail to comprehend information requiring higher level cognitive processes.

Golberg (1987) conducted an extensive literature review of off-line techniques used in the analysis of text comprehension in individuals labeled as autistic savants. The off-line techniques used dealt primarily with answering questions based upon reading a selected portion of text. Goldberg concluded that the studies demonstrated that overall autistic savants are able to comprehend what they have read in passages but they may have dysfunctional procedural memory systems with relatively intact declarative memories.

On-Line Text Comprehension with Autistic Individuals

Snowling and Frith (1986) conducted a second experiment (part of the previous study examined in this chapter) using an on-line strategy to assess whether or not autistic readers were less inclined than normal or dyslexic readers to modify their pronunciation of homographs to fit in with the context of sentences they were reading. The researchers created four sentences, each of which included a homograph. Two of the sentences required the correct use of the homograph in its more frequent English language version and two sentences required the pronunciation in its less frequent way. Snowling and Frith found that "hyperlexic" children with autism make little use of context to disambiguate homographs (see also, Frith & Snowling, 1983; Happe, 1997). This finding, however, is not specific to children with autism as the researchers reported that not all young hyperlexic readers are impaired when reading homographs as compared to young normal readers. The researchers stressed that these findings suggest that individuals who fail this task may adopt a word-by-word reading strategy, rather than integrating words into larger units of meaning.

Snowling and Frith (1986) conducted another experiment comparing the comprehension of units of text differing in size. Two story texts were used in this study. During different intervals of a lengthy text, participants had to choose one out of three given words to complete a "gap" in a sentence. The three words were always of the same grammatical class (noun, verb, adjective, and preposition) but their appropriateness was manipulated systematically. The words were either story appropriate, sentence appropriate, or inappropriate. Within this on-line comprehension task, the readers attention is continuously focused on the exact selection of words and is given explicit alternatives. Snowling and Frith reported that when subjects were required to select words to complete texts they were reading, handicapped children of low verbal ability, whether autistic or nonautistic, did not distinguish systematically between story-appropriate and sentence-appropriate words. These participants were able to reject words that were inappropriate in the immediately surrounding context. Snowling and Frith stated that this may lead one to infer that these participants read in this situation in a word-by-word fashion. The researchers also found that low verbal ability normal children, autistic and nonautistic retarded children of high verbal ability, and normal readers could extract meaning at a level beyond the single sentence which showed evidence of text comprehension. This was indicated by the fact that they preferred story-appropriate over sentence-appropriate choices.

O'Connor and Hermelin (1994) conducted a comprehension study assessing text comprehension in two autistic savant readers. The two readers (one five and the other eight years of age) were given texts that increased in difficulty from passage to passage and were asked to answer questions pertaining to the texts after they had finished reading them. O'Connor and Hermelin assessed comprehension (via the off-line method of answering text-related questions), and reading speeds (an on-line form of assessment). The researchers were interested in the effect text difficulty would have on both comprehension and reading speeds for the two savant readers in comparison with matched controls. O'Connor and Hermelin found that comprehension was appropriate for each participant's developmental status and that their reading speeds were faster than their age-matched controls. Secondly, the researchers reported that when the text was randomized, thereby reducing meaningfulness, an equivalent reduction in reading times was marked for the young autistic child and his matched control. The reading speed reduction was found to be most pronounced for the older control participant. The older autistic participant showed a minimal reduction in reading speed with the randomized texts. The researchers stressed that the results demonstrated that the two individuals with autism had efficient grapheme-phoneme conversion when reading text. Furthermore, O'Connor and Hermelin concluded that this transcoding process is primarily responsible for the fast reading time in the two children with autism.

CONCLUSION AND FUTURE RESEARCH

It seems apparent from the research reviewed that children with autism (who are verbal) are able to learn to pronounce and use words and language but they experience problems using the acquired language to converse appropriately. In fact, spontaneity and diversion from the expected seem to sidetrack and lose individuals. In essence individuals with autism seem unable to follow and understand conversation in this manner.

The above research findings suggest that individuals with autism struggle with comprehending longer sentences that require inferences and request information. It seems as though simple syntax and short utterances are easier for individuals with autism to comprehend. Individuals with autism may appear to be stubborn or to be inattentive when engaging in conversation, when in actuality they may be struggling to comprehend what is being said. When interacting socially with these individuals, it is important to keep these findings in mind because they may be trying to comprehend what the speaker is saying but from the speaker's perspective they seem aloof and uninterested. It is no wonder than that individuals who interact with autistic persons report their conversations as dissatisfying (Dobbinson et al., 1998).

Individuals with autism who acquire language reach linguistic developmental milestones similar to normal children. Problems arise when individuals with autism are required to demonstrate comprehension and social understanding of learned language. Future research and interventions in this area need to focus more attention on the usage of the already learned basic linguistic skills of individuals with autism and teach them to better understand complex and inferential language. This will improve individuals with autism's communication and understanding of other individuals, which will allow them to participate in more socially acceptable ways.

The research reviewed indicates that individuals with autism have the ability to read and comprehend various forms of text. While the studies discussed were adequate at answering some of the questions concerning text comprehension in individuals with autism, they did not point out future research avenues. Future studies could explore some of the problems individuals with autism have with more complex text that may require more inferences to be made in order to understand what is going on within the text. It seems as though individuals with autism comprehend text that is literal and "cut and dry" similar to text in an encyclopedia or dictionary. In contrast, individuals with autism loose insight when the text requires inferences to be drawn based on passed experience or "common sense" types of knowledge.

Future research may want to explore more extensive on-line forms of text comprehension. It may be worthwhile to tap into the "goings on" of individuals with autism as they read and interpret text. This information would prove to be very beneficial to further societies understanding of how individuals with autism process the information as they read and interpret text. Researchers can gain considerable knowledge about how individuals with autism take in and process information by assessing their comprehension of written language. While much has been learned in this area, more information is needed to understand how individuals with autism comprehend written text.

REFERENCES

American Psychiatric Association (1994). *Diagnostic and statistical manual of mental disorders. (DSM-IV)* (4th ed.). Washington, D.C.: Authors.

Balota, D. A., Flores d'Arcais, G. B., & Rayner, K. (1990). *Comprehension processes in reading*. Hillsdale, NJ: Erlbaum.

Bartolucci, G., & Albers, R. J. (1974). Deitic categories in the language of autistic children. *Journal of Autism and Childhood Schizophrenia*, *4*, 131–141.

Bates, E., Bretherton, I., & Snyder, L. (1988). *From first words to grammar*. New York: Cambridge University Press.

Bever, T. G. (1970). The cognitive basis for linguistic structures. In: J. R. Hayes (Ed.), *Cognition and the Development of Language*. New York: Wiley.

Bishop, D. V. M. (1982). *T.R.O.G.: Test for the reception of grammar*. Abingdon, Oxon: Leach.

Brown, R. (1973). *A first language*. Cambridge, MA: Harvard University Press.

Cantwell, D. P., Baker, L., & Rutter, M. (1978). A comparative study of infantile autism and specific developmental receptive language disorder. IV. Analysis ofsyntax and language function. *Journal of Child Psychology and Psychiatry*, *19*, 351–363.

Carparulo, B. K., & Cohen, D. J. (1977). Cognitive structures, language, and emerging social competence in autistic and aphasic children. *Journal of the American Academy of Child Psychiatry*, *16*, 620–645.

De Villiers, P. A., & De Villiers, J. G. (1974). On this, that, and the other: Nonegocentrism in very young children. *Journal of Experimental Child Psychology*, *18*, 438–447.

Dobbinson, S., Perkins, M. R., & Boucher, J. (1998). Structural patterns in conversations with a woman who has autism. *Journal of Communication Disorders*, *31*, 113–134.

Frith, U. (1989). *Autism: Explaining the enigma*. Oxford: Basil Blackwell.

Frith, U., & Snowling, M. (1983). Reading for meaning and reading for sound in autistic and dyslexic children. *Journal of Developmental Psychology*, *1*, 329–342.

Goldberg, T. E. (1987). *On hermetic reading abilities. Journal of Autism and Developmental Disabilities*, *17*(1), 29–44.

Graesser, A. C., & Clark, L. F. (1985). *Structures and procedures of implicit knowledge*. New York: Academic Press.

Happe, F. G. (1994). An advanced test of theory of mind: Understanding of storycharacters' thoughts and feelings by able autistic, mentally handicapped, and normal children and adults. *Journal of Autism and Developmental Disorders*, *24*, 129–154.

Happe, F. G. (1997). Central coherence and theory of mind in autism: Reading homographs in context. *British Journal of Developmental Psychology*, *15*, 1–12.

Happe, F., & Frith, U. (1996). The neuropsychology of autism. *Brain*, *119*, 1377–1400.

Hewitt, L. E. (1998). Influence of question type on response adequacy in youngadults with autism. *Journal of Communication Disorders*, *31*, 135–152.

Keenan, J. M., Potts, G. R., Golding, J. M., & Jennings, T. M. (1990). Which elaborative inferences are drawn during reading? A question of methodologies. In: D. A. Balota, G. B. Flores d'Arcais & K Rayner (Eds), *Comprehension Processes in Reading* (pp. 377–399). Hillsdale, NJ: Erlbaum.

Koegel, R. L., Camarata, S., Koegel, L. K., Ben-Tall, A., & Smith, A. E. (1998). Increasing speech intelligibility in children with autism. *Journal of Autism and Developmental Disorders*, *28*(3), 241–251.

Lee, A., Hobson, R. P., & Chiat, S. (1994). I, you, me, and autism: An experimental study. *Journal of Autism and Developmental Disorders*, *24*(2), 155–176.

Lord, C. (1996). Language in high-functioning adolescents with autism: Questions about deviance and delay. In: D. Cicchetti & S. L. Toth (Eds), *Adolescence: Opportunities and Challenges* (pp. 149–165). Rochester, New York: University of Rochester Press.

Magliano, J. P., & Graesser, A. C. (1991). A three-pronged method for studyinginference generation in literary text. *Poetics*, *20*, 193–232.

McCarthy, D. A. (1930). *The language development of the preschool child*. Minneappolis: University of Minnesota Press.

Mesibov, G. B., Adams, L. W., & Klinger, L. G. (1997). *Autism: Understanding the Disorder*. New York: Plenum Press.

Minshew, N. J., Goldstein, G., & Siegel, D. J. (1995). Speech and language in high-functioning autistic individuals. *Neuropathology*, *9*(2), 255–261.

O'Connor, N., & Hermelin, B. (1994). Two autistic savant readers. *Journal of Autism and Developmental Disorders*, *24*(4), 501–515.

Olson, G. M., Duffy, S. A., & Mack, R. L. (1984). Thinking out loud as a method forstudying real-time comprehension processes. In: D. Kieras & M. Just (Eds), *New Methods in the Study of Immediate Processes in Comprehension* (pp. 253–286). Hillsdale, NJ: Erlbaum.

Paul, R. (1987). Communication. In: D. J. Cohen & A. M. Donnellan (Eds), *Handbook of Autism and Pervasive Developmental Disorders* (pp. 61–84). New York: Wiley.

Peters, A. (1983). *The units of language acquisition*. New York: Cambridge University Press.

Prior, M. R., & Hall, L. C. (1979). Comprehension of transitive and intransitive phrases by autistic, retarded and normal children. *Journal of Communication Disorders*, *12*, 103–111.

Rutter, M. (1978). Language disorders and infantile autism. In: M. Rutter & E. Schopler (Eds), *Autism: A Reappraisal of Concepts and Treatment* (pp. 85–104). New York: Plenum.

Schairer, K. S. & Nelson, N. W. (1996). Communicative possibilities of written conversations with adolescents who have autism. *Child Language Teaching and Therapy*, 164–180.

Schuler, A., & Prizant, B. (1985). Echolalia. In: E. Schopler & G. Mesibov (Eds), *Communication Problems in Autism* (pp. 163–184). New York: Plenum.

Slobin, D. I. (1973). Cognitive prerequisites for the development of grammar. In: C. A. Ferguson & D. I. Slobin (Eds), *Studies of Child Language Development*. New York: Holt, Rinehart & Winston.

Snowling, M., & Frith, U. (1986). Comprehension in 'hyperlexic' readers. *Journal of Experimental Psychology*, *42*, 392–415.

Strohner, H., & Nelson, K. E. (1974). The young child's development of sentencecomprehension: Influence of event probability, nonverbal context, syntactic form and strategies. *Child Development*, *45*, 567–576.

Tager–Flusberg, H. (1981a). On the nature of linguistic functioning in early infantile autism. *Journal of Autism and Developmental Disorders*, *11*, 45–56.

Tager-Flusberg, H. (1981b). Sentence comprehension in autistic children. *Applied Psycholinguistics*, *2*, 5–24.

Tager-Flusberg, H. (1989). A psycholinguistic perspective on language development in the autistic child. In: G. Dawson (Ed.), *Autism: Nature, Diagnosis, and Treatment* (pp. 92–115). New York: Guilford.

Tager-Flusberg, H. (1993). What language reveals about the understanding of minds in children with autism. In: S. Baron-Cohen, H. Tager-Flusberg & D. J. Cohen (Eds), *Understanding Other Minds: Perspectives from Autism* (pp. 138–157). Oxford, England: Oxford University Press.

Tager-Flusberg, H., Calkins, S., Nolin, I., Baumberger, T., Anderson, M., & Chadwick-Denis, A. (1990). A longitudinal study of language acquisition in autistic and Down syndrome children. *Journal of Autism and Developmental Disorders*, *20*, 1–22.

Vetter, H. J. (1995). Language pathology in autism and childhood schizophrenia. In: H. J. Vetter & R. W. Rieber (Eds), *The Psychopathology of Language and Cognition* (pp. 37–59). New York: Plenum Press.

Wahlberg, T. J., & Rotatori, A. (1996). Various treatment modalities for autistic individuals. In: A. F. Rotatori, J. O. Schwenn & S. Burkhardt (Eds), *Advances in Special Education* (pp. 109–131). Greenwich, CT JAI Press.

Wing, E. H., & Secord, W. (1985). *Test of Language Competence*. San Antonio, TX: Psychological Corp.

Woodcock, R. W. (1987). *Woodcock Reading Mastery Tests – Revised*. Circle Pines, MN: American Guidance Service.

AUTISM: MULTICULTURAL PERSPECTIVES

Tina Taylor Dyches, Lynn K. Wilder and Festus E. Obiakor

INTRODUCTION

Since its first use in the early 1900s by Swiss psychiatrist Eugen Bleuler, the term "autism" has been used to describe individuals who exhibit fundamental disturbances of contact with the social world. Bleuler's conceptualization of autism was the foundation on which two Austrian-born professionals in child psychiatry and pediatrics, Leo Kanner and Hans Asperger, were able to suggest a new diagnostic category, distinct from mental retardation and other psychiatric disorders. Today, Kanner's autism and Asperger syndrome are believed to be separate disorders, and the lists of the symptoms defining them have changed frequently during the past 80 years. Yet a few core characteristics have passed the test of time: deficits in social and communication skills, and restricted or unusual behavioral repertoires. The characteristics that currently define autism present extreme challenges to those diagnosed with the disorder and to their families.

A lifelong disorder with symptoms ranging from life-threatening behavior to mild deviancies, autism is also known to co-exist with mental retardation in approximately 75% of the cases (American Psychiatric Association, 1994). Further, approximately half of those with autism do not have functional speech (Prizant, 1996; Wing & Attwood, 1987). Parents raising a child with autism

Autistic Spectrum Disorders: Educational and Clinical Interventions, pages 151–177.

ISBN: 0-7623-0818-4

have reported extreme difficulties in dealing with challenging behaviors, teaching their children to communicate, teaching basic life skills, guarding their children from danger, and preparing their children for adult life (Randall & Parker, 1999). These difficulties appear to be greater among children with autism than among those with other developmental disabilities (Randall & Parker, 1999), warranting study in isolation from other disabilities. Numerous research reports have been published regarding family adaptation to disability (Bennett, DeLuca, & Allen, 1996; Olsen et al., 1999; Seligman, 1999); however little research exists regarding family adaptation to autism specifically, and most research regarding autism emanates from Western cultural perspectives.

The purpose of this chapter is to explore issues surrounding autism and multiculturalism. As little empirical evidence has been published regarding these concerns, the primary intent of this chapter is not to provide answers, but to raise questions for further examination. Issues regarding the identification of individuals with autism among cultural groups, adaptation within families, teaching strategies specific to cultures, and implications for higher education are discussed within the framework of pluralistic societies where multicultural groups are a minority within the dominant (Western or Anglo) culture.

AUTISM WITHIN MULTICULTURAL GROUPS

From its introduction in the 1910s until the present, autism has been enigmatic for both parents and professionals. No topic in the field of autism has gone unchallenged. The professional literature is replete with controversy and even hostility as it explores ways to define the disorder, find potential causes, accurately identify and count individuals with autism, validate effective treatments, and attempt to "recover" or "cure" those with autism. Although concepts that were previously considered controversial may be generally accepted today, an in-depth review of the literature provides cause for further examination. One such issue is the ubiquitous nature of autism. The history of this controversy is explored, along with attempts to validate and defy the claim of ubiquity.

Etiological Theories and Race in Autism

A common position today is that autism occurs across demographic groups. From a statement of the largest professional organization in the field comes this claim: "Autism . . . knows no racial, ethnic, or social boundaries. Family income, lifestyle, and educational levels do not affect the chance of autism's occurrence" (Autism Society of America, 2000, p. 3). This statement is an attempt to disclaim

Kanner's original hypotheses regarding the association between parental characteristics and children with autism. After describing 11 children in his 1943 paper, Kanner made observations regarding their parents: "There is one other very interesting common denominator in the backgrounds of these children. *They all come of highly intelligent families*" (p. 48). In addition, he described many of the parents as being professionals with high levels of education, adding "in the whole group, there are very few really warmhearted fathers and mothers . . . . The question arises whether or to what extent this fact has contributed to the condition of the children" (p. 50).

The above statements have served as a call for research regarding the etiology of autism, with mixed results. Much of the research in the 1950s and 1960s ignored the possibility of genetic or biological causes, focusing on possible psychopathological roots of autism. Bettelheim (1967) championed the psychogenic theory of autism, blaming cold, refrigerated mothers, and removing children from their mothers for treatment. Kanner (1971/1985) disputed the proponents of psychogenesis in autism when he noted that: "Some people seem to have completely overlooked this statement [regarding *inborn* autistic disturbances], however, as well as the passages leading up to it and have referred to the author erroneously as an advocate of postnatal 'psychogenicity' " (p. 230).

In his book *Infantile Autism* (1964), Rimland provided strong evidence against the psychogenic theory of autism. This book was the impetus for removing the blame from mothers of children with autism and formulating the position adopted by the Autism Society of America that specific family characteristics do not contribute to the occurrence of autism. Though such a claim discounted psychogenic etiologies, it still neglected the genetic liability that is currently gaining widespread empirical support in the etiology of some children with autism: "Autism today is thought to be one of the most heritable of all psychiatric conditions" (Szatmari & Jones, 1998, p. 109). Because genetic makeup is such a strong factor in the causation of autism, one might question whether correlations exist between race and autism.

Race has been largely ignored or minimized in the autism literature (Connors & Donnellan, 1998), despite pervasive claims regarding the ubiquitous nature of the condition. A majority of the research in the field of autism has as its foundation Kanner's original group of primarily Anglo Saxon children. In this group of 11 children, two were of Jewish descent, and nine were of Anglo Saxon descent. One child was born in England, but later immigrated to the United States (Kanner, 1943/1985). Throughout his practice in the United States, Kanner observed more children from Anglo families than from other races. Likewise, Asperger studied primarily Anglo children in Vienna, Austria. Because the earliest identification of autism occurred with mainly children of

Anglo descent, the generalizability of research findings for almost 60 years may be called into question in relation to racial and cultural issues. One such query is the prevalence of autism among racial groups.

Prevalence of Autism within Multicultural Groups

Some research has challenged the claim of universality of autism among races (Sanua, 1981a, b, 1984), reporting a low incidence of autism in many Latin American countries (e.g. Peru, Argentina, Brazil and Venezuela) and in several developing countries such as Kenya, India, and Hungary. Sanua hypothesized that autism is more prevalent in Western, highly technological countries, where the nuclear rather than the extended family is predominant. His conclusions and hypotheses, although based primarily on anecdotal evidence, purport psychopathological etiologies of autism. These data may be interpreted differently, however, if a genetic basis for autism is considered.

Although much of the currently published research regarding genetic and biological foundations of autism either ignores or deemphasizes race, some interest in race is emerging. One example comes from studying the effects of diagnosis, race, and age on platelet serotonin levels in individuals with autism and mental retardation (McBride, Anderson & Hertzig, 1998). The neurotransmitter serotonin has been found to be elevated in many individuals with autism, but race has rarely been singled out as a variable for investigation. Results from McBride, Anderson and Hertzig's study indicated that young children with autism had significantly higher serotonin levels than children without disabilities and children with mental retardation. Regardless of diagnosis, however, young white children had significantly lower levels of serotonin than did young Latino or black children. The effects of race and diagnosis were not found in post-pubertal individuals.

Another means of investigating relationships between race and autism is through epidemiological study. Although not as precise as biological studies, epidemiological surveys provide a big picture of the reported incidence and prevalence of autism in a given community. Within a period of 32 years, 19 epidemiological surveys (from the first such study in 1966 until 1997) have indicated prevalence rates ranging from 0.7 to 15 per 10,000, with a median rate at 4.8 (Fombonne, 1998). Conspicuously absent in most of these surveys are data regarding the race of the individuals with autism. Among these surveys, only three provided sufficient data regarding the proportion of "immigrants" in the studies (Fombonne, 1998). A detailed look at some of these studies indicates a high prevalence of autism in children born to immigrants: of the children with autism in an urban city in Sweden, 41% were from Europe, Asia, Africa and South America (Gillberg, Steffenberg & Schaumann, 1991), and 29% of the children with autism in an urban city in the United Kingdom were immigrants, mainly from the Caribbean (Wing, 1980). These rates were high compared to the racial makeup of the respective cities. However, a more recent epidemiological study supports equivalent prevalence rates across races. Data were obtained from two locations in West Midlands, United Kingdom, one with an ethnic population of 20% and the other with only 1% ethnic minority. Prevalence rates between the two areas did not differ significantly (Powell, Edwards, Edwards, Pandit, Sungum-Paliwal & Whitehouse, 2000). However, due to wide confidence intervals, small sample sizes, and variable migration patterns, Fombonne (1998) suggested that such data be interpreted with caution. Following this meta-analysis of epidemiological studies, Fombonne concluded that "the association of immigrant status with autism remains therefore uncertain" (p. 59).

The uncertainty regarding race of individuals with autism results from methodological differences between the studies. First, the accuracy of racial identification is called into question. Parental place of birth is often used; however, this is an "imperfect and ambiguous marker for race, culture and ethnicity" (Goodman & Richards, 1995, p. 367). Second, prevalence data should be analyzed while considering rural and urban areas, as some evidence indicates differences in prevalence rates between minorities in such areas (Gillberg et al., 1991). Third, racial prevalence rates should be interpreted with consideration of the diagnostic criteria used. Prevalence data should not be compared between studies using various editions of the Diagnostic and Statistical Manual of Psychiatric Disorders (DSM) and the International Classification of Diseases, as each edition describes a slightly different population. For example, the criteria of the DSM III-R tended to result in a high rate of false positives, particularly among those with severe mental retardation (Volkmar & Lloyd, 1998). When one follows the DSM III guidelines, the symptoms of children diagnosed with autism more closely resemble Kanner's original descriptions of the disorder, and stronger genetic correlations may be found using the DSM III than using DSM IV guidelines. Finally, methods by which agencies recruit families for screening and identification should be reported in detail, as differences may exist between socioeconomic status and race in recruitment rates.

A good example of the difficulty in interpreting epidemiological data is found in the requirement of the United States Department of Education for an annual reporting of all children who are served under the Individuals with Disabilities Education Act of 1997 (IDEA, 1997). These reports indicate the number and percentage of students served in various disability categories, and just recently these data have been presented according to racial categories. The 22nd Annual Report to Congress on the Implementation of IDEA 1997 reported that based on estimated resident population of the United States and outlying areas (such as American Samoa and Guam), an average of 0.08% of children aged 6–21 were served under the label of autism in 1998–1999. This average is almost twice the median rate of the previously mentioned epidemiological meta-analysis, but falling midpoint of that reported range (Fombonne, 1998). Interestingly, the rate of identification differs across racial categories. Students with autism who were Black or Asian/Pacific Islander were being served at approximately twice the rate (0.12%; 0.10%, respectively) of students with autism who were American Indian/Alaskan (0.06%) or Hispanic (0.06%) (United States Department of Education, 2001) (see Fig. 1).

Comparisons among racial groups of students with autism and students with all disabilities also indicate diagnostic disparities. For example, students who are Asian/Pacific Islanders are being served under the label of autism almost three times as often (4.63%) as the average for the Asian/Pacific Islanders with disabilities (1.72%). Conversely, American Indian and Hispanic students with autism are served under this label less frequently (0.67% and 10.04% respectively) than students within their racial groups having any kind of disability (1.24% and 13.93% respectively). These data are presented in a logarithmic chart to display differences within each reported race rather than between races (see Fig. 2).

It is well known that individual states exert autonomy in classifying students with disabilities, which could explain some of the regional variability found in the following data: Oregon reported 0.26% of the estimated resident population as having autism, where American Samoa reported only 0.01%. Without additional information regarding how these data were obtained and what they actually represent, no firm conclusions can be made. However, some critical questions seem to surface regarding the discrepancies in numbers of minority students who are being served under the IDEA, 1997 label of autism. Are there actual differences in the prevalence of autism across races? How are individuals with autism being categorized ethnically (e.g. Asians and Pacific Islanders being considered as one group under IDEA, 1997)? Are families from some minority cultures reluctant to have their children identified as having autism or identified as having a disability at all? Do families of some socioeconomic groups advocate for a diagnosis of autism rather than mental retardation to avoid a stigma? Are diagnosticians more likely to give the diagnosis of autism to children from some minority cultures than others? Are some characteristics of autism not considered to be problematic by people of some cultures (e.g. avoiding eye contact, or displaying hyperactivity or aggressive behaviors), resulting in the

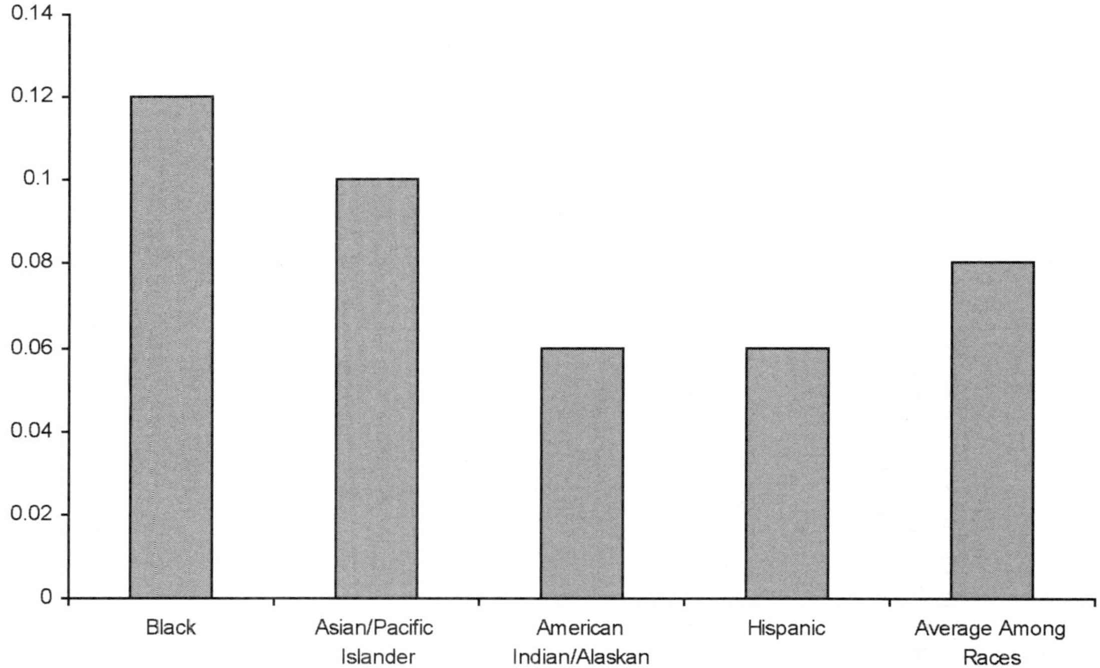

Fig. 1. Percentage (Based on Estimated Resident Population) of Students with Autism aged 6–21 Served under IDEA, Part B, During the 1998–1999 School Year.

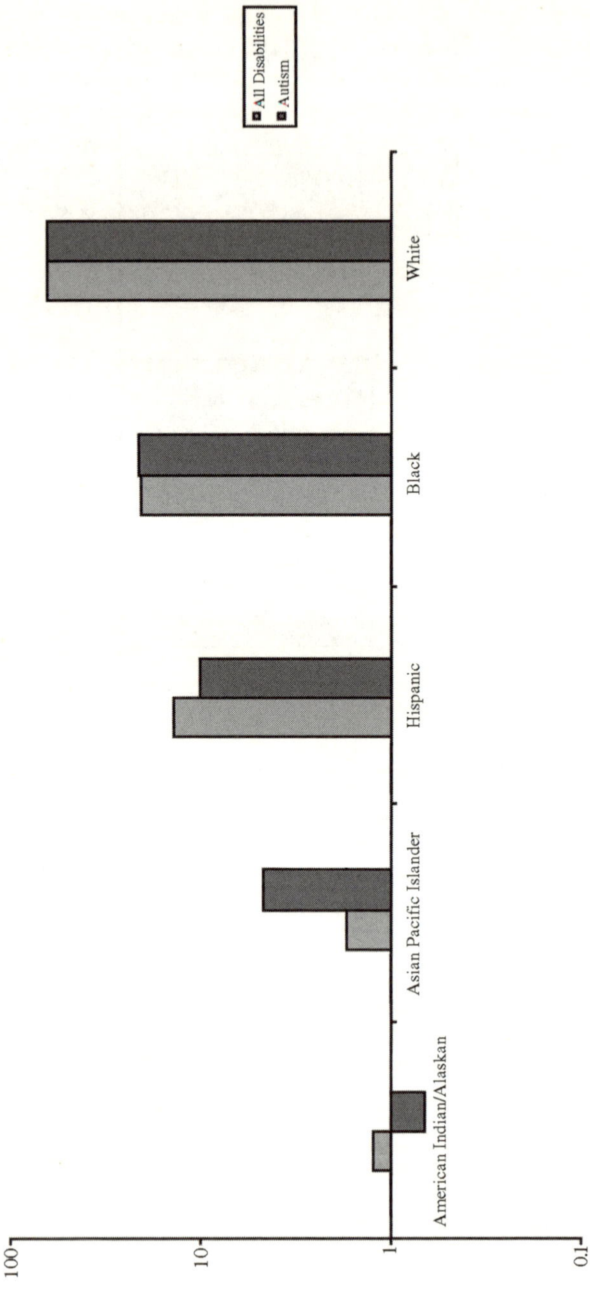

Fig. 2. Percentage of Students with Autism aged 6–21 Served under IDEA, Part B, During the 1998–1999 School Year, by Racial Category.

child not being referred? Are some of these children being served under different classifications (e.g. mental retardation, developmental delay, multiple disabilities, emotional disorder) rather than under the classification of autism?

Clearly, attention to racial classification of individuals with autism, whether they be in Western countries or not, has been largely ignored, and current research has not fully investigated the relationships, if any, between the genetic etiologies of autism and an individual's race. Although research has not supported the psychogenic etiology referred to by Sanua (1981a, b, 1984) when he implicated the isolated family-raising practices in Western civilizations, attention to differences in family adaptation between races is warranted.

MULTICULTURAL FAMILY ADAPTATION TO AUTISM

The literature is replete with reports regarding how families adapt to raising a child with developmental disabilities (Bennett, DeLuca & Allen, 1996; Olsen et al., 1999; Seligman, 1999). Few reports, however, distinguish autism from other developmental disabilities. It is crucial for autism to be isolated as its own group within the adaptation research, as it is known to be a more debilitating disorder than many of the others (Randall & Parker, 1999), thus having different effects on family members' adaptation.

Family adaptation researchers are just beginning to recognize race as a separate variable for exploration. The Resiliency Model of Family Stress, Adjustment, and Adaptation was developed to address issues of ethnicity and culture in the adaptation of multicultural families with low socioeconomic status. The Resiliency Model is an extension of earlier models that were based primarily on the study of Caucasian, middle-class families. It "emphasizes the family's appraisal processes involving ethnicity and culture that facilitate the family's ability to institute new patterns of functioning and achieve harmony while promoting the well-being and development of its members" (McCubbin, McCubbin, Thompson & Thompson, 1998, p. 5). For a full discussion of the Resiliency Model, readers are referred to the 1998 book, *Resiliency in Native American and Immigrant Families* by McCubbin, Thompson, Thompson and Fromer. The Resiliency Model is comprised of two phases: adjustment and adaptation. Within each phase are many interacting components that shape the processes and outcomes for families. In short, family *adjustment* is determined by the interaction between the stressor and the family's vulnerability, patterns of functioning, resources, appraisal of the stressor, and problem-solving and coping strategies. Family *adaptation* to a stressor is determined by the interaction between the pileup of demands created by the situation, the family's resources, appraisal of the situation, paradigms, sense of coherence, schema, and problem-solving and coping repertoire. Two interacting components (i.e. family appraisal of the stressor and social support) are particularly pertinent to discussions in this chapter. These components deserve attention due to cultural differences that appear to exist in appraising disability and in accessing social support. The paucity of research linking race, family adaptation, and autism necessitates the discussion of developmental disabilities in general and autism in particular.

Family Appraisal of the Stressor

A component of the adjustment phase of the Resiliency Model, a stressor has been identified as a "demand placed on the family that produces, or has the potential of producing, changes in the family system" (McCubbin et al., 1998, p. 6). Stressors are not necessarily negative life events, but within the Western context of disability, they are often regarded as such (Connors & Donnellan, 1998). Families raising children with autism are impacted differently by the stressor of receiving the child's diagnosis than are families raising children with other developmental disabilities. Because many children with autism are born without any indication of behavioral, physical, or intellectual abnormalities, their parents have "normal" expectations for them. Unlike parents who are informed of their child's disability near the time of the child's birth (e.g. Down syndrome and cerebral palsy), parents of children with autism deal with the stressor of losing their previously "normal" child. The severity of the stressor is determined by the degree to which it "threatens the stability of the family unit, disrupts the functioning of the family unit, or places significant demands on and depletion of the family's resources and capabilities" (McCubbin et al., 1998, p. 6). It has been stated that "there are few developmental disorders of childhood that create such complex stressors for families as autism (Randall & Parker, 1999, p. 1). These stressors are complex because the disability is hidden behind a normal or even "beautiful" appearance, behavioral manifestations may be physically and emotionally taxing on the family, diagnosis may be difficult to obtain, and coordination of services is often fragmented (see Randall & Parker).

Obviously, when the child's symptoms of autism are extreme, a high level of stress is felt by the family (Bristol, 1984), and the parents are likely to appraise their situation early. Appraisal is defined as "the family's definition of the seriousness of a stressor and its related hardships" (McCubbin et al., 1998, p. 6). The stressor of autism may be appraised differently between and among members of various cultures. These appraisals may be considered to be positive or negative. For instance, a negative appraisal after learning that a child is not developing normally follows the medical model of diagnosing and treating the malady. The child is seen as "not right," "imperfect," or "defective," and thus needing to be "fixed." Other negative appraisals consider the child to be a burden or a threat to the family (Rogers-Dulan & Blacher, 1995). Interestingly, negative appraisals are found across cultures. One type of appraisal is generated by the interpretation of the etiology of a child's disabilities. Green, Sack and Pabrum (1981) reported that some Mojaves believe mental retardation and other birth defects are due to misdeeds of parents. Some Navajos are reported to believe the child's autism may be the fault of parents or a result of witchcraft. Beliefs that the mother may have seen a dead animal while pregnant or that the child was conceived by a man other than the mother's husband have also been reported (Connors & Donnellan, 1998).

Reports of Latino mothers' interpretations of the etiologies of severe disabilities vary from positive to negative appraisal. Young Latino mothers who have immigrated to the United States from Puerto Rico and Mexico report that older generations, "ignorant people," and people from other places still believe mental retardation or developmental disability is a punishment for sin. However, young Latino mothers accept the child as a blessing or gift from God, feeling that they have been found worthy of such a child or that they have been given this challenge to become a better person (Skinner, Bailey, Correa & Rodriguez, 1999). The spiritual and religious paradigm of these mothers, heavily influenced by Catholicism, may have strongly affected their appraisal of their children with disabilities. Much like Mary, Saint and Sufferer, these Latino mothers see themselves as dedicated, sacrificing, and suffering, but good mothers of their children.

The family paradigm within the Native Hawaiian culture regarding the spiritual orientation toward life may facilitate individual families' appraisal that having a child with autism is "normal" and that this child is a valued member of the community, regardless of his or her abilities. Similarly, the Native American paradigm focuses on the functional abilities, albeit minute, of the children, rather than on their disabilities (McCubbin et al., 1998). The Native American/Native Hawaiian assimilation of individuals with disabilities into the mainstream culture is reflected in the absence of native language "labels" or "classifications" for disabilities such as autism. Rather, descriptive statements are commonly used by the Navajos, such as, "she runs away," or "he gets excited" or "he's in his own world" (Connors & Donnellan, 1998, p. 171).

African American families whose religions strongly influence their family paradigms may appraise disability positively. "The optimism and belief that all children are important typifies African American culture and is reflected in family functions and reinforced in church and religious beliefs" (Rogers-Dulan

& Blacher, 1995, p. 234). As it appears, the literature provides some answers regarding appraisal of developmental disabilities within some cultures, however, similar reports are not readily available regarding the appraisal of autism. Because appraisal of autism is directly related to social support and resulting adaptation, research in this area is warranted.

Social Support

Social support is a component of the adaptation phase of the Resiliency Model, and is defined as the community supports and resources "that the family may use to cope with a stressor situation" (McCubbin et al., 1998, p. 20). Social support may include people, such as family and friends, and organizations, such as schools, churches, parent and sibling support groups, and medical services. Social support, which has been studied extensively in the literature, appears to mediate the effects of the stressor on the health of the family (see McCubbin et al., 1998).

Family support. The strong familial support needed to raise a child with developmental disabilities is found in many cultures. Native Hawaiians share a common concern for the wellbeing of all individuals in the tribal structure, which encompasses the immediate and extended family (McCubbin et al., 1998). Similarly, the foundation of the family structure in Filipino American families is built upon cooperation and family support and allegiance, where individual desires are sacrificed for the benefit of the family (McCubbin et al., 1998).

Many individuals within the African American culture perceive care-giving for a dependent member as a responsibility to be shared among siblings and extended family members (Pruchno, Patrick & Burant, 1997). The paucity of adaptation research with African American families who have a member with a disability (Rogers-Dulan & Blacher, 1995) is striking; however, such research on autism is even more rare. In the same dimension, the concept of "familismo" in Hispanic families relates to strong family cohesion. This familial cohesion may circumvent the use of professional services if family values conflict with standards of the majority culture (Blacher, Lopez, Shapiro, & Fusco, 1997). When Latino mothers of children with severe disabilities believe in their spiritual role as "sacrificing mothers," and if they receive strong support from their extended family, they may take upon themselves the responsibility of raising their child with little organizational support (Bailey, Skinner, Rodriguez, Gut & Correa, 1999; Skinner et al., 1999).

Organizational support. Reliance upon organizational support varies according to many factors, including familial support and familiarity with the majority culture. Bailey et al. (1999) reported that Latinos have a lower probability of receiving services than African American families who have children with disabilities, and that the predicting factor is not socioeconomic status, but familiarity with the majority culture. According to the 22nd Annual Report to Congress cited earlier (United States Department of Education, 2001), Hispanic students with autism are served under this label approximately half as often as students with autism who are Black or Asian/Pacific Islander. It appears that for cultural or other reasons, the population of Hispanic students with autism is not being served in ways that other children are being served. Given the reported rate of 40% single parenthood in Latino families with a child with mental retardation, along with twice as much depression as other population estimates (Blacher et al., 1997), it appears that the current social support system may be failing to meet some critical needs of these families.

Highly discrepant rates of identification of multicultural children with autism may be related to the stigma that is attached to receiving a diagnosis. For example, some South Asian families may not refer their children for services, especially if their child is a girl, for fear that they may not be able to arrange a marriage (Raghavan, Weisner & Patel, 1999). Fear of stigma has also been reported in African American families (Pruchno et al., 1997). These African American families tend to access services provided by professional organizations less frequently than the majority culture (see Pruchno et al., 1997) and only after relying on family, friends, religion, and church support (Rogers-Dulan & Blacher, 1995). However, their caregiver burden and level of stress are less than those of Whites, and their satisfaction is greater, while caring for children with developmental disabilities (see Pruchno et al.; Rogers-Dulan & Blacher). As a consequence, professionals in the field of autism should try to ascertain how families from various cultures appraise their child with autism. This knowledge, along with the knowledge of how these families perceive their need for and access to social support, will lead to more effective treatment and education of multicultural students with autism.

Culture-Specific Strategies for Teaching Students with Autism

The differences in prevalence rates across multicultural groups reported in the 22nd Annual Report to Congress provide rationale for teachers to attend to multicultural issues when teaching students with autism. Two reasons for this attention are: (1) the possibility of misclassification, and (2) potential interaction of students with autism with others in the dominant culture.

To explicate the first reason, students with autism may be misclassified, perhaps because of culture. School personnel need to recognize whether the label of autism is occurring more or less frequently with students from various multicultural groups. Since the advent of P.L. 94-142 in 1975, students with autism have been classified and served under disability labels other than autism because the law did not recognize it as a category. In 1990, when the law was reauthorized (IDEA, P.L. 101-476), autism was introduced as a category (Smith, 1998). Students with autism may have been and may still be misclassified as students with mental retardation, multiple disabilities, serious emotional disturbance, communication disorders, or other designations. Proper identification and placement of students with autism are critical to appropriate instructional programming. If some multicultural students (e.g. African Americans) are identified as having autism more frequently than would be expected given the prevalence of autism in other cultures and the assumption that autism occurs across all demographic groups, then professionals should be aware of behaviors that may be interpreted in terms of a cultural base (Obiakor, 1999a). Tantrums, aggression, lack of normal attachment to family members, lack of eye contact, poor social interactions and communication skills, and lack of appropriate emotional expression are behaviors that some students with autism display that may have cultural bases or may indicate other disabilities. Having considered these behaviors in cultural contexts, professionals should be careful that the student is properly classified as having autism. Professionals should be aware that these behaviors might cause a multicultural student to be misidentified as having autism or a student with autism to be misidentified in another disability category.

The second reason multicultural factors should be considered when teaching students with autism is that, like most students, students with autism will probably live and work within the dominant culture. A Western long-term goal for students with autism, even the many who have severe disabilities, is to eventually hold a job in the community (Feldman, 1996; Westling & Fox, 1995). Teachers of multicultural students with autism should be aware that family expectations may be different. Members of some cultures do not value independence and community-based competence, and they should not be forced to adopt such educational goals. However, unless the multicultural child with autism is segregated from the dominant culture, he or she will need to interact with people in this culture. Therefore, if Individualized Education Program (IEP) team members agree, teachers might be encouraged to use strategies that teach students with autism appropriate social interactions and communication skills for the dominant culture within which they may live and work as adults. Since there is a dearth of professional literature delineating culture-specific strategies for teaching students with autism in particular, we have looked at the literature on strategies for teaching multicultural students with disabilities in general and, with caution, have focused that information in terms of the needs of students with autism. Following are universal strategies suggested for teachers who work with multicultural students with disabilities, with implications for teachers of students with autism: cultural understanding, teacher expectations, language issues, and cultural pluralism in curriculum.

Cultural Understanding

The first and foremost consideration for any professional who works with multicultural students with disabilities is to be aware of personal prejudices toward certain groups (Obiakor, 1994). These biases may be toward students of a particular disability, race, gender, socioeconomic status, ethnicity, religion, geographic region, appearance, and national origin. Teachers may feel prejudiced toward students with autism who are dirty, who disrupt class with their unorthodox behavior, who lack social skills valued by the dominant culture, or whose parents are exceptionally verbal in their behalf. Teachers may even engage in prejudice toward students with autism as a disability group because of their difficult behaviors or because the students come from multicultural groups that they dislike. As a result, they must examine personal views and be absolutely certain that their views are not interfering with the effectiveness of their teaching students with autism (Wilder, in press).

Personal and professional biases may substantially affect the education and treatment of individuals with autism. During the psychogenesis era of autism, professional bias against "refrigerated mothers" of children with autism resulted in removal of these children from their homes in order to receive specialized treatment. This bias against mothers is no longer popular; in fact, parents are now requested to be an integral part of the decision-making process for their students with autism (IDEA, 1997). Parents from some multicultural groups may be treated prejudicially by teachers and may be uncomfortable being involved in educational decisions for their children. To deal with these issues either way, it is imperative that teachers examine their own largely Western views regarding multicultural groups and work to gain sensitivity toward their multicultural students and their parents, regardless of the level of parental involvement (Winzer & Mazurek, 1998).

Teacher Expectations

Teacher expectations are powerful determinants of student outcomes, especially in special education (Ford, 1992; Obiakor, 1999b). If a teacher believes that a student with a disability such as autism, from a certain multicultural or socioeconomic group, will perform less effectively in the classroom than the other students in the same class, then that student will probably fulfill the teacher's expectations (Brophy, 1986). When teachers expect high academic and behavioral achievements from their multicultural students, the students tend to deliver (Lucas, Henze, & Donato, 1990). Of course, students with autism may have some limitations related to their disability; however, it is better for teachers to err on the side of expecting too much rather than settling for academic and behavioral achievement that is less than what the student can achieve. A student's multicultural background should never restrict a teacher's expectation of his/her performance or limit his/her future options (Obiakor, 2001).

Language Issues

A discussion of teaching strategies for teaching multicultural students with autism must include consideration of their communication and language abilities and skills. Language is an area on the IEP for most students with autism since problems in communication are common to students with this disability (American Psychiatric Association, 1994). Teaching strategies for multicultural students with autism should be matched with the strengths and difficulties delineated by a comprehensive communication and language assessment using a norm-referenced or criterion-referenced instrument or checklist, an interview, and an observation (Venn, 2000).

If the student's native language is not English, a bilingual diagnostic professional should conduct the assessment, if possible. Assessing any form of communication will be difficult with students with autism for whom English is not their native tongue. The overrepresentation of bilingual students in special education suggests that diagnostic personnel have difficulty distinguishing between disabling conditions and language behaviors characteristic of students learning a second language (Carrasquillo, 1991). Assessment practices identifying such students as having autism should include both a native language and an English language assessment to determine which language should be used to communicate with the student (Delgado & Rogers-Adkinson, 1999). In addition to assessing the student's communication and language abilities, an ecological assessment of the communication needs in the natural environments that the student with autism will encounter assists the IEP team in making decisions regarding language (Westling & Fox, 1995). Diagnostic personnel should be aware that identifying multicultural students with Asperger Syndrome may be problematic since their deficits are in pragmatics and social skills. If assessment of their abilities is confounded with second-language or other cultural behaviors, they may not be accurately identified.

If a student is identified as having autism and determined by the assessment to lack sufficient English fluency to understand academic and behavioral concepts, then an English as a Second Language (ESL) teacher and the special education or general education teacher must collaborate to implement educational and behavioral interventions. Students are likely to benefit from the services of a speech and language pathologist, depending on the results of the assessment. Placing the student with a bilingual special or general educator would be optimal, but the shortage of bilingual educators is extensive (Baca & Cervantes, 1998; Grossman, 1995), causing school administrators to hire bilingual persons in nonprofessional school roles to assist teachers with translation and communication. As a consequence, teaching strategies for students with autism for whom English is not their native language and for other multicultural students should be aligned to assessment results. Strategies to improve communication may include but should not be limited to ESL instruction available in the school district, bilingual special educator instruction (Winzer & Mazurek, 1998), use of picture communication systems or alternative communication (Snell & Brown, 2000), curricular materials in both languages, and periodic ongoing language assessment (see Baca & Cervantes). The development of social skills may be enhanced by using peer buddy or special grouping arrangements, mentor strategies and strategies for teaching resilience (Campbell-Whatley, Algozzine & Obiakor, 1997; Gordon, 1995; Guetzloe, 1997), and cooperative learning, acculturation experiences, and prosocial skills training for the dominant culture (Goldstein, 1999).

Cultural Pluralism in Curriculum

Multicultural students frequently lament that none of the textbooks, stories, or pictures used in their schools included students like them; this actually affects how they feel about themselves (Obiakor, 2001). It is important that those with autism have access to curricular materials that reflect their cultures, so they feel that they belong to the school community just like students from the dominant culture (Winzer & Mazurek, 1998). School assemblies, field trips, classroom visitors, posted text, pictures, flyers, school newsletters, and school personnel should offer a smorgasbord of cultural representation. Multiculturalism should be infused throughout the school context (see Obiakor; Winzer & Mazurek). Besides infusing multicultural representation in schools, teachers need to assess and to teach to individual student cognitive or learning styles to meet the needs of multicultural students with autism. These cognitive styles may be related both to student culture and to disability. Many students with autism prefer to communicate through visual rather than auditory receptive modes. Students from various cultures prefer various culture-relevant cognitive styles. Teachers who ignore the cultural implications of a particular cognitive style will probably be less effective than those who recognize both culture- and disability-related approaches.

Once broad-based strategies and individual strategies are functional, the most valuable strategy of all for teaching multicultural students with autism is to view each individual student positively: as able to progress and willing to learn (Wilder, 2001). Students with autism from multicultural backgrounds should be seen as and treated as valuable members of school communities who are assisted to maximize their human potential. This is the role of a teacher. Kozol (2001) remarked, "Children, whatever the color of their skin or the condition of their birth, bless us by their mere existence on this earth. The great, unanswered question of our age is whether our societies [schools] plan to bless them in return" (p. 2). The critical question is how do teachers develop this positive attitude toward multicultural students with autism? The attitude toward multicultural students with autism begins to form in their training programs.

IMPLICATIONS FOR TEACHER PREPARATION PROGRAMS

Students with autism demonstrate deficits in social skills, communication skills, and behavioral repertoires (Wahlberg, 2000; Wahlberg & Rotatori, 1996). In 1994, the American Psychiatric Association noted that autism coexists with mental retardation in approximately 75% of the cases. Considering the multidimensionality of characteristics associated with autism, it is reasonable to assume that identification, assessment, categorization, placement, and instruction/intervention must be problematic. Although general and special educators are trained to respond to students' unique needs (Obiakor & Algozzine, 1995), they find it difficult to shift their paradigms and try new ideas (Kohl, 1988; Palmer, 1998; Utley & Obiakor, 2001). As a consequence, many multicultural learners with autism are placed in programs prone to frequent misidentification, miscategorization, misplacement, and misinstruction/misintervention (Obiakor, 1999a, 2001). There are underlying reasons for these mishaps. Obiakor and Utley (2001) noted that there is a "severity of the supply-and-demand problem associated with professionals representing different cultural groups in doctoral programs in institutions of higher education" (p. 191). Thus, theoretical rather than practical efforts have been made to change teacher preparation programs. As Obiakor and Utley emphasized, "There is a critical need to rethink traditional teacher preparation programs and develop a culturally responsive teacher preparation program" (2001, p. 191).

Problems for multicultural learners with autism are triple-layered – these students are culturally different, they are linguistically different, and they have an exceptionality that appears loaded with challenging behavioral repertoires. These problems are magnified as teacher preparation programs emphasize a knowledge base in teacher trainees, but spend "very little time teaching the skills that will enable them to effectively apply that knowledge in different classroom settings" (Obiakor & Utley, 2001, p. 192). In addition, negative presumptions about multiculturalism have interfered with the infusion of multicultural curricula in teacher preparation programs. Approximately one decade ago, Obiakor (1993) provided some typical examples:

(1) Universities cannot find qualified culturally diverse faculty for recruitment.
(2) It is a preferential treatment to adopt policies to recruit and retain minority faculty, staff, and students.
(3) Multicultural curriculum is expensive.
(4) Multicultural curriculum is not necessary because racism does not exist anymore.
(5) Advocates of multiculturalism want to lower the quality of education.

These presumptions are counterproductive because they force teacher preparation programs to engage in "fraudulent" multiculturalism by which institutions pay lip service or engage in tokenism.

If the intention is to prepare teachers who can truly serve students with autism, efforts must be made to produce culturally responsive teacher education programs. It is important that students with autism are appropriately identified, assessed, categorized, placed, and instructed, as one simple problem of misreferral can lead to bigger problems of misplacement and misinstruction. Just as it is unfair to use the wrong medication for the right illness or the right medication for the wrong illness (Ysseldyke, Algozzine & Thurlow, 2000), it is a disservice to label students with autism as having mental retardation, behavior disorders, learning disabilities, communication disorders, or other forms of disabilities. General and special educators must be well prepared to be culturally sensitive as they identify and interpret behavioral patterns. Obiakor and Utley (2001) explained that a culturally responsive teacher preparation program involves the following:

(1) Teachers who think and act multiculturally rather than monoculturally.
(2) Teachers who develop curricula that are multicultural rather than monocultural in content.
(3) Teachers who use methods that are congruent with the students' cultural learning styles and who reflect about the relevance of knowledge bases in a variety of cultural contexts.

(4) Teachers who understand that becoming a multicultural educator is a developmental process.
(5) Teachers who understand and respect their own cultural heritage and develop the knowledge, skills, and attitudes to become functional within other ethnic cultures as well as the mainstream culture.
(6) Teachers who understand that multicultural education will enable them to believe in their intrinsic worth, to transcend monoculturalism, and to become multicultural.
(7) Teachers who are willing to learn about customs, belief systems, communication, and linguistic styles, mores, and behavior patterns of different cultural groups. They are willing to internalized a methodology for adapting to and learning about many other cultures from which their pupils may come.
(8) Teachers who are willing to develop a curriculum that includes elements of different cultural groups.
(9) Teachers who identify dominant culturally influenced cognitive styles and how to recognize the individual student variances from the dominant cognitive styles of that student's culture.
(10) Teachers who view multicultural students as capable, motivated and resilient.
(11) Teachers who are change agents who work to fight injustice, social inequality, and inequities (p. 194).

What, then, should be the knowledge base for diversity in teacher education programs? We cannot teach what we do not know (Obiakor, 2001). Earlier, Smith (1998) noted several areas for focus:

(1) Foundations of multicultural education.
(2) Sociocultural contexts of human growth and psychological development in marginalized ethnic and racial cultures.
(3) Cultural and cognitive learning style theory and research.
(4) Language, communication and interactional styles of marginalized cultures.
(5) Essential elements of cultures.
(6) Principles of culturally responsive teaching and culturally responsive curriculum development.
(7) Effective strategies for teaching ethnically diverse students.
(8) Foundations of racism.
(9) Effects of policy and practice on culture, race, class, gender, and other categories of diversity.
(10) Culturally responsive diagnosis, measurement, and assessment.
(11) Sociocultural influences on subject-specific learning.

It is important to note that what happens in classrooms is tied to how teachers are prepared (Obiakor, Karr, Utley & Algozzine, 1998; Obiakor & Utley, 1997, 2001). A child who has autism and who is culturally, racially, linguistically, and socioeconomically different requires a special kind of teacher to effectively address these complex phenomena. Obiakor and Utley (2001) wrote:

> Given the nature of diversity and the dramatic demographic changes within America's classrooms, we are aware that general and special educators will be challenged to provide quality instruction to all children. However, we cannot accept a "deficit orientation" as a fundamental principle upon which we base the implementation of individualized, appropriate educational programs for children with disabilities. . . . General and special educators must be trained to identify alterable factors (e.g. student engagement levels and use of teacher behaviors that decelerate student outcomes) that promote student learning and enhance responsiveness to instruction. Hence, general and special educators must learn through culturally responsive teacher preparation programs to apply pedagogical practices that accommodate students' needs and maximize the academic progress of all children, especially those who come from multicultural backgrounds (p. 204).

Some critical questions should be addressed by teachers, especially as they work with multicultural students with autism in order to meet current demands and challenges:

(1) How do we build on the established knowledge base?
(2) How do we examine the classroom culture?
(3) How do we plan and deliver classroom instruction?
(4) How do we negotiate the roles of teaching?
(5) How do we build self-concepts through self-efficacy?
(6) How do we enhance learning with technologies and resources?
(7) How do we work beyond the classroom?
(8) How do we shift paradigms and powers?

As general and special educators work with students with autism, it is imperative that they know the functional levels of their students. On this issue, teacher preparation programs must be on the cutting edge, requiring at least the following courses for preservice and inservice trainings:

(1) Crisis intervention (e,.g., courses dealing with disruption, disaster, and death)
(2) Collaboration, consultation, and cooperation
(3) Issues and trends in special education
(4) Multicultural psychology and special education
(5) Self-concept development
(6) Parental empowerment strategies
(7) Survey of exceptionality (i.e. opportunities to develop in-depth/overall information about exceptionalities such as autism)

(8) Multidimensional assessment strategies
(9) Multiple intelligences
(10) Comprehensive Support Model (i.e. how the "self," family, school, community, and government can function together for the common good) (see Wilder, in press).

RESEARCH CONCERNS

Professionals who work with multicultural students with autism and their families should be concerned about the relative paucity of research specific to the challenges they face. Published research often determines what will be taught and which interventions will be used with students with autism. First, professionals need to be certain multicultural students are properly classified as having autism. Then, they need to know which interventions work best for them. Because the majority of special education research has been conducted with populations that are predominantly Anglo and because most research has categorized students according to disability and failed to categorize students with autism according to culture, limited data seem to be available to help researchers and practitioners ensure that appropriate services are provided to students with autism from diverse backgrounds. Such limitations may reflect a lack of awareness of cultural issues (Wilder, Jackson & Smith, in press) and of ways that those issues impact students with autism and their families. In addition, such missing information clearly compromises the quality of the fields of professionals who work with multicultural students with autism.

CONCLUSIONS

This chapter has perhaps raised more questions than it has answered, not unusual for the initial examination of an ubiquitous issue. It was not our intention to attempt to solve the problems of multicultural students with autism but to examine multicultural issues for students with autism, their families, and the professionals who work with them. To our knowledge, this comprehensive discussion of these issues is the first of its kind in print. Honestly, we were surprised to see the differences in prevalence rates across races for autism (United States Department of Education, 2001) and assert that further investigation of prevalence disparities is warranted. The questions raised in the beginning of the chapter need to be investigated further. Are there actual differences in the prevalence of autism across races? How are individuals with autism being categorized ethnically? Are families from some minority cultures reluctant to have their children identified as having autism, or identified as having a disability at all? Do families of some socioeconomic strata advocate for a diagnosis of autism rather than mental retardation to avoid the resulting stigma? Are diagnosticians more likely to give the diagnosis of autism to children from some minority cultures than to others? Are some characteristics of autism not considered to be problematic by people of some cultures resulting in some children not being referred? Are some of these children being served under different classifications rather than under the classification of autism? In addition, what are effective teaching strategies for properly classified multicultural students with autism? How can teacher preparation programs attend to multicultural issues for students with autism?

Evidence suggests that multicultural students have more difficulty with the academic and behavioral customs of the school culture than students from the dominant culture. Our examination of multicultural perspectives in autism demonstrates that ethnic diversity may impact students with autism. Students with multicultural backgrounds and autism are challenged on three dimensions: communication, exceptionality, and culture. The professional literature continues to address the first two; it is imperative to now consider the third, multicultural perspectives.

REFERENCES

American Psychiatric Association (1994). *Diagnostic and statistical manual of mental disorders* (4th ed.). Washington, D.C.: author.

Autism Society of America (2000). What is autism? *Advocate: The Newsletter of the Autism Society of America, 33*(6), 3.

Baca, L. M., & Cervantes, H. T. (1998). *The bilingual special education interface* (3rd ed.). Upper Saddle River, NJ: Prentice-Hall.

Bailey, D. B., Skinner, D., Rodriguez, P., Gut, D., & Correa, V. (1999). Awareness, use, and satisfaction with services for Latino parents of young children with disabilities. *Exceptional Children, 65*, 367–381.

Bennett, T., DeLuca, D. A., & Allen, R. W. (1996). Families of children with disabilities: Positive adaptation across the lifecycle. *Social Work in Education, 18*, 31–44.

Bettelheim, B. (1967). *The empty fortress: Infantile autism and the birth of the self.* New York: The Free Press.

Blacher, J., Lopez, S., Shapiro, J., & Fusco, J. (1997). Contributions to depression in Latino mothers with and without children with retardation: Implications for caregiving. *Family Relations, 46*, 325–334.

Bristol, M. M. (1984). Family resources and successful adaptation to autistic children. In: E. Schopler & G. B. Mesibov (Eds), *The Effects of Autism on the Family* (pp. 289–310). New York: Plenum Press.

Brophy J. (1986). Teacher influences on student achievement. *American Psychologist, 41*, 1069–1077.

Campbell-Whatley, G. D., Algozzine, B., & Obiakor, F. E. (1997). Using mentoring to improve academic programming for African American male youths with mild disabilities. *The School Counselor, 44*, 362–366.

Carrasquillo, A. L. (1991). *Hispanic children and youth in the United States: A resource guide*. New York: Garland.

Connors, J. L., & Donnellan, A. M. (1998). Walk in beauty: Western perspectives on disability and Navajo family/cultural resilience. In: H. I. McCubbin, E. A. Thompson, A. I. Thompson & J. E. Fromer (Eds), *Resiliency in Native American and Immigrant Families* (pp. 159–182). Thousand Oaks, CA: Sage.

Delgado, B. M., & Rogers-Adkinson, D. (1999). Educating the Hispanic-American exceptional learner. In: F. E. Obiakor, J. O. Schwenn & A. F. Rotatori (Eds), *Advances in Special Education: Multicultural Education for Learners with Exceptionalities* (Vol. 12, pp. 53–71). Stamford, CT: JAI Press.

Feldman. D. (1996). *Instruction of children and youth who have severe disabilities: A manual for student teachers*. Bloomington, IN: Educational Technology Resources.

Fombonne, E. (1998). Epidemiological surveys of autism. In: F. R. Volkmar (Ed.), *Autism and Pervasive Developmental Disorders* (pp. 32–63). Cambridge, United Kingdom: Cambridge University Press.

Ford, B. A. (1992). Multicultural education training for special educators working with African-American youth. *Exceptional Children, 59*, 107–114.

Gillberg, C., Steffenberg, S., & Schaumann, H. (1991). Is autism more common now than ten years ago? *British Journal of Psychiatry, 158*, 403–409.

Goodman, R., & Richards, H. (1995). Child and adolescent psychiatric presentations of second-generation Afro-Caribbeans in Britain. *British Journal of Psychiatry, 167*, 362–369.

Goldstein, A. P. (1999). *The prepare curriculum: Teaching prosocial competencies*. Champaign, IL: Research Press.

Gordon, K. A. (1995). Self-concept and motivational patterns of resilient African American high school students. *Journal of Black Psychology, 21*, 239–256.

Green, B. E., Sack, W. H., & Pabrum, A. (1981). A review of child psychiatric epidemiology with special reference to American Indian and Alaska Native children. *White Cloud Journal, 2*(2), 22–36.

Grossman, H. (1995). *Special education in a diverse society*. Needham Heights, MA: Allyn & Bacon.

Guetzloe, E. (1997). The power of positive relationships: Mentoring programs in the school and community. *Preventing School Failure, 41*(3), 100–105.

Heller, T., Markwardt, R., Rowitz, L., & Farber, B. (1994). Adaptation of Hispanic families to a member with mental retardation. *American Journal on Mental Retardation, 99*, 289–300.

IDEA (1997). Individuals with Disabilities Act Amendments of 1997, Pub. L. No. 105-17. June 4, 1997 20 U. S. C., 1412.

Kanner, L. (1985). Autistic disturbances of affective contact. In: A. M. Donnellan (Ed.), *Classic Readings in Autism* (pp. 11–52). New York: Teachers College Press. (Original work published 1943.)

Kanner, L. (1985). Follow-up study of eleven autistic children originally reported in 1943. In: A. Donnellan (Ed.), *Classic Readings in Autism* (pp. 223–235). New York: Teachers College Press. (Original work published 1971.)

Kohl, H. (1988). *Growing minds: On becoming a teacher*. New York: Harper Touchbooks.

Kozol, J. (2001). A call to action. *Reaching Today's Youth: The Community Circle of Caring Journal.* [On-line]. Available: www.nesonline.com/rty.call.html

Lucas, T., Henze, R., & Donato, R. (1990). Promoting the success of Latino language-minority students: An exploratory study of 6 high schools. *Harvard Educational Review, 60,* 315–340.

McBride, P. A., Anderson, G. M., & Hertzig, M. E. (1998). Effects of diagnosis, race, and puberty on platelet serotonin levels in autism and mental retardation. *Journal of the American Academy of Child and Adolescent Psychiatry, 37,* 767–776.

McCubbin, H. I., McCubbin, M. A., Thompson, A. I., & Thompson, E. A. (1998). Resiliency in ethnic families: A conceptual model for predicting family adjustment and adaptation. In: H. I. McCubbin, E. A. McCubbin, A. J. Thompson & J. E. Fromer (Eds), *Resiliency in Native American and Immigrant Families* (pp. 3–48). Thousand Oaks, CA: Sage.

Obiakor, F. E. (1993). Multiculturalism: Critical issue facing teacher education programs. In: *Bueno Center for Multicultural Education Monograph Series* (Vol. 9, No. 1, pp. 1–16). Boulder, CO: University of Colorado.

Obiakor, F. E. (1994). *The eight step multicultural approach: Learning and teaching with a smile.* Dubuque, IA: Kendall/Hunt.

Obiakor, F. E. (1999a). Multicultural education: Powerful tool for educating learners with exceptionalities. In: F. E. Obiakor, J. O. Schwenn & A. F. Rotatori (Eds), *Advances in Special Education: Multicultural Education for Learners with Exceptionalities* (pp. 1–14). Stamford, CT: JAI Press.

Obiakor, F. E. (1999b). Teacher expectations of minority exceptional learners: Impact on "accuracy" of self-concepts. *Exceptional Children, 66,* 39–53.

Obiakor, F. E. (2001). *It even happens in "good" schools: Responding to cultural diversity in today's classrooms.* Thousand Oaks, CA: Corwin Press.

Obiakor, F. E., & Algozzine, B. (1995). *Managing problem behaviors: Perspectives for general and special education.* Dubuque, IA: Kendall/Hunt.

Obiakor, F. E., Karr, S., Utley, C., & Algozzine, B. (1998). The requirements and demands of being an educator. In R. J. Anderson, C. E. Keller & J. M. Karp (Eds), *Enhancing Diversity: Educators with Disabilities* (pp. 142–154). Washington, D.C.: Gallaudet University Press.

Obiakor, F. E., & Utley, C. A. (1997). Rethinking preservice preparation for teachers in the learning disabilities field: Workable multicultural strategies. *Learning Disabilities Research and Practice, 12,* 100–106.

Obiakor, F. E., & Utley, C. A. (2001). Culturally responsive teacher preparation programming for the twenty-first century. In: C. A. Utley & F. E. Obiakor (Eds), *Special Education, Multicultural Education, and School Reform: Components of Quality Education for Learners with Mild Disabilities* (pp. 188–207). Springfield, IL: Charles C. Thomas.

Olsen, S., Marshall, E. S., Mandleco, B., Allred, K. W., Dyches, T. T., & Sansom, N. (1999). Support, communication, and hardiness in families with children with disabilities. *Journal of Family Nursing, 5,* 275–291.

Palmer, P. J. (1998). *The courage to teach: Exploring the inner landscape of a teacher's life.* San Francisco: Jossey-Bass.

Powell, J., Edwards, A., Edwards, M., Pandit, B. S., Sungum-Paliwal, S. R., & Whitehouse, B. S. (2000). Changes in the incidence of childhood autism and other autistic spectrum disorders in pre-school children from two areas of the West Midlands, U.K. *Developmental Medicine and Child Neurology, 42,* 624–628.

Prizant, B. (1996). Brief Report: Communication, language, social, & emotional development. *Journal of Autism and Developmental Disorders,* 26, 173–178.

Pruchno, R., Patrick, J. H., & Burant, C. J. (1997). African American and White mothers of adults with chronic disabilities: Caregiving burden and satisfaction. *Family Relations*, *46*, 335–346.

Raghavan, C., Weisner, T. S., & Patel, D. (1999). The adaptive project of parenting: South Asian families with children with developmental delays. *Education and Training in Mental Retardation and Developmental Disabilities*, *34*, 281–292.

Randall, P., & Parker, J. (1999). Supporting the families of children with autism. New York: John Wiley & Sons.

Rimland, B. P. (1964). *Infantile autism*. New York: Appleton-Century-Crofts.

Rogers-Dulan, J., & Blacher, J. (1995). African American families, religion, and disability: A conceptual framework. *Mental Retardation*, *33*, 226–238.

Sanua, V. D. (1981a). Autism, childhood schizophrenia and culture: A critical review of the literature. *Transcultural Psychiatric Research Review*, *18*, 165–181.

Sanua, V. D. (1981b). Cultural changes and psychopathology in children: with special reference to infantile autism. *Acta Paedopsychiat*, *47*, 133–142.

Sanua, V. D. (1984). Is infantile autism a universal phenomenon? An open question. *International Journal of Social Psychiatry*, *30*, 163–177.

Seligman, M. (1999). Childhood disability and the family. In: V. L. Schwean & D. H. Saklofske (Eds), *Handbook of Psychosocial Characteristics of Exceptional Children* (pp. 111–131). New York: Plenum.

Skinner, D., Bailey, D. B., Correa, V., & Rodriguez, P. (1999). Narrating self and disability: Latino mothers' construction of identities vis-à-vis their child with special needs. *Exceptional Children*, *65*, 481–495.

Smith, D. D. (1998). *Introduction to special education: Teaching in an age of challenge* (3rd ed.). Boston, MA: Allyn & Bacon.

Snell, M. E., & Brown, F. (2000). *Instruction of students with severe disabilities* (5th ed.). Upper Saddle River, NJ: Prentice-Hall.

Szatmari, P., & Jones, M. B. (1998). Genetic epidemiology of autism and other pervasive developmental disorders. In: F. R. Volkmar (Ed.), *Autism and Pervasive Developmental Disorders* (pp. 109–129). Cambridge, United Kingdom: Cambridge University Press.

United States Department of Education (2001). *Twenty-Second Annual Report to Congress on the Implementation of the Individuals with Disabilities Education Act*. Washington, D.C.: Author.

Utley, C. A., & Obiakor, F. E. (2001). *Special education, multicultural education, and school reform: Components of quality for learners with mild disabilities*. Springfield, IL: Charles C. Thomas.

Venn, J. J. (2000). *Assessing students with special needs* (2nd ed.). Upper Saddle River, NJ: Prentice-Hall.

Volkmar, F. R., & Lloyd, C. (1998). Diagnosis and definition of autism and other pervasive developmental disorders. In: F. R. Volkmar (Ed.), *Autism and Pervasive Developmental Disorders* (pp. 1–31). Cambridge, United Kingdom: Cambridge University Press.

Wahlberg, T. (2000). Intervention techniques for individuals with autism in inclusive settings. In: F. E. Obiakor, A. S. Burkhardt, A. F. Rotatori & T. Wahlberg (Eds), *Intervention Techniques for Individuals with Exceptionalities in Inclusive Settings* (pp. 217–237). Stamford, CT: JAI Press.

Wahlberg, T., & Rotatori, A. (1996). Various treatment modalities for autistic individuals. In: A. F Rotatori, J. O. Schwenn & S. Burkhardt (Eds), *Assessment and Psychopathology Issues in Special Education* (pp. 109–131). Greenwich, CT: JAI Press.

Westling, D. L., & Fox, L. (1995). *Teaching students with severe disabilities*. Englewood Cliffs, NJ: Prentice-Hall.

Wilder, L. K. (in press). The homeless are people too: Including homeless students in educational programming. In: P. Grant, F. E. Obiakor & E. Dooley (Eds), *Educating All Our Children: Refocusing the Comprehensive Support Model*. Champaign, IL: Charles C. Thomas.

Wilder, L. K. (2001). Success in college for students with disabilities. *Theories and Practices in Supervision and Curriculum*, *12*, 31–34.

Wilder, L. K., Jackson, A., & Smith, T. (in press). Multicultural transition of secondary exceptional learners: A Navajo Native American experience. *Preventing School Failure*, *45*(3).

Wing, L. (1980). Childhood autism and social class: A question of selection? *British Journal of Psychiatry*, *137*, 410–417.

Wing, L., & Attwood, A. (1987). Syndromes of autism and atypical development. In: D. J. Cohen & A. M. Donnellan (Eds), *Handbook of Autism and Pervasive Developmental Disorders* (pp. 3–19). New York: Wiley.

Winzer, M. A., & Mazurek, K. (1998). *Special education in multicultural contexts*. Upper Saddle River, NJ: Prentice-Hall.

Ysseldyke, J. E., Algozzine, B., & Thurlow, M. L. (2000). *Critical issues in special education* (3rd ed.). Boston: Houghton Mifflin.

PART 3:
CLINICAL INTERVENTION CONSIDERATIONS

DIAGNOSIS AND ASSESSMENT OF AUTISTIC SPECTRUM DISORDERS

Julie A. Deisinger

Autistic spectrum disorders (ASD), also known as pervasive developmental disorders (Wetherby & Prizant, 2000), include the diagnostic categories of Autistic Disorder, Rett's Disorder, Childhood Disintegrative Disorder, Asperger's Disorder, and Pervasive Developmental Disorder Not Otherwise Specified (American Psychiatric Association, 2000). Genetic factors, abnormalities in brain structure and biochemistry, and complications during pregnancy have been implicated as possible causes of these syndromes (Alloy, Jacobson & Acocella, 1999; Papalia, Olds & Feldman, 2001; Wing, 1997). Epidemiological studies conducted since 1970 estimate that ASD affect from 0.1% to 1% of the general population (Kadesjo, Gillberg & Hagberg, 1999; Tanguay, 2000). Each of these conditions involves serious impairments in social interaction and communication skills, accompanied by restricted interests or repetitive behaviors (American Psychiatric Association, 2000).

The most recent revision of the *Diagnostic and Statistical Manual of Mental Disorders* (DSM-IV-TR; American Psychiatric Association, 2000) provides specific guidelines for the classification of autistic spectrum disorders. The most commonly occurring of these, Autistic Disorder, requires that five diagnostic criteria be met. First, at least two aspects of social interaction must be deficient, such as lack of eye contact, inappropriate use of facial expression or body language, difficulties in developing and maintaining friendships, or failure to exhibit social reciprocity. Second, there must be significant impairment in communication skills, as evidenced by either a lack of spoken language or a delay in language development, inability to initiate or sustain conversations, a

Autistic Spectrum Disorders: Educational and Clinical Interventions, pages 181–209.

ISBN: 0-7623-0818-4

tendency to repeat certain words or phrases, or the lack of imaginative or imitative play. The third diagnostic criterion for Autistic Disorder specifies either the presence of an unusual pattern of interests (such as an abnormal preoccupation with a particular topic or a persistent fascination with parts of objects), a rigid adherence to unusual routines, or repetitive patterns of unusual bodily movements (such as flapping or twisting the hands or fingers). Fourth, the aforementioned symptoms must be apparent before three years of age. Finally, Autistic Disorder cannot be diagnosed if criteria for either Rett's Disorder or Childhood Disintegrative Disorder are met.

Rett's Disorder occurs far less often than Autistic Disorder and reportedly affects only females (American Psychiatric Association, 2000; Harris, Glasberg & Ricca, 1996). Individuals with this condition appear to be developing normally until five months old. Between five months and four years of age, however, a decline in the rate of head growth occurs. In addition, persons with Rett's Disorder display a loss of purposeful hand movements and a decline in social interaction, accompanied by the appearance of repetitive hand-wringing gestures, uncoordinated gait, and slowed movements. These individuals also exhibit serious deficits in both expressive and receptive language.

Childhood Disintegrative Disorder is very uncommon, but is more typically found among males (American Psychiatric Association, 2000; Filipek et al., 1999). Persons who receive this diagnosis develop normally through two years of age, after which they demonstrate significant losses in the areas of language, motor skills, adaptive behavior, play, and bladder or bowel control. These decrements in ability must be evident by ten years of age. Furthermore, problems with social interaction and communication as well as restricted interests or repetitive mannerisms must be present.

Studies on the prevalence of Asperger's Disorder suggest that at least 80% of affected persons are male (Harvard Mental Health Letter, 1999). This condition shares two of the criteria required for Autistic Disorder, namely, marked deficits in social interaction and the presence of either restricted interests or stereotyped movements. Such impairments must seriously hinder social, occupational, or other types of functioning. In contrast to Autistic Disorder, however, persons with Asperger's Disorder do not exhibit significant delays in language or cognitive development. Additionally, a diagnosis of Asperger's Disorder cannot be made if criteria are met for another ASD or for schizophrenia (American Psychiatric Association, 2000).

In some instances, symptoms associated with ASD may be evident but all of the criteria needed for any single diagnostic category may not be present. For example, age of onset may be later than usual, or symptoms of the disorder may be atypical or of milder severity. Such cases are classified as a Pervasive

Developmental Disorder Not Otherwise Specified (PDD-NOS; American Psychiatric Association, 2000).

IMPORTANCE OF ACCURATE DIAGNOSIS

According to Lord and Risi (2000), the diagnosis of ASD accomplishes several ends. First, it facilitates the scientific study of such disorders so that noteworthy differences among these conditions can be identified. In addition, a diagnostic classification enables clear communication among professionals who work with developmentally disabled individuals. Perhaps most importantly, diagnosis may allow families of persons with an ASD to obtain treatment services.

Unfortunately in many cases, correct identification of an ASD may not occur for several years (Bax, 1999). A recent survey of 770 families in the United Kingdom (Howlin & Asgharian, 1999) revealed that parents of children with Autistic Disorder or Asperger's Disorder began to notice developmental abnormalities when their children were 18 months and 30 months of age, respectively. Despite these parents' efforts to learn the nature of their children's difficulties, however, the average age of diagnosis was $5\frac{1}{2}$ years for children with Autistic Disorder and 11 years for those with Asperger's Disorder. Similar delays in diagnosis reportedly exist in other European countries and in North America (Bax, 1999).

Some individuals with ASD may not be correctly identified until adulthood. In the sample surveyed by Howlin and Asgharian (1999), 28 individuals reportedly were not diagnosed as having either autism or Asperger's Disorder until they were over 20 years old; one of these did not receive the proper diagnosis until age 41. Misdiagnosis also may occur, due to similarities in the symptoms of these and other psychiatric disorders. For example, features of Asperger's Disorder such as eccentric behaviors, fluctuating mood, and rigid habits may be mistaken for symptoms of schizophrenia, mania, anxiety disorders, obsessive-compulsive disorder, or schizoid personality disorder (Perlman, 2000; Ryan, 1992; Wolff, 1991). The possibility that an ASD may coexist with another psychiatric condition (e.g. see Atlas & Gerbino-Rosen, 1995) further complicates the process of diagnosis.

Serious adverse consequences may result from delayed identification of ASD. Parents of affected individuals may be unable to access services for their children and obtain support for themselves. They may not receive information about effective methods of behavioral management, thus compounding their children's behavioral problems. Also, because ASD have an underlying genetic basis (Filipek et al., 1999; Simonoff, 1998; Tanguay, 2000; Volkmar, Klin & Pauls, 1998; Wing, 1997), these parents need to be informed about the possibility that their other offspring might be affected. Furthermore, children with developmental delays who are not identified as such may not receive appropriate instruction at school. If these children's teachers are unaware of their diagnoses, they may use unsuitable teaching methods or may punish these children for unusual behaviors. Such circumstances could then lead to rejection by peers, loss of self-esteem, or depression (Howlin & Asgharian, 1999).

Delayed diagnosis makes negative outcomes more likely (Howlin & Asgharian, 1999). Therefore, if an ASD is suspected, an accurate diagnosis should be obtained as soon as possible. A comprehensive assessment can help to identify specific symptoms, thereby facilitating a differential diagnosis among the various subtypes of pervasive developmental disorder. Additionally, a thorough assessment allows for the identification of individual strengths and deficits so that an appropriate course of treatment can be devised and implemented. The assessment process should include specialists with expertise in ASD from a variety of disciplines such as psychiatry, psychology, neurology, pediatrics, occupational therapy, physical therapy, speech pathology, and special education (Filipek et al., 1999; Greenspan & Wieder, 1999). Interdisciplinary collaboration is important due to the variety of needs and problems that families of children with pervasive developmental disorders may experience. However, one treatment provider should be designated to oversee and coordinate the assessment, so that duplication of effort can be avoided (Filipek et al, 1999; Volkmar et al., 1999). Also, parents of children suspected of having an ASD should be closely involved throughout the assessment process (Filipek et al., 1999; Klin, Sparrow, Marans, Carter & Volkmar, 2000).

GENERAL SCREENING PROCEDURES

Screening for an ASD is usually the first step in the assessment process. Primary care providers should routinely screen all infants, toddlers, and preschoolers to check for the presence of a pervasive developmental disorder (Filipek et al., 1999). Filipek et al. (1999) recommended that initial evaluation should involve the use of such general developmental screening instruments as the Ages and Stages Questionnaire, Second Edition (Bricker & Squires, 1999), the Child Development Inventories (Ireton, 1992), the Parents' Evaluation of Developmental Status (Glascoe, 1998), or the Brigance Screens (Brigance, 1986). The latter instrument can be used to check for developmental problems in children aged two to seven years and has demonstrated a high degree of accuracy in identifying preschoolers with developmental difficulties (Glascoe, 1997). All of the aforementioned questionnaires have been found to have good reliability and validity and can be completed by parents in about 10 minutes or less (Filipek et al., 1999).

Parental reports about a child's behavioral problems, difficulties with social development, or delays in speech or language development should be assessed more completely. In addition, the presence of the following behaviors in children warrants further assessment immediately: absence of babbling or gesturing by one year of age, failure to use single words by age 16 months, the lack of spontaneous two-word speech by age two years, or any loss of language or social skills at any age (Filipek et al., 1999).

Routine care providers also should carefully evaluate any child who has an older sibling that has already been diagnosed with an ASD, even if parents report no concerns about the younger child. If an older child in the family has severe symptoms of such a disorder, parents may not recognize milder symptoms in a younger sibling. As emphasized by Filipek et al. (1999), family history is one of the most important determinants of at-risk status for an ASD, due to the absence of definitive signs or tests for these disorders.

Children with identified developmental delays should receive an audiologic evaluation to determine whether language delays are due to hearing loss. However, it is important to recognize that autism and hearing loss can co-occur, and to consider other factors such as impaired social functioning and unusual behaviors when making a differential diagnosis (Filipek et al., 1999).

Some children with developmental delays may exhibit a condition called pica, characterized by persistent eating of nonnutritive substances (American Psychiatric Association, 2000). These children should be periodically screened for lead poisoning, since elevated levels of lead in the bloodstream may play a role in the onset or exacerbation of autistic symptoms (Filipek et al., 1999).

SPECIFIC SCREENING INSTRUMENTS FOR AUTISTIC SPECTRUM DISORDERS

When general screening measures indicate the need for further assessment, follow-up evaluations may involve other screening instruments that have been specifically designed to detect symptoms associated with ASD. One such instrument is the Checklist for Autism in Toddlers (CHAT; Baron-Cohen, Allen & Gillberg, 1992). The first section of this measure contains nine questions for parents, such as whether their child appears interested in other children, seeks interaction with parents, or engages in imaginative play. The second section consists of five observations that can be made by an evaluator, such as whether the child expresses interest in a toy, complies with a request, or participates in a pretend game. Results of one study (Cox et al., 1999) indicated that 18-month-old children who were identified as autistic on the basis of the CHAT were found to have either autism or other language delays at 42 months of age;

however, this instrument failed to detect 60% of children in that study who were later diagnosed with autism (Tanguay, 2000). Also, other authors (e.g. Baird et al., 2000; Filipek et al., 1999) reported that the CHAT may fail to identify children with Asperger's Disorder or PDD-NOS.

An as-yet unpublished instrument called the Pervasive Developmental Disorders Screening Test-Stage 1 (PDDST; Siegel, 1998, cited in Filipek et al., 1999) is available through its author and can be used in primary care settings to evaluate children up to three years of age. This measure gathers information not tapped by the CHAT, by including questions about developmental regression and the presence of positive as well as negative symptoms. For example, the PDDST asks parents whether their child performs unusual repetitive movements, which might not be witnessed by an evaluator during an assessment session (Filipek et al., 1999).

The Autism Screening Questionnaire (ASQ; Berument, Rutter, Lord, Pickles & Bailey, 1999), offers the advantage of being available in two versions: one for persons under six years of age and another for those over age six. Its 40 questions are based on items from a semistructured clinical interview called the Autism Diagnostic Interview-Revised (ADI-R; Lord, Rutter & LeCouteur, 1994). These items examine aspects of reciprocal social interaction, communication, and repetitive behaviors. Both the reliability and validity of the ASQ are reportedly good, and the instrument succeeds in differentiating pervasive developmental disorders from other kinds of diagnoses. However, it cannot be used to distinguish between autism and other forms of developmental disorders (Berument et al., 1999).

Because the preceding three instruments are not specifically intended to detect Asperger's Disorder, two other screening measures can be used. The High-functioning Autism Spectrum Screening Questionnaire (ASSQ; Ehlers & Gillberg, 1993, Ehlers, Gillberg & Wing, 1999) is a 27-item checklist that assesses for Asperger's Disorder and other forms of high-functioning autism by asking parents and teachers about symptoms such as restricted interests, literal interpretation of metaphors, clumsiness, social naivete, and difficulties with peer relationships in spite of a desire for friendships. Both the parent and teacher forms of the ASSQ have been found to successfully distinguish children with ASD from those with attention-deficit or other disruptive behavior disorders. Cut-off scores of 13 for parent ratings and 11 for teacher ratings identified approximately 90% of mild cases of ASD in a recent study (Ehlers et al., 1999). The likelihood of failure to detect a true case of Asperger's Disorder in using the ASSQ is reportedly small (Kadesjo et al., 1999). Still, the authors of this instrument cautioned that it must not be used as the sole measure for diagnosis (Ehlers et al, 1999).

Another measure that can be used to screen for Asperger's Disorder is the Australian Scale for Asperger's Syndrome (ASAS; Garnett & Attwood, 1995, cited in Attwood, 1998). Like the ASSQ, this instrument can be completed by parents, teachers, and other treatment providers who are well acquainted with the child being assessed. Respondents are asked to rate various aspects of the child's social, emotional, cognitive, and motor behaviors on a 0-to-6 scale, with scores of 0 indicating that the behavior in question is rarely evident and scores of six denoting that it is frequently observed. If the majority of items are rated two or higher, further evaluation is indicated (Attwood, 1998).

A screening instrument used to differentiate Autistic Disorder from other developmental disorders is being developed. The Screening Tool for Autism in Two-Year-Olds (STAT; Stone, 1998, cited in Filipek et al., 1999) differs from the screening devices previously discussed in that it is an observational method rather than a questionnaire. Administration of the STAT involves a 20-minute play interaction to examine pretend and reciprocal play, imitation of movements, and nonverbal communication. Filipek et al. (1999) reported that in a pilot study using the STAT, 100% of children with autism and 97% of children with other forms of developmental delay were correctly classified. This instrument is being further refined to determine optimal scoring procedures.

INTERVIEWS TO ASSESS ASD

If screening devices suggest that an in-depth assessment is necessary, detailed information should be gathered concerning the child's birth, developmental, medical, and family histories (Filipek et al., 1999; Klin et al., 2000; Volkmar et al., 1999; Wicks-Nelson & Israel, 2000). Mild obstetrical complications (e.g. toxemia, vaginal bleeding, induced labor, breech position, forceps or cesarian delivery, among others) have been largely ruled out as causal factors in the development of ASD (Filipek et al., 1999). Nevertheless, several authors (e.g. Filipek et al., 1999; Klin et al, 2000; Volkmar et al., 1999) indicated that information concerning the pregnancy and neonatal period should be obtained.

Information pertaining to developmental history should note ages at which important developmental milestones were achieved and whether the child has exhibited any regression in development at any time. Previous evaluations should be reviewed to obtain an impression about the course of development over time (Klin et al., 2000; Volkmar et al., 1999). Klin et al. (2000) recommended that questions about developmental history should be tied to specific memorable events (e.g. the child's birthdays) to improve parents' recall in relation to developmental issues.

Questions about medical history should inquire about unusual physical features, seizures, possible exposure to lead, and disturbances in sleep, eating, or mood. Medical examination should check for the presence of unusual muscle tone, poor coordination, and repetitive motions (Filipek et al., 1999). A mental status exam should be performed on the client being evaluated, with particular attention devoted to assessing the person's social and communication abilities, adaptability to change, patterns of restricted interest, unusual mannerisms, distractibility, and mood (Filipek et al., 1999; Volkmar et al., 1999).

When obtaining background about family history, it is essential to ask whether any members of either the nuclear or extended family have been diagnosed with autism, mental retardation, Fragile X syndrome, or tuberous sclerosis. As was reported earlier, ASD tend to run in families (Filipek et al., 1999). Children with Fragile X syndrome, a condition caused by malformation or breakage of the X chromosome (Alloy et al., 1999), often exhibit symptoms associated with autism (Filipek et al., 1999). Tuberous sclerosis, which manifests in the form of abnormal tumor-like growths in the cerebral cortex, skin, heart, kidneys, and other organ systems, also has been linked to autism. Medical examination for this condition involves examination of the skin for characteristic lesions that are visible only under ultraviolet light (Filipek et al., 1999).

Two structured clinical interviews exist for the purpose of assessing ASD. The Parent Interview for Autism (PIA; Stone & Hogan, 1993) is comprised of 118 items that assess social behavior, communication abilities, and repetitive movements. Administration of this measure requires about 30 to 45 minutes (Mesibov, Adams & Klinger, 1997), and its psychometric properties are reportedly adequate (Filipek et al., 1999).

The second clinical interview for pervasive developmental disorders is the Autism Diagnostic Interview-Revised (ADI-R; Lord et al., 1994). Its five sections can be used to examine communication abilities, social development, play behavior, repetitive movements, and behavioral problems in individuals from ages 18 months through adulthood. This semistructured interview, which was designed in accordance with DSM-IV diagnostic criteria for autism (Lord et al., 1994), is reported to have good psychometric properties (Volkmar & Marans, 1999). In fact, the ADI-R has been called the "gold standard" diagnostic instrument for use in research on ASD (Filipek et al., 1999, p. 459). However, it is not widely used in clinical practice due to the time requirement of an hour or more for its administration, as well as the need for special training in its administration and scoring (Filipek et al., 1999; Lord et al., 1994; Volkmar & Marans, 1999).

CHECKLISTS AND RATING SCALES

One of the earliest rating scales devised to assess autism is the Childhood Autism Rating Scale (CARS; Schopler, Reichler, DeVellis & Daly, 1980), which can be used to assess children over two years of age (Western Psychological Services, 2001). It consists of 15 items that examine behaviors associated with autism such as impairment in relationships, use of stereotypic movements, resistance to change, lack of eye contact, and unusual verbalizations such as echolalia and pronoun reversal (Schopler et al., 1980). A professional evaluator observes a child during the initial diagnostic appointment. Immediately afterward, he or she rates each CARS scale on a 4-point continuum from 1 (behavior within normal limits) to 4 (severely abnormal behavior). Total scores for the CARS range from 15 to 60, with scores of 30 or more indicating a diagnosis of autism. Reliability and validity for this rating scale are reported to be good (Schopler et al., 1980; Trevarthen, Aitken, Papoudi & Robarts, 1996; Volkmar & Marans, 1999), although Volkmar and Marans (1999) mentioned that inter-rater reliability has not been adequately examined. A problem associated with use of the CARS is its tendency to incorrectly classify non-autistic children with mental retardation as autistic (DiLavore, Lord & Rutter, 1995; Volkmar & Marans, 1999). Therefore, this rating scale may be more appropriately utilized as a screening device rather than as a diagnostic measure (Volkmar & Marans, 1999).

The Autism Behavior Checklist (ABC; Krug, Arick & Almond, 1980, cited in Volkmar & Marans, 1999) is an instrument intended for use by teachers as a component of educational planning. Comprised of 57 items, this measure evaluates sensory and relational symptoms of autism, use of the body and objects, language use, and self-help abilities (Volkmar & Marans, 1999). ABC items have different weights assigned to them, with higher weights given to items more strongly associated with autism (Yirmiya, Sigman & Freeman, 1994). The ABC was designed to distinguish persons with autism from the general population, as well as from persons with mental retardation, blindness, deafness, or serious emotional disturbance. A total score of 67 or more suggests probable autism, whereas a score between 55 and 67 indicates possible autism. Advantages of this checklist include its ease of administration and scoring; however, questions have been raised about its reliability and validity (Volkmar & Marans, 1999).

Like the CARS, the ABC may be better used as a screening device than as a diagnostic method (Volkmar & Marans, 1999). In addition, because both the CARS and the ABC were designed for use with severely handicapped populations, neither of these instruments should be used to assess milder forms of ASD such as Asperger's Disorder (Klin et al., 2000; Luteijn, Luteijn, Jackson, Volkmar & Minderaa, 2000; Yirmiya et al., 1994).

A checklist that can be used to diagnose persons with autism is the Gilliam Autism Rating Scale (GARS; Gilliam, 1991, cited in Carr, 1999; Pro-Ed, 2001). This measure examines autistic symptoms and their severity in persons aged 3 through 22 years. Scale items were created to correspond with DSM-IV criteria for autism, and are grouped into three core subtests: Stereotyped Behaviors, Communication, and Social Interaction. An optional fourth subtest, Developmental Disturbances, gathers information about developmental history from birth to age three. Intended for use by parents, teachers, and mental health professionals, this rating scale can be completed in five to 10 minutes. Reliability and validity information about the GARS suggest that it is psychometrically strong (Pro-Ed, 2001).

For children who have already been diagnosed with autism, the Revised Behavior Summarized Evaluation Scale (BSE-R; Barthelemy et al., 1997) can be employed to examine behavior change and responses to treatment across time. This measure is intended for use by members of a treatment team, such as psychiatrists, psychologists, teachers, and therapists. These professionals rate each of the BSE-R's 29 items on a 5-point scale to indicate the frequency of symptomatic behaviors. Examples of behaviors that are assessed by this scale include problematic social interaction, poor eye contact, failure to communicate verbally, use of stereotyped utterances and movements, resistance to change, sleep disturbances, and difficulties with mood (Berthelemy et al., 1997).

Recently, three instruments were created specifically to assess children with less severe forms of pervasive developmental disorder. One such measure, the Gilliam Asperger's Disorder Scale (GADS; Gilliam, 2001, cited in Pro-Ed, 2001; Online Asperger Syndrome Information and Support/OASIS, 2000), can be completed by parents or by professionals who are familiar with a child suspected of having Asperger's Disorder (Pro-Ed, 2001). Normed on over 100 individuals with Asperger's Disorder, the 40-item GADS contains scales to examine a child's early developmental history, cognitive patterns, restricted behaviors, and pragmatic abilities (OASIS, 2000; Pro-Ed, 2001). Test responses yield standard scores and percentiles that can be evaluated to determine the likelihood that a child has Asperger's Disorder (Pro-Ed, 2001).

The Asperger Syndrome Diagnostic Scale (ASDS; Myles, Bock & Simpson, 2001, cited in Pro-Ed, 2001; OASIS, 2000), contains 50 yes/no items designed to assess language, cognitive abilities, social interactions, maladaptive behaviors, and sensorimotor functioning in persons aged five to 18 years. Parents, teachers, speech-language pathologists, and mental health providers can complete the instrument in 10 to 15 minutes. Respondents' answers on the ASDS can be deemed valid only when they are well acquainted with the person being evaluated. This instrument yields an "AS Quotient" (Pro-Ed, 2001, p. 30) that denotes the likelihood of Asperger's Disorder, with higher scores indicating an increased probability of the disorder. Other uses of the ASDS include identification of specific behaviors to target for intervention, and measurement of treatment outcomes (Pro-Ed, 2001).

A third new rating scale is the Children's Social Behavior Questionnaire (CSBQ; Luteijn, Jackson, Volkmar & Minderaa, 1998; Luteijn et al., 2000), which was devised specifically to assess for the presence of PDD-NOS. The CSBQ can be completed by parents or caregivers of children with ASD. Its 96 items comprise five subscales that examine disruptive behavior, social interaction problems, difficulties in recognizing social cues, resistance to change, and stereotyped behaviors. The authors of this instrument stated that its reliability and validity are satisfactory. However, discriminant analyses that were reported in Luteijn et al. (2000) indicated that only about 27% of children diagnosed as PDD-NOS could be correctly classified on the basis of the CSBQ, with almost 29% misclassified as autistic and roughly 24% misclassified as having Attention Deficit Hyperactivity Disorder. In addition, correlations between CSBQ scales and DSM-IV criteria for PDD were reportedly weaker than expected. Therefore, this instrument may require further development to investigate the effects of such factors as age, gender, and IQ on CSBQ scores (Luteijn et al., 2000).

OBSERVATIONAL ASSESSMENT METHODS

Naturalistic observations should be a component of the assessment process when evaluating someone for the possibility of an ASD. Such observations should not be limited to interactions between the person and the evaluator, but should include interactions between the examinee and familiar individuals such as family members and peers. By making observations in a variety of situations, the evaluator can gain a better understanding of the examinee's communicative and social skills (Filipek et al., 1999).

Wicks-Nelson and Israel summarized the steps needed to conduct an evaluation of environmental factors that might be pertinent to the functioning of children with autism. These included: (1) identification of environments usually encountered by the child, (2) division of these environments into sub-environments, (3) identification of important activities associated with cach subenvironment, and (4) identification of skills needed so that the child can participate in these activities. Wicks-Nelson and Israel (2000) listed the following procedures to evaluate skills that a child with autism might need for a given activity. These include: (1) analysis of skills that persons with normal development use during the activity, (2) use of observation to identify skills that the child can perform, (3) comparison of the child's performance to that of individuals with normal development in order to identify missing abilities, and (4) evaluation of possible adaptations that might be used to assist the child during the activity.

Videotaped observations also can play an important part in a comprehensive assessment by allowing evaluators to view the behaviors of persons with ASD on multiple occasions and in a variety of settings (Volkmar et al., 1999). Videotapes of very young children may even provide early indications of ASD. In a 1998 study, Teitelbaum, Teitelbaum, Nye, Fryman, and Maurer systematically analyzed videotapes of 17 children with autism who had been diagnosed at approximately three years of age. The videotapes, recorded during the children's infancy, reportedly revealed developmental disturbances in sitting, crawling, and walking that were evident long before a diagnosis of autism was made. Some children displayed movement disturbances as early as four to six months old, and others reportedly demonstrated movement disturbances at birth. Teitelbaum et al. (1998) asserted that analysis of movement disturbances might enable early diagnosis of autism, thereby making it possible to begin therapeutic interventions during the first months of life.

The Autism Diagnostic Observation Schedule (ADOS; Lord, Rutter, DiLavore & Risi, 2001, cited in Western Psychological Services, 2001), permits standardized observations of persons suspected of having ASD. The current version of the ADOS combines two previously separate instruments (see DiLavore et al., 1995, and Lord et al., 1989) into one measure consisting of four modules (Lord et al., 2000). Each module contains a series of structured activities to be observed over a 35 to 40 minute period. Only one module is administered to an examinee, depending on the person's age and language abilities. The first module is intended for use with nonverbal children, the second is to be used with children who speak in phrases but are not verbally fluent, and the third is for children who have fluent language abilities. Module 4 is designed for use with verbally fluent adolescents and adults. The only group of persons with ASD who cannot be assessed with the ADOS are nonverbal teens and adults (Western Psychological Services, 2001).

Observations recorded during an ADOS administration are scored to determine the examinee's DSM-IV diagnosis, with defined cut-off scores for both Autistic Disorder and the broader concept of ASD (Filipek et al., 1999; Lord et al., 2000). This measure reportedly has excellent reliability and good discriminant validity (Lord et al., 2000). Like the Autism Diagnostic Interview-Revised (ADI-R), the ADOS is considered a "gold standard" instrument for the diagnosis of ASD, especially for research purposes (Filipek et al., 1999, p. 459). However, because it can be administered more quickly than the ADI-R, the ADOS is more likely to be used for clinical diagnoses (Filipek et al., 1999). Potential users should be aware that the ADOS requires specialized training in administration and scoring procedures before it can be used (Western Psychological Services, 2001). However, according to Klinger and Renner

(2000), such efforts are worthwhile because structured observations allow for valid detection of autistic symptoms across various evaluators. In addition, such observations supplement diagnostic information obtained from instruments that rely solely on parental reports.

INTELLECTUAL ASSESSMENT

From 76 to 89% of persons with autism have IQs below 70 (Alloy et al., 1999). Therefore, evaluation of intellectual functioning to identify or rule out the presence of mental retardation is a necessary element of a comprehensive assessment for persons with ASD (Klin, Carter & Sparrow, 1997, cited in Carter et al., 1998).

The Wechsler intelligence scales are among the most widely used instruments for the assessment of intellectual functioning (Alloy et al., 1999). These scales consist of subtests to assess an examinee's verbal and nonverbal intellectual capacities (Sattler, 1992). Several studies have investigated the use of Wechsler scales to examine cognitive abilities in persons with ASD.

Ehlers et al. (1997) administered the Wechsler Intelligence Scale for Children-Revised (WISC-R; Wechsler, 1974, cited in Ehlers et al., 1997) to a sample of 120 children who ranged in age from five to 15 years old. Forty of these participants had been diagnosed with Asperger Syndrome, 34 with Autistic Disorder, and 36 with attention disorders. Examination of the test profiles indicated that participants with autism demonstrated peak scores on the Block Design subtest. In comparison to persons with autism, participants with Asperger Syndrome did significantly better on the Comprehension and Picture Arrangement subtests. However, persons with Asperger's performed poorly on the Object Assembly, Coding, and Arithmetic subtests (Ehlers et al., 1997).

Statistical analyses of participants' subtest scores allowed correct classification of almost 58% of the children with Asperger Syndrome, almost 80% of those with Autistic Disorder, and about 51% of those with attention disorders. Overall, 63% of the participants were correctly classified on the basis of subtest scores. However, Ehlers et al. (1997) emphasized the heterogeneity of the Wechsler profiles in their study, and commented that subtest patterns pertained to group findings rather than to individual profiles.

Siegel, Minshew, and Goldstein (1996) also reported variability in the Wechsler profiles of 45 children and 36 adults who had been diagnosed with autism on the basis of the Autism Diagnostic Interview. All of the participants in the study had Full Scale IQ and Verbal IQ scores of 70 or greater. For these individuals with high-functioning autistic disorder, the Comprehension subtest was usually the lowest score among the Verbal subtests, and either Picture

Arrangement or Coding/ Digit Symbol was typically the lowest subtest among the Performance subtests. High scores were usually obtained on Digit Span and Block Design. Still, no single Wechsler profile predominated. In contrast to what had typically been reported in earlier literature, most of the participants in this study did not exhibit significant differences between Verbal and Performance IQ scores. When significant differences did occur, VIQ>PIQ and PIQ>VIQ patterns were equally likely. Siegel et al. noted that in their study, the variability in IQ scores among persons with autism was similar in magnitude to the VIQ-PIQ differences found in the general population.

Barnhill, Hagiwara, Myles, and Simpson (2000) reported similar results in a study of 37 children with Asperger syndrome. These researchers found a high mean scaled score on the Block Design subtest and a low mean score on Coding. However, Wechsler profiles of the sample in this study did not reveal significant differences between Verbal and Performance IQ scores (Barnhill et al.).

Since there does not appear to be a typical pattern of Verbal versus Performance IQ scores associated with ASD, Siegel et al. (1996) cautioned that Wechsler tests should not be used to diagnose autism but should be administered for the purposes of educational placement or neuropsychological assessment. Item analysis of Wechsler protocols and review of examinees' behaviors and comments during the test administration may provide additional information about examinees' intellectual strengths and deficits (Barnhill et al., 2000).

The Stanford-Binet Intelligence Scale, Fourth Edition (SB:FE; Thorndike, Hagan & Sattler, 1986, cited in Sattler, 1992) is another commonly used test for the assessment of intellectual functioning. Intended for examinees aged 2 through 23 years, this instrument contains 15 subtests that measure verbal reasoning, abstract/visual reasoning, quantitative reasoning, and short-term memory (Sattler, 1992). According to Harris, Handleman, and Burton (1990), the SB:FE can provide helpful information about the cognitive abilities of children with autism. These authors found that children with autism obtained a characteristic profile on this battery. The Absurdities subtest, which measures attention to detail as well as social reasoning (Sattler, 1992), was typically their lowest score. Children with autism performed best on the Pattern Analysis subtest, which examines visual-motor and visual-spatial abilities (Harris et al., 1990; Sattler, 1992).

The intellectual functioning of non-verbal autistic children may be estimated by administering the Performance IQ subtests of the Wechsler instruments, or performance measures from either the SB:FE or the Kaufman Assessment Battery for Children (K-ABC; Kaufman & Kaufman, 1983, cited in Sattler, 1992). The latter test, which can be administered in 45 to 75 minutes, can be used with children ages two years, six months through 12 years, five months. One of its four scales, the Nonverbal Scale, consists of subtests from two other scales (Sequential Processing and Simultaneous Processing) that do not require language. The examiner gives instructions for this scale through gestures, and an examinee can respond by making appropriate movements (Sattler, 1992).

Another way to estimate the intelligence of non-verbal, minimally verbal, or deaf children with autism is through administration of the Leiter International Performance Scale (Leiter, 1948; Sattler, 1992; Wicks-Nelson & Israel, 2000). This measure, which can be administered in about 30 to 45 minutes, consists of 54 tasks arranged in an age-scale format from age two to 18. Like the Nonverbal Scale of the K-ABC, instructions for the Leiter are demonstrated through the use of gestures. The examinee must select blocks that display certain symbols and correctly arrange them on a frame. This test yields a Mental Age that can be used to calculate an IQ score, which correlates fairly well with scores from the Wechsler Intelligence Scale for Children (Sattler, 1992).

The Raven's Coloured Progressive Matrices (Raven, Court & Raven, 1986, cited in Sattler, 1992) is another tool that can be used to examine the reasoning abilities of children with autism who have minimal or no expressive language (Wicks-Nelson & Israel, 2000). This test contains 36 items that can be used with children ages five through 11 years. Each item presents the examinee with an array of symbols, in which one part is missing. The examinee must choose the missing piece from several options presented below the array. This test can be completed in about 15 to 30 minutes (Sattler, 1992).

The Bayley Scales of Infant Development (Bayley, 1969, 1993, cited in Papalia et al., 2001) may be used when evaluating the intellectual functioning of young or very low-functioning children with autism (Wicks-Nelson & Israel, 2000). The 1993 revision of this instrument can be administered to children from one month to $3\frac{1}{2}$ years of age, to examine mental, motor, and behavioral functioning (Papalia et al., 2001).

ASSESSMENT OF ADAPTIVE FUNCTIONING

Adaptive functioning refers to an individual's ability to handle common demands of daily living (American Psychiatric Association, 2000), as manifested in the domains of interpersonal relationships, performance at school or work, and use of leisure time (Bird, 1999). Evidence of significant deficits in adaptive functioning is needed to assign a diagnosis of Autistic Disorder, and to make a differential diagnosis between Autistic Disorder and Asperger's

Disorder (American Psychiatric Association, 2000). Also, as noted earlier, a majority of individuals with autism have significantly below-average IQ scores. To determine whether an extremely low IQ score is indicative of mental retardation, deficits in adaptive skills also must be present (American Psychiatric Association, 2000). Thus, an assessment of adaptive functioning should be included in a comprehensive evaluation of ASD.

In addition to diagnosis of mental retardation and ASD, evaluation of adaptive functioning serves several other important purposes. These include identification of an examinee's strengths and weaknesses for purposes of educational and treatment planning, monitoring of progress over time, and documentation about the usefulness of interventions (Carter et al., 1998).

Several instruments exist to facilitate examination of adaptive functioning. A general rating of functioning in children from four to 16 years of age can be assigned using the Children's Global Assessment Scale (CGAS; Shaffer et al., 1983). This rating scale resembles the Global Assessment of Functioning scale that is used when making a DSM-IV-TR multiaxial diagnosis. A clinician can use the CGAS to rate a child's adaptive functioning on a scale from 1-100. The scale is divided into 10 levels, each consisting of 10-point brackets. High scores are associated with good to superior functioning, and scores in the range of 71–80 indicate no more than mild impairment. Scores below 70 denote clinically significant difficulties in functioning, with lower scores representing serious impairments (Bird, 1999). Another version of this instrument has been devised for use by non-clinicians. Both versions of the scale are reported to have good psychometric properties (Bird, 1999).

The Columbia Impairment Scale (CIS; Bird et al., 1993) is another tool for rating functional abilities in children. One version of this measure can be administered directly to a child or adolescent. A similar version, with better psychometric properties, can be completed by a parent or another respondent who is very familiar with the examinee. The 13 items of the CIS inquire about difficulties with family and other social relationships, mood, behavior at school or work, and leisure activities (Bird, 1999). Each item is rated on a 5-point scale ranging from "no problem" to "a very bad problem" (Bird, 1999, p. 220). Scores of 15 or higher on the parent version of the CIS indicate impairment in functioning (Bird, 1999).

A semistructured interview is the format of the Social Adjustment Inventory for Children and Adolescents (SAICA; John, Gammon, Prusoff & Warner, 1987). This measure of adaptive functioning can be used by trained clinicians to gather information about respondents who are six to 18 years of age. The SAICA contains 77 items to assess functioning at school and at home, peer relationships, and leisure pursuits (Bird, 1999). Although it can provide detailed information about an examinee's abilities in the areas described above, a drawback of the SAICA is the length of time needed to administer the interview, which may vary from 30 to 75 minutes (Bird, 1999).

The Vineland Adaptive Behavior Scales (VABS; Sparrow, Balla & Cicchetti, 1984) is a measure for the assessment of adaptive functioning that appears frequently in the literature on ASD (for example, see Carpentieri & Morgan, 1996; Gillham, Carter, Volkmar & Sparrow, 2000; Hundert, Morrison, Mahoney, Mundy & Vernon, 1997; Njardvik, Matson & Cherry, 1999; Panerai, Ferrante & Caputo, 1997; Roberts, McCoy, Reidy & Crucitti, 1993; Schatz & Hamdan-Allen, 1995; Stone, Ousley, Hepburn, Hogan & Brown, 1999; Szatmari, Archer, Fisman & Streiner, 1994; VanMeter, Fein, Morris, Waterhouse & Allen, 1997; Vig & Jedrysek, 1995; Volkmar, Carter, Sparrow & Cicchetti, 1993; Wicks-Nelson & Israel, 2000). This instrument is available in three versions, two of which are an interview format for parents or caregivers; the third version is a questionnaire to be completed by an examinee's teacher (Sattler, 1992). The VABS can be used to examine the competence of children and adolescents in the following four domains: communication, daily living skills, socialization, and motor skills. An Adaptive Behavior Composite also can be obtained by combining results from all four areas (Sattler, 1992). Predictably, persons with ASD are likely to obtain low scores on the socialization domain (Carpentieri & Morgan, 1996; Gillham et al., 2000).

Gillham et al. (2000) examined the utility of the VABS as a tool for identification of autism in children aged four to 13 years. Using regression analyses, they calculated adaptive behavior scores that would be expected on the basis of either chronological age or mental age, and compared these to actual VABS scores. These authors found that socialization scores for persons with autism were significantly below expected levels. By creating an index based on the ratio of actual to predicted socialization scores, they were able to correctly classify over 85% of both autistic and nonautistic participants in their study. Therefore, Gillham et al. speculated that comparisons of actual to predicted socialization scores could be useful when diagnosing autism.

Carter et al. (1998) provided additional information regarding the pattern of VABS scores obtained by persons with autism. These authors reported that in addition to significant socialization deficits, autistic individuals obtain relatively strong scores in daily living skills and intermediate scores in communication (Carter et al.). They also noted that within each VABS domain, persons with autism reveal more variability in their functioning than would be seen in either well-functioning or mentally retarded individuals.

Given the characteristic pattern of VABS scores typically found among persons with autism, Carter et al. (1998) created a set of special norms for the VABS to be used when evaluating autistic individuals. These norms were developed from a sample of 684 persons with autism. The total sample was divided into four normative groups: persons under age 10 who are verbal, persons under age 10 who are mute, persons over age 10 who are verbal, and those over age 10 who are mute. However, because 95% of persons over age 10 in this study were less than 35 years old, Carter et al. indicated that these norms should not be used with individuals who are older than 35.

According to Carter et al. (1998), the purpose of designing special norms for persons with autism was to enable clinicians to identify appropriate goals for improvement of social functioning in this population. Since deficits in socialization are a core feature of autism, using the special norms provides additional information about socialization deficits relative to other persons with autism. Such information can help to determine what types of modifications in adaptive behavior may be realistically attainable. Use of national norms will still be needed, however, to document mental retardation in persons with autism (Carter et al.).

ASSESSING THEORY OF MIND

Socialization deficits associated with pervasive developmental disorders may occur because persons with ASD lack a "theory of mind" (Muris et al., 1999, p. 67). Theory of mind refers to an ability to understand the thoughts, feelings, and intentions of other people, as well as a capacity to use such knowledge to anticipate what other people might do (Muris et al., 1999). Recently, two measures have been created to examine social understanding in persons with ASD.

The Theory-of-Mind test, or TOM test (Muris et al., 1999) is an interview for use with children between the ages of five and 12. It contains 78 items pertaining to stories and drawings about which a child has to answer questions. Test items assess for recognition of emotions, understanding of false beliefs, and understanding of humor. Each TOM item is scored as a pass (1) or a failure (0). Thus, a total of 78 points can be obtained on the test, with higher scores indicating a more advanced theory of mind.

Another measure to assess theory of mind is the Awkward Moments Test devised by Heavey, Phillips, Baron-Cohen, and Rutter (2000). This test was developed using adults with autism or Asperger Syndrome who ranged in age from 22 to 51 years old. The test involves viewing eight brief segments from British television programs or televised commercials; these film excerpts are presented to the examinee on a computer. The first film clip is a practice item, while the last seven constitute the actual test. Each of the test segments depicts a person experiencing a socially awkward event. Immediately following each film segment, the computer presents the examinee with a question about the mental state of the person in the film clip, as well as a control question about either an observable feature in the film or information that was given in the film dialog.

Heavey et al. (2000) compared the Awkward Moments Test performance of participants with pervasive developmental disorders to that of a matched control group with no history of PDD. These authors found that respondents with ASD correctly answered fewer of the questions about film characters' mental states and intentions than did the control group. They concluded that the Awkward Moments Test may be used as a way to identify interpersonal difficulties in persons with ASD, by allowing an assessment of social information processing that approximates a real-life social situation.

NEUROPSYCHOLOGICAL ASSESSMENT

Certain types of neuropsychological deficits are frequently observed among persons with ASD. These include difficulties with motor functioning, verbal reasoning, complex memory, and planning, among others (Filipek et al., 1999, Minshew, Goldstein, Muenz & Payton, 1992; Minshew, Goldstein & Siegel, 1997; Szatmari, Tuff, Finlayson & Bartolucci, 1990). A neuropsychological assessment can identify the nature and severity of these problems so that appropriate interventions can be implemented (Filipek et al., 1999).

Gross and fine motor development of children aged $4\frac{1}{2}$ to $14\frac{1}{2}$ years can be examined with the Bruininks-Oserestsky Test of Motor Proficiency (Bruininks, 1978, cited in Sattler, 1992; Western Psychological Services, 2001). This test consists of eight subtests containing a total of 46 items (Western Psychological Services, 2001). Gross motor skills can be evaluated using subtests that assess running speed, balance, bilateral coordination, and limb strength. Subtests of response speed, visual-motor control, and upper-limb speed and dexterity measure fine motor skills. A subtest for upper limb coordination measures both gross and fine motor abilities (Sattler, 1992). The full battery can be administered in 45 to 60 minutes, and a short form containing 14 items can be completed in 15 to 20 minutes (Western Psychological Services, 2001). Subtest scores, a Gross Motor Composite, a Fine Motor Composite, and a Battery Composite score can be obtained. Age-based standard scores, percentile ranks, stanines, and age equivalents also are available when using this test (Western Psychological Services, 2001).

Visual-motor performance can be screened with the Bender Visual Motor Gestalt Test (Bender, 1938, cited in Sattler, 1992). The test contains nine cards depicting geometric shapes. Each card is presented in succession, and the examinee is instructed to copy each design on a sheet of paper. The Bender usually can be completed in about five minutes, although some children may require longer periods of time to finish the test (Sattler, 1992). According to Sattler (1992), children with autism may make errors of fragmentation, omission, substitution, and collision, or they may include unusual doodling or scribbling on their Bender protocols.

Another widely used measure of visual-motor skills is the Developmental Test of Visual-Motor Integration (VMI; Beery, 1982, cited in Sattler, 1992; Western Psychological Services, 2001). This test requires examinees to copy 24 geometric forms that are arranged in a test booklet from lesser to greater complexity. It can be administered either individually or in a group, and can be completed in 10 to 15 minutes. Age norms for this instrument range from 28 weeks up to 17 years of age; standard scores and percentiles also are provided (Western Psychological Services, 2001).

Two studies (Carpentieri & Morgan, 1994; Carpentieri & Morgan, 1996) used the SB:FE to assess verbal reasoning abilities in children with autism. The SB:FE broadly assesses these skills through the use of four subtests: Vocabulary, Comprehension, Absurdities, and Verbal Relations (Sattler, 1992). Both the 1994 and 1996 studies by Carpentieri and Morgan reported that children with autism had low verbal reasoning scores. Findings of the 1994 study revealed that children with autism scored low on Absurdities (described earlier, in the section on intellectual assessment) and on the Comprehension subtest, which measures social skills and knowledge about solutions to common problems (Sattler, 1992). The 1996 study indicated that autistic children's verbal reasoning ability was lower than that of a matched group of nonautistic children with mental retardation.

Complex memory functioning in persons with ASD has been studied through the use of the California Verbal Learning Test (CVLT; Delis, Kramer, Kaplan & Ober, 1987, cited in Minshew & Goldstein, 1993). This instrument measures such memory abilities as recall, recognition, learning strategies, learning rates across trials, vulnerability to interference, retention of information after either short or long delays, and learning errors (Delis, Freeland, Kramer & Kaplan, 1988). Minshew and Goldstein (1993) compared the performance of 21 matched pairs of persons with high-functioning autism and controls on 33 variables derived from the CVLT (e.g. the number of words correctly remembered from word lists on free-recall and recognition tasks, or the number of errors made during these tasks). Results indicated that the participants with autism in this study performed worse than controls on 30 of the 33 variables, although only six of the 33 variables yielded significant differences. The authors interpreted their findings as evidence of mild problems with verbal memory for persons with autism.

Another study (Bennetto, Pennington & Rogers, 1996) compared adolescents and young adults with high functioning autism with a matched sample of control subjects on various types of memory skills. They found that subjects with high functioning autism did significantly worse on tasks pertaining to temporal order memory, source memory, free recall, and working memory. The latter finding was corroborated by Pennington and Ozonoff (1996), who also reported evidence of deficits in working memory for persons with autism.

Memory for faces also is impaired in children with autism (Hauck, Fein, Maltby, Waterhouse & Feinstein, 1998; Szatmari et al., 1990). According to Hauck et al. (1998), children without ASD found it easier to recall faces than objects, while children with autism demonstrated equal recall of faces and objects. These authors indicated that recognition of faces was highly and consistently correlated with other measures of adaptive skills and social development.

Russell and Jarrold (1999) compared the abilities of children with autism, children with learning disability and children without disabilities on a memory task associated with self-monitoring. These researchers asked participants to remember whether they had performed a certain action or whether someone else had. Specifically, they asked subjects to remember whether they or the experimenter had arranged a group of picture cards in a particular order. Participants with autism did much worse than the other two groups on this task. The authors of this study commented that these results lent support to the existence of monitoring deficits in persons with autism.

Self-monitoring is one of the executive functions of the brain (Luu, Collins & Tucker, 2000), which also include such abilities as planning, cognitive flexibility, and self-regulation (Luu et al., 2000; Ozonoff, 1995). The literature on autism consistently reports that this disorder is associated with deficits in executive functions (Klinger & Renner, 2000; Penington & Ozonoff, 1996).

The Wisconsin Card Sorting Test (WCST; Berg, 1948, cited in Ozonoff, 1995) has been used to study cognitive flexibility and abstract reasoning in persons with autism. When taking this test, an examinee is given a deck of 128 cards depicting designs that vary according to color, shape, and number. He or she must match the cards with one of four stimulus cards that are similar to the cards in the deck. The examinee is not told the matching criterion, but must determine the sorting principle on the basis of feedback from the test administrator, who tells the examinee whether each card was correctly or incorrectly placed. After 10 consecutive cards have been sorted correctly, the examiner changes the sorting rule and the procedure begins again. The test concludes when either six categories have been correctly sorted or when the deck runs out of cards (Ozonoff, 1995). Ozonoff (1995) cited seven previous studies that used the WCST to investigate executive functioning in subjects with autism. In five of those studies, participants with autism scored lower than control subjects on this measure, suggesting that impairment in executive functions is a key feature of autism (Ozonoff).

A neuropsychological assessment that has been used to study planning ability in persons with autism is called the Tower of Hanoi (Simon, 1975, cited in Aman, Roberts & Pennington, 1998; Wicks-Nelson & Israel, 2000). Equipment for this test consists of two identical boards: one for the test administrator and the other for the examinee. Each board has three vertical pegs in a straight line and three or four plastic rings of varying sizes that fit over the pegs. The rings on the examinee's board are configured differently at the beginning of each trial; the examiner's board displays the desired end state. The examinee's task is to move the rings to achieve the same configuration as seen on the examiner's board. Rings are moved according to a set of rules: (1) a large ring cannot be placed on top of a smaller ring. (2) only one ring at a time can be moved, and (3) rings cannot be moved to the table or to the examiner's board, but must always be moved to another peg (Aman et al., 1998). Aman et al. reported persons with autism performed more poorly than control participants on this measure of executive functioning. According to Wicks-Nelson and Israel (2000), impairment in executive functions may account for the cognitive rigidity that is typically associated with ASD.

Although neuropsychological assessment can provide valuable information regarding an individual's strengths and deficits, Manjiviona and Prior (1999) reported an important caveat pertaining to this assessment method. These authors compared the neuropsychological functioning of children and adolescents who had been diagnosed with either autism or Asperger syndrome. They reportedly found no differences in the neuropsychological profiles of the two groups, other than the general finding that participants with Asperger syndrome had higher IQ scores than those with autism. Based on these results, they concluded that neuropsychological evaluation of persons with ASD should not be used for the purpose of differential diagnosis.

SUMMARY

Because language deficits are often present among individuals with pervasive developmental disorders, evaluation of language abilities is an essential part of a comprehensive assessment. According to Wetherby, Prizant, and Schuler (2000), assessment of language skills for persons with autistic spectrum disorders must focus on three broad areas of concern: linguistics, social and emotional communication, and language-related cognitive functions. Linguistic evaluation includes assessment of both expressive and receptive language. Examination of social and emotional communication must assess reciprocity of social interaction, understanding and expression of emotion, and regulatory strategies to manage emotional arousal. Finally, evaluation of language-related cognitive domains must include an assessment of the use of symbolic representations and imitation (Wetherby et al.).

REFERENCES

Alloy, L. B., Jacobson, N. S., & Acocella, J. (1999). *Abnormal psychology: Current perspectives* (8th ed.). Boston, MA: McGraw-Hill College.

Aman, C. J., Roberts, R. J., & Pennington, B. F. (1998). A neuropsychological examination of the underlying deficit in attention deficit hyperactivity disorder. *Developmental Psychology, 34*(5), 956–969.

American Psychiatric Association (2000). *Diagnostic and statistical manual of mental disorders* (4th ed., text revision). Washington, D.C.: Author.

Atlas, J. A., & Gerbino-Rosen, G. (1995). Differential diagnosis and treatment of an inpatient adolescent showing pervasive developmental disorder and mania. *Psychological Reports, 77*, 207–210.

Attwood, T. (1998). *Asperger's syndrome: A guide for parents and professionals*. Philadelphia, PA: Jessica Kingsley Publishers.

Baird, G., Charman, T., Baron-Cohen, S., Cox, A., Swettenham, J., Wheelwright, S., & Drew, A. (2000). A screening instrument for autism at 18 months: A 6-year follow-up study. *Journal of the American Academy of Child and Adolescent Psychiatry, 39*(6), 694–702.

Barnhill, G., Hagiwara, T., Myles, B. S., & Simpson, R. L. (2000). Asperger syndrome: A study of the cognitive profiles of 37 children and adolescents. *Focus on Autism and Other Developmental Disabilities, 15*(3), 146+. Retrieved November 16, 2000 from Infotrac database on-line (Article A65773318) on the World Wide Web: http://infotrac.galegroup.com

Baron-Cohen, S., Allen, J., & Gillberg, C. (1992). Can autism be detected at 18 months? The needle, the haystack, and the CHAT. *British Journal of Psychiatry, 161*, 839–843.

Barthelemy, C., Roux, S., Adrien, J. L., Hameury, L., Guerin, P., Garreau, B., Fermanian, J., & Lelord, G. (1997). Validation of the Revised Behavior Summarized Evaluation Scale. *Journal of Autism and Developmental Disorders, 27*(2), 139–153.

Bax, M. (1999). Diagnoses made too late. *Developmental Medicine and Child Neurology, 41*(12), 795.

Bennetto, L., Pennington, B. F., & Rogers, S. J. (1996). Intact and impaired memory functions in autism. *Child Development, 67*(4), 1816–1835.

Berument, S. K., Rutter, M., Lord, C., Pickles, A., & Bailey, A. (1999). Autism Screening Questionnaire: Diagnostic validity. *British Journal of Psychiatry, 175*, 444–451.

Bird, H. R. (1999). The assessment of functional impairment. In: D. Shaffer, C. P. Lucas, & J. E. Richters (Eds), *Diagnostic Assessment in Child and Adolescent Psychopathology* (pp. 209–229). New York: Guildford Press.

Bird, H. R., Shaffer, D., Fisher, P., Gould, M. S., Staghezza, B., Chen, J. Y., & Hoven, C. (1993). The Columbia Impairment Scale (CIS): Pilot findings on a measure of global impairment for children and adolescents. *International Journal of Methods in Psychiatric Research*, *3*, 167–176.

Bricker, D., & Squires, J. (1999). *The Ages and Stages Questionnaire* (2nd ed.). Baltimore, MD: Paul H. Brookes.

Brigance, A. (1986). *The BRIGANCE Screens*. North Billerica, MA: Curriculum Associates.

Carr, A. (1999). *The handbook of child and adolescent clinical psychology: A contextual approach*. New York: Routledge.

Carpentieri, S. C., & Morgan, S. B. (1994). Brief report: A comparison of patterns of cognitive functioning of autistic and nonautistic retarded children on the Stanford-Binet: Fourth Edition. *Journal of Autism and Developmental Disorders*, *24*(2), 215–223.

Carpentieri, S., & Morgan, S. B. (1996). Adaptive and intellectual functioning in autistic and nonautistic retarded children. *Journal of Autism and Developmental Disorders*, *26*(6), 611–620.

Carter, A. S., Volkmar, F. R., Sparrow, S. S., Wang, J. J., Lord, C., Dawson, G., Fombonne, E., Loveland, K., Mesibov, G., & Schopler, E. (1998). The Vineland Adaptive Behavior Scales: Supplementary norms for individuals with autism. *Journal of Autism and Developmental Disorders*, *28*(4), 287–302.

Cox, A., Klein, K., Charman, T., Baird, G., Baron-Cohen, S., Swettenham, J., Drew, A., & Wheelwright, S. (1999). Autism spectrum disorders at 20 and 42 months of age: Stability of clinical and ADI-R diagnosis. *Journal of Child Psychology and Psychiatry*, *40*(5), 719–732.

Delis, D. C., Freeland, J., Kramer, J. H., & Kaplan, E. (1988). Integrating clinical assessment with cognitive neuroscience: Construct validation of the California Verbal Learning Test. *Journal of Consulting and Clinical Psychology*, *56*(1), 123–130.

DiLavore, P. C., Lord, C., & Rutter, M. (1995). The Pre-linguistic Autism Diagnostic Observation Schedule. *Journal of Autism and Developmental Disorders*, *25*(4), 355–379.

Ehlers, S., & Gillberg, C. (1993). The epidemiology of Asperger syndrome: A total population study. *Journal of Child Psychology and Psychiatry*, *34*(8), 1327–1350.

Ehlers, S., Gillberg, C., & Wing, L. (1999). A screening questionnaire for Asperger syndrome and other high-functioning autism spectrum disorders in school age children. *Journal of Autism and Developmental Disorders*, *29*(2), 129–141.

Ehlers, S., Nyden, A., Gillberg, C., Sandberg, A. D., Dahlgren, S. O., Hjelmquist, E., & Oden, A. (1997). Asperger syndrome, autism, and attention disorders: A comparative study of the cognitive profiles of 120 children. *Journal of Child Psychology and Psychiatry*, *38*(2), 207–217.

Filipek, P. A., Accardo, P. J., Baranek, G. T., Cook, E. H. Jr., Dawson, G., Gordon, B., Gravel, J. S., Johnson, C. P., Kallen, R. J., Levy, S. E., Minshew, N. J., Prizant, B. M., Rapin, I., Rogers, S., Stone, W. L., Teplin, S., Tuchman, R. F., & Volkmar, F. R. (1999). The screening and diagnosis of autistic spectrum disorders. *Journal of Autism and Developmental Disorders*, *29*(6), 439–484.

Gillham, J. E., Carter, A. S., Volkmar, F. R., & Sparrow, S. (2000). Toward a developmental operational definition of autism. *Journal of Autism and Developmental Disorders*, *30*(4), 269–278.

Glascoe, F. P. (1997). Do the Brigance Screens detect developmental and academic problems? *Diagnostique*, *22*(2), 87–103.

Glascoe, F. P. (1998). *Collaborating with parents: Using parents' evaluation of developmental status to detect and address developmental and behavioral problems*. Nashville, TN: Ellsworth & Vandermeer.

Goldstein, G., Minshew, N. J., & Siegel, D. J. (1994). Age differences in academic achievement in high-functioning autistic individuals. *Journal of Clinical and Experimental Neuropsychology, 16*(5), 671–680.

Greenspan, S. I., & Wieder, S. (1999). A functional developmental approach to autism spectrum disorders. *The Journal of the Association for Persons with Severe Handicaps, 24*(3), 147–161. Retrieved January 10, 2001 from FirstSearch database on-line (Number BEDI99031457) on the World Wide Web: http://FirstSearch.oclc.org

Harris, S. L., Glasberg, B., & Ricca, D. (1996). Pervasive developmental disorders: Distinguishing among subtypes. *School Psychology Review, 25*(3), 308–315.

Harris, S. L., Handleman, J. S., & Burton, J. L. (1990). The Stanford Binet profiles of young children with autism. *Special Services in the Schools, 6*(1–2), 135–143.

Harvard Mental Health Letter (1999, October). *What is Asperger's Disorder?* Retrieved November 16, 2000 from Infotrac database on-line (Article A59007796) on the World Wide Web: http://infotrac.galegroup.com

Hauck, M., Fein, D., Maltby, N., Waterhouse, L., & Feinstein, C. (1998). Memory for faces in children with autism. *Child Neuropsychology, 4*(3), 187–198.

Heavey, L., Phillips, W., Baron-Cohen, S., & Rutter, M. (2000). The Awkward Moments Test: A naturalistic measure of social understanding in autism. *Journal of Autism and Developmental Disorders, 30*(3), 225–236.

Howlin, P., & Asgharian, A. (1999). The diagnosis of autism and Asperger syndrome: Findings from a survey of 770 families. *Developmental Medicine and Child Neurology, 41*(12), 834–839.

Hundert, J., Morrison, L., Mahoney, W., Mundy, F., & Vernon, M. L. (1997). Parent and teacher assessments of the developmental status of children with severe, mild/moderate, or no developmental disabilities. *Topics in Early Childhood Special Education, 17*(4), 419–434.

Ireton, H. (1992). *Child Development Inventories.* Minneapolis, MN: Behavior Science Systems.

John, K., Gammon, G. D., Prusoff, B. A., & Warner, V. (1987). The Social Adjustment Interview for Children and Adolescents (SAICA): Testing of a new semistructured interview. *Journal of the American Academy of Child and Adolescent Psychiatry, 26*, 898–911.

Kadesjo, B., Gillberg, C., & Hagberg, B. (1999). Autism and Asperger syndrome in seven-year-old children: A total population study. *Journal of Autism and Developmental Disorders, 29*(4), 327–331.

Klin, A., Sparrow, S. S., Marans, W. D., Carter, A., & Volkmar, F. R. (2000). Assessment issues in children and adolescents with Asperger syndrome. In: A. Klin, F. R. Volkmar & S. S. Sparrow (Eds), *Asperger Syndrome* (pp. 309–339). New York, NY: Guilford Press.

Klinger, L. G., & Renner, P. (2000). Performance-based measures in autism: Implications for diagnosis, early detection, and identification of cognitive profiles. *Journal of Clinical Child Psychology, 29*(4), 479–492.

Lord, C., & Risi, S. (2000). Diagnosis of autism spectrum disorders in young children. In: A. M. Wetherby & B. M. Prizant (Eds), *Autism Spectrum Disorders: A Transactional Developmental Perspective* (Vol. 9, pp. 11–30). Baltimore, MD: Paul H. Brookes Publishing Company.

Lord, C., Risi, S., Lambrecht, L., Cook, E. H. Jr., Leventhal, B. L., DiLavore, P. C., Pickles, A., & Rutter, M. (2000). The Autism Diagnostic Observation Schedule-Generic: A standard measure of social and communication deficits associated with the spectrum of autism. *Journal of Autism and Developmental Disorders, 30*(3), 205–223.

Lord, C., Rutter, M., Goode, S., Heemsbergen, J., Jordan, H., Mawhood, L., & Schopler, E. (1989). Autism Diagnostic Interview Schedule: A standardized observation of communicative and social behavior. *Journal of Autism and Developmental Disorders, 19*(2), 185–212.

Lord, C., Rutter, M., & LeCouteur, A. (1994). Autism Diagnostic Interview-Revised: A revised version of a diagnostic interview for caregivers of individuals with possible pervasive developmental disorders. *Journal of Autism and Developmental Disorders, 24*(5), 659–685.

Luteijn, E., Jackson, S., Volkmar, F. R., & Minderaa, R. B. (1998). The development of the Children's Social Behavior Questionnaire: Preliminary data. *Journal of Autism and Developmental Disorders, 28*(6), 559–565.

Luteijn, E., Luteijn, F., Jackson, S., Volkmar, F., & Minderaa, R. (2000). The Children's Social Behavior Questionnaire for milder variants of PDD problems: Evaluation of the psychometric characteristics. *Journal of Autism and Developmental Disorders, 30*(4), 317–330.

Luu, P., Collins, P., & Tucker, D. M. (2000). Mood, personality, and self-monitoring: Negative affect and emotionality in relation to frontal lobe mechanisms of error monitoring. *Journal of Experimental Psychology, 129*(1), 43–60.

Manjiviona, J., & Prior, M. (1999). Neuropsychological profiles of children with Asperger syndrome and autism. *Autism, 3*(4), 327–356.

Mesibov, G. B., Adams, L. W., & Klinger, L. G. (1997). *Autism: Understanding the disorder*. New York, NY: Plenum Press.

Miller, J. N., & Ozonoff, S. (2000). The external validity of Asperger disorder: Lack of evidence from the domain of neuropsychology. *Journal of Abnormal Psychology, 109*(2), 227–238.

Minshew, N. J., & Goldstein, G. (1993). Is autism an amnesic disorder? Evidence from the California Verbal Learning Test. *Neuropsychology, 7*(2), 209–216.

Minshew, N. J., Goldstein, G., Muenz, L. R., & Payton, J. B. (1992). Neuropsychological functioning of nonmentally retarded autistic individuals. *Journal of Clinical and Experimental Neuropsychology, 14*(5), 749–761.

Minshew, N. J., Goldstein, G., Taylor, H. G., & Siegel, D. J. (1994). Academic achievement in high functioning autistic individuals. *Journal of Clinical and Experimental Neuropsychology, 16*(2), 261–270.

Minshew, N. J., Goldstein, G., & Siegel, D. J. (1997). Neuropsychological functioning in autism: Profile of a complex information processing disorder. *Journal of the International Neuropsychological Society, 3*(4), 303–316.

Muris, P., Steerneman, P., Meesters, C., Merckelbach, H., Horselenberg, R., van den Hogen, T., & van Dongen, L. (1999). The TOM test: A new instrument for assessing theory of mind in normal children and children with pervasive developmental disorders. *Journal of Autism and Developmental Disorders, 29*(1), 67–80.

Muris, P., Steerneman, P., & Ratering, E. (1997). Interrater reliability of the Psychoeducational Profile (PEP). *Journal of Autism and Developmental Disorders, 27*(5), 621–626.

Myles, B. S., Bock, S. J., & Simpson, R. L. (2001). *ASDS: Asperger Syndrome Diagnostic Scale*. Pro-Ed.

Njardvik, U., Matson, J. L., & Cherry, K. E. (1999). A comparison of social skills in adults with Autistic Disorder, Pervasive Developmental Disorder Not Otherwise Specified, and mental retardation. *Journal of Autism and Developmental Disorders, 29*(4), 287–295.

Online Asperger Syndrome Information and Support/O.A.S.I.S. (2000). *Diagnostic rating scales for Asperger Syndrome*. Retrieved December 28, 2000 from O.A.S.I.S. on the World Wide Web: http://www.udel.edu/bkirby/asperger/DX_scales.html

Ozonoff, S. (1995). Reliability and validity of the Wisconsin Card Sorting Test in studies of autism. *Neuropsychology, 9*(4), 491–500.

Papalia, D. E., Olds, S. W., & Feldman, R. D. (2001). *Human development* (8th ed.). Boston, MA: McGraw-Hill.

Panerai, S., Ferrante, L., & Caputo, V. (1997). The TEACCH strategy in mentally retarded children with autism: A multidimensional assessment: Pilot study. *Journal of Autism and Developmental Disorders, 27*(3), 345–347.

Pennington, B. F., & Ozonoff, S. (1996). Executive functions and developmental psychopathology. *Journal of Child Psychology and Psychiatry and Allied Disciplines, 37*(1), 51–87.

Perlman, L. (2000). Adults with Asperger disorder misdiagnosed as schizophrenic. *Professional Psychology: Research and Practice, 31*(2), 221–225.

Pilowsky, T., Yirmiya, N., Shulman, C., & Dover, R. (1998). The Autism Diagnostic Interview-Revised and the Childhood Autism Rating Scale: Differences between diagnostic systems and comparison between genders. *Journal of Autism and Developmental Disorders, 28*(2), 143–151.

Pro-Ed. (2001). *2001 spring catalog*. Austin, TX: Author.

Roberts, C., McCoy, M., Reidy, D., & Crucitti, F. (1993). A comparison of methods of assessing adaptive behaviour in pre-school children with developmental disabilities. *Australia and New Zealand Journal of Developmental Disabilities, 18*(4), Special Issue, 261–272.

Russell, J., & Jarrold, C. (1999). Memory for actions in children with autism: Self versus other. *Cognitive Neuropsychiatry, 4*(4), 303–331.

Ryan, R. M. (1992). Treatment-resistant chronic mental illness: Is it Asperger's syndrome? *Hospital and Community Psychiatry, 43*(8), 807–811.

Sattler, J. M. (1992). *Assessment of children: Revised and updated third edition*. San Diego, CA: Author.

Schatz, J., & Hamdan-Allen, G. (1995). Effects of age and IQ on adaptive behavior domains for children with autism. *Journal of Autism and Developmental Disorders, 25*(1), 51–60.

Schopler, E., Reichler, R. J., DeVellis, R. F., & Daly, K. (1980). Toward an objective classification of childhood autism: Childhood Autism Rating Scale (CARS). *Journal of Autism and Developmental Disorders, 10*(1), 91–103.

Shaffer, D., Gould, M. S., Brasic, J., Ambrosini, P., Fisher, P., Bird, H., & Aluwahlia, S. (1983). A Children's Global Assessment Scale (CGAS). *Archives of General Psychiatry, 40*, 1228–1231.

Siegel, D. J., Minshew, N. J., & Goldstein, G. (1996). Wechsler IQ profiles in diagnosis of high-functioning autism. *Journal of Autism and Developmental Disorders, 26*(4), 389–406.

Simonoff, E. (1998). Genetic counseling in autism and pervasive developmental disorders. *Journal of Autism and Developmental Disorders, 28*(5), 447–456.

Sparrow, S. S., Balla, D. A., & Cicchetti, D. V. (1984). *Vineland Adaptive Behavior Scales*. Circle Pines, MN: American Guidance Service.

Steerneman, P., Muris, P., Merckelbach, H., & Willems, H. (1997). Assessment of development and abnormal behavior in children with pervasive developmental disorders. Evidence for the reliability and validity of the revised Psychoeducational Profile. *Journal of Autism and Developmental Disorders, 27*(2), 177–185.

Stone, W. L., & Hogan, K. L. (1993). A structured parent interview for identifying young children with autism. *Journal of Autism and Developmental Disorders, 23*, 639–652.

Stone, W. L., Ousley, O. Y., Hepburn, S. L., Hogan, K. L., & Brown, C. S. (1999). Patterns of adaptive behavior in very young children with autism. *American Journal on Mental Retardation, 104*(2), 187–199.

Szatmari, P., Archer, L., Fisman, S., & Streiner, D. L. (1994). Parent and teacher agreement in the assessment of pervasive developmental disorders. *Journal of Autism and Developmental Disorders, 24*(6), 703–717.

Szatmari, P. Archer, L., Fisman, S., Streiner, D. L., & Wilson, F. (1995). Asperger's syndrome and autism: Differences in behavior, cognition, and adaptive functioning. *Journal of the American Academy of Child and Adolescent Psychiatry, 34*(12), 1662–1671.

Szatmari, P., Tuff, L., Finlayson, A. J., & Bartolucci, G. (1990). Asperger's syndrome and autism: Neurocognitive aspects. *Journal of the American Academy of Child and Adolescent Psychiatry, 29*(1), 130–136.

Tanguay, P. E. (2000). Pervasive developmental disorders: A 10-year review. *Journal of the American Academy of Child and Adolescent Psychiatry, 39*(9), 1079+. Retrieved November 6, 2000 from Infotrac database on-line (Article A65329815) on the World Wide Web: http://infotrac.galegroup.com

Teitelbaum, P., Teitelbaum, O., Nye, J., Fryman, J., & Maurer, R. G. (1998). Movement analysis in infancy may be useful for early diagnosis of autism. *Proceedings of the National Academy of Sciences in the United States, 95*(23), 13982–13987.

Trevarthen, C., Aitken, K., Papoudi, D., & Robarts, J. (1996). *Children with autism: Diagnosis and interventions to meet their needs.* Bristol, PA: Jessica Kingsley Publishers.

VanMeter, L., Fein, D., Morris, R., Waterhouse, L., & Allen, D. (1997). Delay versus deviance in autistic social behavior. *Journal of Autism and Developmental Disorders, 27*(5), 557–569.

Vig, S., & Jedrysek, E. (1995). Adaptive behavior of young urban children with developmental disabilities. *Mental Retardation, 33*(2), 90–98.

Volkmar, F. R., Carter, A., Sparrow, S. S., & Cicchetti, D. V. (1993). Quantifying social development in autism. *Journal of the American Academy of Child and Adolescent Psychiatry, 32*(3), 627–632.

Volkmar, F. R., Cook, E. H. Jr., Pomeroy, J., Realmuto, G., Tanguay, P., and the Work Group on Quality Issues (1999). Practice parameters for the assessment and treatment of children, adolescents, and adults with autism and other pervasive developmental disorders. *Journal of the American Academy of Child and Adolescent Psychiatry, 38*(2), 32+. Retrieved November 7, 2000 from Infotrac database on-line (Article A58531554) on the World Wide Web: http://infotrac.galegroup.com

Volkmar, F. R., Klin, A., & Pauls, D. (1998). Nosological and genetic aspects of Asperger syndrome. *Journal of Autism and Developmental Disorders, 28*(5), 457–463.

Volkmar. F. R., & Marans, W. D. (1999). Measures for assessing pervasive developmental and communication disorders. In: D. Shaffer, C. P. Lucas & J. E. Richters (Eds), *Diagnostic Assessment in Child and Adolescent Psychopathology* (pp. 167–205). New York, NY: Guilford Press.

Western Psychological Services (2001). *Catalog 2001.* Los Angeles, CA: Author.

Wetherby, A. M., & Prizant, B. M. (2000). Introduction to autism spectrum disorders. In: A. M. Wetherby & B. M. Prizant (Eds), *Autism Spectrum Disorders: A Transactional Developmental Perspective* (pp. 1–7). Baltimore, MD: Paul H. Brookes.

Wetherby, A. M., Prizant, B. M., & Schuler, A. L. (2000). Understanding the nature of communication and language impairments. In: A. M. Wetherby & B. M. Prizant (Eds), *Autism Spectrum Disorders: A Transactional Developmental Perspective* (pp. 109–141). Baltimore, MD: Paul H. Brookes Publishing Company.

Whitehouse, D., & Harris, J. C. (1984). Hyperlexia in infantile autism. *Journal of Autism and Developmental Disorders, 14*(3), 281–289.

Wicks-Nelson, R., & Israel, A. C. (2000). *Behavior disorders of childhood* (4th ed.). Upper Saddle River, NJ: Prentice Hall.

Wing, L. (1997). The autistic spectrum. *Lancet, 350*(9093), 1761–1766. Retrieved November 22, 2000 from Lexis-Nexis Academic Universe database on the World Wide Web: http://web.lexis-nexis.com/universe/

Wolff, S. (1991). 'Schizoid' personality in childhood and adult life: I. The vagaries of diagnostic labeling. *British Journal of Psychiatry, 159*, 615–620.

Yirmiya, N., Sigman, M., & Freeman, B. J. (1994). Comparison between diagnostic instruments for identifying high-functioning children with autism. *Journal of Autism and Developmental Disorders, 24*(3), 281–291.

COUNSELING ISSUES FOR PARENTS OF CHILDREN WITH AUTISTIC SPECTRUM DISORDERS

Sandra Burkhardt

with contributions from Mary Ellen Bucci

INTRODUCTION

Professionals committed to assisting children with Autistic Spectrum Disorders (ASD) and their families are often confronted with a daunting array of conflicting theories, recommendations, and personal convictions about the origins and treatment of ASD. Autism is a serious developmental disorder and, as such, children with autism and their parents face monumental challenges. Although the origins of autism are biological (American Academy of Pediatrics, 2001), psychological theories persist that implicate parents in the development and maintenance of symptoms (e.g. Fonagy & Target, 1996).

Environmental influences at home and school are likely to play some part in the expression of the communicative and behavioral dysfunction associated with ASD. Thus, professionals who counsel families need to understand the unique features of ASD and identify opportunities for intervention. In the absence of prevention and cure of ASD, environmental intervention, including psychopharmacology, is essential to management of the disorders and improved quality of life for persons with ASD and their families.

Autistic Spectrum Disorders: Educational and Clinical Interventions, pages 211–233.
2001 by Elsevier Science Ltd.
ISBN: 0-7623-0818-4

The psychoanalytic, behavioral, cognitive, and biological paradigms of psychology have offered theories and practices regarding ASD with varying degrees of utility. Historically, parents, particularly mothers, were blamed for the abnormal social and emotional functioning of their children with ASD, including poor attachment and lack of reciprocity in social interactions (Bettelheim, 1967; Kanner, 1943). Too often unsubstantiated beliefs led to ineffective treatment and exacerbation of guilt and suffering for parents who were told that somehow *they* were responsible for the persistence of ASD symptoms. Pioneers in treatment, such as Bruno Bettelheim and O. Ivar Lovaas, saw their initial treatment programs challenged as brutal and inhumane (e.g. Ekstein, 1991; Lovaas, 2000; Schopler, 1971, 1988). Through theories and therapies, the symptoms of ASD continued to display enduring resilience.

Recently, the Committee on Children with Disabilities of the American Academy of Pediatrics released guidelines for the pediatrician's increased role in the identification of ASD (American Academy of Pediatrics, 2001). Their report provides substantial reassurance that parental practices are not the cause of ASD and that care should be taken to support rather than indict parents regarding their children's difficulties. The report challenges professionals to listen to parents and provide them with as much information and assistance as possible given the current lack of definitive treatment standards.

To that end, this chapter encourages compassion and caution on the part of professionals who help children with ASD. Parents and siblings of persons with ASD are at risk themselves for stress reactions related to the demands of managing the person with ASD, often with lack of social support for their efforts. Professionals who serve persons with ASD and their families should provide accurate information, appropriate diagnosis, effective treatment strategies and social support whenever possible.

THEORETICAL PERSPECTIVES ON THE ROLE OF PARENTS OF CHILDREN WITH ASD

The history of psychosocial interventions for persons with autism and their families is sobering. Mothers in particular have been heavily implicated in the etiology, development, and maintenance of the child's abnormal relational and attachment behaviors (Bettelheim, 1967). Early psychoanalytic theories cited mothers' treatment of their children as the actual cause of autistic disorder and codified the tendency to blame mothers for the children's difficulties, including disruptive behaviors, poor social-emotional functioning and inadequate communication. Theories that indicted parents were based upon a belief that unconscious rejection of the child led the child to withdraw from the real world

(Bettelheim, 1967; Nolen-Hoeksema, 1998). Fonagy and Target (1996) provide a contemporary psychoanalytic perspective that continues to propose parental treatment of the child as a causative factor in the social-emotional deficits demonstrated by children with autism.

In sum, the psychodynamic perspective saw the child with autism as exiled to psychological separateness by an emotionally inadequate "refrigerator" mother (Bettelheim, 1967). Kanner, who first described autism, suspected fathers as the cause of the disorder (Nolen-Hoeksema, 1998). Thus, the very presence of a child with ASD in a family raised suspicion that inadequate, intrusive, negligent or harsh parental practices caused the poor attachment demonstrated by the child with the disorder.

Subsequent theories moved blame from the realm of the mother's unconscious rejection of the child to misguided or inadequate efforts to properly manage the child's unusual behaviors (Schopler, 1971). Presuming that all children responded similarly to rewards and punishments from their environment, behaviorists implied that stauncher, more consistent applications of behavior management than parents typically provided would reduce the undesirable excessive behaviors associated with autism, such as self-stimulation (e.g. Lovaas, 1977; Lovaas, Schaeffer & Simmons, 1965). Aversive conditioning was used to promote social behavior (Lovaas et al., 1965). Recent trends encourage parents to recruit and support a regimen of home trainers to provide intensive and promising behavioral treatment for young children with ASD to address communicative, social-emotional and behavioral deficits (Smith, Eikeseth, Klevstrand & Lovaas, 1997; Smith & Lovaas, 1998). Parental concerns about the children's lack of normal social functioning, including expressions of love, affection, and friendship, were relocated to a lesser priority than the professionals' mandate that unacceptable behaviors be extinguished.

Cognitive theories focused upon the development of normal reasoning and judgement, including social cognition, the ability to reason about the social world. The theory of mind, discussed elsewhere in this volume, refers to the development of social reasoning abilities and the deficits exhibited by children with ASD (Attwood, 1998; Baron-Cohen, 1995). This model for understanding ASD suggests that practice in the tasks associated with social reasoning will assist in the remediation of social skill deficits.

Important progress has been made in emphasizing the biological origins of ASD and disputing psychogenic theories of etiology (Volkmar, 2001), however, biological intervention, including effective pharmacological treatment, remains elusive.

In sum, over the course of 60 years, the recommendations of professionals who treat autism have ricocheted from removing children with autism from their parents' pathogenic care to endorsing that parents turn their homes into therapeutic treatment centers for up to 40 hours per week. Some professionals, including teachers, physicians, counselors and speech therapists, continue to interpret the resilience of the symptoms of ASD as evidence of parental inadequacy. However, the position can be taken that the persistence of ASD symptoms, often in the presence of heroic parental efforts, is evidence of the severity of ASD. Parents, humbled by the extent of their children's dysfunction (lack of language, attachment, and socially appropriate behavior as well as intellectual limitations), have been defenseless targets for blame as their best efforts yielded little progress for their children. At some junctures, well-intentioned professionals have made the situation worse for parents, adding guilt, shame and anger to their existing burden of worry and disappointment.

PARENTS' PERSPECTIVE ON ASD

Parents of children with ASD are not in an enviable position. No specific guidelines for diagnosis or treatment of ASD exist (American Academy of Pediatrics, 2001). Parents are left to navigate a host of standard and alternative treatments (American Academy of Pediatrics, 2001). There is agreement that issues related to diagnosis, early intervention, appropriate eligibility for special educational programs, teacher compliance with IEP goals, social skills training, discipline and preparation for independent living in adulthood are essential. However, there are few publicly funded programs or endorsed steps offered by the medical, educational or mental health communities to provide parents with clear options for effectively treating their children.

The Policy Statement of the American Academy of Pediatrics (2001) makes a resounding endorsement for professionals *to listen to parental concerns*. The Committee states that parents are often correct about abnormalities in their children's development. These concerns should be viewed as "flags" that guide professionals to evaluate for ASD. Anecdotes from parents of children with ASD abound with references to professionals, beginning with the pediatrician or preschool teacher, who dismissed maternal worries about a toddler's failure to talk or relate socially as excessive anxiety on the part of the mother. In fact, parental concerns are often prognostic for the later identification of developmental disorders (Glascoe, 1994, 1997; Glascoe & Dworkin, 1995; Glascoe, MacLean & Stone, 1991).

Health care professionals and educators may view autism with a curious mixture of blame and hopelessness. The demeanor of some parents may be anxious, edgy, tearful, or demanding which can lead professionals either to offer false reassurance or to dismiss parental concerns as products of worry rather than astute observation. The American Academy of Pediatrics' current policy statement is likely to make headway in legitimizing parental reports as reliable sources of diagnostic information (American Academy of Pediatrics, 2001).

Still, the endless list of unanswered, and, as yet, unanswerable questions for parents of children with ASD, is likely to create psychosocial stress. Parents frequently wonder: Will my child have friends? Will he or she marry? Will he or she have a job? Where will we find people outside the family (or within) who understand my child? The very ruminations which plague parents may lead professionals to view parental attempts at protecting their children as coddling, sabotaging progress toward improved functioning, "enabling" dependent behavior or "being in denial" about their children's prognosis. Those professionals who listen carefully to many parents, however, may hear the pain of confused and desperate people who receive little support and much implied criticism from others.

In the past, professionals were willing to indict parents for their inability to successfully change the characteristics of ASD despite the dismal record of professional intervention itself. Previous interventions cast suspicion upon parents, even recommending removal of the child from the mother's influence. Parents bore not only the daily stresses of caring for a child with a mysterious disability, but also the burden of suspicion that they made their child ill. It is not surprising that this unfortunate muddle of misunderstanding and blame has added pain, shame and confusion to the grief of a diagnosis of ASD.

The current understanding of ASD has removed much of the traditional blame of parents, especially mothers. However, residual elements remain. As parents seek help for their children, they continue to experience a lack of consensus regarding diagnosis of ASD, especially for children with mild impairments. Even more sobering, parents must chose among treatments that offer hope but little certainty of helpfulness. As children's conditions improve, it may be that they move *up* but not *out of* the spectrum of autistic disorders. One consistent feature of ASD is that the symptoms related to social and emotional functioning are almost as enduring as the parents' concern for the future of their child.

In sum, there is a need for clear guidelines for how parents of children with ASD should proceed in the management of their child. However, such guidelines will not be forthcoming until research confirms the efficacy of treatment or prevention. Compassion is needed regarding the significant issues that parents of children with ASD face, including the dearth of uniform, consistent, effective and affordable intervention offered to them by professionals. Factual information is needed to help parents make decisions about intervention and to protect them from claims that exploit the lack of standardized treatment. Finally, professionals should advocate, on behalf of families, for improved availability and affordability of services and research regarding the prevention, etiology, prognosis, and treatment of ASD.

THE PROFESSIONALS' ROLE

From the perspective of the professional, ASD presents a monumental challenge. A child has an incurable disorder of unknown origins that stalls the development of social and emotional functioning, the very heart and soul of human existence. Physicians and teachers who offer false reassurance to parents may do so in an effort to protect parents from unfavorable but inevitable truths – that despite current treatment, their children may not be fine.

Educators may become discouraged in working with children with ASD. As teachers try to help, their efforts may go seemingly unacknowledged by both the child with ASD who displays limited positive regard for them and parents who anxiously focus upon the deficits that remain, rather than the progress that has been made. Similarly, physicians may find it difficult to address disabilities related to social and emotional functioning during the routine office visit. It is particularly easy with young children to wait and see if nature, taking its course, resolves developmental delays through maturation. Current medical management strategies do not reward ordering extensive diagnostic procedures or upsetting parents with potential bad news. It is understandable that the routine well or sick child check-up has not always included a discussion of pervasive developmental disorder (American Academy of Pediatrics, 2001).

Professionals face awkward decisions in the diagnosis and treatment of ASD. The significance and resilience of the symptoms of ASD in the absence of definitive diagnostic and treatment recommendations place undue burdens upon professionals who are in the forefront of helping families with children with ASD, but have few tools for doing so.

COUNSELING ISSUES SPECIFIC TO ASD

Professionals working with families of children with ASD may be called upon to offer assistance in the management of the child's disorder. Management issues often include two areas: treatment options and family accommodation to the child's special needs. The current discussion includes an examination of research related to the family environment that may be important to the management of a family member with ASD.

Social-emotional functioning is at the very heart of relationship. Families of persons with ASD cannot rely upon typical interpersonal strategies, such as reciprocity (you have to do this for me because I did it for you) and affection (do this and I will like you, don't do it and I won't) to guarantee interpersonal effect. Family life with ASD involvement, including the parent-child relationship, means that many of the usual rules of social engagement are off. "Fairness" is not a concept that occurs to persons with ASD and they seem particularly unable to learn important social lessons from past mistakes. Thus, the family member with ASD may not improve his or her social behavior in response to other family members' social responses, such as ignoring, arguing, payback or discussion. Additionally, the characteristics of ASD, including lack of reciprocity, dysphoric mood, inflexibility and communication difficulties, are especially difficult for siblings to tolerate.

At the same time, not all families of children with ASD are the same. Research in the area of families' interpersonal characteristics and their effects on a family member with a disorder such as schizophrenia, depression or anxiety suggests that family characteristics predict relapses. Thus, patients with similar levels of pathology appear to be more or less vulnerable to recurring episodes of their illness depending upon the emotional climate in the family.

In the past, parents of children with ASD have been the focus of suspicion regarding their children's symptoms. Professionals and parents themselves continue to wonder and worry about the part that parents play in the children's behavior. Children with even mild ASD symptoms occasionally display self-stimulatory and self-injurious behaviors that appear to be triggered by environmental demands.

Paradoxes abound. For instance, children with ASD are believed to eschew change, for example, becoming violent and agitated if a toy is removed from its preferred location. In this case, one would presume that environmental accommodation that keeps the child's world consistent and that only strategically introduces change would result in flawless management of the child. This type of accommodation does, in fact, work to a certain degree. However, the parent of any child with ASD will tell stories of their child's extreme agitation at having to do routine, mundane daily activities, such as homework or going to bed, which one would think the child should have assimilated to quite readily. Environmental demands, even routine and benign ones, may trigger affective and behavioral disruptions, which this author euphemistically calls "meltdowns".

Meltdowns include a distinctive mix of cognitive, affective and behavioral excesses and deficiencies. Excesses may include tantrums, threats of violence to self or others, aggression, screaming and repetitive questioning. Deficiencies may include lack of reasonableness, inability to soothe self or be soothed by others, and poor self-regulation of thoughts, feelings and actions. Meltdowns make management of persons with ASD particularly stressful for family members.

Before proceeding to discuss how the emotional climate in the family may contribute to behavioral excesses and deficits, it must be clear: it is erroneous to *blame* parents for causing the behavioral dysfunction seen in their children with ASD. Usually, parents manage the emotional ways of their children to the best of their ability. Temperament, personality, genetics, environmental resources, and situational stress all contribute to how a child acts and a parent responds. Thus, the role of parents, while important, may not be as deterministic as once believed. Because ASD by definition impairs social and emotional functioning, parents of children with ASD may face a greater ordeal when trying to manage their children's behavior than the parents of other children who can more capably regulate their own social behaviors. The parents of children with ASD cannot rely on the establishment of the proverbially "good" relationship with their child to insure consistent compliance and improved behavior. Thus, parents of children with ASD are in the position that their own efforts may not significantly improve their children's behavior, but that mismanagement of the child with ASD will make a bad situation worse. It is in the service of trying to make difficult situations for persons with ASD better that the research on *expressed emotion* (EE) is presented as a possible blueprint for intervention for families of children with ASD.

THE POTENTIAL ROLE OF EXPRESSED EMOTION (EE) IN BEHAVIORAL SYMPTOMS OF ASD

Research in the area of *expressed emotion* (EE), or how people display their feelings with others, offers potential insight into the role that families, particularly parents, may play in triggering and managing behavioral excesses and deficits. *Expressed Emotion* (EE) is the descriptive title of a constellation of interpersonal activity that includes criticism and hostility (NEE, negatively expressed emotion) and intense and intrusive emotional overinvolvement (EOI) (Mueser et al., 1993). Mueser et al. (1993) determined that family affective behaviors influenced social problem-solving and assertiveness in psychiatric patients

Research in EE suggests that families with members with mental illnesses, such as schizophrenia, depression and anxiety, vary in the ways in which they relate to the ill family member. Families who display high levels of *negatively expressed emotion* (NEE), such as non-constructive criticism, sarcasm, put-downs, and hostility, or *emotional overinvolvement* (EOI), such as extreme self-sacrifice, lack of objectivity and dramatic displays of emotion, place ill family members at risk of relapse (Mueser et al., 1993). The relapse rate of people from families with a high level of NEE or EOI is greater than the relapse rate for people from families without NEE or EOI, *even when the severity of the illness is the same in the sick family member*. Thus, the effect of EE on patients with mental illnesses may parallel the effects that EE has on persons with ASD. It is possible that altering the level of EE in the families (and classrooms) of persons with ASD may help to reduce the intensity, frequency and duration of problem behaviors, including self-injurious and self-stimulatory behavior. Further, reducing the behavioral excesses and deficiencies that persons with ASD exhibit within the family is likely to lower the interpersonal stress created for all members of the family.

A TYPICAL ASD FAMILY INCIDENT

A hypothetical case is presented to illustrate a typical family incident in a family with a child with ASD.

The family is a middle class family with adequate financial resources. Bill and Mary are the parents of Paul, age 9, with ASD and Jack, age 11 without ASD. Bill tends to get impatient with the children. Mary gets critical and harsh with Bill, but not usually with the children. Paul regularly has tantrums that begin with verbal complaints and escalate to crying, yelling, threats of self-injury and targeting rage against persons who have nothing to do with the precipitating event. Jack, 11, impatient like his father, becomes critical and sarcastic when provoked.

Today the conflict involves Paul complaining that the mustard on his hot dog is the wrong kind. Mother scurries to locate the "right" mustard in an attempt to ward off a tantrum by Paul and a confrontation with Bill. Bill is impatient with Paul's demands regarding inconsequential things such as mustard. Bill believes Paul should learn to be more tolerant and that Mary should not cater to the boy quite so much. Bill becomes irate and commands Paul to eat the hot dog as is or go without lunch as a disciplinary action. Mary, whose efforts to deflect conflict have now been undermined by Bill's command, becomes irritated with Bill for escalating the conflict. Mary's comment "Thanks a lot" toward Bill causes Bill to roll his eyes in exasperation and to withdraw from the lunch table in disgust. Jack, who is feeling anxious and confused by the rapid deterioration of the family meal, targets his brother's complaints as the cause of the conflict and calls Paul "a big stupid jerk" and "a crybaby". When Mary demands that Jack "mind his own business" and refrain from calling his brother names, Jack sasses his mother and is sent to his room. Jack leaves the lunch table muttering under his breath how unfair his mother is and how stupid his brother is. Bill, hearing Jack's disrespect, reprimands Jack for talking back to his mother. Mary, having located the right mustard from the back of the refrigerator, eats lunch with a placated Paul who is happy to have mom all to him self. Paul looks over, sees Mom crying, and tells her "Daddy is mean. Jack's a troublemaker".

(Perhaps readers unfamiliar with children with ASD will find the above incident absurd, as if no family could be rendered this dysfunctional over mustard. Readers *with* children with ASD may believe the author has eavesdropped on their home.)

EE PRINCIPLES APPLIED TO AN ASD TYPICAL INCIDENT

Research regarding the characteristics of ASD and the effects of EE offer insight into the family incident. Paul's reaction to the mustard is directly related to ASD. He is sensitive to sensory input, such as taste, and cannot readily accommodate difference. Bill's reaction, from a practical point of view, makes sense; his children should learn to eat what is provided without tantrums. However, Bill's tendency toward NEE begins the downward spiral of interpersonal exchanges. Mother should not have to cater to insignificant whims, but perhaps a pattern of OEI leads her to vigilance regarding Paul's need for routine. Mary's EOI gives her radar for antecedents to Paul's tantrums, and when she senses the gathering of clouds she takes action to avoid the storm.

When Bill and Jack express negativity toward Paul in the form of criticism, they earn Mary's disapproval because she wants their help in preventing Paul's tantrum. From her point of view, a peaceful lunch is more important than challenging an escalating Paul over the issue of mustard. Mary accurately assesses that Bill and Jack have greater social reasoning capacities than Paul does and she holds them to a higher standard in terms of social problems solving. She is angry with them when they do not help further her agenda – a peaceful meal. Bill could contain himself, but his tendency toward NEE in the face of his son's poor judgement and his wife's accommodation to Paul's nonsense infuriates him. Jack, at 11, is likely to see his brother as spoiled and his mother as favoring Paul.

The research related to EE would predict that Paul's tantrums are most likely to escalate when his family members express critical opinions, display hostility, or overly involve themselves in response to him or in his presence.

A counselor who understands the relative contributions of EE may be able to help Bill, Mary and Jack understand that while their emotional reactions are quite understandable given the circumstances, that those very normal reactions may precipitate more intense meltdowns for Paul. As Paul's behavior deteriorates and there is more reason to express negative emotion toward him, Paul is likely to relapse in a downward spiral of self-injurious, threatening, oppositional and unreasonable tantrum.

Thus, the counselor can help the family to set goals and priorities in managing the symptoms of ASD in the face of both NEE and EOI.

First, the parents need to construct a hierarchy of goals for behavior change for their child with ASD. There are several possible goals that emerge from the incident that was just described. These include: having a peaceful meal, teaching the children manners, training Paul to be more flexible about food, teaching parents to concur regarding discipline, supporting the expression of honest thoughts and feelings among family members, and studying the effects of negative interactions among family members. Although preventing Paul's tantrums may feel like a priority, particularly to Mary, it may not be a sufficient goal for all members of a family. However, the family learning that the management of NEE may have a positive impact on reducing Paul's tantrums may be a goal that the family can support.

Thus, the family, beginning with the parents, needs to set an agenda with several possible goals. For example, Bill and Mary may agree that Paul needs to limit unreasonable requests for food at mealtime. Once Mother and Father agree, Paul and Jack should be informed that this goal is for the whole family. The goal should be concretely defined. For example, "unreasonable requests" from any family member means demanding items that are not already on the table or foods that have not been prepared for the current meal. The children should be brought in on the plan, explaining the goal in concrete terms and identifying the interpersonal rewards of the goal, such as "so your family will like to eat together" or "show cooperation" or "get along better".

The counselor may need to work with family members separately and together, helping validate Jack's impression that his brother does overreact to mustard, but that the family is going to be working on helping Paul do better and that Jack's patience will help. Similarly, Bill and Mary may decide that mealtime is not the time for the teaching and learning of lessons, and they can agree to accommodate to Paul's need for familiar foods in order to keep the peace at mealtime. Introducing options is likely to reduce family stress and offer face-saving escapes from the selection of goals that are not readily achieved.

Finally, Bill and Mary can decide to offer each other respite when conflict begins. If Bill's NEE leads to tantrums then a back-up plan should be created, such as, Bill eating elsewhere without making negative comments to Mary or Paul. Although this leaves Mary to accommodate Paul, Mary must refrain from attacking Bill for his impatience. Thus, a peaceful meal can be accomplished. If Bill is better suited to offer Mary respite from Paul's demands in some circumstances, such as homework or bedtime, then he may repay the lunchtime debt during him more patient times.

THE ROLE OF EE IN FAMILY FUNCTIONING

A relationship between expression of negativity by parents, particularly mothers, and behavior of the child has been explored (e.g. Dowdney & Pickles, 1991). Findings have generally supported the notion that parents' affective expressions affect their offspring. It has been suggested that maternal intrusiveness is associated with child noncompliance (Johnson & Lobitz, 1974; Lobitz & Johnson, 1975). Expressions of criticism, hostility, sarcasm and anger by others, such as parents, teachers, siblings and acquaintances, may have particularly detrimental effects upon persons with ASD.

There is evidence that children's behavior affects parental behaviors (Cook, Kenny & Goldstein, 1991). Thus, the person with ASD is likely to affect other family members as well. For instance, maternal anger, irritability, and aggression have been reported to increase in the face of persistent opposition by the child (Dowdney & Pickles, 1991). Such opposition is a characteristic of persons with ASD who resist change, intrusion into their agendas, and redirection of their theories of the motivations of others.

Family dynamics, or patterns of interactions, may contribute to the development of downwardly spiraling negativity. Mueser et al. (1993) found that patients with highly critical relatives were themselves more likely to make non-constructive criticisms and demands. Thus, persons who lack the skills to effectively manage emotion-charged conflict situations are prone to launch harsh counterattacks when criticized. Long strings of criticism followed by counter criticism were found in highly critical families but not is less critical families.

Assertiveness may play an important role in terminating negative interaction sequences; that is, patients who speak up against those who harshly criticize them effect an end to the criticism sequence. Assertiveness can be defined as the ability to express oneself in a direct, honest and appropriate manner in order to ensure one's personal rights (Lange & Jakubowski, 1976). Harsh, overly critical or non-negotiable communication, such as non-constructive criticisms, demands, or commands, are not considered assertive (Mueser et al., 1993). EE may result in relapse for persons with mental illness because of patients in high EE families either lacking assertiveness (can not defend themselves) or choosing not to be assertive based upon a history that has taught the patient that such attempts are ineffective (do not even try). Counselors may intervene in families with EE by: (a) increasing assertiveness in persons with ASD, and/or (b) decreasing EE in the family system. Because there is a discrepancy between assertive behavior displayed in role play and behavior displayed in a naturally occurring situation, such as a family interaction, the use of videotaped family interactions without the counselor present may be preferable for family training sessions aimed at reducing EE.

Relatives with high warmth ratings were less likely to offer non-constructive criticism compared to relatives without high warmth ratings. Interestingly, however, warm relatives were not less critical or demanding during family interactions (Mueser et al., 1993). *What* the warm relatives chose to criticize differed less than *how* they acted when being critical.

Cook et al. (1991) found that parental affective style was influenced by an adolescent's tendency to elicit negativity from others and was not predicted by the mother's negativity, although fathers' negative affective style resulted in elevated negativity in the entire family. Adolescents were found to express greater negativity toward their mothers rather than fathers. Children with characteristics associated with eliciting negativity were found to do so from their own parents, even parents who were not negative by disposition. Cook et al. stated that their findings dispelled the notion that negativity in disturbed families is caused by maternal personality traits.

Cook et al. (1991) conclude that "for treatment purposes it is equally important to intervene on both sides of this reciprocal pattern of interaction, training parents to be less reactive to adolescent negativity and assisting adolescents to elicit less negativity by lowering the levels at which they produce it." (p. 500).

Sources of problematic interactions in families include the following: family members disposed toward negative behavior, family members whose behavior evokes negative reaction, relationship factors which negatively influence behavior, and reciprocity in relationships, that is, treating someone the way they treat you (Cook et al., 1991). These findings may be of particular significance for families of children with ASD, who find themselves driven to function within a narrow range of affective expression by the dramatically poor reactions that persons with ASD display in the presence of EE.

In families inclined to display high levels of EE, the functioning of the child with ASD may well be compromised, although the family believes itself to only be displaying "natural" reactions to everyday events or the unacceptable behavior of other family members. Family members may become pitted against each other in their attempts to openly express feelings (I'm furious, I'm frustrated, I'm upset) while maintaining the stable functioning of a family member with ASD who does not respond well to NEE. Further, should levels of NEE be directed at a person with ASD, immediate or delayed behavioral symptoms such as tantrums or self-stimulatory behaviors occur. These symptoms themselves may become a precipitant that evokes more NEE from family members, leading to a vicious cycle of expression, reaction to expression, reaction to reaction, etc.

Such cycles of interpersonal dysfunction are likely to leave persons with ASD and their families quite depleted. Further, maladaptive exchanges may contribute to the appearance that family members, especially parents, create autistic symptoms. Fong (1991) determined that high-stress mothers of adolescents with autism were more likely to appraise their children's actions as threatening in comparison to low-stress mothers of adolescents with autism. Thus, the cognitive appraisal of a family member regarding the behavior of a person with autism may affect his or her interpersonal approach.

Family members may easily become pitted against one another. Those members of the family who wish to maintain peace, or the status quo, may become punitive of family members who display NEE because of the subsequent deterioration in the behavior of the person with ASD. Other family members may see their personal expression of NEE as justified or even essential to setting limits on the behaviors of the person with ASD. A frustrated parent or misunderstood sibling is apt to resist the notion that *their* own authentic negative expressions of disapproval (yells, screams, slaps, pushes, taunts or threats) are the cause rather than the result of the "bad" (unreasonable) behavior of the person with ASD.

When NEE is present, families may need to be counseled to prepare for a possible "relapse" in the person with ASD. The person targeted during the "relapse" may not be the person who precipitated the incident. Thus, a safety plan for all, which includes time out, distance and distraction may need to be developed. Family members may need to be dissuaded from an attitude that blames someone for sabotaging family functioning when good efforts do not result in good outcomes.

TYPICAL RESPONSES TO ASD

It may be that ASD, with its mysterious combination of features, is an ultimate challenge to families and service providers. The disorders strike at the very heart of interpersonal interactions – the ability to communicate, to show gratitude, to form attachments, and to generalize what has been learned in one setting into another. Thus, parents, teachers, siblings and peers are likely to find that their efforts to connect with a person with ASD are not enthusiastically or consistently repaid. This social inequity may be associated with the development of hostile feelings. Persons with ASD have a tendency to expect, demand or encourage greater patience or understanding from others than the person with ASD is able to give. Others, such as other adult family members, teachers and peers, accurately perceive that persons with ASD get more than they give in terms of emotional support. Such observations are apt to precipitate negative responses.

In sum, EE in the environment makes a potential contribution to the management of persons with ASD. An understanding of the effects of EE may assist the professional in determining appropriate points of intervention and providing family members with a rationale for why it is useful for them to moderate their negatively expressed emotion or emotional overinvolvement during interactions with the person with ASD. EE may be higher in families with members who have mental illness, however, families with mentally ill members may feel they have more reason to express intense emotion. Counselors may need to take an interactionist approach to intervention, identifying the family member with the most resources to initiate needed changes in the family's emotional climate.

In addition to the contributions made by the social environment, it may also be helpful to review what capacities lie with the person with ASD for coping with interpersonal interactions. Here the discussion turns to a review of the development of social cognition.

THE DEVELOPMENT OF SOCIAL COGNITION IN PERSONS WITH ASD

Children achieve developmental milestones throughout the childhood period. These milestones include sitting up, walking, talking and toilet training to name but a few. Children develop the ability to think and reason about the outside world. Piaget described the stages of cognitive development which children can be expected to achieve (Piaget & Inhelder, 1963).

Similarly, *social cognition* develops beginning in childhood. Social cognition's simplest definition may be "cognition about people and their doings" (Flavell, 1985, p. 119). Social cognition involves internal mental processes associated with the efforts of people to know themselves, others and themselves in relationship to others. Social cognition includes interpersonal relations, social customs, and social ritual. Unlike thought and reasoning about the material world, social cognition involves thoughts and understanding about concepts that are subtle, abstract and internal (Flavell, 1985).

A basic tenet of the literature related to social cognition is that observation of social phenomenon leads to inference regarding the "intentions, attitudes, emotions, ideas, abilities, purposes, traits, thoughts, perceptions, and memories . . . *inside* the person and strictly psychological" (Flavell, 1985, p. 119).

The defining characteristics of ASD suggest that persons with ASD do not "observe" social phenomenon as others do. Gaze avoidance, limited verbal and non-verbal communication, and preoccupation with objects suggest that persons with ASD lack predisposition to the development of social cognition.

Three *preconditions* have been identified relative to the development of social cognition: existence, need and inference (Flavell, 1984). It is proposed that this framework provide some insight into the deficits in social functioning displayed by persons with ASD and some opportunities for intervention for professionals working to improve their social functioning.

Existence. Existence has been defined as "a person's basic knowledge that a particular fact or phenomenon of the social world exists as one of life's possibilities." (Flavell, 1985, p. 120). The child with ASD is not aware that others have thoughts, motives, desires and intentions. Thus, the child with ASD will not display acts of social reasoning or judgement if there is no apparent reason to do so. For example, a person with ASD may not offer to cooperate because he or she has no intrinsic desire to please others. It may not occur to a child with ASD to share or show gratitude since "kindness" and "appreciation" are necessarily concepts related to perceiving how someone else will interpret another's social actions.

The lack of awareness of a person with ASD may lead others to conclude that the person is deliberately rude, inconsiderate, selfish or manipulative. For example, Yirmiya, Solomonica-Levi, and Shulman (1996) found persons with autism less able to predict the outcome of deceptive action than persons with mental retardation. Given their incredible level of social naivete, blaming the person with ASD for unawareness of social expectations is like blaming a person with visual impairment for failing to return a served volleyball. It seems apparent that persons with ASD often fail to "see" the social cues that signal the need for a social response.

Persons with autism may miss their chance to engage in appropriate social and emotional interactions. Persons with ASD can initiate social interactions when *they* are aware of the existence of their own desire to communicate, however, they do not consistently respond to the expectations of others because they may not perceive the cues that signal a response is needed. These missed opportunities for social engagement may result in eventual social avoidance or rejection by others, targeting the person with ASD for social ridicule.

Need. Once a person becomes aware of the existence of social phenomenon, it typically follows that the person "senses the need to attempt an act of social cognition" (Flavell, 1985, p. 121). People may or may not make an effort to understand the social acts of which they are aware. Thus, the child with ASD may be aware that the child next to him wants to play. Still, the child with ASD may not make the effort to respond to the perceived social expectation because he or she feels no need to do so. Autism, by its very definition, often includes a desire to be alone or to function without social response to others. Thus, even when cued to the existence of a social demand, (i.e. "Mary wants to play cars with you"), the child with ASD may not respond to the opportunity, lacking an intrinsically motivating reason to do so. Unlike shyness, where social anxiety, once overcome, results in some pleasure in social acceptance and interaction, the person with ASD may experience a type of social separateness that reflects a very limited need to establish social connection. Thus, spinning the wheels of the cars may suffice for play instead of pretending to race the cars with Mary. Motivational deficit may lead to lack of social responsiveness even in the presence of social cues that make the existence of a social expectation perfectly clear.

Inference. Inference has been defined as "the capacity to carry off a given form of social thinking successfully." (Flavell, 1985, p. 121). Often the person with ASD is aware of the existence of social opportunities and experiences the need to interact, but lacks ability to engage in social exchanges. The inability to apply social knowledge to social tasks may emanate from two types of deficits. *Skill deficits* may be described as "I don't know what to do or say". *Performance deficits* can be defined as "I know what to do but I don't know when or how to do it". Social awkwardness may result when a person with ASD makes an attempt to engage others by talking incessantly about his or her pet interest as a means of engaging in social interaction, while failing to react to the other person's complete boredom regarding the topic. Such imperfect applications reflect the limited social understanding that defines ASD.

Given these definitions of *existence, need and inference*, it becomes evident that individuals with ASD do not readily understand the psychological states of others. As described by Frith (1991), the person with ASD is unable to form accurate or consistent inferences about others. Thus, they may be able to learn to act in empathic ways toward others in certain circumstances, but the feeling state associated with empathy does not generalize to other situations and persons with ASD may not recognize when it is natural to experience empathy.

Treatment goals include modeling, rewarding and encouraging appropriate social actions and positive emotional expressions. In this way, social "behaviors" are produced in response to both external contingencies and internal schemas. Improved social understanding is presumed to occur with practice. In sum, as families provide much of the social environment in which children with ASD live, the children's difficulties with the development of social cognition present challenges to others who try to socially engage them.

TREATMENT ISSUES FOR PARENTS

There is no cure for ASD and no treatment guarantees recovery (American Academy of Pediatrics, 2001). Intensive behavioral programs based upon the work of O. Ivar Lovaas address the communication and social deficits associated with autism and this form of treatment is emerging as a most effective treatment to date (McEachin, Smith & Lovaas, 1993; Smith, Wynn & Lovaas, 1997). Speech is learned naturally for most children during the first three to four years of life and becomes *more* difficult to acquire with age. (Anyone who has tried to learn a second language as an adult knows this from experience.) Thus, if a child has not learned to speak by age six or seven, it is extremely difficult to help them acquire language, perhaps because a neurological "window of opportunity" for learning language closes (Nichols, Martin & Wallace, 1992). Early intervention allows for greater gains in younger children because the neural pathways needed for acquisition of language are still intact, or that the "pruning" of unneeded connections has not yet occurred (Cohen, 1994).

It was reported that 47% (9 out of 19 children) of a group with ASD treated with Lovaas's methods achieved "normal functioning" after two to three years of treatment (Lovaas, 1987). Longitudinal findings indicated that at age 12, eight of the nine children had maintained typical functioning (McEachlin et al., 1993). More recently, a look at these same children as young adults indicates maintained gains without intervening treatment (Gresham & McMillan, 1998). The outcomes of Lovaas's methods suggest that early detection and intervention may substantially improve the prognosis for persons with ASD.

The Lovaas (1987) approach to autism is similar to the approach taken with severe learning disability. Instruction is accomplished by breaking down complex tasks into specific pieces that enable the child to learn one well-defined skill at a time, with each skill a steppingstone to further learning. The treatment initially targets the child's extreme isolation and resistance to social interaction, followed by language and communication skills.

An individualized treatment plan is needed for each child with autism because each child is unique. Some commonly targeted behaviors include paying attention, imitating others, and compliance with instructions. The method developed by Lovaas (1987) relies upon visual presentation of directions and minimal verbal instruction because most children with autism have limited receptive language skills. The format for presentation of material, defined in behavioral terms as "discrete trials", is consistent: SD>R>SR, where "SD" represents the discrete stimulus being presented, "R" represents the response of the individual and "SR" represents the reinforcing stimulus, or consequence, to the response. Lovaas programs address behavioral excesses and deficits using the SD>R>SR formula as direct instruction. For example, a therapist commands, "Come here" (SD), the child comes (R), and the therapist hugs the child and says "very good" (SR). An emphasis is placed upon the child succeeding at least 90% of the time, meaning the desired response should be one the child is fairly able to perform. Using the above example, if the child did *not* join the therapist, the child would be prompted to merely move closer to the therapist, so that even a limited response would be rewarded. The child enjoys the therapy and the child's behavior is shaped in the appropriate direction by rewards for approximations of the desired behavior.

A benefit of the methods proposed by Lovaas (1987) is the infusion of hope and optimism for helping even the most impaired person with ASD. Because intervention begins at the current functional level of the child, small steps are introduced and improvement is displayed. The Lovaas approach focuses less on what the child cannot do and more on what progress the child makes. This important emphasis may serve to encourage and sustain families battling demoralization about their children's deficits. A current drawback to the Lovaas approach is that it is costly, labor intensive, and may be inconvenient for families who must have a trainer in the home applying the methods.

Other treatment considerations include the work of Koegel, Koegel and McNerney (2001) who suggest that the concept of pivotal areas for intervention replace specific skills as the focus of treatment. Three general areas of impairment are involved in ASD: social interaction, verbal and nonverbal communication and stereotyped patterns of behavior, interests and activities (Koegel et al.). In a similar vein, Koegel & Koegel (1996) recommend child-initiated communication intervention as part of their Natural Language Paradigm to replace adult-initiated communication methods.

Treatment to address social cognitive deficits may include social skills training as well as intervention aimed at improving social understanding (Attwood, 1998; Bowler, 1992; Frith & Happe, 1994; Ozonoff & Miller, 1995). No psychosocial programs with definitive treatment effects have been identified to date, although emerging trends are promising.

In general, treatment options for parents should be carefully weighed, with current research findings consulted. Fantastic claims, clinical anecdotes and personal testimonials should be received with caution, as the history of treatment of ASD is filled with false promise and misguided good intentions.

COUNSELING GUIDELINES FOR ASD: CHALLENGE TO THRIVE, ACCOMMODATE TO SURVIVE

Recent advances in treatment of ASD show families are in the forefront of managing persons with ASD. Home services, school planning, job support and community living rely on the cooperation, resources and availability of family members to provide not only the physical but the psychosocial environment that support a person with ASD. The psychosocial stress for the family with a member with ASD should be considered a risk factor for the family members themselves.

Based upon the defining characteristics of ASD and families, the following counseling guidelines are suggested:

(1) Help families engineer for success by understanding the role Expressed Emotion, including Negatively Expressed Emotion and Emotional Over-involvement may play in the triggering, prolonging or escalating of dysfunctional interactions within the home. The research on NEE suggests several guidelines for families of persons with ASD that may be helpful to reduce and manage tantrum behavior: make criticism of persons with ASD as benign and constructive as possible, avoid NEE when possible, offer family members constructive outlets for their frustration, hostility and disappointment to reduce NEE, and have a safety plan in place to respond to tantrums following exposure to high levels of EE.
(2) Challenge to thrive. Introduce new behavior goals in the family environment to increase the likelihood that the child with ASD will make progress in social and emotional functioning. Accepting or accommodating to deficits will not help the person with ASD to improve.
(3) Accommodate to survive. It has been established that the behavioral symptoms of ASD are resilient. Thus, the outcome of a single incident will not make or break the future. When necessary, families can be encouraged to preserve resources by containing symptoms to survive the incident and planning to improve appropriate behavior in the immediate future. Preserve parental resources through respite, planning, support and encouragement.
(4) Create options for success for families of persons with ASD by defining a hierarchy of goals to be worked on. If the goal of teaching flexibility about wearing different clothing to school is not successful this morning, then perhaps the goal of peacefully starting the school day while wearing yesterday's shirt can be celebrated.
(5) Review the limitations in the development of social cognition that characterize ASD. Help family members to understand the difference between the inability of persons with ASD to identify and respond to social expectations and an insensitive refusal to be considerate of others. The important distinction between "can't" and "won't" may reduce the frustration of family members who feel treated unfairly by the person with ASD or by the accommodations made on that person's behalf.

SUMMARY

Families of persons with ASD face significant challenges. A history of theoretical and treatment efforts which have indicted parents as instrumental to the development of their children's disorders has been replaced with clear statements regarding the biological basis of ASD. However, family influences may contribute to the management of ASD symptoms, and highlights from the literature on Expressed Emotion were discussed for their relevance to management of persons with ASD. Consideration of the deficits associated with the development of social cognition in persons with ASD was given in the service of fostering improved understanding of specific points of intervention. A review of the basic elements of the Lovaas (1987) method was presented as a foundation for understanding current trends in treatment. Suggestions for counselors of families of persons with ASD concluded the chapter.

REFERENCES

American Academy of Pediatrics Committee on Children with Disabilities (2001). Policy Statement: The pediatrician's role in the diagnosis and management of autistic spectrum disorder in children (RE060018). *Pediatrics*, *107*(5), 1221–1226.

Attwood, T. (1998). *Asperger's syndrome: A guide for parents and professionals*. London: Jessica Kingsley Publishers.

Baron-Cohen, S. (1995). *Mindblindness: An essay on autism and theory of mind*. Cambridge, MA: Bradford, MIT Press.

Bettelheim, B. (1967). *The empty fortress*. New York: Free Press.

Bowler, D. M. (1992). "Theory of Mind" in Asperger's syndrome. *Journal of Child Psychology and Psychiatry*, *33*, 877–893.

Cohen, I. (1994). An artificial neural network analogue of learning in autism. *Biological Psychiatry*, *36*, 5–20.

Cook, W. L., Kenny, D. A., & Goldstein, M. J. (1991). Parental affective style risk and the family system: A social relations model analysis. *Journal of Abnormal Psychology*, *100*(4), 492–501.

Dowdney, L., & Pickles, A. R. (1991). Expression of negative affect within disciplinary encounters: Is there dyadic reciprocity? *Developmental Psychology*, *27*(4), 606–617.

Ekstein, R. (1991). Bruno Bettelheim. *American Psychologist*, *46*(10), 1080.

Flavell, J. H. (1985). *Cognitive development* (2nd ed.). Englewood Cliffs, New Jersey: Prentice-Hall.

Fonagy, P., & Target, M. (1996). A contemporary psychoanalytic perspective: Psychodynamic developmental therapy. In: E. D. Hibbs & P. S. Jensen (Eds), *Psychosocial Treatments for Child and Adolescent Disorders: Empirically Based Strategies for Clinical Practice*. Washington, D.C.: APA Press.

Fong, P. (1991). Cognitive appraisals in high- and low-stress mothers of adolescents with autism. *Journal of Consulting and Clinical Psychology*, *59*(3), 471–474.

Frith, U. (1991). Asperger and his syndrome. In: U. Frith (Ed.), *Autism and Asperger Syndrome*. Cambridge: Cambridge University Press.

Frith, U., & Happe, F. (1994). Autism: Beyond "Theory of Mind". *Cognition*, 50, 115–132.

Glascoe, F. P. (1994). It's not what it seems: The relationship between parents' concerns and children with global delays. *Clinical Pediatrician, 33*, 292–296.

Glascoe, F. P. (1997). Parents' concerns about children's development: Prescreening technique or screen test? *Pediatrics, 99*, 522–528.

Glascoe, F. P., & Dworkin, P. H. (1995). The role of parents in the detection of developmental and behavioral problems. *Pediatrics, 95*, 829–836.

Glascoe, F. P., MacLean, W. E., & Stone, W. L. (1991). The importance of parents' concerns about their child's behavior. *Clinical Pediatrician, 30*, 8–11.

Johnson, S. M., & Lobitz, G. K. (1974). Parental manipulation of child behavior in home observations. *Journal of Applied Behavior Analysis, 7*, 23–31.

Kanner, L. (1943). Autistic disturbances of affective contact. *Nervous Child, 21*, 217–250.

Koegel, L. K., & Koegel, R. L. (1996). The child with autism as an active communicative partner: Child-initiated strategies for improving communication and reducing behavior problems. In: E. D. Hibbs & P. S. Jensen (Eds), *Psychosocial Treatments for Child and Adolescent Disorders: Empirically Based Strategies for Clinical Practice*. Washington, D.C.: American Psychological Association.

Koegel, R. L., Koegel, L. K., & McNerney, E. K. (2001). Pivotal areas in intervention for autism. *Journal of Clinical Child Psychology, 30*(1), 19–32.

Lange, A. J., & Jakubowski, P. (1976). *Responsible assertive behavior*. Champaign, IL: Research Press.

Lobitz, G. K., & Johnson, S. M. (1975). Parental manipulation of the behavior of normal and deviant children. *Child Development, 46*, 719–726.

Lovass, O. I. (1977). *The autistic child: Language development through behavior modification*. New York: Irvington.

Lovaas, O. I. (1987). Behavioral treatment and normal educational and intellectual functioning in young autistic children. *Journal of Consulting and Clinical Psychology, 55*, 3–9.

Lovaas, O. I. (2000). Concerns about misinterpretation and placement of blame. *American Psychologist, 44*(9), 1243–1244.

Lovaas, O. I., Schaeffer, B., & Simmons, J. Q. (1965). Experimental studies in childhood schizophrenia: Building social behaviors in autistic children by the use of electric shock. *Journal of Experiemntal Research in Personality, 1*, 99–109.

McEachin, J. J., Smith, T., & Lovaas, O. I. (1993). Long-term outcome for children with autism who received early intensive behavioral treatment. *American Journal on Mental Retardation, 97*, 359–372.

Mueser, K., Bellack, A., Wade, J., Sayers, S., Tierney, A., & Haas, G. (1993). Expressed emotion, social skill, and response to negative affect in schizophrenia. *Journal of Abnormal Psychology, 102*(3), 339–351.

Nicholls, J. G., Martin, A. R., & Wallace, B. G. (1992). *From neuron to brain: A cellar and molecular approach to the function of the nervous system* (3rd ed.). Sunderland, MA: Sinaner Associates.

Nolen-Hoeksema, S. (1998). *Abnormal psychology*. Boston: McGraw Hill.

Ozonoff, S., & Miller, J. (1995). Teaching theory of mind: A new approach to social skills training for individuals with autism. *Journal of Autism and Developmental Disorders*, 25, 415–433.

Piaget, J., & Inhelder, B. (1963). *The child's conception of space*. London: Routledge and Paul.

Schopler, E. (1971). Parents of psychotic children as scapegoats. *Journal of Contemporary Psychotherapy, 4*, 17–22.

Schopler, E. (1988). Concerns about misinterpretation and uncritical acceptance of exaggerated claims. *American Psychologist, 43*, 658.

Smith, T., Eikeseth, S., Klevstrand, M., & Lovaas, O. (1997). Intensive behavioral treatment for preschoolers with severe mental retardation and pervasive development disorder. *American Journal of Mental Retardation*, *102*, 238–249.

Smith, T., & Lovaas, O.I. (1998). Intensive and early behavioral intervention with autism: The UCLA young autism project. *Infants and Young Child*, (10), 67–78.

Smith, T., Wynn, J., & Lovaas, O. I. (1997). Outcome in adulthood. Paper presented at the Early Intervention Conference. Los Angeles, CA.

Volkmar, F. R. (2001). Pharmacological interventions in autism: Theoretical and practical issues. *Journal of Clinical Child Psychology*, *30*(1), 80–87.

Yirmiya, N., Solomonica-Levi, D., & Shulman, C. (1996). The ability to manipulate behavior and to understand manipulation of beliefs: A comparison of individuals with autism, mental retardation, and normal development. *Developmental Psychology*, *32*(1), 62–69.

COUNSELING TECHNIQUES FOR INDIVIDUALS WITH AUTISTIC SPECTRUM DISORDERS

Michele R. Arthur, Anthony F. Rotatori and Tim Wahlberg

INTRODUCTION

Educational and environmental interventions available for children with Autism Spectrum Disorders (ASD) are many and varied (see Attwood, 1998; Cumine, Leach & Stevenson, 1998; Falvey, Grenot-Scheyer, Coots & Bishop, 1995: Greenspan & Wielder, 1997; Hyman & Levy, 2000; Intagliata, 2001; Koegel & Koegel, 1995; Myles & Simpson, 1998; Nichel, 1996; Rogers, 2000; Safran, 2001, Starr, 1998; Williams; 1995; Wolf-Schein, 1994). Early interventions often include home-based therapy accompanied by speech therapy (see Chaplop & Haymes, 1994; Wisconsin Autism Project, 1995), behavior modification (see Lovaas, 1987; Luiscelli, Taras & Lovaas, 1998), and special education services (see Ryan, 2000).The transition to adulthood often involves vocational training or advanced education, continued skills training, and perhaps, residential placement (see Myles & Simpson, 1998). All services are tailored to the individual, however, counseling is frequently an adjunct service that may be requested by the individual, family, or agency serving the individual with ASD. Therefore, counselors, therapists, and social workers must be aware of the clinical symptoms and behavioral characteristics of ASD and effective techniques to assist these individuals.

Autistic Spectrum Disorders: Educational and Clinical Interventions, pages 235–254.

ISBN: 0-7623-0818-4

CLINICAL SYMPTOMS AND BEHAVIORAL CHARACTERISTICS OF INDIVIDUALS WITH ASD

Counselors and mental health professionals increasingly use the term ASD to describe clients with the following pervasive developmental disorders: Autistic Disorder; Rett Disorder: Childhood Disintegrative Disorder; Asperger Disorder and Pervasive Develomental Disorder Not Otherwise Specified (American Academy of Pediatrics, 2001; Greenspan & Wielder, 1999; Prizant & Rubin, 1999; Wetherby & Prizant, 2000). The primary features of ASD are: impaired communication, impaired social interaction, and restricted repetitive behaviors, interests, and activities (see American Psychiatric Association, 1994). Individuals with ASD have a range of conditions. For example, 75% of individuals with autism are dually diagnosed with mental retardation and approximately half of all autistic individuals are non-verbal (Sigman & Capps, 1997). In contrast, clients with Asperger Disorder do not exhibit a clinically significant intellectual delay (Bock & Myles, 1999). Due to these varied conditions, counselors must integrate knowledge about mental retardation, communication disorders, and mental illness.

In individuals with mental retardation, behavior is recognized as a form of communication. The same principle must be kept in mind when treating individuals with ASD. Teaching effective communications skills, appropriate ways to express feelings, and methods to gain impulse control are strategies implemented to reduce undesirable behaviors. Similar to individuals with mental retardation, individuals with ASD have difficulty understanding abstract ideas and language. Therefore, techniques such as speaking in concrete terms and asking specific questions would also be effective with individuals with ASD (see Greenspan & Wielder, 1997; Hurth, Shaw, Izeman, Whaley & Rogers, 1999; Smith & Lovass, 1998; Wetherby & Prizant, 1999).

However, it is important for clinicians to realize that greater impairments in adaptive skills are found in individuals with ASD (except Asperger Disorder) than in children with mental retardation (Carpentieri & Morgan, 1996; Schatz & Hamdan-Allen, 1995). In fact, "large increases in IQ have only modest effects in increasing social skills for children with autism" (Schatz & Hamdan-Allen, 1995).

The communication deficits found in ASD are highly variable as well. As mentioned previously, half of all individuals with autism are nonverbal, however, individuals with Asperger Disorder can not be diagnosed as having this disorder if there is a clinically significant delay in language (American Psychiatric Association, 1994). For individuals with autism, who do acquire language, the acquisition is significantly delayed. In other clients with autism, adequate speech may develop, but is hindered by an inability to initiate or sustain conversation. In fact for many with autism, language is frequently used in stereotyped or idiosyncratic ways and is accompanied by impairments in nonverbal communication. It is difficult to separate the communication deficits in ASD from the social impairment. Social and emotional reciprocity may be lacking.

Often individuals with ASD exhibit a failure of peer relationships and a deficit in sharing interests, achievements, and enjoyment with others (American Psychiatric Association, 1994). Frequently, individuals with ASD manifest a preoccupation with stereotyped and restricted patterns of interest, inflexible routines or rituals, repetitive motor mannerisms, or focus on parts of objects. This limited repertoire negatively impacts social relations.

The repetitive behavior and obsessive thoughts of adults with ASD appears similar to symptoms of obsessive-compulsive disorder (Baker, Koegel & Koegel, 1998). However, one study (McDougle et al., 1995) found a specific subset of traits among a group with autism. The most commonly reported repetitive behaviors of the autistic group were: repeating, need to touch/ tap/ rub, ordering, or hoarding. In the group with obsessive-compulsive disorder the most frequent compulsions were checking, cleaning, and repeating. The most frequently endorsed obsessions of the autistic group were: need to know or remember (often-labeled self-doubt), hoarding, and contamination. In contrast, those with obsessive-compulsive disorder most often had obsessions about aggression, contamination, and symmetry. Despite these differences, similar treatment is effective including serotonin reuptake inhibitors and behavior therapy (McDougle et al., 1995).

In addition to cognitive, communication, social, and behavioral deficits, ASD is further compounded by abnormal sensory and perceptual processing. Several theories may help the practitioner gain an understanding of ASD. They are: "Theory of Mind," "Executive Function," "Central Coherence," "Social Impairment" and "Control Theory of Autism".

Theory of Mind (Rutter, 1999) suggests that the social impairments seen in ASD may be associated with an inability to understand subjective mental states (to appreciate what others think, believe, desire, and intend). This theory would account for the inability of clients with ASD to share joint attention and perspective as well as their weak interpretation and relatedness failure to attach motivational value to take another's point of view. One study taught persons with autism about mental states, but improvement in social communication skills was not demonstrated (Hadwin, Baron-Cohen, Howlin & Hill, 1997). The authors suggested communication skills did not improve because the learned task did not generalize. Positively, Dahlgren and Trillingsgaard (1996) stated children with ASD improve in this capacity with higher levels of cognition, verbal ability and chronological age. Thus, counselors who decide to use theory of mind clinical interventions may be more successful when these techniques are applied to older, smarter and more verbally fluid clients.

Another theory suggests problems with *Executive Function* in persons with ASD. Executivefunction is defined as an ability to maintain an appropriate problem-solving framework (Bailey, Phillips & Rutter, 1996). It includes the following abilities: "to disengage from the external context; inhibit inappropriate responses; plan and generate sequences of willed actions; sustain an appropriate cognitive set for staying on task; monitor own performance and make use of feedback; flexibly shift attentional set" (Bailey, Phillips & Rutter, 1996, p. 101). Deficits in executive function would account for the difficulties that clients with ASD have related to the following; learning from ones mistakes from past experience, changing ones opinion of a certain social situation (inflexibility), socially impulsive critical responding of others behavior and engagement in repetitive behaviors.

A third theory, *Central Coherence*, has been proposed to explain deficits seen in weak drive for persons with ASD. This theory proposes that these individuals have a weak drive for central coherence, a tendency to process information in pieces rather than in context, thus resisting the "gestalt" (Frith, 1989, as cited in Bailey, Phillips & Rutter, 1996). Deficits in central coherence may account for the following symptoms in clients with ASD: savant skills; inherent insistence on sameness; specific odd interests; poor text comprehension; and failure to extract and use global meaning from written context. Finally, it is suspected that difficulty seeing the whole may hinder interpersonal understanding such as comprehension of facial expressions.

A fourth theory, *Social Impairment*, suggests deficits in social insight (Happe & Frith, 1996: Mundy, 1995). According to this theory, individuals with ASD have developmental anomalies in their neurological systems which impact negatively on affective and cognitive processes related to social development. Such anomalies may account for the following social behaviors in clients with ASD their: inability to recognize the emotional state of others, failure to share the focus of social attention, and difficulties in putting themselves in another's shoes.

The last theory, *Control Theory*, as proposed by Wahlberg (see chapter 2 in this book) hypothesizes that neurological deficits exist in individuals with ASD which causes them to suffer from environmental over-stimulation. According to Wahlberg, this over-stimulation forces individuals with autism to process incoming stimulus in a different manner than normal individuals. According to this view, clients with ASD take in environmental information in a way to screen out anything that is over stimulating. This leads these clients to behave in a way to create order within the "chaos" of the world. Due to their striving for control, clients with ASD, insist upon sameness and exhibit rigid and inflexible behaviors. When environmental situations are too pressing, they engage in "zoning out" or stereotypic behaviors to remove themselves from the over stimulating social situations or react with emotional discomfort to auditory, visual or tactile stimulation that is painful to themselves.

The aforementioned theoretical frameworks may help explain the deficits witnessed in individuals with ASD. However, in clinical practice, altering behavior patterns and teaching adaptive skills is usually emphasized. It is clear that counseling these individuals vary greatly depending on developmental stage, intelligence, and severity of autism.

The term ASD acknowledges the broad range in severity of symptoms (see American Academy of Pediatrics, 2001). ASD is a complex spectrum disorder, with symptoms occurring on a continuum from mild to severe which effect cognitive, communication, social, and behavioral domains. Due to this complexity, behavioral specialists are often consulted for treatment of individuals with ASD (see Attwood, 1998; Lovaas, 1987; Lovaas & Smith, 1988; Luiselli, Taras & Lennon, 1998; Mash & Barkley, 1996; McEachin, Smith & Lovaas, 1993). Traditional counseling services would be limited to those individuals with sufficient verbal and cognitive skills to benefit from such services. Counselors, in addition to utilizing their knowledge and expertise of counseling strategies and cognitive-behavioral interventions must also integrate their expertise of developmental delays, communication disorders, mental retardation, and mental illness. In addition, counselors will need to modify traditional therapy to adapt to the special needs of these individuals.

CHARACTERISTICS AND COUNSELING INTERVENTIONS

The challenge in counseling is not only to alter behavior, but also to help the client gain insight. Therefore a guide to characteristics frequently seen when counseling clients with ASD will follow. Common characteristics that counselors need to address include deficit patterns of communication, faulty social development, problematic emotional responses, and difficulty making decisions. Treatment strategies and suggestions to address these maladaptive functioning deficits are included. Some of the techniques suggested are borrowed from educational practices (see Kunce & Mesibov, 1998; Marks et al., 1999; Matson & Swienzy, 1994). Others merely emphasize particular counseling techniques (see Intagliata, 2001; Luiselli et al., 1998; Marriage, Gordon & Brand, 1995; Ozonoff & Miller, 1995; Myles & Southwick, 1999). The ideas presented are not exhaustive but simply a guide based on the theoretical frameworks, current research, and the experiences of clinicians familiar with ASD. Many of the examples were gathered from the authors' clinical experience.

Initial Session Concerns

As in any initial counseling session, roles must be clarified, ethical and legal considerations discussed, and consent obtained. Goals must be clearly established and prioritized through a collaborative effort. With younger clients, parental involvement in goal setting is highly advantageous (see Starr, Foy & Cramer, 2001). At times the counselor may need to set an educational goal, such as educating the client about ASD (see Attwood, 1998) but it is vital that the client agree to the goal. In counseling situations with "higher functioning" individuals, the deficits often appear as treatment goals. Concurrently, the deficits also demand modification of the counseling process. A counselor who is aware of how ASD affects perception, thought processes, and also hampers communication and socialization will be prepared to alter the counseling process to address these special needs.

Enhancing Communication

Communication deficits, including deficits in receptive and expressive language, often interfere with comprehension and, therefore, the counseling process. The implication when counseling individuals with communication deficits is two-fold. The counselor must monitor frequently his own use of language as well as the client's level of comprehension.

Specific characteristics of ASD that interfere with communication include the following; mirrored adaptive responses, halted reception, processing deficits, and inability to comprehend the abstract. Mirrored adaptive responses interfere with communication because individuals with ASD have learned to adapt to social societal norms. For example, clients may be adept at appearing as though they follow conversations. Simply inquiring, "do you understand?" may evoke "yes" in response. However, the meaning may *not* be understood. A better approach would be to ask the individual with ASD to repeat or paraphrase previous comments made by the counselor. This provides the counselor an opportunity to clear up any misperceptions before proceeding further. The use of reflective listening, paraphrasing, and clarifying questions by the counselor also serves as a model for the client.

At times halted reception interferes with communication. Halted reception may occur when certain stimuli catch the attention of the client preventing the individual from attending to further input. The individual may perseverate on certain sentences or words that interfere with communication processing. For example, a client with ASD wanted to discuss some carpentry concerns with a counselor. The counselor, who had some experience with carpentry, attempted to answer the client's questions. The counselor made reference to a hammer early in his statement. Inquiring for comprehension, the counselor discovered the word "hammer" had interfered with the client's ability to focus on the explanation. When questioned further the client indicated that the word "hammer" triggered a visualization of a childhood memory. The visualization prevented him from following the conversation any further. The client reported that this type of derailing happened often. In such cases, the counselor must be cognizant of body language to ascertain if the client is attending. Questioning the client regarding comprehension or asking the client to paraphrase previous statements would also be useful.

Unlocking Communication

At other times, during processing delays, individuals with ASD appear to "freeze." It seems these individual need extended time periods to process auditory information and formulate a response. Counselors must speak explicitly in concrete terms, use a minimum of words, and reduce the number of social signals given (such as facial expressions and gestures that accompany language), as well as allow sufficient time for clients with ASD to process information and formulate a response. Quickly restating or rephrasing the question may contribute to stimulation overload and confuse the thought process of the clients even further.

Inability to understand abstractions may also interfere with comprehension. Individuals with ASD communicate and interpret language quite literally. One client with ASD, who was informed that a residential move was necessary because the current home was "shrinking", subsequently experienced difficulty sleeping. The cause, when discovered, was fear and worry that the house was literally closing in and about to harm the family. Another example occurred when a client with ASD was told by a counselor, "we will see about a group to help with obsessive thoughts and compulsive behaviors." The individual refused to leave the session, but insisted to the counselor, "You wanted to show me something!" A third example demonstrates the use of literal language by a client. This child with ASD reported his reluctance to befriend a peer because the peer "vibrated." In actuality the peer rested the ball of his foot on the floor and rapidly bounced his leg up and down.

Understanding How Clients With ASD Think

The previous examples demonstrate ways for counselors to clarify statements and modify their use of language to improve communication to clients with ASD. The following examples, in contrast, will assist the counselor to understand clients with ASD. Understanding how the client with ASD thinks and perceives situations may help the counselor build rapport and generate effective problem solving and coping strategies. First-hand accounts given by individuals with ASD often indicate that they are either visual or numeric thinkers (see Grandin, 1995; Willey, 1999). Asking how a particular individual thinks may provide information useful to the counselor. A high functioning individual with ASD may be able to state their style of thinking while a lower functioning individual with ASD may need concrete examples of various thinking styles such as thinking in pictures, numbers, or words.

A technique for helping a client with ASD who thinks in numbers may be to use a numeric rating system to quantify and self-monitor emotions (Attwood, 1998). Assigning numerical values to the benefits and drawbacks of particular solutions to problems would help the individual evaluate situations in a mathematical manner. Progress toward a goal could also be evaluated on a numerical continuum.

In addition to thinking differently, individuals with ASD often experience altered sensory and perceptual abilities. Intense sensory perceptions may cause reactions to particular sights, sounds, smells, or tactile sensations. An example of this occurred with a child with ASD who felt physically warm during the school day and began to cry. The child, however, was too embarrassed to acknowledge over-stimulation as the cause of the tears.

Dealing With Misperceived Social Interactions

The difficulties clients with ASD have related to communication, different thinking styles, and altered perceptions contribute to their tendency to misperceive social interactions. Delays in social development are typical (see Gray, 1998; Gray & Garand, 1993; Gresham, 1998; Marks et al., 1999; Robertson, Tanguay, L'ecuyer, Sims & Waltrip, 1999). Social situations are frequently misperceived (Attwood, 1998; Happe & Frith, 1996; Hobson, 1993). Furthermore, the ability to comprehend the subtleties of social contexts is often fragmented. Delayed social development in ASD occurs despite measured intelligence at or above the mean and adequate speech. Within a structured counseling session, a client with ASD may function quite well, but when he is observed in groups among peers with greater cognitive and verbal deficits, the social awkwardness of the client becomes apparent. Therefore, it is important for the counselor not to raise expectations beyond the capabilities of the individual with ASD.

In addition to delayed social skills, often the perception and therefore reporting about social situations is faulty. An example of this occurred with a client who had great difficulty with spontaneous telephone conversations. To assist the client in being more spontaneous during telephone conversations, mock conversations were role played during counseling sessions. The individual practiced various scenarios. For a homework assignment, he called to inquire about a social group for adults with ASD. He reported that the secretary treated him in a rude manner. The counselor asked the client to review the phone conversation. The client related that when he asked for information about the social group, the receptionist put him on hold, which he interpreted as extremely rude. Another client with ASD reported a teacher had been "verbally abusive." In fact, the client had interrupted the teacher who was attending to the needs of another student. The teacher requested that the client be seated and indicated she would provide assistance momentarily. It is apparent that counselors, in order to effectively assist clients with ASD, need to verify their own understanding of the client through use of clarifying and probing questions, reflective listening, and paraphrasing.

Fragmented Social Skills

In addition to having social developmental delay and misperceptions of social interactions, clients with ASD have social skills that are fragmented in nature, perhaps because of the lack of central coherence. Many times clients with ASD seem to grasp bits and pieces of social context while leaving out important social imperatives or they try and learn effective ways to "fit in" with others. For example, individuals with ASD may inadvertently offend others by being brutally honest rather than following social conventions of polite behavior. An individual with ASD may laugh at inappropriate times during conversations, violating the norms governing social interactions. Conversely, an individual with ASD may have adaptively learned to laugh when others in the social setting smile or laugh, although not comprehending the humor. Others become a teasing target. For example, a client with ASD, who attempted to complete his assigned task of closing a gate before school began, did not grasp that the older children sitting on the gate were teasing him. He simply reported that his job was very difficult because the fence was very heavy and hard to push. In situations such as the above, it is important for the counselor to interpret the social situation for the client with ASD so that he can correct his fragmented response.

Techniques To Improve Social Skills

Various counseling strategies may be effective to assist the client with ASD to improve social skills. Training in basic conversation skills and social skills is one method to teach socially appropriate behavior, learn social conventions, and avoid offending others. Social skills training programs that incorporate demonstrations, modeling, rehearsal, performance feedback (see Luiselli et al., 1998), role playing (see Marriage et al., 1995) and in vivo exercises (see Attwood, 1998; Marriage et al., 1995) allow the client with ASD to witness appropriate interactions, practice social skills in a safe environment, gain instantaneous feedback, and hone skills before completing social skill homework independently. For example, the client who interpreted being put on hold as rude, may have benefited from rehearsing the telephone calls with the counselor present providing immediate feedback regarding standard procedures in such a situation. Utilizing sequenced pictures of social situations (see Edelson, 1995; Edelson, 1999; Gray, 1998; Gray & Garand, 1993), social scripts (see Attwood, 1998; Schafer, 1996; Swaggart & Gagnon, 1999), or conducting social autopsies would also provide opportunities to assess and correct social misperceptions.

Individuals with ASD, often are deficit in social skills that promote friendship (Attwood, 1998). For example, it is not uncommon for these individuals to exhibit the following negative behaviors which interfere in the development of friendships: difficulty taking turns, critical of others mistakes or weaknesses, rudeness, interest in solitary and idiosyncratic pursuits, clumsy and ill-coordinated recreational skills, poor pragmatic communication abilities, and a desire to have complete control over a situation (see Attwood, 1998; Bock & Myles, 1999; Rodier, 2000; Ryan, 2000; Safran, 2001). Counselors can be very helpful in training and encouraging friendship skills for individuals with ASD. Attwood (1998) described a training program that used behavioral and cognitive strategies to assist clients with ASD acquire and develop friendship skills. The program involved the following steps: (a) assess which skills are observed or absent; (b) assess the quality and range of expression; (c) perform a task analysis of the skills while identifying prompts, shaping strategies and positive reinforcement; and (d) teach the skills. To teach the skills, Attwood employed videotaped role plays of being and not being a friend along with social stories, comic strip conversation and a friendship diary. To increase the likelihood of developing friendships, Attwood matched clients with ASD based on similar interest and hobbies. Additionally, Attwood encourages the development of local pen pal registries and internet chat lines as a means of increasing friendships.

Dealing With Faulty Emotional Responses

Given the aforementioned difficulties with communication and social interactions it is not surprising that clients with ASD often have extreme or faulty emotional responses to situations. Clients with ASD may experience a range of emotions including sadness, disappointment, and fear. But they are particularly likely to display these emotions as frustration, verbal and physical aggression, anger and/or violence (see Baron-Cohen, 1988; Mawson, Grounds & Tantum, 1985; Scragg & Shah, 1994). In fact, the ASD condition tends to cultivate anger. Bock and Myles (1999) stated that violence in individuals with Asperger Disorder may be linked to their lack of empathy. However, Ghaziuddin, Tsai and Ghaziuddin (1991) reported that violence in individuals with Asperger Disorder has occurred in only a small sample of persons with this disorder. Because of this fact, these researchers cautioned mental health professionals to be careful about generalizing that clients with Asperger Disorder are violent as such a label may result in a stigma and stress for these individuals.

The negative emotional response is often triggered by misperceptions, behavioral preseverations, and frustrations regarding social situations as well as by changes in routine and transitions. For example, an event is initially misperceived, such as the child thinking the teacher was verbally abusive for not attending to his needs immediately. This perceived wrongdoing is further compounded by the child's rumination about the event. It may appear the event has been exaggerated and that the individual is overreacting. However, the emotional response is often proportionate to the client's perception of the event.

Cognitive distortions are prominent in clients with ASD and repeatedly contribute to their emotional reactions such as anger. The emotional response may be exacerbated by excessive rumination. During this rumination about the perceived wrongdoing of others, the faulty perception may become entrenched and anger overdeveloped. This can occur due to clients with ASD limited ability to manage negative feelings especially frustration, their lack of empathy and self control to moderate their reaction, their immature conflict resolution and their limited vocabulary to express negative emotions (Attwood, 1998). Counselors may allow a client with ASD to vent this emotion, however, emotional venting about the perceived wrongdoing of others needs to be focused on a particular theme or utilized to point out self-management or coping techniques that could be transferred to similar situations. At times counselors can make clients with ASD assess their anger by using what Attwood (2001) refers to as a "angerometer". This is a rating scale of one to ten with assigned points for most anger (ten) verse little anger (one). When a client goes above seven, it is recommended that he engage in one of the following: anger reduction technique such as relaxation: using a grievance book to make complaints: going to a sanctuary area: or engaging in thought switching by reading a pleasant book (Attwood, 1998).

The ongoing frustration that accompanies the cognitive misperceptions, altered sensory perceptions, misunderstandings in communication, and cognitive deficits also contribute to heightened emotional responses. In addition, constant difficulty perceiving the "gestalt" and maintaining an appropriate problem solving set contribute to the over-development of anger.

Changes and transitions also lead to heightened emotional response. Individuals with ASD prefer the consistency and predictability found in routine. Routine helps control anxiety, whereas changes in routine increase anxiety. Increased anxiety may lead to increased intensity and frequency of obsessive thoughts and compulsive behavior, which are utilized as coping techniques by clients with ASD. An example of this occurred with the client who role played telephone calls with his counselor. The client, wanting to be prepared for any contingency, continually desired to alter the role-play, stating, "What if the person says this?" Since one cannot be prepared for every possibility, individuals with ASD often find themselves anxious and angered by the changes that occur.

Some techniques to assist the individual with ASD to manage their emotions include teaching compensatory techniques such as checking out perceptions with a trusted support person. Utilizing educational techniques to teach about cognitive distortions through analyzing current life experiences, beliefs about those events, and the emotional reaction that accompanies them may be necessary (see Kunce & Mesibov, 1998; Williams, 1995). Discovering the root of the emotion through analyzing the event and the beliefs about the event that triggered the emotion is likely to be beneficial (see Harris, Belchic, Blum & Celiberti, 1994). In addition, the client with ASD may self-monitor emotional reactions by keeping a chart noting the event, belief, and accompanying emotion (see Attwood, 1998; Luiselli et al., 1998). Examining those situations during subsequent counseling sessions can be helpful. Assisting the client with ASD to learn cognitive reframing strategies to restate thoughts in a positive way may also be advantageous (see Attwood, 1998). Counselors must be prepared to use reality orientation to help clients with ASD see how rigidity or misperceptions contribute to their emotional reactions such as anger. Correctly identifying emotions and helping clients to expand their vocabulary to more accurately reflect emotional states may also be helpful.

Myles and Southwick (1999) indicated that a client with ASD may go into a rage or meltdown when provoked, or when under high stress or anxiety levels. These researchers reported that the following interventions may be effective in quieting the client who is experiencing a tantrum, rage or meltdown: (a) temporarily removing the client from the situation; (b) standing near the client to offer support; (c) touching the client as a form of comfort; (d) making the client laugh; (e) redirecting the client to another activity; (f) giving the client a choice of going to a identified safe place for a few minutes; and (g) going for a brief walk with the client. When the rage is intense, Myles and Southwick recommend that the client be removed to a safe room where he can calm down.

Improving Decision Making

While social situations present particular problems for a client with ASD, decision-making is also a task that causes difficulties. Decision-making may be hampered by deficits in executive function, lack of comprehension, rigidity, obsessive thinking, and anxiety. A client with ASD may attempt to apply literal thinking strategies to abstract situations. Compound questions may not be understood as either/or choices. Anxiety may trigger ritualistic behavior or obsessive thinking. The need to know or remember is a particular obstacle to decision making as a client may search exhaustively for all possible solutions to a problem or obsessively generate pros and cons without reaching a decision. However, the client's obsessing behavior must be viewed by the counselor as an intellectual response to anxiety. On the other hand, a client may perceive only one solution and be unable to imagine other alternatives.

Counselors can use the following to assist clients with ASD in making better decisions: teaching a formal problem solving procedure; utilization of rating systems, such as numbers to rate feelings about a particular decision; listing pros and cons in a time limited fashion; implementing thought stopping to interrupt obsessive thinking; and placing a time limit on decision making. Other possibilities include systematic desensitization to help the client cope with the heightened anxiety of making a decision, cognitive reframing such as informing the individual that a decision will satisfy the need to know, and encouraging flexibility through the experience of learning that most decisions are reversible

Supporting Parents of Clients With ASD

Parents of clients with ASD benefit from support and education (see Attwood, 1998; Myles & Southwick, 1999; Starr, Foy & Cramer, 2001). For example, a survey by Starr et al. found that parents of students with ASD "appeared to want their children in inclusive classrooms, and for the most part are satisfied with their children's class performance, however, it is evident that there are numerous concerns regarding educational planning and programming for their children within the general education setting" (p. 67). Counselors can be helpful in assisting and supporting parents in their efforts to implement effective inclusion strategies via parent-teacher team collaboration (see Wolf-Schein, 1994).

Similarly, Myles and Southwick (1999) recommended that counselors can work with parents to develop a home plan that speaks to concerns such as agreeing on the cause of a maladaptive behavior, designing a structured daily routine, organizing individual family members responsibility and discipline. They suggest parents may need to join a support group or arrange for respite care. Counselors can be helpful to these parents by providing names and addresses for such referrals. Also, Myles and Southwick indicate that counselors can teach parents to use the "lasting word" technique to help them avoid inevitable arguments and power struggles with their child. The lasting word technique involves the following rule: "Say what you mean and mean what you say; say it only twice in a calm voice; verify the child's understanding; stop talking and take action" (p. 93).

Another area of concern is the problematic frequency of suicidal ideation in individuals with ASD. Attwood (2001) reported that the rate of suicidal ideation among individuals with Asperger Disorder is three to four times that of normal individuals. The authors own clinical experience support this rate. In our practice, we have witnessed eight to nine year old clients' talk about suicide. Generally, this talk is due to a recent social frustration the client has experienced and it is done for effect and attention. However, when clients with ASD enter junior high, they have more difficulty establishing positive social relationships. Even though they put considerable effort into making friends, they are unsuccessful due to their ASD characteristics. This can result in a meltdown and active suicidal ideation and intention. Thus, counselors need to educate parents of clients with ASD about assessing the level of their child's suicidal ideation and intention and securing emergency treatment if needed.

CONCLUSION

It is clear that the diagnosis of ASD has far reaching effects for a client – impacting family, social, educational, and vocational domains as well as impacting one's sense of happiness and well being. Therefore, counselors must be cognizant of the particular needs of clients with ASD based on the developmental stage, cognitive abilities, communication abilities, and severity of symptoms as well as counseling techniques that diminish social skill deficits and problematic emotional reactions. In addition, the counselor must prioritize treatment goals in collaboration with the client to choose effective techniques to implement, evaluate progress, and flexibly alter treatment strategies when necessary. For younger clients with ASD, it is recommended that parents be included in treatment goal settings.

Working with clients with ASD taxes the resources of counselors. Coping with the client's lack of reciprocity and positive feedback presents a particular challenge for counselors. Collaborating with other mental health professionals or working as a team member may assist the counselor to maintain emotional equilibrium and generate positive ideas for treatment strategies.

REFERENCES

American Academy of Pediatrics (2001). Committee on Children With Disabilities. Technical report: The pediatrician's role in the diagnosis and management of autistic spectrum disorder in children. *Pediatrics, 107*(5) (URL: http//www.pediatrics,org/cgi/content/full/107/5/e85).

American Psychiatric Association (1994). Diagnostic and statistical manual of mental disorders (4th ed.). Washington, D.C.: American Psychiatric Association.

Attwood, T. (1998). *Asperger's syndrome: A guide for parents and professionals*. London, England: Jessica Kingsley Publishers Ltd.

Attwood. T. (2001). *Asperger's syndrome: Current research and clinical applications*. Workshop presentation at Oak Park Public Schools, River Forest, Il.

Bailey, A., Phillips, W., & Rutter, M. (1996). Autism: Toward an integration of clinical, genetic, neuropsychological, and neurobiological perspectives. *Journal of Child Psychology and Psychiatry, 37*(1), 89–126.

Baker, M. J., Koegel, R. L., & Koegel, L. K. (1998). Increasing the social behavior of young children with autism using obsessive behavior. *The Journal of the Association for Persons with Severe Handicaps, 23*, 300–308.

Baron-Cohen, S. (1988). An assessment of violence in a young man with Asperger's syndrome. *Journal of Child Psychology and Psychiatry, 29*, 351–360.

Bock, S. J., & Myles, B. S. (1999). An overview of characteristics of Asperger syndrome. *Education and Training in Mental Retardation and Developmental Disabilities, 34*, 511–520.

Carpentieri, S., & Morgan, S. B. (1996). Adaptive and intellectual functioning in autistic and nonautistic retarded children. *Journal of Autism and Developmental Disorders, 26*(6), 611–620.

Chaplop, M. H., & Haymes, L. K. (1994). Speech and language acquisition and intervention: Behavioral approaches. In: J. L. Matson (Ed.), *Autism in Children and Adults: Etiology, Assessment, and Intervention* (pp. 213–240). Pacific Grove, CA: Brooks/Cole.

Cumine, V., Leach, J., & Stevenson, G. (1998). *Asperger syndrome: A practical guide for teachers*. London, U.K.: David Fulton.

Dahlgren, S. O., & Trillingsgaard, A. (1996). Theory of mind in non-retarded children with autism and Asperger's syndrome: A research note. *Journal of Child Psychology and Psychiatry, 37*, 759–763.

Edelson, S. M. (1995). *Theory of mind*. Salem, OR: Center for the Study of Autism.

Edelson, S. M. (1999). Social behaviors in autism spectrum disorders. *New Development, 5*, 5.

Falvey, M. Grenot-Scheyer, M., Coots, J., & Bishop, K. (1995). Services for students with disabilities: Past and present. In: M. A. Falvey (Ed.), *Inclusive and Heterogeneous Schooling: Assessment, Curriculum, and Instruction* (pp. 23–40). Baltimore, MD: Paul H. Brookes.

Ghaziuddin, M., Tsai, L., & Ghaziuddin, N. (1991). Brief report: Violence in Asperger syndrome, a critique. *Journal of Autism and Developmental Disorders, 21*, 349–354.

Grandin, T. (1995). *Thinking in pictures and other reports from my life with autism*. New York: Doubleday.

Gray, C. A. (1998). Social stories and comic strip conversations with students with Asperger syndrome and high-functioning autism. In: E. Schopler, G. B. Mesibov & L. J. Kunce (Eds), *Asperger Syndrome or High-functioning Autism?* (pp. 167–198). New York: Plenum.

Gray, C. A., & Garand, J. D. (1993). Social stories: Improving responses of students with autism with accurate social information. *Focus on Autistic Behaviors*, *8*, 1–10.

Greenspan, S. I., & Wielder, S. (1997). Developmental patterns and outcomes in infants and children with disorder of relating and communicating: A chart review of 200 cases of children with autistic spectrum diagnoses. *Journal of Developmental and Learning Disorders*, *1*, 87–141.

Greenspan, S. I., & Wielder, S. (1999). A functional developmental approach to autism spectrum disorders. *The Journal of the American Association of Persons with Severe Handicaps*, *24*, 147–161

Gresham, M. M. (1998). Social skills training: Should we raze, remodel, or rebuild? *Behavioral Disorders*, *24*, 19–25.

Hadwin, J., Baron-Cohen, S., Howlin, P., & Hill, K. (1997). Does teaching theory of mind have an effect on the ability to develop conversation in children with autism. *Journal of Autism and Developmental Disorders*, *27*(5), 519–537.

Happe, F. G., & Frith, U. (1996). The neuropsychology of autism. *Brain*, *119*, 1377–1400.

Harris, S. L., Belchic, J., Blum, L., & Celiberti, D. (1994). In: J. L. Matson (Ed.), *Autism in Children and Adults: Etiology, Assessment, and Intervention* (pp. 127–146). Belmont, CA: Brooks/Cole.

Hobson, R. P. (1993). Understanding persons: The role of affect . In: S. Baron-Cohen, H. Tager-Flusberg, & D. Cohen (Eds), *Understanding Other Minds: Perspectives from Autism*. New York: Oxford University Press.

Hyman, S. L., & Levy, S. E. (2000). Autistic spectrum disorders: When traditional medicine is not enough. *Contempoary Pediatrics*, *17*, 101–116.

Hurth, J., Shaw, E., Izeman, S. G., Whaley, K., & Rogers, S. J. (1999). Areas of agreement about effective practices among programs serving young children with autism spectrum disorders. *Infants and Young Children*, *12*, 17–26.

Intagliata, S. (2001). Therapeutic interventions. *Milestones*, *3*, 2–4.

Koegel, R., & Koegel, L. (1995). *Teaching children with autism: Strategies for initiating positive interventions and improving learning opportunities*. Baltimore, MD: Paul H. Brookes.

Kunce, L., & Mesibov, G. B. (1998). Educational approaches to high-functioning autism and Asperger syndrome. In: E. Schopler, G. B. Mesibov & L. J. Kunce (Eds.), *Asperger Syndrome or High-Functioning Autism?* (pp. 227–261). New York: Plenum.

Lovaas, O. I. (1987). Behavioral treatment and normal educational and intellectual functioning in young autistic children. *Journal of Consulting and Clinical Psychology*, *55*, 3–9.

Lovass, O. I., & Smith, T. (1988). A comprehensive behavioral theory of autistic children: Paradigm for research and treatment. *Journal of Behavioral Therapy and Experimental Psychiatry*, *20*, 17–29.

Luiselli, J. K., Taras, M., & Lennon, L. (1998). Behavioral support for persons with Asperger Disorder. *Mental Health Aspects of Developmental Disabilities*, *1*, 1–9.

Marks, S. U., Schrader, C., Levine, M., Hagie, C., Longaker, T., Morales, M., & Peters, I. (1995). Social skills for social ills: Supporting the social skills development of adolescents with Asperger's syndrome. *Teaching Exceptional Children*, *32*, 56–61.

Marriage, K. J., Gordon, V., & Brand, L. (1995). A social skills group for boys with Asperger syndrome. *Australian and New Zealand Journal of Psychiatry*, *29*, 58–62.

Mash, E. J., & Barkley, R. A. (Eds) (1996). *Child psychopathology*. New York: Guilford Press.

Matson, J. L., & Swienzy, N. (1994). Social skills training with autistic individuals. In: J. L. Matson (Ed.), *Autism in Children and Adults; Etiology, Assessment, Intervention* (pp. 241–260). Pacific Grove, CA: Brooks/Cole.

Mawson, D. G., Grounds, A., & Tantum, D. (1985). Violence and Asperger's syndrome. *British Journal of Psychiatry, 147*, 566–569.

McDougle, C. J., Kresch, L. E., Goodman, W. K., Naylor, S. T., Volkman, F. R., Cohen, D. J., & Price, L. H. (1995). A case-controlled study of repetitive thoughts and behavior in adults with autistic disorder and obsessive-compulsive disorder. *American Journal of Psychiatry, 152*(5), 772–777.

McEachin, J. J., Smith, T., & Lovaas, O. (1993). Long term outcome for children with autism who received early intensive behavioral treatment. *American Journal on Mental Retardation, 97*, 359–372.

Mundy, P. (1995). Joint attention and social-emotional approach behavior in children with autism. *Developmental Psychopathlogy, 7*, 63–82.

Myles, B. S., & Simpson, R. L. (1998). Asperger syndrome: A guide for educators and parents. Austin, TX: PRO-ED.

Myles, B. S., & Southwick, J. (1999). Asperger syndrome and difficult moments: Practical solutions for tantrums, rage, and meltdowns. Shawnee Mission, KS: Autism Asperger Publishing Company.

Nichel, R. E. (1996). Controversial therapies for young children with developmental disabilities. *Infants and Young Children, 8*, 29–40.

Ozonoff, S., & Miller, J. N. (1995). Teaching theory of mind: A new approach to social skills training for individuals with autism. *Journal of Autism and Developmental Disorders, 25*, 415–433.

Prizant, B. M., & Rubin, E. (1999). Contemporary issues in interventions for autism spectrum disorders: A commentary. *The Journal of the Association for Persons with Severe Handicaps, 24*, 199–208.

Robertson, J. M., Tanguay, P. E., L'ecuyer, S., Sims, A., & Waltrip. C. (1999). Domains of social communication handicap in autistic spectrum disorders. *Journal of the American Academy of Child and Adolescent Psychiatry, 38*, 738–745.

Rodier, P. M. (2000). The early origins of autism. *Scientific American, 2*, 56–64.

Rogers, S. J. (2000). Interventions that facilitate socialization in children with autism. *Journal of Autism and Developmental Disorders, 30*, 399–409.

Rutter, M. (1999) The Emmanuel Miller Memorial Lecture 1998: Autism: Two-way interplay between research and clinical work. *Journal of Child Psychology and Psychiatry, 40*(2), 169–188.

Ryan, J. (2000). *When you have a student with autism in your classroom*. Chicago: Office of Specialized Services.

Safran, S. (2001). Asperger syndrome: The emerging challenge to special education. *Exceptional Children, 67*, 151–160.

Schafer, R. (1996). *Help from social stories*. Ontario, Canada: Hyperexia Association.

Schatz, J., & Hamdan-Allen, G. (1995). Effects of age and IQ on adaptive behavior domains for children with autism. *Journal of Autism and Developmental Disorders, 25*(1), 51–59.

Scragg, P., & Shah, A. (1994). Prevalence of Asperger's syndrome in a secure hospital. *British Journal of Psychiatry, 165*, 679–682.

Sigman, M., & Capps, L. (1997). *Children with Autism*. Cambridge, MA: Harvard University Press.

Smith, T., & Lovaas, O. I. (1998). Intensive and early behavioral intervention with autism: The UCLA young autism project. *Infants and Young Children, 10*, 67–78.

Starr, E. (June, 1998) When the best thing about finishing school is "No more teasers." Teachers need training to help students with autism. *Professionally Speaking: The Magazine of the Ontario College of Teachers*, 18–20.

Starr, E. M., Foy, J. B., & Cramer, K. M. (2001). Parental perceptions of the education of children with pervasive developmental disorders. *Education and Training in Mental Retardation and Developmental Disabilities*, *36*, 55–68.

Swaggart, B. L., & Gagnon, E. (1995). Using social stories to teach social and behavioral skills to children with autism. *Focus on Autistic Behavior*, *10*, 1–16.

Willey, L. H. (1999). *Pretending to be normal: Living with Asperger's syndrome*. London, England: Jessica Kingsley.

Williams, K. (1995). Understanding the student with Asperger syndrome: Guidelines for teachers. *Focus on Autistic Behavior*, *10*, 9–16.

Wetherby, A., & Prizant, B. (1999). Facilitating language and communication development in autism: Assessment and intervention guidelines. In: D. B. Zager (Ed.), *Autism: Identification, Education, and Treatment*. Hillsdale, NJ: Lawrence Erlbaum.

Wetherby, A. M., & Prizant, B. M. (2000). *Autism spectrum disorders: A transactional developmental perspective*. Baltimore, MD: Paul H. Brookes.

Wolf-Schein, E. (1994). Treatment of the autistic-spectrum disorder: Where are we now? *Developmental Disabilities Bulletin*, *22*, 35–53.

Wisconsin Early Autism Project, Inc. (1995). *Training Sheet*. Madison, WI: Wisconsin Early Autism Project.

RESOURCES

Autism Society of America, Inc.
7910 Woodmont Avenue, Suite 300
Bethesda, MD 20814-3015
800-3-AUTISM (328-8476)
(301) 657-0881
Fax: (301) 657-0869
http://www.autism-society.org/
(National organization that provides information packages and referral services to the public, newsletter published 6 times yearly, first issues of each year lists resources, has 223 chapters in 48 states.)

Autism Research Institute
4182 Adams Avenue
San Diego, CA 92116
(619) 281-7165
(Provides information about methods of treatment of autism, quarterly newsletter.)

CAN (Cure Autism NOW)
5225 Wilshire Blvd., Suite 226
Los Angeles, CA 90036
(323) 549-0500
Fax: (213) 549-0547
http://www.canfoundation.org
(Parent founded organization funds research on biological treatments for autism.)

Division TEACCH
University of North Carolina, Chapel Hill
School of Medicine
310 Medical School, Wing E, CB 7180
(919) 966-2174
e-mail: teacch@unc.edu
http://www.unc.edu/depts/teacch/teacch.htm
(Training workshops for teachers and other professionals.)

The Family Connection
Beach Center on Families and Disability
3111 Haworth Hall
University of Kansas
Lawrence, KS 66045
(800) 854-4938
e-mail: Family @ dole.lsi.ukans.edu
http://www.lsi.ukans.edu/beach/beachhp.htm
(Focus on challenging behavior, referral to 20 states with positive behavioral training teams or parent and professionals in their area skilled in utilizing positive behavioral supports.)

The Indiana Resource Center for Autism
Indiana University Institute for the Study of Developmental Disabilities
2853 East Tenth Street
Bloomington, IN 47405
(812) 855-6508
(Info on autism, training for professionals, paraprofessionals, & family members.)

Journal of Autism and Developmental Disorders
published by Plenum Press
233 Spring Street
New York, NY 10013

National Alliance for Autism Research
414 Wall Street
Research Park
Princeton, NJ 08540
(888) 777-NAAR (6227)
(609) 430-9160
Fax: (609) 430-9163
http://www. naar. org

Virginia Autism Resource Center
P.O. Box 1300
Stephens City, VA 22653
Toll Free: (877) 667-7771
(540) 869-0300 (information, resources)

www.autism-resources.com

http://www.autism-pdd.net/

Autism Book Recommendations
http://web/syr.edu/~jmwobus/autism/autism-books.htm\

THE ROLE OF MEDICATION IN THE MANAGEMENT OF AUTISTIC SPECTRUM DISORDERS

Marlin Hoover, Ph.D.*

INTRODUCTION

Over the past 50 years there has been substantial improvement in the manner in which psychoactive (mental health) medications work. The medications are more specific in the ways in which they adjust the functioning regions of the brain and nervous system that produce and control behavior and thought processes. This has led to more carefully targeted intended effects while producing fewer unpleasant side effects (Bezchlibnyk-Butler & Jeffries, 2000; Julien, 2001; Stahl, 2000).

With the introduction of major tranquilizers, individuals who once had difficulty managing the stimulation of everyday life are better able to cope with social interactions and life tasks, to manage their own affairs, and to cope with circumstances that would have been too stressful previously. Likewise, with the development of effective antidepressant medications, individuals who suffered episodes of great personal distress, psychological discomfort, internal anxiety, and an inability to approach their lives in a hopeful way could relatively quickly begin feeling and sleeping better, become more physically active, and take a more active role in solving their life problems. While these medications have not replaced the necessary social support, education, wise counsel, personality transformations, and individual effort necessary to cope with conditions that

* Marlin Hoover, Ph.D. is a clinical psychologist.

Autistic Spectrum Disorders: Educational and Clinical Interventions, pages 255–267.
2001 by Elsevier Science Ltd.
ISBN: 0-7623-0818-4

have such a pervasive impact on a person's psychological functioning, the fact that the modern psychoactive medications can have such a beneficial impact serves to illustrate the degree to which our psychological and biological functions are interdependent. Modern mental health medications (psychoactive drugs) have proven to be of great value in assisting many people to feel and cope better (Dipiro et al., 1999).

The effectiveness of the medications appears to have grown more rapidly than the public acceptance of the use of mental health medications. Yet many people are afflicted with conditions that diminish the quality of life of the individual and the person's family, friends, teachers, and co-workers. However, only a minority of those individuals are willing to take these medications or are aware that an appropriate psychoactive medication would be beneficial to them. Additionally, only about one-third of the people who would benefit from medication actually seek the assistance of a prescribing professional and comply with recommendations for pharmacotherapy. This avoidance of a potentially beneficial form of therapy is not unique to the avoidance of the use of mental health medications but is true also of the frequency with which people seek and accept psychological and social therapies (Druss, Hoff & Rosenheck, 2000).

Problems associated with being identified as having a "mental illness" are explored extensively in texts in abnormal psychology and sociology. The stigma that comes from being identified as having a problem and being the subject of therapeutic intervention is understood to place an extra burden of difficulty on an individual who is labeled as having an undesirable characteristic or to belong to a socially undesirable group. While there may be a considerable cost to such an identification, it seems to many that the benefits of receiving appropriate biological, psychological, and social interventions outweighs the cost for conditions that have a pervasive damaging impact on a person's ability to learn, relate to others, manage the affairs of life, and become independent. The identification or labeling acknowledges problems that the person and the person's family, peers, teachers, and friends have already recognized.

Sometimes the recognition of those problems by others is less thoughtful, reasoned, and helpful and causes many more difficulties for the person than a professional diagnosis. This is especially true if a professional diagnosis leads to helpful therapies. It is not unusual for the social problems of individuals with an autistic spectrum disorder (ASD) to lead to avoidance of the person by peers, family, and friends; these problems also may lead to criticism of the individual and blaming the individual for behaviors the person cannot control.

In summary, avoidance of professional labeling and intervention does not mean that the individual will not be labeled. It more often means that the labels that will be applied by the person's acquaintances and significant others are likely to be more damaging and are more likely to lead to destructive responses to the individual and a highly negative or hostile attitude on the part of the individual. What is needed is the understanding that would come from information provided to the person and his or her significant others by professionals.

VALUE OF MENTAL HEALTH MEDICATIONS

Most people who have had a personal experience with a loved one or acquaintance who suffers from one of the more severe mental illnesses find that ordinary human compassion dictates the use of any effective and constructive means to alleviate that person's suffering and enhance her well-being. However, many people are simply unaware of the large body of scientific knowledge, clinical experience, and personal successes brought by modern mental health medications. This leaves many people vulnerable to antiscientific prejudices, the old myths about mental illnesses, and naïve assumptions about the individual's ability to transcend his or her biology.

Every thought, action, and subjective experience is supported by biological changes in the human organism. Our biology makes psychological processes possible at the same time that it imposes limits on us. Every psychological event produces biological changes in us. Our decisions can alter our biology in obvious and subtle ways. Our biological and psychological processes are interdependent, and by the chance of our particular biology we may or may not be fortunate in the abilities and limits imposed by our own biological being.

Mental health medications make it possible to alter our biological, and therefore our psychological, functioning in ways that are beneficial and that alter our biological processes in a direction more closely approximating the ideal that nature intends. These medications work primarily by urging the brain, which is the primary psychological organ, to manage its various tasks in the optimum manner, by increasing activity in locations and communication routes that are underperforming and reducing the amount of activity in locations and communication routes of the brain that are overactive. Mental health medications either enhance or mimic naturally occurring events in order to perform their work.

As mental health medications have become better targeted (making more precise alterations in the location or system needing a change) and cleaner (producing the desired effect without problematic side effects), it has become possible to use them to enhance the functioning of individuals with more subtle, but none-the-less problematic, conditions (Julien, 2001). Therefore, although most would agree that mental health medications should be used by an individual who is self-injurious in order to protect him from harm, it is also important to consider the benefits of medications in conditions like the ASDs, where the individual's behavior may be better adapted as a result of their use.

The overall goal of the administration of mental health medications in these conditions is to allow the individual to learn, love, play, and work in a more fulfilling and adaptive manner. At times the medication will be targeted toward a symptom that results from too little activity in a region of the brain (e.g. not enough activity in the pre-frontal region to sustain attention) or too much activity (e.g. overactive limbic system producing extreme emotionality). At other times the medication will smooth or enhance the transmission of information (e.g. not enough neurotransmitter, or fluctuations in the speed of transmission due to membrane instability). A more complete description of the mechanisms of action of mental health medications and of the functioning of the brain in relation to behavior is beyond the scope of this chapter and is the subject matter of many texts and the focus of a tremendous research effort (Bezchlibnyk-Butler & Jeffries, 2000; Julien, 2001; Stahl, 2000). For the purpose of this chapter, it is enough to know that the conditions that are referred to as ASDs result from problems in brain structure and function that are subtle but real and which interfere with the brain's ability to function in the manner we believe to be optimum. The mental health medications either increase or decrease the activities in one or another area of the brain in a way that enhances or mimics a natural process in an attempt to bring brain function to an optimum level. Psychological functioning is only optimum when brain functioning also is optimum.

Learning and experience alter brain structure and functioning. If this assertion sounds contradictory, then remember that the biological processes in the brain and the psychological processes in the mind are interdependent. We learn because there are physical changes in the brain as a result of learning. All the symptoms of the ASDs can be altered by biological changes as well as by psychological interventions. Neural transmission is enhanced by antidepressants and by increased physical activity and pleasant social and cultural experiences. A person can be taught to engage in social activities in a more satisfying manner at the same time that her anxiety can be reduced biologically while she is in social situations, making it easier for her to learn social skills. Biological, psychological, and social approaches to ameliorating the symptoms of the ASDs enhance and reinforce each other. There is substantial evidence for many symptoms that a combination approach is more effective than any individual approach alone, and interventions with individuals are most effective when the approaches are combined (American Academy of Pediatrics Technical Report, 2001).

Do mental health medications make people dependent? The medications used for the treatment of the symptoms of the ASDs do not produce physical addictions when used as directed. In fact, the psychostimulants are the only category of these medications that might be abused when used improperly (Julien, 2001). Continued use of the medication may be necessary to maintain the gains made by the individual through the enhanced functioning made possible by the medication. However, cessation of use does not lead to a craving for the medication. The medications used for these conditions are not addictive in that sense.

Do these mental health medications make people "zombies"? When the best medication is administered in the right dosage, it is only sedating when the person needs sedation in order to avoid destructive behaviors or to be able to sleep. The medications that may have the most dramatic impact on the individual in altering activity levels and manner of relating are the major tranquilizers. These are properly used only when the individual's problems justify the impact of the medication.

Many of these medications increase a persons ability to be focused, to mobilize energy, to work or interact, and to be more productive. When a person's reaction to a medication is not beneficial, the reaction usually disappears if the medication is stopped. This allows for adjustments to be made in the specific kind and amount of medication used.

CURRENT USE OF MENTAL HEALTH MEDICATIONS IN TREATING ASDS

In order to understand how psychoactive medications can assist the person with an ASD it is helpful to understand the common signs and features as well as the differences among the disorders. Most medications are supplied for symptoms that are not the unique features of either an individual ASD or the family of ASDs (Volkmar, 1999). Rather, the targeted problems or symptoms may be experienced by individuals without any of these disorders and may co-exist with these ASDs (Campbell, Cueva & Hallin, 1996).

The features of each of the ASDs are discussed elsewhere in this volume. This brief review serves as a framework for understanding some of the similarities and differences in featured behaviors and symptoms among the ASDs. Table 1 presents similarities and differences taken from the DSM-IV, the Diagnostic and Statistical Manual of the American Psychiatric Association (1994.) They are autistic disorder (AD), Asperger's disorder (AspD), Rett's disorder (RD), childhood degenerative disorder (CDD), and atypical pervasive developmental disorder (AtypPDD).

Table 1. Characteristic Features of Autistic Spectrum Disorders.

	AD	AspD	RD	CDD	AtypPDD
Problems with social skills	+	+	+	+	+
Problems with fine motor skills	+	+	0	0	+
Problems with gross motor skills	+	+	0	0	+
Problems in language development	+	0	+	+	+
Stereotyped mannerisms and motor behaviors	+	+	+	+	+
Mental retardation	+	0	+	+	0

Note: AD = autistic disorder; AspD = Asperger's disorder; RD = Rett's disorder; CDD = childhood degenerative disorder; AtypPDD = atypical pervasive developmental disorder.
+ = feature present; 0 = feature absent.

As Table 1 shows, the primary distinctions among the various disorders are in the areas of fine and gross motor skills, in the presence or absence of substantial language development, and in the usual presence of mental retardation. All of the symptoms and features listed in Table 1 can cause difficulties for the child with the named disorder and his family. However, at the present time, these cardinal symptoms cannot be effectively eliminated by medications. The problem of stereotyped behaviors can be improved in some cases with treatment with certain antidepressant medications, and problems with social skills can be ameliorated to a modest degree with treatment with either major tranquilizers or antidepressant medication (Campbell et al., 1996; Martin, Scahill, Klin & Volkmar, 1999; McDougle et al., 1998).

Some of the problems exhibited by individuals with each of the ASDs may be relatively unique to that ASD. For instance, the developmental language delay that is a common feature of autistic disorder is usually not present in Asperger's disorder. So pharmacological intervention that might assist a child with autism would only be used with an individual with that particular disorder.

Many problems are not unique to any one of the ASDs but may be experienced by a person with any of the disorders as well as a person with a wide variety of other disorders. For instance, depression in one of its many forms may coexist with any of the ASDs (Damore, Stine & Brody, 1998; Ozbayrak, 1997; Storch, 1999; Volkmar, Cook, Promeroy, Realmuto & Tanguay, 1999). It might even result from the person's struggle to cope with the ASD. Treatment for coexisting conditions may enhance functioning of the individual with an ASD even though a variety of problems that cannot be affected by medications remain.

To understand the role of psychoactive medications, it is necessary to identify the key symptoms or problems in functioning that will be the target of medical intervention. These symptoms or problems experienced by a person with an ASD may respond to a variety of interventions, including medication when appropriate. Psychological symptoms and problems common among persons with ASDs listed in Table 2 are amenable to medication treatment at this time (Campbell et al., 1996; Rapin, 1997).

Obviously absent from Table 2 are some prominent features of the ASDs that do not seem to respond to current mental health medications, e.g. mental retardation and verbal and nonverbal learning disabilities (Volkmar et al., 1999). It is hoped that future advances in the understanding of brain functioning will make more dramatic constructive alterations in brain function possible so that conditions that are now beyond medical treatment can be ameliorated.

At the present time, the psychoactive medications used in the treatment of individuals with each of the disorders are targeted toward the improvement of specific observed symptoms rather than toward the disorder itself. Table 3 presents the categories of psychoactive medications most commonly used to benefit individuals with an ASD with a few of the most commonly used examples of each type (Campbell et al., 1996; McDougle, 1997; Volkmar et al., 1999).

Which medication is selected depends on the professional judgment of the prescriber. The decisions about whether to medicate and which medication is appropriate are made in light of the individual's biological status and condition

Table 2. Specific Symptoms Targeted for Treatment.

Target Symptom	Medication Type
Agitation; self-injurious behavior	Major tranquilizers
Aggressiveness; temper tantrums and/or explosive anger	Major tranquilizers and/or antidepressants and/or mood stabilizers and/or anticonvulsants and/beta blockers
Stereotyped behaviors	Major tranquilizers and/or antidepressants
Social fears; dysphoric mood and depression obsessions and compulsions; generalized anxiety	Antidepressants; long-acting anxiolitic
Hyperactivity	Psycho-stimulants; antidepressants; naltrezone
Attention deficit; impulsivity	Psycho-stimulants and/or antidepressants

Table 3. Categories of Psychoactive Medications.

Medication Type	Generic Name	Brand Name
Major tranquilizers	Halperidol; thioridazine; risperidone; olanzapine	Haldol; Mellaril; Risperdal; Zyprexa
Long-acting anxiolitic (tranquilizer)	Buspirone	Buspar
Antidepressants	Amitriptyline; fluoxetine; paroxetine; clomipramine	Elavil; Prosac; Paxil; Anafranil
Antidepressants that can act as psychostimulants	Imipramine; buproprion	Tofranil; Wellbutrin
Psychostimulants	Methylphenidate pemoline d- and 1-amphetamine	Ritalin; Cylert; Adderall
Mood stabilizers	Lithium carbonate; valproic acid	Lithonate; Depakote
Anticonvulsants	Carbamazepine; phenytoin	Tegretal; Dilantin
Beta blockers	Propanolol; nadolol	Inederal; Corgard

and with regard to the general health of the individual, especially considering other coexisting medical conditions that might be affected by the medication and also considering the person's ability to absorb and eliminate the medication and its breakdown products.

Minor tranquilizers are a major category of psychoactive medication that is usually not used for any of the ASDs. The anxieties associated with the ASDs tend to be chronic, with long-standing patterns, and are not effectively treated by the minor tranquilizers (like Xanax) because tolerance can rapidly develop and because these medications can precipitate depression (Volkmar, 1999).

USE OF SPECIFIC CATEGORIES OF MEDICATIONS TO AFFECT SPECIFIC SYMPTOMS

A number of studies have documented beneficial effects of the various psychotropic medications for the ASDs (Volkmar et al., 1999). There are examples of individuals from each of the separate diagnostic categories benefiting from the categories of medications listed above. However, patterns emerge across studies suggesting that, in general, some medication types are more beneficial than others for specific symptoms.

Table 4 presents the general trends for which medications are most often used in each of the diagnostic categories (Campbell et al., 1996; McDougle, 1997; Volkmar, 1999). However, the use of only some specific medications has been thoroughly researched so far. Additionally, some medications have not been used in documented research with some of the specific types of ASD. A review of the literature suggests that a systematic analysis of the effects of only one of the major tranquilizers and several of the types of antidepressants have been completed in AD, AspD, and RD (Wiener, 1996). There is less information about the effects of medications on RD, CDD, and AtypPDD.

The most common findings indicate that the major tranquilizers are of benefit to some individuals with AD and also to individuals who have RD, CDD, and AtypPDD. However, they are useful primarily when the person is experiencing specific symptoms like agitation, self-injurious behavior, and aggression. The major tranquilizers usually are not found to benefit individuals with Asperger's disorder (Volkmar, 1999). The psychostimulants seem to produce untoward effects in individuals with AD but can be useful to individuals with Asperger's disorder who have problems with attention. In general, the antidepressants can be of assistance to individuals across all categories if the individual is depressed, but seem to be used most often with individuals with AspD.

There are current anecdotal reports of some treatment success for medications developed for use with dementias. These medications (Aricept etc.) are reported to produce learning benefits. However, trials with these medications appear to be in early stages (Bandoletti, 2001).

A high proportion of individuals with ASDs (especially AD) are taking one or more mental health medications and appear to benefit substantially (Campbell et al., 1996; Volkmar, 1999). These medications can make it possible for the persons to engage in study, play, social interactions, and self-direction and to

Table 4. Prevalence of Type of Medication by Diagnostic Category.

	AD	AspD	RD	CDD	AtypPDD
Major tranquilizers	+		+	+	+
Antidepressants		+			
Psychostimulants		+			
Mood stabilizers	+	+			

Note: AD = autistic disorder; AspD = Asperger's disorder; RD = Rett's disorder; CDD = childhood degenerative disorder; AtypPDD = atypical pervasive developmental disorder.
+ = feature present; 0 = feature absent.

feel more satisfied in their daily lives. However, it is important to remember that these medications are not a substitute for psychological, social, and educational interventions. Rather, they enhance the individual's ability to benefit from those interventions.

BENEFITS AND HAZARDS OF MENTAL HEALTH MEDICATIONS

No fair consideration of the use of psychoactive medications can ignore the hazards of some of these medications for the person's physical functioning. For the most part, the side effects are related to the dosage of the medication, with greater doses causing more side effects, and the side effects disappear if the medication is discontinued. The professional who prescribes the medication will weigh the potential benefits and side effects of the medications with the person and/or the family of the child. A decision to give a mental health medication to a person or a child is a statement that, to the professional's and the person or the parent's best knowledge, the potential benefits outweigh the known and anticipated hazards of taking the medication. Although this is a difficult decision to make, at least some direction comes from answering the question, Is doing this worth the risk? It is important to remember that we make decisions like this about ourselves and our loved ones continuously. The decision to drive one's child to a movie theater is based on the calculation that the potential benefit of seeing the movie is worth the risk of injury in a car accident while driving to the theater. Even though we put ourselves and our children at risk by the decisions we make to provide them with growth opportunities, it is still important to understand the risks of these medications.

The following brief review is not exhaustive, and the consideration of whether or not a particular medication should be tried is one that must be left to the prescribing professional in consultation with the individual, or the person responsible for the individual, after a careful consideration of the potential benefits and the specific and known hazards of the medication. The hazards themselves are well documented in the training of the prescribing professional, pharmacists, and informational literature provided to the individual considering the medication. The following general findings provide a brief review of the known side effects and potential problems associated with taking mental health medications.

Major tranquilizers have the highest incidence of known side effects, with the extrapyramidal side effects being most common. This class of side effect involves symptoms that look like Parkinson's disease and include muscular and motor problems. These side effects can be diminished by the administration of a second medication that makes these side effects much more tolerable. A second condition, akathesia, looks like agitation or anxiety but results from the medication and necessitates an alteration in the medication (Bezchlibnyk-Butler & Jeffries, 2000; Dipiro et al., 1999; Julien, 2001; Ozbayrak, 1997; Stahl, 1997).

The most serious side effects of these medications may be irreversible. The patient or the patient's agent must be informed of this possibility and must consider it before accepting treatment using a major tranquilizer.

Another side effect of the major tranquilizers is shared with some of the antidepressant medications. That type, anticholinergic side effects, includes dry mouth, constipation, difficulty in urinating, and blurry vision. These anticholinergic side effects are present with only some of the major tranquilizers and with only some of the antidepressants.

A third side effect of some major tranquilizers and some antidepressants is sedation. This side effect may actually be useful because it may assist a person who is having difficulty sleeping to obtain more restful sleep. The prescribing professional can choose a medication with or without this side effect, depending on whether it might be of assistance to the individual.

Another class of side effect occurs with the psychostimulants. These medications can cause sleeplessness, weight loss, and an increase in motor tics as well as Tourette's symptoms. These side effects usually disappear when the medication is discontinued. With weight loss and sleeplessness, the prescribing professional and the individual will make a decision regarding the relative benefits of continuing the medication when considering its impact on weight and sleep.

A potentially more serious side effect of the psychostimulants is the risk of seizure. Though small, this risk is considered by prescribing professionals and should be considered by the individuals involved. Additionally, these medications present a risk for abuse when self-administered in an improper fashion. Psychostimulants are unique in abuse potential among the psychoactive medications commonly utilized for the ASDs.

Individual medications may pose unique known risks that will be reviewed and discussed by the prescribing professional when the administration of a medication is considered (Damore et al., 1998). In general, there is a risk of toxicity with any of the medications when too much is taken, and that risk must also be considered in selecting the medication and in making a decision about the manner in which the medication will be administered.

Although there is reason for caution in observing the physical and psychological response of an individual to a mental health medication, this mode of treatment has proven beneficial in many clinical trials. Under the direction of an appropriate prescribing professional, the benefits of utilizing a biological as well as psychological and social modes of intervention justify the risk.

It is customary to consider the medical risks of using mental health medications. There are also psychological risks involved, including the self-perception of the individual using the medication and the reaction of significant others to the individual's use of this mode of treatment. Most harm comes from a negative impression of the meaning of utilizing medication. Often the counselor, teacher, or parent can model an appropriate and accepting attitude, suggesting the wisdom of using medication by defining it as a resource for strengthening one's body – like vitamins, food, exercise, reading new information, and trying new approaches to a problem. Each of these is something outside ourselves that we did not invent but that, when incorporated, enhances our functioning.

SUMMARY

Mental health medications are used to treat a broad range of symptoms that can be experienced by individuals with one of the autistic spectrum disorders (ASDs). The psychoactive medications are targeted toward the specific symptom rather than the disorder itself. The medications work either by enhancing or mimicking a natural process, and they either increase or decrease the activity in an area of the brain or affect a communication route within the brain.

Many clinical trials have demonstrated the usefulness of mental health medications for altering the psychological and biological functioning of the individual treated. Medications work best in conjunction with and coordinated with psychological, educational, and social interventions designed to enhance the individual's functioning. No medication is without side effects, and an analysis of the potential benefits and risks of the use of a medication must be undertaken when medication to enhance an individual's functioning is considered.

REFERENCES

American Academy of Pediatrics Technical Report, Committee on Children with Disabilities (2001). The pediatrician's role in the diagnosis and management of autistic spectrum disorder in children. *Journal of Pediatrics*, *107*, 5.

American Psychiatric Association (1994). *Diagnostic and statistical manual of mental disorders* (4th ed.). Washington, D.C.: American Psychiatric Association.

Bandoletti, M. (2001). Doctor fights autism on a new front. *Pioneer Press*, May 17.

Bezchlibnyk-Butler, K. Z., & Jeffries, J. J. (2000). *Clinical handbook of psychotropic drugs*. Seattle: Hogrefe & Huber.

Campbell, M., Cueva, J. E., & Hallin, A. H. (1996). Autism and pervasive developmental disorders. In: J. M. Weiner (Ed.), *Diagnosis and Psychoparmacology of Childhood and Adolescent Disorders* (2nd ed., pp. 151–192). New York: Wiley.

Druss, B., Hoff, R., & Rosenheck, R. (2000). Underuse of antidepressants in major depression: prevalence and correlates in a national sample of young adults. *Journal of the American Medical Association*, *61*, 234–237.

Damore, J., Stine, J., & Brody, L. (1998). Medication-induced hypomania in Asperger's disorder. *Journal of the American Academy of Child and Adolescent Psychiatry*, *37*, 248–249.

Dipiro, J. T., Talbert, R. L., Yee, G. C., Matzke, G. R., Wells, B. G., & Posey, L. M. (1999). *Pharmacotherapy: A pathophysiologic approach*. Stamford, Ct.: Appleton & Lange.

Julien, R. M. (2001). *A primer of drug action*. New York: W. H. Freeman.

Martin, A., Scahill, L., Klin, A., & Volkmar, F. R. (1999). Higher-functioning pervasive developmental disorders: Rates and patterns of psychotropic drug use. *Journal of the American Academy of Child and Adolescent Psychiatry*, *38*, 820–828.

McDougle, C. J. (1997). Psychoparmacology. In: D. J. Cohen & F. R. Volkmar (Eds), *Handbook of Autism and Pervasive Developmental Disorders* (2nd ed., pp. 707–729). New York: Wiley.

McDougle, C. J., Brodkin, E. S., Naylor, S. T., Carlson, D. C., Cohen, D. J., & Price, L. H. (1998). Sertraline in adults with pervasive developmental disorders: A prospective open-label investigation. *Journal of Clinical Psychoparmacology*, *18*, 62–66.

Ozbayrak, K. R. (1997). Sertraline in PDD. *Journal of the American Academy of Child and Adolescent Psychiatry*, *36*, 7–8.

Rapin, I. (1997). Autism. *New England Journal of Medicine*, *337*, 97–104.

Stahl, S. M. (2000). *Essential psychopharmacology: Neuroscientific basis and practical applications* (2nd ed.). Cambridge: Cambridge University Press.

Storch, D. D. (1999). Medication-induced hypomania in Asperger's disorder. *Journal of the American Academy of Child and Adolescent Psychiatry*, *38*, 110–111.

Volkmar, F. (1999). Asperger's disorder: Neurobiology and treatment. Presented at the National Association for Continuing Education Conference, "Across the Spectrum: Learning Disabilities, ADHG and Asperger's Disorder." Fort Lauderdale, Fl., April.

Volkmar, F. (2001). Pharmacological interventions in autism: Theoretical and practical issues. *Journal of Clinical Child Psychology*, *30*, 80–87.

Volkmar, F., Cook, E. H. Jr., Pomeroy, J., Realmuto, G., & Tanguay, P. (1999). Practice parameters for the assessment and treatment of children, adolescents, and adults with autism and other pervasive developmental disorders. American Academy of Child and Adolescent Psychiatry, Working Group on Quality Issues. *Journal of the American Academy of Child and Adolescent Psychiatry*, *38*(12 Suppl.), 32S–54S.

Wiener, J., (Ed) (1996). *Diagnosis and psychopharmacology of childhood and adolescent disorders* (2nd ed.) New York, NY: John Wiley & Sons.

INTERVIEW WITH A HIGH FUNCTIONING ADULT WITH AUTISM

Tim Wahlberg and Anthony Rotatori

INTRODUCTION TO CASE STUDY

John is a forty-two year old man who was diagnosed with autism six years ago. He agreed to do an interview with the author in order to tell his side of the story and to answer any questions the author had. Prior to the interview John was assessed on a number of measures which included the following: Kaufman – Brief Intelligence Test (K-BIT), Stanford-Binet memory for sentences, and the Kaufman Test of Educational Achievement (K-TEA) reading comprehension subtest. Intellectual testing resulted in an average IQ scored of 99, as well as average scores on the Stanford-Binet memory for sentences and the K-TEA comprehension subtests. Presently, John is employed as a maintenance assistant in a large retail store in the Midwest. He has been employed in this capacity for about ten years. He lives in a garage apartment adjacent to his sister's home and communicates with her via a short wave radio. John has had a number of psychiatric hospitalizations since his teenage years primarily due to the need for his medication to be adjusted. John attended college and earned an associates degree majoring in sociology. His primary social contacts are with his sister, his girlfriend and associates at work. John's early school years were very difficult and he had increasing social difficulties as he progressed through school. As a way of masking his social difficulties and oddities, John would take on the "persona" of a "hippie" even though he did not partake in the typical beliefs and activities related to this stereotype 1960's generation.

Autistic Spectrum Disorders: Educational and Clinical Interventions, pages 269–300.

ISBN: 0-7623-0818-4

What follows is a four and a half-hour interview with John in which he was asked a variety of structured questions. John was allowed to digress spontaneously on his own topics as they arose during the questioning period. To make the dialog easier to read, the author took the liberty to edit some of the grammatical context or order of what was said during the interview. The author did not change the context of the conversation at any point.

INTERVIEW

Author: Lets talk a little bit about your background. You were first diagnosed early on in school. What was your first diagnosis?

John: What they did was they decided that I had some kind of hyper kinetic disorder and that I had attention and concentration types of problems and stuff like that.

Author: Like Attention Deficit Disorder.

John: Well back then it wasn't called that. After I looked at the documents that they gave to my parents. As I learned about ADHD, I could see that that's what they were reporting that they were finding in me at that time. They even wanted to put me on Ritalin.

Author: What kind of services did you receive in school?

John: I had trouble with certain sounds. I wasn't only having trouble saying things. This is one thing my speech teacher never knew because I could never express it. I was getting a whirlpool of things just spinning around in my head where I could not keep the letters straight in my head to be able to say them. I would not always say what the speech teacher would want me to repeat back.

Author: So what was being said to you by people was often jumbled and confused.

John: Yes. Unless they repeat things over and over again, I would start to repeat the things they were saying. It also mentioned in the reports that I had trouble keeping saliva under control. I am not sure why that is important. They said that this was part of the reason why I could not pronounce things.

Author: So you received speech services as a young child. Tell me what your school years were like? Maybe we can move through your grade school, high school, and college educational experiences.

John: Well I wasn't talking until I was about seven years old. There are some people in my family that think it was before that but I am the one that has experienced it and I know when I started talking. I repeated first grade after a teacher had somehow reached me and got me to do oral reading and stuff. She opened the doors you could say for me to start learning.

Author: How do you think she reached you?

John: Well, she, her name was Mrs. Starwalt and I liked Walt Disney movies. I looked at her as being part of Walt Disney because of the Walt in her name. Plus her dog's name was Star and one of my favorite songs was 'Wish Upon A Star' and so I would repeat that song over and over and this dog became that song. The dog was important to me. I saw my teacher as someone that could connect to me. Someone she could reach me by her dog.

Author: Do you think it had something to do with the fact that you felt you could trust her because of her name?

John: Yes. That is where it came from because I remember that it felt like I could trust her because that's the way my thinking was. She was like Walt Disney. That's the way I thought.

Author: That was first grade, how did the rest of grade school turn out for you?

John: Well, I had to go to special speech therapy and a lot of different programs. These other programs go under the name of Domain and Delacato. There were a lot of different things. I remember going into a bag and feeling for a bunch of different things and objects. And I would have to guess what they were by touch and so they did a lot of sensory type of exercises. They got me to talk and say things by having me look at a card and see it as something like a table. For me it was just nothing. What they would show me was going nowhere. Then they decided to take the word table and place it directly on a table, and I started associating with that being a table, and chair and everything in the house that was labeled.

Author: So everything in the house was labeled.

John: Right. I needed something that was real.

Author: Did you have any friends in grade school?

John: No, I didn't. Well, I had one friend his name was Darrel. He became my friend, because I liked the way he smiled. That is why I picked him as a friend, I like the way he smiled. Also, he would copy me and do the same things I would do and I like that too. I don't know if he understood that he was more like something to copy and interact with. It was more like I would do something and he would copy me and I would do something else and he would copy me. We would just like mirror each other, that is why I liked him. And then he got another friend. I could not accept the other friend. I could not take in two people, at one time.

Author: So would that overload your system?

John: Yes, So I started to not want to be with him. He wanted this other friend with him. This other friend would not copy what I would do and it was frustrating for me because it was like magic, things were working for me and Darrel but this other friend wasn't working out. I decided that I didn't want to be friends with Darrel because he decided that he wanted this other friend to be with him. I could not deal with two people at one time.

Author: How were your high school years?

John: Well in high school, I didn't like people touching and teasing me. I guess I was somebody to make fun of. Some thought me to be retarded.

Author: Why did you not like to be touched? What did that do to you?

John: Well, if somebody touched me it was like, it is hard to explain, but its like my whole body would be full of all these waves. Energy just driving me nuts.

Author: Would this overload the system?

John: Oh, yah.

Author: Did this make you nervous because someone was invading your space?

John: No, it wasn't because they were invading my personal space. It was that they were causing some kind of sensory type of reaction in me. That would make me try to withdrawal from them because touch was more hurtful to me than helpful. It was a painful thing. Everyone would grab my arm or slap me on the back and say hey how's it going, and I didn't like that. Also, there is something about touching my hair. It is stimulating to me and very calming. When I grew up it was like people in the neighborhood did not like me. I think it was because my eyes were different. My eyes were glassy like and it scared people. I would not look at people when I talked to them. People were afraid of me.

In some cases, stimulation calm's me down. I am currently taking Adderal and it calms me down. It has been helpful. I am also on Risperdal, which the doctor says control the autistic tendencies like rocking back and forth, repeating things, and biting my skin. All these things calm me down. None of this makes sense to me. But I guess my mind and body knew what it was doing so it made me do these things.

Author: Do you suppose that doing these things allowed you to stimulate yourself and in doing so you removed the external environment that was overt-simulating to you?

John: Well, It was my way of blocking out what was around me, especially noise. Noise doesn't mean horns honking and stuff. To me noise was colors being bright, light being bright. Everything was so overpowering. Like the TV being on. When I was doing the Doman and Delacato thing, they told me no TV, no radio, none of that stuff, because they had an effect on me.

Author: You made an interesting comment that you thought your body was taking care of what it thought it needed to. Do you suppose your body knew it was over-simulated and that's how it copes with the over-stimulation?

John: Yes. I would do things that normally I would not want to like banging my head on the wall. This happened to me even a few years ago. I went to a Halloween party and the lights flashing, music, people laughing, and the noise was just to much. I had to get out of there and I wasn't able to physically remove myself. It was like my body was withdrawing from what was happening and pulling me in to something that teachers mentioned in psychology, enigma. I am just caught into that and totally away form what's happening and you just stay there. Sometimes my body starts to rock back and forth and/or my head bangs on something. Other times, I bite myself or something like that. I can't explain it.

Author: But it removes that stimulation?

John: Yah, it did and but it never made any sense. But I knew and tried to tell these doctors that told me that if I calmed down I could control the situation. I tired to explain to them look, it's not me that's making the movement, its my body that's doing it.

Author: So it's just a reaction.

John: Right, it's my body that's doing it. I wasn't the one doing it. If I was the one doing it, I would have stopped it.

Author: So you made it through high school. Was it a struggle to make it through?

John: It really was. What happened is I had to go to night school as things were happening. Later the doctors told me that I was having depth perception problems. It wasn't that I was hallucinating as some doctor's thought. What would happen is a truck would go by the school and it would kind of pick up and stay in the air. All I was aware of was that I saw what I saw. It was coming towards us it was coming right towards the window. I told everybody move out of the way that a truck is coming and I meant to protect people. But it didn't happen and they thought I was on drugs or something. They couldn't figure out what was going on. I couldn't understand it either because it kind of scared me when I finally calmed down and realized that I was on the second floor. I thought how could I have seen that truck coming towards me?

Author: Did you first hear the truck coming?

John: No, I first saw the truck and it was like an angle. Sometimes I see angles I almost need a mirror for me to see it correctly. I wasn't seeing it as going away from the building but coming toward it. If a mirror was there, I would have seen the truck going way as opposed to toward the building.

Author: So it was a perceptual problem.

John: Right, it was a perceptual disorder, and I had a lot of that. My parents couldn't understand why I did not like to go in the car as things would happen and change around. I can remember this happening when I was five years old. Things would move yet they weren't really moving. I knew that but yet I would see things move. I couldn't understand why these things were happening. When I would be in the car, all of a sudden we would be ready to go onto a bridge and the way we were going, or maybe the angle we were going, the bridge stops or disappears and all I can see is a void there and I would scream and my parents couldn't understand why I was screaming. I couldn't explain to them that I was having this perception that the bridge was not there. They didn't know what to think. They felt that I was deliberately trying to get attention or something.

Author: John, did you understand once you drove over the bridge that it was okay?

John: What would happen is that I would start to blink my eyes and I couldn't understand why I was doing that but I would blink my eyes and slow things down. I would then be taking in pieces. Bit by bit by flashing my eyes. I could start to see things moving at a slower pace and I could see that everything was ok.

Author: So you learned to do that in order to slow down the intake of information.

John: Right, but my parents didn't like that I would constantly blink my eyes all the time.

Author: So you went to night classes and got through school.

John: I barely made it. I had to take classes pass-fail. It is to believe that I even graduated from high school because I had difficulty with reading. It didn't make sense to me later how I could have possibly made it through high school.

Author: What was hard about reading?

John: Because the words are so cluttered together on a page. It was not like looking through a window at one line, word by word. I would look at all this stuff all at once. It was all this information thrown at me. It was overwhelming and overestimating.

Author: What would happen when you looked at a page?

John: If there was a picture, I would start to get lost in that picture. It would take me away form all the print that was underneath it. So I would get lost in the picture. I would get deeply absorbed into it. I wouldn't be able to see what the class was doing. I remember when I was taking physical science. I remember the book, it was a green cover with bright green lines and red lines and it said physical science, but the thing about the book was I couldn't understand it. I couldn't get it to make sense. The school gave me classes to substitute for other classes, like cooperative work agreement for biology. They had me in special audio-visual classes where I set up my own program of study using audio-visuals. They sort of made things simpler but they didn't really help me with the problem I was having. I needed to be able to read. And they didn't help me with that.

Author: Who helped you learn to read?

John: Well it wasn't until I went to the Mayo Clinic in St. Paul, Minnesota. They did some tests and they could see that I wasn't able to be attentive to what I was reading. I wasn't able to comprehend what I was reading. They had me in these language skills classes that also involved reading. You would take small pieces and be able to look at some piece and eventually they would add more and more to it. They gradually worked me into being able to read a whole page. I still have trouble with reading. I can read something if there is pictorial information.

Author: So you need a picture to go with the text?

John: No, I need something that can present a picture. Like one word that would be a picture word. A word that would make me think of a picture, would cause me to remember.

Author: So you made it through high school, what about college?

John: Yes, I have an associate degree in science. Because I am a repetitive person I was able to make it through college by my repetitive memory. Constantly going over things, I would go through things receptively over and over and it would be amazing about the large amounts of information I could take in and just completely reproduce it on a page. One of my teachers, I remember her using my work on the test as an example of how thorough you can be. Well, what she didn't understand was that I had looked at those charts and just went over them repetitively to where all I had to think of was charts and what I would be writing about. What my brain would do, it would take those three charts and would log them together like a computer would do and log together into one program to where I would see this guys philosophy. I did not purposely cause myself to remember it that way but my brain had taken all that information and made it into a picture form and it presented it to me in that way. When I wrote this information down I was not using any applied information I was just writing exactly what I was seeing in my brain. They found out later after I graduated form college that I wasn't applying what I had learned. It was really just memorization. Nothing learned at all. Again, unless I can connect to what it is, there is no learning. I have to be able to connect to it. If I can't make a connection, if something that presents itself as a picture to where I can relate to it, it is nothing but memorized lists.

Author: Did you have any classes in college that presented problems for you?

John: Yah, Sociology class. She did not use visualizations. She was just talking and I could not understand how people were getting any information out of her talking. There was no picture to connect with so I was not able to learn anything. Because of this experience I dropped out of school. I wanted to get out of there. I could see no reason to go on because I was getting nothing form the class.

My grade was going form a C to a D and I didn't want it to get to an F so I withdrew.

Author: So that's your experience with school and the school process. You mentioned to me before this interview that you were able to teach a young boy with autism to eat. How did you do that?

John: Yah, well he had trouble feeding himself. I wasn't going to listen to what the other teachers were telling me that he was just never going to be able to do this and that someone was always going to have to feed him. I thought about what they said and I remembered. I had trouble with learning and this could be the same problem he was having because nobody was taking the time to repeat the same thing over and over and over then adding another step. Finally making it into a complete whole so that he sees the picture and is able to follow through.

Author: You had said earlier that you had trouble looking at people. Could you elaborate on that?

John: Yes, to look at ones face is overwhelming because the face never stays straight, it is always changing. The eyes are moving or blinking, the nose is twitching, the mouth is moving, and if you can look away from all that and just look at one thing that is moving you can concentrate. So if someone is moving their hands while they are talking you are able to look at their hands and actually hear what they are saying as compared to looking at their face.

Author: So the face is just too over-stimulating. There is too much that can change.

John: Right. At my current job, they sometimes tell me to look at the customer when I am talking They don't understand that the worst thing I could do is look at the customer because I can't talk to the customer if I am looking straight at them. So by looking away from the customer and looking at something close to them or something close to their face, they think your looking at them, but you are not really looking at them. Then you are able to talk to them. It is another thing if someone forces me to look at someone in the eye. This has happened in counseling sessions. The therapist would want me to look at his eyes while I was talking. I would get so to the point where I would just drill right into him with my eyes and block out everything around him. That bothered him. He felt like I was peering right through him.

Author: Another thing is you mentioned before the interview began that you need patterns and sequencing in order to learn.

John: Yes everything I do is done in a pattern or sequence. What I have told people is that I am a very patternistic type person. I need to have things go a certain way or else I become lost. I need to follow a pattern. When I was little, I could cope with what was going on around me by making a system.

Author: What kind of a system?

John: People would tell me that I need to do that and I need to do this and I got fed up because I could not remember it all so I had to find a way to be able to remember. I decided to start with a few things. I started with one or two things and then finally eventually got to three things. I got to three things and being comfortable with that. I tried to go to four things and I couldn't do it. So I went to three things and then I went from three things into breaking that down into three more things. I would constantly break these things down into threes because I knew three works for me. So would take the three things and they would all be related to each other. I would see a picture in my head. I would see the three things together and then another three things underneath each other. That's why I was able to remember because it became a picture. It was no longer instructions that had to be followed in a certain order but it was a picture that needed to be followed in a certain order. That worked for me. At work they have let me do things the way that worked for me and that means they don't give me a schedule. They give me a time that I work but they don't tell me what I need to do. They let me run the program. Because I am so precise, I am able to do everything the same way and still get everything done. They are amazed that it works so they don't bother me and tell me that I need to do something different.

Author: Another thing you had talked with me about before the interview was the problems you had with pronoun reversal and the difficulties you had with learning pronouns. Could you tell me about that?

John: The problem with pronouns was first of all people would want me to say "I" and I would think of an eye, someone's eye looking at me. I could not see eye as being the letter "I", it wasn't working for me. When they would say "I", I would turn back at them and say me. They would get upset with me because I refuse to say "I". Because I was having frustration with that letter "I", I would just repeat to them me. I wouldn't say I. If they were to say he/she they, it would really confuse me because first of all I knew that there was a boy, there was a girl, there was a he, she but they started adding more and more. It was overwhelming. They were giving me too much information. I remember that they would say what happens to this boy or something and I would say to them, boy he, man whatever. As I got older and older, they started putting more pressure on me to conform. I was getting to the point where I was throwing and kicking things, I couldn't deal with it anymore. My life was overwhelming enough and I didn't need the pressure of having to make changes. I hated making changes. I didn't like changes. I wanted things to stay the same.

Author: Why?

John: Because if things stayed the same you know that everything is going to work. Nothing is going to fail. It's all going to work. When you make changes you are no longer able to follow the pattern. So you don't know where to go. You are lost. The only way to get back to what I would call reality for me was being able to be on a clear path so I know where I am going. The only way I was able to get back on track was to put myself right back to where I was even if it meant completely withdrawing from the situation going on.

Author: You spoke earlier about how you felt that individuals with autism feel like they do not have control. Is what you just described a way for you get control back?

John: Yes, I would try to take back the control because I had followed what they had wanted me to do. I needed to pull back because I was getting lost, overwhelmed. I needed to pull out. It wasn't that I wanted to take the control back, it was that I needed to take the control back.

Author: You spoke earlier about doing things to prevent you from becoming fixated so that your brain would not shut off. Could tell me more about that?

John: I remember even in high school that I would be staring at stuff. The sun would be coming in the window. People couldn't see what I could see. They couldn't see the colors that I could see that were in the rays of the sun. So I got to the point where I saw stuff and people thought I was on drugs. I started to let them believe it because I thought that maybe it was better to be seen as somebody that was taking drugs than somebody that was crazy. I didn't want to be seen as crazy. So I would pretend that I was on something. I would stretch things a little. I would not only say I was seeing something purple, I would say that I was seeing a purple squirrel. I wasn't seeing a purple squirrel, but I was seeing colors.

Author: You were talking about doing stuff to prevent yourself form getting fixated.

John: Yes, I would do something repetitively to break myself away from that fixation. I did not want to be fixated because it made me look strange and weird. So I would do things to try and bring myself out of it. Trying to keep myself from being fixated kind of got me noticed to. I would make repetitive sounds, tap my hand or something.

Author: Did you find that many things in the classroom over-stimulated you?

John: There was way to much stimulation. More than I ever wanted. I could not wait to get out of school. I couldn't wait to get back into my room where it was quiet because I made it quiet. Or I could go and listen to my record player and watch the record spin around and around. Sometimes I would put objects on it like a toy car and watch it spin around and then watch it fly off into the air. It was like taking a problem and spinning it around nonstop making it come to an end. To see that car fly would relax me. Repetition was my answer to withdrawal. If I wasn't repetitive, I would become withdrawn and stereotypic. I would get caught into doing stuff with my hands or flicking my fingers or shaking my hand up and down, rocking back and forth. I didn't want to do this stuff so I had to do other things to break away from all that. The only way to do it was to do things repetitively. It also got to where I was taking numbers and I was just taking numbers and constantly going through and scanning numbers on lists. Whatever it took to keep me in the world. I didn't want to withdraw. I didn't want to and yet everything was causing me to.

Author: So this is what you mean by autism controlling you.

John: Right.

Author: You spoke about lining things up because everything around you was moving so fast that this slowed things down. Could you tell me more?

John: I would line up my toy cars. In fact I still do that. I still line up my cars. It is hard on me if somebody moved them because they disturbed the pattern. This is like a thing of calmness. These cars are lined up in a certain way to where they match each other. But if somebody moved the cars, it would totally cause me to lose confidence. People didn't know the things they could do to help me. Sometimes they were actually taking me away and I couldn't express it. I was a child without expression. I could not express what was going on. I don't know if it's because of different medicine but now I am able to express myself. This is like the first time I have been able to.

Author: You said it is hard to talk to people who are not autistic because they are not rhythmic and symbolic. Could you elaborate on that?

John: Okay, you work out for me because you are perfect. I don't know what it is about you but your are able to be quiet at the right time and be able to talk at the right time. You don't impose or go against the pattern. You allow it to be a 'Question and Answer' session. It works for me. Others can be talking and they cut in and say, "Well what do you mean?" That completely throws me off. You don't do that. You are easy to talk to, plus you don't force me to look at you so I don't have to feel overwhelmed because I don't need to look at you. You don't tell me look at you when I am talking. So I am able to talk to you. Other people who don't understand autism have a hard time talking to me because their first rule is to make eye contact. I hate that rule. I wish somebody would get rid of it because I don't think its fair. I don't think that rule is a fair social rule, because not everybody can make eye contact.

Author: Do you have problems with decision making?

John: Oh yah.

Author: So what do you do about that? How do you resolve it?

John: I have to take a paper and write things down, then make a chart. Sometimes it takes me, the whole day to make a decision, because I just make list after list until I can finally get it down to making a decision in three. I have narrowed it down to three choices. Sometimes I have to make a heavy-duty decision. Any kind of change to me is a heavy-duty decision. I know it is going to take my whole day and maybe the next day before I can finally get everything to work. So, I make lists that give me picture after picture. Finally, I draw up a chart that is simple and narrowed it down to three choices. Then, I have those three choices. What do I do, I take and make another picture. I have lines one, two, and three from the first choice then a second choice of one, two, and three lines down again. Then the third choice is one, two, and three lines again. That way my decision making is complete. That is how I see it. Three is complete. So, I have got three reasons here for the first choice, three reasons for the second and three reasons for the third. I do not go beyond three because I know if I do I will get overwhelmed and lost. I look at these three things on each one then I do a comparison. I compare the three things and then when I start to make the comparison, I ask myself which would be of more benefit.

Author: Is this like a rule that you follow?

John: Yes but people don't know what I go through to make decisions. They don't know how hard it is. I use tons of paper when I am writing.

Author: Do you feel like you have to analyze every angle? Every single possibility before you can come up with a decision? Do you think that's part of it? Do you have any idea?

John: I don't know. Sometimes, I wonder if it's an obsession. I am so caught into doing things through my system and because my system has proved itself to work for me. That is the only way I will do it. Its almost like I don't want to make the decision. If it's a decision of yes and no, that's easy for me. But if it's a decision where I have to pick things that's when I got to make those charts.

Author: What would happen if I said, "you could have anything to eat for dinner tonight"?

John: Oh-boy! Don't do that to me.

Author: That would be very difficult for you.

John: Oh yah, definitely. To other people I know that's a simple thing for them. But for me it's not. It's a very complicated thing.

Author: What do you do when you go to a restaurant?

John: Oh-boy. You are not going to believe this, well maybe you will. Would you believe that I order the same thing.

Author: What do you order?

John: Well one thing I always look for on the menu is a Rueben sandwich. So that's what I look for. If I find the restaurant does not have a Rueben sandwich, I want to leave. Now with McDonald's, I always get a Big Mac value meal. The reason why I get it is because that's what I always get. I just get what I always get. No decision making needed. I wouldn't like it if they canceled out the Big Mac value meal. I would have a hard time and I may not go back to that restaurant. My sister has noticed that about me. She says "you need to get something different. You can't always get the same thing all the time. How are you going to be able get some variety". What she doesn't realize is, I don't want variety in my life. I want things simple where I can follow them where it is a pattern. I like it that way, I can follow it and I don't have to get all confused and overwhelmed. So it's always the same thing most of the time. I'd say most of the time because sometimes people put pressure on me. When that happens I order what they ordered. That's how I solve that but I didn't make the decision. They made it for me.

Author: John, have you ever felt depressed in your life?

John: Yes, I have to keep reminding myself that it's not my fault that things aren't making sense to me. That with time and with not being afraid to ask people for help, I can do it. Because I know sometimes it's going to mean that I need to ask somebody, what do you mean what are you talking about. I have to. Because otherwise what will happen is I will become withdrawn because I can't connect to the world. I can't connect to people.

Author: Have you ever felt suicidal?

John: Yes, in fact that happened when I was 16 years old. I had threatened to my parents that I was going to hurt myself. I didn't want to live anymore and it was because I had to make all those tough decisions. To other people the decisions I had to make were very simple, but for me they were very tough. Like for example, I had gotten into a pattern where at that time I had been dressing in bell bottom pants and flowered shirts not because I wanted to be a hippie, but I liked patterns and flowered shirts had a pattern. Bell bottom pants were patterns. The belts that you wore, they were all patterns. People didn't know that's why I liked them. Some people thought I was trying to become a hippie or one of the flower children or something from the sixties. When it came to make a change that meant coming out of the pattern look. It was a hard decision for me because it would mean that I could no longer follow something that I was comfortable with. I would have to go into chaos and try to pick something out of chaos to make chaos work. That did not work for me, so it was a tough decision. It was hard.

Author: What would you have done to hurt yourself? Did you have a plan or did you really want to die?

John: October 31 of 1995, I did die but I was brought back to life. I wanted to die then. All those other times, I don't believe I wanted to die.

Author: What did you do on October 31, 1995?

John: Since I had control over all these things and my system had control of shutting things off or making things shut down, I started applying it to my physical body. I don't know how I was able to do it but I was able to stop everything and shut down in my body. I was mentally willing that everything must shut down in my body. It would all come to an end. I willed it to a point to where I can't understand how it happened. They found that my heart did stop, my breathing did stop and I remember that I was counting the time away. Getting higher and higher with the numbers. When they revived me they said I was counting. Isn't that interesting. They said I was counting and they said they don't remember what number I stopped at but the counting that you were doing seemed to have revived you out of what was happening. They told me that they had tried everything. They even tried reviving me by shocking my chest. When I am withdrawn nothing reaches me. Nothing can touch me and nothing can hurt me. So those shocks, I did not feel. I was totally completely withdrawn. Deep inside myself I got to where I was just going to shut everything down. I knew my system had worked, and I tried that system deep inside to make everything shut off.

Author: On that day you didn't want to live anymore?

John: I didn't want to live, I didn't want to live.

Author: Do you think you could have hurt yourself with something else other than shutting your system down? What if that didn't work?

John: Well, I don't know but I knew it would and I don't know how I knew. I do know this that it had a lot to do with how I was able to take control my mind. I knew that I could use my mind to make things stop and because I knew I could do that, I decided to apply my mind to my body and just start shutting things off.

Author: Where were you when this was happening?

John: I was at a hospital and they thought they had lost me.

Author: But who found you? How did you end up there? Where did you shut down?

John: What happened was this kid, Andy, was taking advantage of me and he wanted to have control over my car. I wouldn't let him have control over the car and get into the drivers seat and drive. So he started beating up on me and since I didn't like his touch, I withdrew completely from the situation. I was getting to where I was getting tired of it. I didn't want anybody touching me anymore. I didn't like it. I don't like it even when I go into the hospital. People would touch me. Why? Why couldn't they just leave there hands off me. So I knew that no matter what, I was going to be touched. Nobody was going to leave me alone and that I would be better off dead. Just totally better off away form everybody. Just gone. And that's how it started.

Author: So were you home or where were you?

John: In my car. Andy had never seen me with closed eyes and he went and told somebody and they got the paramedics. They rushed me to the hospital. They thought I was suffering form some sort of heart attack or something. They weren't sure what was happening. The way I was reached was it took this one guy, I remember this, I would be counting down. I call it counting down to get to 999. Other people would call it counting up. But I call it counting down. While I was counting this one guy I don't know what it was about him but he wasn't going to let go of me. He said, "John please don't go there are so many people who could benefit from the gifts that you have" and I would try to not listen. He said that he felt that there was something special about me and that I need to come back because there is a reason for everything that has happened. I will tell you this that I would hear other hospital staff when I was shutting everything off in my body. I was hearing them say things like "he is not breathing. There are no vital signs of life'. I would hear them say this stuff and then came this guy. It was like this guy was not going to let go of me. So that's when I started remembering, counting backwards and making the whole process stop just to come back to see what this guy wanted. That's how it happened.

Author: Have you ever felt that way since then?

John: No but I am scared to death to know that I am able to shut down. I don't like the idea that the mind can be that dangerous.

Author: Well, I think you need to be careful of that. If you ever feel that way you need to call somebody or let your sister know.

John: Yes, I know.

Author: John do you have a lot of anxiety? Do you know what anxiety is? Would you describe yourself as having anxiety?

John: Anxiety, I don't worry about what is going to happen to me, but I do get overwhelmed and that causes me to want to run. I get a panic kind of feeling and I got to get away. I would actually do that when I was working for a toy store. I would run out of the store onto the street just to get away. But lately I have found other ways of doing that without looking like I was going berserk.

Author: Like what? What do you do?

John: Well what I do is go to a quiet place. I go into the break room where things are quieter. I don't have to hear this noise. I call it noise because it overwhelms me. The sights and sounds are noise. So to get away, I go into the break room, cover my eyes and just lay down. I don't have to run out of the store anymore.

Author: Have you done anything to get your way?

John: I will say this that I don't like it when anyone tried to control my life so I will actually take the control away from them. By doing something, something totally irrational like taking bottles (I have done stuff like this) and smashing them together just weird stuff that I would do and they would get scared that I was going to take the glass and cut my wrist. I wasn't planning to do that but yet that behavior would scare them to where they would hospitalize me. But I gained the control back.

Author: If you think something is unfair what do you do to change it?

John: If something is unfair and yet it is with in my pattern, I let it be that way. If it is unfair and it causes me to come out of the pattern that I am comfortable in then I will resist, I will try to get away from it. I do not combat it, because I don't want to hurt anybody. I will hurt myself. I will take it inward and start pounding and hitting myself. That's how I would deal with it.

Author: Using a rating scale of one to ten, how do you feel right now?

John: Well first of all, I don't use a rating scale of one to ten. I would use a rating scale of zero to nine because it goes with my system.

Author: So with your system of zero to nine, how do you feel right now with lets say overall happiness? Nine being as happy as you've ever been.

John: I would say I am at a seven. A seven to me is more than average. Five is right where it is balanced out. I would say that being able to finally express myself and let people know what it is like is tremendous. It takes so much pressure off me. Stuff that I have always wanted to express, I am able to express now. So that puts me at a seven.

Author: Do you think using a rating scale is a good thing to use when asking individuals with autism how they feel?

John: Yes but you have to make sure that they don't have some other number system that they have developed. If you are within their system of things, they will not be able to come up with a number. They will either guess it or they will they say that they can't come up with anything.

Author: But otherwise you think it is a good idea? Do you like that sort of rating scale?

John: Yes because you can see the scale. You can see it. It's like a picture.

Author: You said you have a girlfriend. When did you become aware of your own sexuality?

John: Well that's a problem.

Author: You don't have to talk about that if you don't want to.

John: No, what the thing is I am still trying to become aware. I know that my girlfriend wants to have kids when we get married, and I don't know how to tell her this but I feel very uncomfortable about having sex with her. I am afraid that I am going to get overwhelmed, and I am not going to want her to hold me or touch me, so that is one of my fears. I don't know how that's going to work. Also, people in the past when I was in special schools would molest me. So touch is to me a very hurtful thing. So sexual wise, I don't know how I should feel. I will tell you this that these things that people say your supposed to have that are supposed to be natural feelings when you are getting closer and closer to your girlfriend, those feelings aren't in me at all. They are just not there.

Author: Do you remember going through puberty?

John: I remember. I know what it is because I went to classes. I learned a few years ago that puberty had to do with growth of hair and other things, but those other things they were talking about were getting so confused and mixed up in my brain that I couldn't comprehend what they were talking about. I am confused about where the baby comes from. I sometimes wonder if it is form the stomach or is it somewhere else. The information was presented to me so quickly and so much at one time that I couldn't understand anything. All I understand is bits and pieces like ovaries, Fallopian tubes estrogen, androgen and it's okay somehow that all this stuff makes something work.

Author: Do you yourself remember going through puberty as a young man?

John: Actually, I remembered having to shave and stuff. I never did experience this thing that they call wet dreams. I think that a lot of it has to do with the fact that my brother had molested me. He knew I didn't like to be touched but he also felt like he had control over me and I was afraid of him so I would not try to get away from him. So that might be part of the reason why I never went through this natural thing I was supposed to go through.

Author: Do you know what ruminating is? Like going over something over and over in your head like when you get angry about things. Does that ever happen to you?

John: What happens with me when I get upset is my brain races ahead of me and then I don't even know what happened. It just happens. I end up going into sort of a dead stage, sort of like I am totally out of it. My thinking has stopped and I am just sitting there sometimes for hours.

Author: So it's like a shutdown.

John: Shutdown, exactly.

Author: Do you shutdown when you get angry?

John: Yes but its not just when I get angry. When I am overwhelmed, it happens. When I get angry, I get overwhelmed because I don't want to be overwhelmed.

Author: So its kind of like one or the other.

John: Right.

Author: You talked earlier about eye contact. Do you work at that? You looked at me quite a bit even though I did not request that of you.

John: Yes, I try, but I side glanced you. I didn't look completely at you.

Author: But sometimes you do.

John: When I feel that what I have to say is extremely important, then I can focus on you like just now. If it is not extremely important, I won't look directly at you. That's the way it is.

Author: Is eye contact a comfort level based on the person? Is it easier for you to look at your sister?

John: Once you become more familiar to me and I know what you are going to do and what actions you are going to do with you face, I will get more comfortable. But you would need to constantly come to me to get used to you.

Author: When you take medication such as Adderal and Risperdal, do you feel your body changing?

John: Well I will tell you that the Tofernal helped stop the part where I don't notice bodily changes where I could possibly wet my bet. Tofernal stopped it. The doctor just simply decided well lets try something that is used for children that normally stops bed wetting and it worked.

Author: But do you feel a physical change in your body when you take the Risperdal and Adderal such as a sense of warmth?

John: The Risperdal allows me to be able to stay with people. When I am not on the Risperdal, I am more withdrawn from people. The Adderal stops the rocking back and forth because it stimulated whatever part of my brain needs so I don't need to rock back and forth. My body doesn't feel it needs to rock back and forth and that's what I want to get at. My body doesn't want to rock back and forth. It's not something I have control over when I rock back and forth. But when I rock back and forth that's a sign to my doctor immediately that the medication is not balanced. The Adderal causes me to be able to make better contact with people. I have better eye contact with people. But the doctor has not been able to make it to where I can make complete eye contact. He feels that there is some kind of degree of Attention Deficit Disorder along with autistic disorder and he feels that if he could give me more Adderal that it would make a difference in my concentration abilities. He also feels that if he could give me more Risperdal that I would be able to be in a situation where I could probably take on a job with more risks and changes. This is what my doctor believes. I don't know. It hasn't been tested out to see whether that is so or not. But he feels that I would do better with more medication, however, my sister is opposed to it. The reason why is that I have been on medication that has caused stuff like temporary blindness. I would completely loose sight. Everything would go black. I would see all these black dots forming and then all of a sudden my vision was gone. Because of what drugs have done to me, my sister is very concerned about different medicines. She knows Risperdal has side effects such as tardive dyskinesia. She doesn't want me on a lot of Risperdal to where I develop tardive dyskinesia. She says to my doctor she doesn't care if it is only 1% of developing tardive dyskinesia, she doesn't want her brother to be one of those 1% that get it. So she feels that the dosage should be kept low.

Author: So you don't mind taking medicine in general?

John: I don't like taking drugs. That's what I call them too. I know that I should look at them as medicine but they take that control away from me but then again without the medicine, autism takes the control away from me. It's a topsy-turvy thing. Its like you have to do one or the other.

Author: Do you like the feeling of water? Do you like to take showers or baths?

John: I love water. I love to go underwater. When you go underwater all noise are drowned out, they are gone. It is the most comfortable place to be is under the water. You don't have to do anything, you can be so happy and content. There is no need to do something stimulating to get oneself away from something. Because you are already under the water and it is all drained out. It's all drowned. It's gone. The muffled sound is comfortable to handle.

Author: How does the water feel against your skin when you are in the pool? Is that soothing?

John: I love water. If I get under too much stress, I will hold my hand under the water and sometimes I will just go and hit myself with the water on my face because somehow that relaxes me. I don't understand how it does. I just do it because I know it works.

Author: You talked about various things that you do when you get over-stimulated with me today. How do you know when you are getting close to being overstimulated?

John: Oh boy. What happens is you can feel a chemical change occurring in your body. It's a wavering you feel something is not right in your body and you know its not right. You just can sense it. I don't know how to explain it.

Author: You don't feel something in your stomach, head or anything?

John: Oh no! It's your whole entire body. It's like you know you feel like it. It was like a week or two ago, my medication was thrown off and I was afraid I was going to have to go into the hospital because I could feel myself loosing control. I was getting to where I couldn't think strength. Things weren't making sense to me. Communication was harder for me. Talk words were coming out incorrectly when I would talk to people. The employees at my work saw this a few years ago and I had to tell them I was autistic. Now they understand why there are times when I can't communicate with them. You know because you are not able to stay keyed to what's happening and what's happening also is outside of you. For example, the exhaust fans at work get louder than peoples' voices and things get out of whack. Your senses are taking information in incorrectly instead of taking it in all balanced. There are times where I will not call my doctor because I am afraid he is going to hospitalize me. I don't like to be hospitalized. Some of the people, even though my doctor tries to get everyone to be aware that John does not like to be touched, rube my back or something to try and make me feel better. I just need to withdraw. This is what happens when I am in the hospital. So I don't like being in the hospital.

Author: Do you have any strategies to calm yourself down when you feel overwhelmed?

John: What I do when this occurs at work is I say things over and over to myself but quietly trying to make sure that nobody overhears it so I can still do something repetitive yet not be heard.

Author: So you use self talk such as 'It's going to be okay" to calm yourself?

John: Right. But sometimes I can't go through a self talk thing and I have to first just do something repetitive. After things calm down, I say okay things are getting better now. Sometimes, I am at a point where I can't do it right away. But I know what works and I use that and it helps me to be able to be calm enough to where I can then start using self talk.

Author: Do you ever swear?

John: I don't like swearing. I have a hard time with that. I don't know what it is but to me there is no point, no reasoning, there is no rhyme. There is nothing that makes sense to it. You say a word that totally is contrary to what you are really talking about. Okay people were trying to explain to me that these swear words meant something but I visualize it as that. For example like a female dog. I told them I see a female dog as a female dog or as a dog. I can't place that other word (Bitch). I can't make sense out of it. So I don't use it.

Author: Does it bother you when people swear around you?

John: Yes, especially when they are using words, like the 'F' word for example. When they use that and I am like why are they saying that when they are not doing that? So why are they saying that?

Author: So it is frustrating?

John: Right. So people frustrate me when they swear. Because they are taking language, and making it be something totally false. It is not describing what it really is.

Author: Do you have any information on what type of behaviors other people can do to make it easier for individuals with autism to make them feel better?

John: The one most important thing is and I clearly stress this, is first you need to understand. You need to understand what autism is what it does to people and second of all you need to give them time. Time to adjust. Whatever it is you need to give them time and if you want them to make changes you need to allow them to make them gradually according to their built in time table, not according to a deadline. It just doesn't work. Understanding has to come first, otherwise they can not really understand why they need to do these things. They need to know the why. Once they got the why then they need to give it time.

Author: How do you figure out something you don't understand such as slang?

John: Well, I went through a speech and language clinic and they went over all these different things with me with different pictures. That's how they showed me. They would show me the picture of what this means and then they would show me two other pictures of how this is silly if it really means that. I was able to see that was silly so I would look at the other thing. I never knew that there was another side to it. I never knew that there was another picture to it. When I saw these two other pictures, I started to see that it makes more sense than the other. So by them using pictures and having me compare the pictures, I was able to slowly start to put the words together with the picture.

Author: What do you do now?

John: Sometimes, I still slip. Like somebody says "what's up" and because I hear it first literally, I will look up. I don't mean to but I do it because I hear it first in a literal way. Then, I realize oh wait a minute, I need to break this down into what they really mean. What are they asking me. Oh yah, they are trying to see how am I doing. That's what happens. But I need to think and that's why time is needed. That's why sometimes people ask me something and I will be quiet because I am not ready to answer yet. When I am ready to answer things just work out. The employees know I have autism and I have explained to them what it is for me. They have been able to accept me, work with me, and talk with me. They think that it's the greatest thing to be able to talk to me. They think it's special. They call me their toys are us kid. That's what they call me. They look at me as a special person and you know I have got to tell you these employees do not like anyone doing me wrong. They don't like anybody messing with me or tricking me or laughing at me and they are good friends. They are not just employees. They stick up for me when I am not able to do something because I become overwhelmed by the situation. I am in a good place. I've tired to explain to my sister, when she says that there are other jobs where you could get paid better, that this job works for me. This job lets me follow my pattern. This job gives the time to understand autistic people and to work with me and accommodate all my special needs. They want to see me succeed within my means. You don't find very many employers like that. There is no reason to leave. If they started to get to where they weren't accepting me or trying to make changes with the way I am, then I would have to leave but since things are working out that's why I need to stay. Money doesn't mean anything to me, even though I know you got to have it. I know that is more important in this world to stay stable and balanced. Sticking with a job with less pay but the added benefits that you wouldn't get elsewhere, it's worth it.

Author: Do you collect anything?

John: I collect Hot Wheel cars because I like lining things up. I also like to see the cars go round and round in circles and I like it that I can have the control over them. You know over the spinning actions, all that stuff that I can be in control of it. It seems like I almost an obsession with Hot Wheel cars and track. I don't buy any other cars. This is an obsession that I've had since my childhood and haven't come out of it yet.

Author: Is it calming to you?

John: Yes, it is. Those motors, the noise that the motors make. The way those motors are is a constant sound, a whirring sound. I like the whirring sound that you get form the motors. So, I am comfortable when I do Hot Wheel cars.

Author: Do you watch any TV?

John: I have a TV and I watch one show Star Trek voyager and sometimes I will watch the news because I know that I need to listen to the weather. I need the weather to know what to wear the next day or what I am going to have to do at work. For example, I need to know if it's a snow day. I may need to shovel or something. Otherwise, if I don't get the weather I can't plan ahead and then I am lost. If I come to work and there is snow, I am totally lost. I need to know that it is going to snow first so that I can be ready for it.

Author: What if the weather reports snow tomorrow and it doesn't? Does that bother you?

John: No because I just go back to my regular routine. But it is frustrating when they tell me that it is not going to snow and it snows. This throws my entire routine off completely.

Author: What do you do on days like that?

John: You know what I do. I become absorbed in the work of working outside shoveling snow and breaking the ice. I perseverate in it to the point of excluding all the other duties. So there are days where they have to put up with me as I don't do everything that I normally do. I overhead them one time and they said 'oh no it snowed', and I overheard them say 'oh no this is going to interrupt his routine for sure'.

Author: What do you like about Star Trek Voyager?

John: Well, I like the music. I like the theme music to Start Trek Voyager. Also, I like that they try and do everything as peaceful as they can. The captain tries to make sure that everyone is happy and content and then everyone is able to meet each other's needs. I like seeing a show like that even though I know that it's not realistic. I it is comforting for me to see the spaceship on the picture just gliding and then when it goes over Saturn When I see that shadow and those lights, it just reminds me of how it is with me and the sunlight. I get so engrossed in the light and the colors and then as the ship goes forward and moves on, it reminds me of how I am going forward and moving on. So it is always a comfort to see Start Trek Voyager on TV. As for watching all the other stuff that's too much information. I can't take all that. I am better off sitting down watching a washing machine spin rather than trying to absorb all that stuff that is on TV. So, I am very comfortable with, sitting down in front of a washing machine and watching it spin. I try to watch it without letting people know that I am watching it because it relaxes me and calms me down even though others do not see it as normal.

Author: Do you ever go to the movies or anything like that?

John: Yes, but I have a rule about going to the movies. I need to be in the middle of a row and nine seats away from the front because nine is a multiple of three.

Author: You said you have a car, do you drive?

John: Yah, I do and the only car I feel that I am able to drive is a Geo Metro. Why, because the engine sound is perfect. I am able to focus. The engine sound helps me focus and I am able to drive because the steering is so easy to drive a Geo it just glides across the road. The car is so small that I am able to make turns and I can come in and out of traffic with no problem. Any other car I don't think I could drive.

Author: So you wouldn't like to drive my big truck.

John: No way. I want something small. I want something that has a Geo Metro engine sound. It is very important that it has that kind of engine sound because certain engine sounds distract me to where I can't concentrate on the road. I need to have a gentle purring engine. This is extremely important.

Author: It sounds like a lot of what you do in everyday functioning follows certain patterns and rules. Do you create them?

John: Yes, they are my own design. They are my own world. That makes me function in this life. Just because on an aptitude test, autistic people do not appear gifted, I think the way we have been able to cope with this world that we do have gifted ability. We are able to take our intelligence and make something work. Before the Domain and Delacato method, I was labeled as retarded and I have come a long way since then and I am continually making strides and I am being flexible where I can in what I have done with my number three system that I call Zystem Three. Don't ask me why but for some reason it has to be called Zystem Three because the letter 's' has to be backwards so it's the way I think. With Zystem Three, I've allowed it to become my three plus one system. What does this do? It allows me flexibility. I have allowed myself to go three plus one with the understanding that I don't need to go beyond a one. I can go and add one thing at a time and gradually what happens is that I am able to get more and more stuff to fit into my pattern. But I have to do it gradually. It takes time and patience on other peoples' part. My sister understands me so well. She gives me time to think. She gives me time to come up with a decision even if it takes me two or three days. She just will not push me. She wants me to do the right thing and she knows that with me sometimes it is very hard. She knows that when we go to a restaurant that it is not good for someone to say to me, "I'm going to have the pork are you going to have the chicken or the beef taco?" She knows that for them to do that is not helpful to me. And so what she does is say, "Do you want your taco hard or soft?" She just makes it a two way thing, one or the other. I am picking from those two things not choosing from a whole selection of stuff. Then, she doesn't say do you want chicken, beef or pork, she doesn't just throw that at me like that. She says, "do you want dark meet or white meat?" Do you see what she is doing? She is taking it gradually and then she is saying "okay now chicken has both dark meet and white meat". She explains this stuff to me because for some reason I forget these things. By her going through it with me, I am able to understand. This can take up to three minutes. However, I come to a decision say that I will have the pork because at that time, I was not feeling like I wanted white meat and pork unlike the beef, you are not talking white or dark meat, you are talking about rich meat, and I didn't want that so we went with the pork which was milder so I was able to pick that. She takes her time with me. She has taken the place of my mother and my sister still worries about what would happen to me if something were to ever happen to her. She has got me living right next to her because she told me she can not stand it when she tries to live without knowing what's going on with me. She doesn't like it when I am far away from her. She wants me right there so she can check on me. She wants to make sure that I am okay. She is a very good sister.

CLINICAL SYNOPSIS

John's case illustrates, in many ways, the experiences of adults with autism that the authors have counseled. His experiences have resulted from the fact that his diagnosis occurred recently and he was not provided any school related services for his autistic characteristics. While he did receive some services for learning disabilities, which were probably helpful for the development of his reading capacity and comprehension, John's social skill deficits were never addressed. Fortunately for John, his adjustment to society has been more functional due to the use of psychotropic medication. Medication, such as Risperdal, has provided a calming effect that has allowed him to keep a job for the past ten years, as well as develop some meaningful relationships with his sister and girlfriend. In many ways John is functioning much higher in social and vocational areas than would be typical for an adult with autism who did not receive autism specific services as a child. In the following sections, we highlight aspects of John's experiences which emphasis possible counseling concerns. Again, we have found these concerns to be common among individuals with autism who have been diagnosed later in life.

Perceptual Difficulties

In the case study, John referred to a number of instances where he described distortions in his visual perceptions. The reader may recall his description and fear while driving in a car with his parents that a bridge was going to end. Certainly, family member, teachers, and clinicians may be quick to label John's visual perceptual experience as being indicative of a psychotic episode. In our clinical practice, visual perceptual distortions such as John's are not that uncommon in individuals with autism. As such, clinicians must be comprehensive in their questioning related to a client's perceptual distortions so that they can distinguish a psychotic episode as opposed to a visual perceptual distortion. Questions related to the frequency and content of the client's other visual perceptual distortions would be helpful in answering this concern. It is unlikely that one would be having frequent visual perceptual distortions in a variety of areas if one has a psychotic condition. As we analyze John's case, he did refer to other visual perceptual distortions that he had experienced. The reader may recall his description of the bus coming into his classroom and the sun's reflections. The content of his visual distortions appeared to focus on angles and the brightness of the perception.

Decision Making

It has been the authors' experience in working with both children and adult individuals with autism that they have a difficult time making decisions about life situations. Typically, clinicians work with clients with autism to develop a workable decision making system. John was able to create his own decision-making system. While the content and parameters of John's decision making are difficult for the reader to follow, it works for him. Interestingly, John's system involves numbers. Using numbers has allowed John to break up information into smaller units and then eliminate the small units so that an overall decision can be made. It seems as though the use of numbers allows John to take information that may be 'complex' and 'gray' and convert it to 'black and white' information. Interestingly, John's sister will assist him socially in his decision making by breaking down social questions into a black and white context. Clinicians can also use this strategy when their clients are struggling and frozen by having to make a social decision.

Conversation

As the interview progressed, it was obvious to the reader that John experienced difficulty at times due to his literal interpretation of spoken language. For example, he had to learn not to respond to a literal expression such as another work employee saying, "What's up?" Other examples included, how common cursing expressions made no sense to him because he would have a visual picture of the curse word and it would make no sense in the context of its use in conversation.

Clinically this points out the need for clinicians to provide a strategy for their client to employ when presented a literal expression. It is also critical that clinicians avoid the use of figurative statements during a therapy session with an individual who has autism as they may lose the client's attention and concentration as he struggles with understanding the statement's meaning. Interesting, John described a useful strategy for understanding such statements. The strategy involved the use of pictures which showed him how a statement could have a variety of meanings. Clinicians are reminded that the use of pictures is meaningful for comprehension because individuals with autism frequently think in pictures. During the interview the flow of conversation at times became one way due to John's preservation on a topic. This is a common experience when counseling clients with autism. A strategy that clinicians may find useful when this happens is to allow the client to perseverate and wait for an opportunity to redirect the conversation topic back to the original concern. Abruptly disrupting or inhibiting the client's preservation may cause the client to become angry as he/she may view the clinician as being rude or inconsiderate.

Routines and Transitions

What the case study illustrated is John's craving for routine and sameness. Routine becomes a way of life for individuals with autism. For example, John listens to the weather every night to arrange his clothes for work the next day. He orders the same restaurant food (e.g. McDonalds Big Mac). John drives the same car and route to work. He eats meals at the same time every day and only watches a select few programs not necessarily for content but for visual effects that calm him (Star Trek beginning). John arranges "hot wheels" cars to watch them spin off a record playing (which has gone on since he was a child). If there is a change in John's routine, he experiences considerable stress. His discussion of what happens when it does snow and it was not forecasted the night before is a good example of this. In this situation, John could not adapt to the different weather situation that day because it changed his routine at work. Fortunately for John, his fellow work associates and supervisor are able to accommodate his difficulty by allowing him to engage in a work activity that calms him down. Clinicians can be helpful in orientating family members and employers in ways to accommodate the client with autism during significant changes in routine to reduce the likelihood of a stressful reaction. Clinicians can also be helpful to family members and employers in stressing the gradual transitioning of the client during changes in routines. For example, providing the worker with autism sufficient lead-time can greatly reduce stress during a transitional period. Also, breaking down the transition into phases is more easily tolerated by clients with autism.

Relationships

The case study illustrated the difficulty John has in one to one relationships. For instance, John was befriended by one student in grade school, however, when this friend introduced John to another student, John was not able to share time with this friend due to the presence of the other student. Furthermore, the struggle with keeping friendships resulted in John being taken advantage of. Clinically, this illustrates the fact that individuals with autism do attempt to have social relationships, however, due to the complexities of friendships, they may not be able to spontaneously interact or accommodate the changes that are needed in the friendship. John did report having a girlfriend and he related conversation about marriage. A concern John related to marriage centers around intimacy. He described the confusion he has related to how a woman has a baby. His confusion is related to how a child is conceived biologically. It appears that he is struggling with creating a visual picture of how conception and birth occur. Clinically, this highlights the potential confusion that a client with autism may have in terms of understanding the need to compromise and accept responsibilities related to the sharing of ones life with another. In the authors' experiences, it is not common for individuals with autism to marry. We have counseled clients with autism that have been married and have children, however, their marital relations and parenting skills were dysfunctional. A positive relationship that John has is with his sister. John described the numerous ways that she assists him in his adjustment and adaptation to the world. For example, she assists him in ordering at a restaurant and acts as an advocate when his physician considers a medication change. It appears that his sister consciously arranges aspects of John's environment that will allow him to be more successful. It has been the authors' experience that clients with autism who have a family member who is vigilant and positive about their care and success seem to adapt better in their life situations. Thus, it is important for clinicians to identify interested family members who are willing to work closely with the client in their daily living situations related to educational or employment experiences.

Over-stimulation and Overload

A common theme John related was how he could be overwhelmed or overloaded by common environment experiences (e.g. learning pronouns). John explained different techniques he uses to calm himself down when overstimulated or overloaded. For the most part, John is able to detect when he is becoming over-stimulated and he takes steps to reduce the stimulation so that a problematic outcome is reduced. Clinically, it is important to understand the magnitude of over-stimulation for individuals with autism. Teaching them techniques for detecting the onset of over-stimulation and what to do about it can greatly enhance their livelihood and functionality.

INDEX